Monographs of the Hebrew Union College

1. Lewis M. Barth, *An Analysis of Vatican 30*

2. Samson H. Levey, *The Messiah: An Aramaic Interpretation*

3. Ben Zion Wacholder, *Eupolemus: A Study of Judaeo-Greek Literature*

4. Richard Victor Bergren, *The Prophets and the Law*

5. Benny Kraut, *From Reform Judaism to Ethical Culture: The Religious Evolution of Felix Adler*

6. David B. Ruderman, *The World of a Renaissance Jew: The Life and Thought of Abraham ben Mordecai Farissol*

7. Alan Mendelson, *Secular Education in Philo of Alexandria*

8. Ben Zion Wacholder, *The Dawn of Qumran: The Sectarian Torah and the Teacher of Righteousness*

Monographs of the
Hebrew Union College
Number 8

———

The Dawn of Qumran
The Sectarian Torah and the
Teacher of Righteousness

Ben Zion Wacholder

The Dawn of Qumran

*The Sectarian Torah and the
Teacher of Righteousness*

Hebrew Union College Press
Cincinnati 1983

Library of Congress Cataloging in Publication Data

Wacholder, Ben Zion.
  The dawn of Qumran.

  (Monographs of the Hebrew Union College, ISSN 0190–
5627 ; no. 8)
  Includes bibliographical references and indexes.
   1. Temple scroll—Criticism, interpretation, etc.
2. Teacher of Righteousness. I. Title. II. Series.
BM488.T44W33 1983   229'.918   83–275
ISBN 0-87820-407-5

Published with the assistance of the
Henry Englander—Eli Mayer Publication Fund,
established in their honor by
Esther Straus Englander and Jessie Straus Mayer

Designed by Noel Martin
Manufactured in the United States of America
Distributed by KTAV Publishing House, Inc.
New York, New York 10013

Dedicated to
Truesdell S. Brown
Scholar, Teacher, and Friend

Column LVI of the Qumranic Torah. Reproduced here and on the jacket with the kind permission of the Israel Exploration Society from Plate 71 in *The Temple Scroll,* ed. Yigael Yadin (Jerusalem, 1977), Volume Three.

Contents

Acknowledgments xi

Preface xiii

Abbreviations xvii

Chapter 1
A Second Torah at Sinai? 1
    The Pronouns "I," "Thou," and They" 4
    The Pronoun "Thou" Addressed to Moses 7
    Purpose 9
    Composition 13
    Unity 16
    "Torah" 17
    The Future Sanctuary (Column 29) 21
    Conclusion 30

Chapter 2
The Sectarian Torah in Qumranic Literature 33
    Enoch 33
    The Book of Jubilees 41
        Introduction 42
        Legal Lore 48
        The Calendar 53
        Heavenly Tablets 60
        Jacob's Dream 61
    Eupolemus 62
    The War Rule 77
    The Literature of the Commune (Yaḥad) 83
    סרך היחד (Community Rule) 84
        Hodayot 88
        Pesherite Commentaries 89
        Pesherite References to the Second Torah 91
    The Copper Scroll and New Jerusalem 94

Chapter 3
Who is Zadok? 11Q Torah and the Teacher of Righteousness . . . 99
    The Copper Scroll 99
    The Damascus Document 101
        The Structure and Date of the Damascus Document . . . 105
            Introduction: 391–410 after the Exile 105
            The Body of the Treatise 110
        "Until the Rise of Zadok" 112
        Israel's Three Sins and the Qumranic Torah 119

The New Covenant in Damascus 129
The *Moreh Ṣedeq* and the *Beney Ṣadoq* in the Texts of the
Commune 135

Chapter 4
    Zadok in Talmudic and Karaite Writings 141
        Zadok and Baethus, the Disciples of Antigonus of Soko . . . 141
        Al-Qirqisani on Zadok and Baethus 148
        Zadok and Anan. The Qumranic Torah and the Karaites . . . 155
        Allusions to the Qumranic Sect in the Talmudic Literature . 160
        Greek Evidence 167

Chapter 5
    Chronology 171
        The Succession of the High Priests and the Tobiads 171
        The Chain of the Qabbalah 173
        Chronography at Qumran 176
        The Sect's Own Timetable 178
        The First Twenty Years of the Sect: 196/195–177/176 181
        Pesher Habakkuk: Faith in the *Moreh Ṣedeq* in spite of Dashed
        Expectations 185
            The Wicked Priest in the Habakkuk Commentary 193
        Pesher Nahum 199
        Is Daniel's Reference to the Unfulfilled Vision an Allusion to
        Qumran? 200
        The Date of Zadok and the Qumranic Torah 202
        Persian Culture during the Hellenistic Period 212
        Zadok in the Literary Context of His Time 218
        Challenging Mainstream Judaism 222

Notes 231

Indices 283
    Citations 283
    Modern Authors 301
    Subjects 305

Acknowledgments

I am deeply indebted to many individuals without whose devoted help this book would not have been written. The members of the seminar on the "Temple Scroll"—William Hartfelder, Jack Love, and John Kampen—helped crystallize some of the leading ideas found in this study. My colleague, Stephen Kaufman, criticized early drafts of this manuscript. John Kampen's labors in the making of this book exceed my own; he has assisted in the research, the editing, and the annotation of the typescript. His keen perception of what is and what is not cogent has been invaluable. Professor Moshe Assis assisted in the rendition of the Arabic text of al-Qirqisani. Dr. Elizabeth Krukowski, Jancy Jaslow, and Rabbis Michael Berk and David Bouganim edited the typescript and assisted in the production of a more coherent and readable text.

This study benefited from a session at the centennial meeting of the Society of Biblical Literature held in Dallas on November 7, 1980. The members of the panel, Jacob Milgrom, Joseph Baumgarten, and the chairman, John Strugnell, most graciously praised the draft in public and privately supplied me with many pages of annotation. John Strugnell has also most kindly shared with me his notes on the hitherto unpublished fragments of the sectarian Torah. The notes of Professor Sid Z. Leiman, who originally served as an anonymous advisor of the Press, were kindly made available to me. The public and private comments of these eminent scholars have been enormously helpful in the preparation of the final draft and have contributed greatly to the cogency of the argumentation. Of course the final responsibility remains my own.

Dr. Alfred Gottschalk, president of the Hebrew Union College—Jewish Institute of Religion, and Dean Samuel Greengus have lent the moral and financial support without which my work could not have been done. Special thanks are due to Mrs. Miriam Weiss and her staff for their patient reproduction of successive typescripts. I am indebted to the members of the Publications Committee of the Hebrew Union College Press, and in particular to its chairman, Dr. Michael A. Meyer, for their deep interest in this manuscript. My wife, Touby, and my children, Nina, Sholom, David, and Hannah, have been a source of inspiration and were immensely helpful in the various stages of the production of this work.

I have dedicated this volume to my mentor and friend Professor Truesdell S. Brown. Dr. Brown's renown rests on his contributions to the study of Greek historiography. Much of the methodology employed in this work comes directly from his mentor, Felix Jacoby (1876–1959), an intellectual giant I would wish to have known.

Preface

This book interprets the largest and the most recently recovered of the manuscripts found in the Judaean wilderness which are also known as the Dead Sea Scrolls. An analysis of this newly found text, its form and content, together with the ancient references to it, leads to a hypothesis regarding the scroll's apparent and real author. If correct, our hypothesis opens new vistas within a vast literary treasure which is still as enigmatic today as it was when first found in the 1940's. Many passages in the major Qumranic texts assume a new meaning, giving them a historical concreteness hitherto unimagined. Moreover, this monograph presents the evidence for tracing the genesis of the sect and its literature. The discussion of the allusions to our manuscript in the Qumranic, talmudic, and Karaite writings suggests an outline of the history of the sect that stretches from 200 B.C.E. to 1000 C.E.

The reader will note that I do not refer to this manuscript by the title made famous by Professor Yigael Yadin, who has called it *Megillat-Hammiqdaš*, or "The Temple Scroll." Yadin's contributions to the discovery, decipherment, and understanding of this ancient parchment are so prodigious that they would ordinarily call for honoring the name given by him to the scroll. His voluminous introduction and commentary in Hebrew illumine every line of the recovered text. At the time of this writing, Yadin's promised English translation of his entire work has not yet appeared, although German, French, and Spanish translations of the ancient scroll are now available.

In my view, "The Temple Scroll" is an inappropriate title for this manuscript. It is certainly true that there are sections of the scroll devoted to a new sanctuary, its sacred city and its ritual. On the other hand, the bulk of its subject matter relates to topics other than the temple. In fact, most of the themes found in the Mosaic Torah are reiterated in our scroll. The appelation given to it by Yadin seems to reflect an archaeological perspective. It tends to obscure the prominence of such themes as the royal charter or the additional feasts of the new wine and new oil. But the basic objection to Yadin's title comes from ancient testimony. The author of this text, as well as references to it in other Qumranic manuscripts, apparently designate our scroll as the *Torah* or *Seper Torah,* the Book of the Law. Such a title may seem grandiose to the modern reader but no one has the right to alter it. According to Damascus Document 5:1–5, this *Seper Torah* had been entrusted to Joshua and Eliezer, who placed it into an ark where it reposed for centuries until it was unsealed by the founder of the sect. The contents, language, and form tend to confirm our understanding of the ancient testimony that the work before us was presented not merely as another of the pseudepigraphs that filled the caves of Qumran but as a rival to the Five Books of the Torah which God had handed down to Moses. Accordingly, I refer to this work as the Qumranic or sectarian Torah. The term sectarian as used in this monograph has no pejorative connotation. Neither is it necessarily synonymous with *Yaḥad* (Commune) or *Beney Ṣadoq* or any other appellation of the Qumran community. What it does mean is that whereas the canonical Torah was recognized as being of divine origin by all of Israel, the *Seper Torah* found at Qumran was so considered by only a part of Israel. The siglum adopted here is 11Q Torah, although it should be added that the provenance of the cave where the main manuscript of the sectarian Torah was found is uncertain.

The significance of this text is attested by the fact that until now remnants of four or more manuscripts of this Qumranic Torah have been identified, all of them by Yadin. The single exception is a group of fragments from Cave 4 in the possession of John Strugnell, and these fragments are evidently the oldest, dating from circa 150 B.C.E. Interestingly, the main text, now reposing in Jerusalem's Shrine of the Book, consists of what had originally been two manuscripts, columns 2–5 belonging to Scribe A and columns 6–66 to Scribe B. Since columns 5 and 6 in part duplicate themselves, there can be no doubt that the two scripts are the remains of two originally independent scrolls.

The title *Seper Torah* suggests the paramount status of this work in the eyes of the sect. By 200 B.C.E. the Five Books of Moses had long been recognized as the most sacred division of Scripture. Their wording has come down in a number of versions: the Septuagintal, the Samaritan, and the Masoretic recensions, as well as in the remnants of the Qumranic library. In spite of their divergence, the essential similarity of all these versions attests to the acceptance of the same Torah as the most sacred book of Israel. The text of our manuscript, however, cannot be classified as still another version, but must be viewed as a new Torah. As there is no reason to suppose that the Qumranic community repudiated the traditional Torah of Moses, the question arises as to how the community related the *Seper Torah* before us to the Torah accepted by Israel as a whole. The answer is given in the body of this study. Here it suffices to say that, as I see it, it was the acceptance of this sectarian work as the word of God at Sinai in addition to the ancestral Scriptures that characterized the ideology of the sect. The scribes of Qumran copied the scriptural books as well as the immense number of biblical commentaries, apocalypses, pseudepigraphs, histories, and rules of the community. None of these writings, however, sacred as they were, could compare with the holiness ascribed to this scroll. If the traditional Torah was regarded as holy, the *Seper Torah* was considered the holy of holies. The Commune of Qumran related to the sectarian Torah as has mainstream Judaism to the Five Books of Moses, the law of Israel.

Zadok emerges as the main personality of this monograph. Until now ignored or treated with disdain in Qumranic and talmudic studies, he is to be regarded as one of the leading figures of the Second Temple. The identification of Zadok as the probable author of the sectarian Torah opens a new approach to the study of post-biblical literature. The large body of post-exilic writings misnamed the Apocrypha and Pseudepigrapha has been treated as if it had no authors, merely compilers who pasted together older materials. The identification of Zadok as the author of the sectarian Torah marks, I hope, the beginning of an attempt to search deeper into the origins and authorship of post-biblical literature.

Our hypotheses concerning the role of the hidden Torah at Qumran may lead to a radical understanding of the Commune and its literature. These texts frequently refer to secrets and mysteries of the Law to which only members of the sect were privy. The sectarian Torah, because of its pivotal role in the formation of the sect, seems to be the key to resolving the problems raised by these enigmatic allusions. It provides the solution, as well, to the puzzling problem of how the sect originated and developed. This monograph proposes both a relative and absolute chronology, not only for the sectarian Torah, but also for the Book of Jubilees, the Damascus Document, and other Qumranic writings. If some of these hypotheses are accepted, much of the Judaean history of the last three centuries of the pre-Christian era will have to be rewritten.

Although this is a monograph intended for the specialist, an attempt has been made to present the subject-matter in a manner accessible to anyone seriously interested in the history and literature of Qumran, particularly those who wish to gain an acquaintance with the newly found sectarian Torah. My faithful assistant, John Kampen, has assembled an exhaustive bibliography relating to this scroll which I have named the "Sectarian Torah." It is to be found in the notes to chapter 1, especially notes 6–8.

Abbreviations

AcOr	*Acta Orientalia*
AJ	*Jewish Antiquities*
ALUOS	*Annual of the Leeds University Oriental Society*
ARN	Abot de-Rabbi Nathan
ARNA	Abot de-Rabbi Nathan, Version A
ARNB	Abot de-Rabbi Nathan, Version B
APOT	*The Apocrypha and Pseudepigrapha of the Old Testament*, R. H. Charles (ed.)
ASTI	Annual of the Swedish Theological Institute
B.	Babylonian Talmud
BA	*Biblical Archaeologist*
BASOR	*Bulletin of the American Schools of Oriental Research*
BDB	*The Hebrew and English Lexicon of the Old Testament* by F. Brown, S. R. Driver, and C. A. Briggs
BJ	*The Jewish War*
BJRL	*Bulletin of the John Rylands Library*
CA	*Against Apion*
CBQ	*Catholic Biblical Quarterly*
CRAIBL	*Comptes Rendus de l'Académie des inscriptions et belles-lettres*
CRINT	*Compendia rerum iudaicarum ad novum testamentum*
DJD	*Discoveries in the Judaean Desert*
DSSE	*The Dead Sea Scrolls in English* by Geza Vermes (1962 ed.)
DTT	*Dansk Teologisk Tidsskrift*
EJ	*Encyclopaedia Judaica*
ETL	*Ephemerides theologicae lovanienses*
ETR	*Etudes théologiques et religieuses*
ExpT	*Expository Times*
FGrH	*Die Fragmente der griechischen Historiker* by Felix Jacoby
HTR	*Harvard Theological Review*
HUCA	*Hebrew Union College Annual*
IB	*Interpreter's Bible*
IDB	*Interpreter's Dictionary of the Bible*
IDBS	*Interpreter's Dictionary of the Bible*, Supplementary Volume
IEJ	*Israel Exploration Journal*
J.	Jerusalem Talmud
JAAR	*Journal of the American Academy of Religion*
JANES	*Journal of the Ancient Near Eastern Society, Columbia*
Jastrow	*A Dictionary of the Targumim, the Talmud Babli and Yerushalmi, and the Midrashic Literature* by Marcus Jastrow
JBL	*Journal of Biblical Literature*
JE	*Jewish Encyclopedia*

JJS	*Journal of Jewish Studies*
JLA	*Jewish Law Annual*
JQR	*Jewish Quarterly Review*
JSHRZ	*Jüdische Schriften aus hellenistisch-römischer Zeit*
JSJ	*Journal for the Study of Judaism*
JSS	*Journal of Semitic Studies*
JTS	*Journal of Theological Studies*
JZWL	*Jüdische Zeitschrift für Wissenschaft und Leben*

Koehler-Baumgartner   *Lexicon in Veteris Testamenti libros* by L. Koehler and W. Baumgartner

Levy	*Wörterbuch über die Talmudim und Midraschim* by J. Levy
LM	*Lutherische Monatshefte*
M.	Mishnah
NEB	*New English Bible*
PAAJR	*Proceedings of the American Academy of Jewish Research*
PE	*Preparatio Evangelica* of Eusebius
RB	*Revue Biblique*
REJ	*Revue des études juives*
RHPR	*Revue d'histoire et de philosophie religieuses*
RSV	*Revised Standard Version*
Schürer I	*The History of the Jewish People in the Age of Jesus Christ* by Emil Schürer, revised and edited by G. Vermes and F. Millar et al., vol. I.
Schürer II	Ibid., vol. II
T.	Tosefta
TDNT	*Theological Dictionary of the New Testament*
ThS	*Theological Studies*
TS	*The Temple Scroll* by Yigael Yadin, vols. I–III and Supplement
VT	*Vetus Testamentum*
VTSup	*Supplement to Vetus Testamentum*
WHJP	*World History of the Jewish People*

Qumran Texts

CD	Damascus Document
1QH	*Hodayot* (Thanksgivings)
IQM	War Rule
IQpHab	Pesher Habakkuk
4QpNah	Pesher Nahum
1QS	Community Rule
IQSa	Messianic Rule
IQSb	Blessings
3Q 15	Copper Scroll
IIQ Torah	Qumranic Torah (Temple Scroll)

Chapter 1
A Second Torah at Sinai?

Bearing the provocative title *Fragments of a Zadokite Work,* Solomon Schechter's publication in 1910 of the text of twenty sheets from the Cairo Genizah was considered sensational.[1] Were these fragments part of a lost work emanating from the medieval sect known as the Karaites, as some scholars maintained, or were they, as others argued, the work of a group who had flourished in Judaea before and during the advent of Christianity?[2] The answer to this question came in 1947 with the discovery of a remarkably extensive library of a pre-Christian Jewish sect in the Judaean desert. The works in this library have turned out to be the sacred writings of a sect which identified itself as *Yaḥad* (Commune). They have revealed a plethora of details concerning its organization and beliefs.[3] These writings are characterized not only by their abundance, but also by a variety of genres. In addition to the books found in the Masoretic collection, this library preserved several works previously available only in Greek or Ethiopic translation, such as the Book of Jubilees and the Testaments of the Twelve Patriarchs.[4] While Josephus had noted the fecundity of Essene literary activity,[5] we were still not prepared for the numerous commentaries on what may have constituted the entire Scripture. Within this collection are also the remains of books which, though not directly sectarian, were influential in the development of the *Yaḥad.*

Despite this generally prolific literary activity, the particular contents of sixty-seven columns of the work published by Yigael Yadin and named "The Temple Scroll" still seem extraordinary.[6] The exceptional significance of this discovery lies in the contents of the book, for it contains what seems to be another version of the legal lore found in the Mosaic books, in some respects resembling sections of Exodus, Leviticus, Numbers, and Deuteronomy. At the same time, it also contains pericopes which have no counterpart in the traditional Pentateuch.[7] The first dozen columns have been heavily damaged, with col. 1 missing entirely.[8] It seems, nevertheless, that the author of 11Q Torah began with an allusion to or summary of Exodus 24 and 34, which described the source and purpose of his work. After the introduction, the writer began with a description of the structure of a sanctuary, the main theme of cols. 3–13 and continued in cols. 30–46. Columns 13–29 prescribe the calendar of the sacrificial ritual as mandated in Leviticus 23 and Numbers 28–29. The next major section, cols. 47–52, is devoted essentially to the laws of defilement, which include also the rules of the holy city and the observance of dietary laws and related matters. Columns 52–66 deal with subjects found in Deuteronomy 13–23. Certain subjects receive a column or two, sometimes three, while others are given one or two lines. Certainly, as the title "The Temple Scroll" indicates, the sanctuary and its precincts form a principal topic of the book.

A glance at the fragments of 11Q Torah will suffice to indicate that its author invested major effort in its composition. Its unequaled length of 8.148 meters with a minimum of sixty-seven columns makes it by far the longest work discovered in the Judaean wilderness.[9] It is, however, in the contents of the book that the efforts of the author can be really appreciated. In an overwhelming number of passages the traditional text undergoes major changes or is even entirely new.[10] In relatively few passages does he merely copy the scriptural exemplar, and even in those places he usually makes alterations. These alterations or innovations do not concern themselves with mere generalizations but supply numerous details. What seems remarkable is not so much that the author prescribes the dimensions of a sanctuary whose likeness was so disparate from the tabernacle recorded in the Hebrew Scripture, but that the ordinances pertain to the erection of a whole precinct with perhaps half a dozen structures, the location and dimensions of each given in minute detail.[11] Certainly, the prescriptions for the sacrificial rites in the Temple Scroll exceed those recorded in the Priestly Code of Leviticus and Numbers.[12] Once the author finds a favorite subject, such as the royal charter, he tirelessly delves into its numerous laws.[13] On the other hand, he can be succinct where the traditional Torah is quite expansive.[14] But whether lengthening or shortening the traditional text, there seems to be little doubt that the author of 11Q Torah was intent on putting forth a work of major proportions. Yadin's extensive commentary has shed much light on the contents, construction, and style of this unique text.[15] However, basic questions as to the nature, purpose, and authorship of the Temple Scroll need further investigation.

What was the author's purpose in composing this book? This question, relevant to any major work, is particularly crucial for understanding the essence of a work which was intended to be taken as a sacred text.[16] It is to this problem that the remainder of this chapter addresses itself.

Yadin's response to this question, explicated at length in both his commentary and his introduction, may be summarized in a single word: editorship. Like Josephus, the sages of old, and the modern student of Scripture, the author of the Temple Scroll recognized the numerous repetitions and duplications in the Mosaic books, some of them lacking coherence and others appearing to be contradictory. Citing numerous examples, Yadin shows how 11Q Torah, through conflation and harmonization, succeeds in fusing related passages into a harmonious unity.[17] Even in sections which at first glance seem to be nothing but a copy of the traditional Torah, the author uses paraphrase to remove obscurities and add elucidations. A legalist, the writer accomplished his editorial work with skill and subtlety. What the Deuteronomist did for the preceding three Mosaic books, the author of 11Q Torah proposed to do for the Law as a whole, including Deuteronomy. Thus the writter of 11Q Torah, according to Yadin, regarded himself as an editor whose chief task was to present the reader with an integrated text containing as few flaws and ambiguities as possible.[18] The reader could now find a fair summary of the Mosaic law without repetition or contradiction.

The sections of the Temple Scroll which have no archetype in the Pentateuch are regarded by Yadin as supplements, incidental to the main task of editing.[19] There had existed old traditions, alluded to in 1 Chronicles and talmudic literature, which ascribed the design and furnishings of the Solomonic sanctuary to the direct command of God, as revealed to Moses and the prophets.[20] Relying on such traditions, Yadin says, the author of 11Q Torah reworded the accounts concerning the construction of the sanctuary and ascribed them to God. What is true of the design of the sanctuary in the Temple Scroll applies also to the other material not found in the Mosaic exemplar. The author believed that he had found them in authentic sources. Surely he considered the royal charter to be in the very spirit of Deut. 17:11–20.[21] Other subject matter not found in Scripture could be located in the lore that circulated among certain isolated groups, an example of which is the Qumranic library itself. It no doubt contained many additional laws of purity not recorded in the Mosaic Torah. Observances practiced since antiquity, such as the offering of woods, recorded only in Nehemiah, received wording characteristic of the traditional Torah.[22] Thus the task which the author of 11Q Torah set for himself, according to Yadin, was not very different from that of the sages of the Mishnah.[23] The Mishnah and the Halakic Midrashim contain numerous halakot not recorded in the Pentateuch, but which the rabbis ascribed to Moses who they said received them at Sinai. No one would suppose that the rabbis ascribed equality with Scripture, much less superiority, to the Halakah. The rabbis aimed at elucidation and amplification. Elucidation and amplification, according to Yadin, were also the purpose of 11Q Torah's author.[24] The reading of his composition would make Scripture appear more complete and perfect than ever.

Learned and detailed though Yadin's argument is, its validity seems questionable. His proposition, which ascribes to the author the purpose of editing a coherent and harmonious Pentateuch, makes little sense. Yadin finds parallels to the Temple Scroll in the composition of Deuteronomy as well as in a number of pseudepigraphs, all of which claimed divine authority.[25] But neither Deuteronomy nor pseudepigraphs such as Enoch or Jubilees may be regarded as proper models for 11Q Torah. It is generally agreed that the composition of Deuteronomy, which evidently occurred in the seventh century B.C.E., antedates the acceptance of a more or less canonized Torah ascribed to Moses. When the "canonization" did take place, evidently in the exilic or post-exilic period, the Book of Deuteronomy's Mosaic authorship was taken for granted. The Samaritan and Greek versions of the Pentateuch attest to the fact that centuries before the Temple Scroll, dated by Yadin circa 100 B.C.E., the canonicity of the Mosaic Torah was fully recognized throughout Israel. And nothing contained in any of the extracanonical books alters this fact, since none of the pseudepigraphic treatises alluded to by Yadin assumes the form of a reedited Torah. Even in Yadin's own definition of the purpose of the Temple Scroll, it is extraordinary that it appeared in the post-exilic epoch, especially in the aftermath of the Maccabean victory, when the prestige of the tradition reached new heights. Thus, even if the author's main purpose was the editing of a more harmonious Torah, such an act would have been no less daring than for Luther to have composed a "Fifth Gospel." Though it is true, as Yadin has shown, that the author employs harmonization and conflation, the editing of a more readable Torah does not seem to have been the author's real purpose. There is a possibility, nay a likelihood, that the task which he set for himself was more grandiose. Could it be that the author proposed to present the reader with another Torah, even more faithful to the word of God and more authoritative than its Mosaic archetype? The following pages outline the evidence for such a view.

11QTorah has not one but two authors: (a) the person who wrote the book, and (b) its alleged composer. This chapter deals exclusively with the latter, the fictive authorship. The real author concealed his identity by advancing the claim that his writings were of a divine source, not as conveyed by any mortal, but revealed directly by God, in the same way as the Torah had been revealed to Moses. By presenting his work as the word of God, the author played for high stakes: he might be glorified as a divine messenger or damned as an agent of Satan. An examination of the syntax and structure of his work will explicate the intent of this writer.

The Pronouns "I," "Thou," and "They"

The author of 11Q Torah not only conceals his own identity, but also attempts to convince the reader that this scroll is not a human composition, that every word had indeed been uttered by God. This becomes evident in the use of the first-person singular throughout the text. The "I" passages are quite numerous, as the following list, by no means exhaustive, indicates. Special notice is given to clauses in which the text of the Mosaic source is altered from the third person to the first.

1. 2:1 אנ[ו]י עוש]ה—"[I] am do[ing]."
2. 29:3–4 בבית אשר א[שכין] שמי עליו—"In the house upon which I will cause My name [to dwell]."
3. 29:6 אשר יביאו לי—"which they will bring to Me."
4. 31:9 ככול אשר אנוכי מדבר אליכה—"according to all which I tell thee."

5. 39:10–11 לי אחר יבואו מבן עשרים [שנ]ה—"to Me, afterwards they can enter from twenty year[s of age]."

6. 45:10 ולוא יבואו בנדת טמאתמה אל מקדשי—"They shall not come into My sanctuary when they are sexually impure."

7. 45:12 אשר אשכין שמי בה—"wherein I shall cause My name to dwell."

8. 45:14 כי אני יהוה שוכן בתוך בני ישראל לעולם—"for I the Lord reside among the Israelites forever."

9. 46:3–4 בתוך מקדשי לעו[לם] ועד כול הימים אשר א[ני שוכ]ן בתוכם—"within My sanctuary forev[er] throughout all the days that [I resi]de in their midst."

10. 46:7–8 אשר יהיו עולים אליו לבוא אל מקדשי—"so that the Israelites will ascend it to enter into My sanctuary."

11. 47:3–4 והעיר אשר אקדיש לשכין שמי—"the city which I shall sanctify causing My name to reside."

12. 47:9 ואל עיר מקדשי לוא יביאו—"they shall not bring (them) into My holy city."

13. 47:11 אנוכי משכן את שמי ומקדשי בתוכה—"I cause My name and My sanctuary to dwell in its midst."

14. 47:12–13 יהיו מביאים . . . לעיר מקדשי—"They shall bring . . . to My holy city."

15. 47:15–16 אם במקדשי תזבחוהו יטהר למקדשי—"If you slaughter it in My sanctuary, it shall be pure for My sanctuary."

16. 47:17–18 ולוא תטמאו את מקדשי ועירי בעורות פגוליכמה אשר אנוכי שוכן בתוכה—"Do not defile with the hides of your abominations My sanctuary and My city in which I reside."

17. 52:10 לוא תזבחנו לי—"Do not sacrifice it to Me."

18. 52:14–15 קרוב למקדשי דרך שלושת ימים כי אם בתוך מקדשי תזבחנו—"within a three days' journey of My sanctuary, but rather within My sanctuary art thou to slaughter it."

19. 52:16 במקום אשר אבחר לשום שמי עליו—"in the place which I will choose to place My name thereon."

20. 53:14–21 ואיש כי ידור נדר לי . . . ואשה כי תדור נדר לי . . . ואנוכי אסלוח לה—"If a man will make a vow to Me . . . If a woman will make a vow to Me . . . I shall forgive her."

It should be noted that this passage demonstrates an explicit rewriting of Num. 20:3–5, changing the third-person "God" references into the first person. This is also true in some of the following examples.[26]

21. 55:15–17 אם ימצא בקרבכה באחד שעריכה אשר אנוכי נותן לכה איש או אישה אשר יעשה את הרע בעיני לעבור בריתי . . .—"If there be found in your midst, in one of your settlements which I grant to you, a man or a woman who does evil in My sight, transgressing My covenant . . ."

In this passage there is a change from Deut. 17:2.

22. 56:17–18 ואנוכי אמרתי לכה לוא תוסיף לשוב בדרך הזואת עוד—"I have said to you, 'Do not ever return that way again.'"

Here again there is a change from Deut. 17:16.[27]

23. 60:10–11   כי במה בחרתי מכול שבטיכה לעמד לפני ולשרת ולברך בשמי —"For them have I chosen from all of your tribes, to stand before Me, to serve and to bless in My name."

24. 63:3 . . .   ונגשו הכוהנים בני לוי כי בהמה בחרתי לשרת לפני ולברך בשמי —"The priests, the sons of Levi, shall then draw near, for them have I chosen to serve in My presence and to bless in My name. . . ."
    This passage involves a change from Deut. 21:5.

The first extant letter in the fragments, which begin with col. 2,[28] is interpolated by Yadin as אנ]י, or what is more probable, אנוכ]י, thus identifying its fictive author. These words in col. 2 are taken from Exod. 34:10, and clearly it is God who is uttering them. The remaining phrases presumably reproduce the covenant between God and Israel as revealed to Moses in the tablets mentioned in Exod. 34:1. While Yadin has recognized the role of the first person in the scroll,[29] he sees it as a mere rhetorical device to add authoritativeness to the Mosaic transmission of the text.[30] However, the "I" in this book does not seem to be merely a stylistic device or affectation. Rather, it advances a claim for divine authorship. The Temple Scroll is not to be characterized as an epitome attempting to paraphrase, conflate, or supplement Moses' legal corpus, but rather as a code of laws uttered by God Himself on Mount Sinai which claims at least equality to and probably superiority over the Mosaic Torah. Unnoticed by Yadin and other scholars, the real significance of the first person can only be appreciated if it is analyzed in conjunction with the author's use of the second and third persons.

Virtually all the passages commanding the construction of the temple employ ועשיתה (thou shalt make), תעשה (thou shalt make), תתן (thou shalt put), ונתתה (thou shalt put), and תבנה (thou shalt build). Beginning with the first column the author emends the text of Exod. 34:10 to the second-person singular, a practice which he generally follows.[31] Equally significant is the employment of the third-person plural, utilized as a rule to add information to the direct prescription. While the second-person singular is the introductory imperative, the third-person plural seems to indicate supplementary commands. The main structure of the book consists of a syntax built on these three pronouns.[32] The following passages exemplify the use of the book's elemental personae:

1. 3:4–8   בי]ת לשום שמי עליו כ[ול] . . . בו כסף וזהב מכול א . . . ולוא תטמאנו כי אם מן ה   טהו]ר . . . [נחו]שת וברזל ואבני גזית לב . . . ואת כול כלי יעשו זהב זהב—". . . ho]use upon which to place My name, a[ll] . . . silver and gold from all . . . thou shalt not defile it, but rather of . . . [bro]nze and iron and hewn stone . . . all its vessels let them make of pu[re] gold."

2. 46:6–8   ושתים עשרה מעלה תעשה לו אשר יהיו עולים בני ישראל אליו לבוא אל מקדשי—"Thou shalt make twelve steps which the Israelites will ascend to enter My sanctuary."

3. 46:9–12 ועשיתה חיל סביב למקדש רחב מאה באמה אשר יהיה מבדיל בין מקדש הקודש
לעיר ולוא יהיו באים בלע אל תוך מקדשי ולוא יחללוהו וקדשו את מקדשי ויראו ממקדשי
אשר אנוכי שוכן בתוכמה—"Thou shalt make a rampart around the sanctuary
a hundred cubits wide, which will separate the holy sanctuary from the
city, so they may not in confusion enter My sanctuary and profane it, but
they shall rather hold My sanctuary sacred and be in awe of My sanctuary, wherein I reside in their midst."

4. 51:6–7 ולוא יטמאו בהמה אשר אני מגיד לכה בהר הזה ולוא יטמאו—"they shall
not defile themselves with those things which I declare to you on this
mount; they shall not defile themselves."

5. 52:19–21 לוא תואכל בשר שור ושה ועז בתוך עירי אשר אנוכי מקדש לשום שמי בתוכה
אשר לוא יבוא לתוך מקדשי וזבחו שמה וזרקו את דמו על יסוד מזבח העולה ואת חלבו
יקטירו—"Thou shalt not eat within My city which I sanctify, placing My
name within it, the flesh of bull, sheep, or goat, which does not come into
My sanctuary, where they shall slaughter and sprinkle its blood upon the
base of the altar of the burnt offering and offer up the fat."

As has already been shown, the scroll is composed in the first-person singular.
In a number of places, the second-person singular and the third-person
plural are used in conjunction. The following examples, therefore, are also
indicative of the work's syntax:

1. 32:12–15 [ו]עשיתה תעלה . . . ולוא יהיה נוגעים בהמה כול אדם כי מדם העולה מתערב
במה—"Thou shalt make a water-course . . . and none shall touch it (the
water), for some of the blood of the burnt offering is mixed with it."

2. 46:13–16 ועשיתה להמה מקום יד חוץ מן העיר אשר יהיו יוצאים שמה לחוץ לצפון
המערב לעיר בתים ומקורים ובורות בתוכמה אשר תהיה הצואה יורדת אל תוכמה ולוא תהיה
נראה לכול רחוק מן העיר שלושת אלפים אמה—"Thou shalt make for them a
place of the hand outside of the city whither they are to go out—
northwest of the city; buildings with springs[33] and cisterns within them
into which the excrement will descend, not within sight—a distance of
3,000 cubits from the city."

In spite of some exceptions, the scroll is characterized by the I-thou-they
style, in which "I" is God. This syntax is adopted to advance a consistent
claim for the divine origin of the scroll, the same claim which is made in the
Pentateuch. The supposition that 11Q Torah is another Torah finds further
support in the Mosaic identity of the second-person singular.

The Pronoun "Thou" Addressed to Moses

As had been recognized, the first person refers to the Deity, but whom does
the second-person "thou" specify? In the legal parts of the Torah, the
second-person singular frequently refers to the collective you, i.e., Israel.[34]

However, the author of the scroll evidently borrowed the I-thou syntax from
the account of the tabernacle, which is closely connected with the content of
the scroll.[35] There the "thou" refers to Moses exclusively since the same
material is duplicated in Exodus when the lawgiver repeats these commands
to Israel and is reiterated a third time when they actually complete the task. Is
the subject of the second person throughout the scroll also Moses, or does
"thou" lose its original sense to refer to Israel as a collectivity? The answer is
clear. In this scroll, the subject of "thou" is the same throughout; as in many
passages of the Pentateuch—Moses. In col. 44:5, we find the passage לבני אהרון
אחיכה (for the sons of Aaron, thy brother).[36] "Thy brother" is clearly an addition to emphasize the identity of the addressee, Moses. This identity also
becomes manifest with the use of מדבר (speak) in col. 31:9. The construction
מדבר אליכה necessarily refers to God speaking to Moses, as is shown in Deut.
5:24-25. In its present context in the scroll, this line appears to be a paraphrase of Exod. 25:9, which reads ככול אשר אני מראה אותך—"In accordance
with all I show thee." In both cases, the verb is describing the activity of divine
revelation to Moses. The foregoing identity finds further confirmation in 11 Q
Torah 51:6-7, which reads as follows: "They shall not be defiled by these
things of which I tell thee on this mount." "This mount" refers to none other
than Mount Sinai, as it does in Exod. 26:30 and elsewhere. Since this is not a
passage copied directly from Deuteronomy, we can take it as evidence of the
author's intention, i.e., to show that the Lord is speaking directly to Moses on
Mount Sinai. This claim is extraordinary since many of the passages refer to a
temple and cult which will only become operative following the conquest.[37]
Still the use of ועשיתה (thou shalt make), referring to Moses, points out that
whoever erected the sanctuary or executed its cultic prescriptions would be
acting as Moses' agent.

Here syntax fuses with theological content. The I-thou-they formulation
which permeates the text was clearly borrowed from sections of Exodus,
where two duplicate accounts prescribe the sanctuary in the wilderness.
Exodus 25-34 contains divine ordinances given to Moses commissioning its
construction, and Exodus 35-40 relates their execution by the Israelites.[38]
11 Q Torah uses the pronominal forms found in the first account, purposefully
avoiding stylistic resemblances to the chronicle of the tabernacle's actual construction by the people. This appears to be more than a stylistic peculiarity.
While the biblical account attests to the execution of these ordinances, the
author of the scroll wishes to convince his contemporaries that these prescriptions have never been executed. What the author seems to imply is that the
sanctuary prescribed in this text is to be identified with neither the wilderness
tabernacle nor the Solomonic structure.[39] In contrast to the account in Exod.
35-40, the author stresses the point that the execution of these commandments has never been completed in the past and is to be fulfilled in the days to
come.

Other aspects of style reinforce the thesis that the writer wished his work to be considered of Sinaitic origin. Morphology and orthography are fused with syntax to produce an impression that the text before us emanates from God, as dictated to Moses on Sinai.[40] Rather than the more prosaic אני, God refers to himself with the majestic אנוכי, as in Exod. 20:2. As Milgrom has noted, the Tetragrammaton is always written in the square alphabet, as in the canonical scrolls found at Qumran, not in the paleo-Hebrew script used for the Divine name in other Qumran texts.[41] Characteristic of the Temple Scroll is the *hey* ending of the second- and third-person plural verbal afformatives, e.g., וספרתמה (ye shall count),[42] והקרבתמה (ye shall present),[43] and וקדשתמה (ye shall sanctify),[44] as well as the second- and third-person plural pronominal suffixes, e.g., לכמה (to you),[45] מושבותיהמה (their habitations),[46] דורותיהמה (their generations),[47] and ידיהמה (their hands).[48] Kutscher and Qimron have called attention to these endings in the Isaiah Scroll and other biblical texts emanating from Qumran.[49] These artificial lengthenings are borrowed from the cohortative אתנה (let me give)[50] and the lengthening with the archaic מו ending, e.g., תבאמו (thou shalt bring them).[51] While some of these and other endings seem to reflect current trends in spelling, many of these variants must be explained as the author's attempt to give his work an appearance of antiquity and authority.[52]

Purpose

Style harmonizes with purpose in 11Q Torah. Unfortunately, the book's prologue and epilogue have perished; however, many pericopes end with a statement of intent for the commandments enjoined therein.[53] These summary statements reveal a pattern exemplified in the following citations:

to place my name (לשום שמי)

1. 3:4   לשום שמי עליו—"To place My name upon it."
2. 52:16   ושמחתה לפני במקום אשר אבחר לשום שמי עליו—"thou shalt rejoice before Me in the place which I shall choose to place My name upon it."

to choose (לבחור)

3. 52:9   לפני תואכלנו שנה כשנה במקום אשר אבחר—"Before Me thou shalt eat it every year, in the place which I shall choose."
4. See no. 2 above.
5. 56:4–5   ויגידו לכה באמת מן המקום אשר אבחר לשכין שמי עליו—"They shall tell thee truthfully from the place upon which I will choose to cause My name to reside."
6. See no. 34 below

to atone (לכפר)[54]

7. 17:2–4   וישמחו כי כופר עליהמה . . . [מקרא קודש יה]יה היום הזה להמה [חוקות עולם לדורותיהמה] בכול מושבותמה וישמחו . . .—"They shall rejoice as atonement is

made on their behalf . . . [a holy convocation] this day will be for them, [a statute forever for their generations] in all their habitations, they shall rejoice . . .''

8.   21:8–9   [ביו]ם הזה יכפרו על התירוש וישמחו בני ישראל לפ[ני] יהוה [חוק] עולם לדורותיהמה בכול מושבותיהמה ושמחו בי[ום הזה] . . .—"[For on] this day, they shall atone over the new wine, the Israelites shall rejoice bef[ore] the Lord, [an institution] forever for their generations in all their habitations. They shall rejoice on [this day] . . .''

9.   26:7   . . . וכפר בו על כול עם הקהל—"And by means of it, he will atone for all the people of the community . . .''

10.   32:6   לכפר על העם—"to atone for the people . . .''

to sanctify (לקדש)

11.   See no.16 below.

12.   27:8–9   מקרא קודש יהיה לכמה היום הזה וקדשתמה אותו לזכרון בכול מושבותיכמה—"A holy convocation will this day be for ye, ye shall sanctify it as a memorial in all your habitations.''

13.   35:8–9   וקדשתה את ס[בי]ב למזבח ולהיכל ולכיור ולפרור והיה קודש קודשים לעולם ועד—"thou shalt sanctify the area ar[oun]d the altar, the sanctuary, the laver and the storehouse, so that it will be a holy of holies forever.''

14.   See no. 22 below.

15.   See no. 20 below.

to not defile (לוא יטמא)

16.   16:5   [לוא] יטמא כי קדו[ש הוא ליהוה] . . .—"[not] shall it be defiled, for holy [it is to the Lord] . . .''

17.   45:12–14   כול איש עור לוא יבואו לה כול ימיהמה ולוא יטמאו את העיר אשר אני שוכן בתוכה כי אני יהוה שוכן בתוך בני ישראל לעולם ועד—"No blind men may enter it (i.e., the city) throughout their lifetimes, so that they shall not defile the city within which I reside, for I, the Lord, reside among the Israelites for-ever.''

18.   See no. 22 below.

19.   See no. 23 below.

20.   51:6–8   ולוא יטמאו בהמה אשר אני מגיד לכה בהר הזה ולוא יטמאו כי אני יהוה שוכן בתוך בני ישראל וקדשתמה והיו קדושים—"They shall not defile themselves with those things which I declare to you on this mount; they shall not defile themselves. For I, the Lord, reside among the Israelites. Thou shalt sanctify them and they shall be holy.''

to purify (לטהר)

21.   45:4–7   ולוא [יהי]ו מתערבים אלה באלה . . . משמר אל מקומו וחנו זה [ב]א וזה יוצא ליום השמיני ומטהרים את הנשכות זואת אחרי זאת [ל]עת תצא הראישונה ולוא תהיה שמה תערובת—"Ye [shalt] not mingle with one another, . . . each watch shall remain at its post. One [co]mes and another goes on the eighth day. They

shall purify the chambers one after another, [at the] time that the first one
leaves so there not be any mingling there."

22. 47:3-7 [והיו] עריהמה טהורות וש[כנתי . . . אתמ]ה לעולם והעיר אשר אקדיש לשכין
שמי ומקד[שי בתוכה] תהיה קודש וטהורה מכול דבר לכול טמאה אשר יטמאו בה כול אשר
בתוכה יהיה טהור וכול אשר יבוא לה יהיה טהור יין ושמן וכול אוכל וכל מושקה יהיו
טהורים—"Their cities [shall be] pure. I will d[well . . . with the]m forever.
The city, which I will sanctify causing my name and my sanctuary to
reside therein shall be holy and pure of anything unclean by which defilement occurs. Everything within it shall be pure and everything which
comes into it shall be pure, wine and oil as well as all food and drink shall
be pure."

23. 50:17-19 וכוּל כלי חרש ישברו כי טמאים המה ולוא יטהרו עוד עד עולם—"They
shall break all earthenware vessels, for they are defiled, and may never be
purified."

do not mix (לוא יערב)

24. 32:14-15 ולוא יהיה נוגעים בהמה כול אדם כי מדם העולה מתערב במה—"No one
shall touch it (the water), for the blood of the burnt offering is mixed with
it."

25. 35:11-13 מובדלים זה מזה לחטאת הכוהנים ולשעירים ולחטאות העם ולאשמותמה ולוא
יהיו מערבים כולו אלה באלה כי מובדלים יהיו מקומותמה זה מזה—"They shall be
separate from one another, the sin-offering of the priests and the he-
goat from the sin-offerings of the people and their guilt-offerings. None
of these shall they mix with one another, for separate shall their locations
be from one another."

26. 37:11-12 ולוא י[י]תערבו זבחי שלמי בני ישראל בזבחי הכוהנים—"The peace
offerings of the Israelites may not be mixed with the sacrifices of the
priests."

27. See no. 21 above.

to separate or set apart (להבדיל)

28. See no. 25 above.

29. 46:9-10 ועשיתה חיל סביב למקדש רחב מאה באמה אשר יהיה מבדיל בין מקדש הקודש
לעיר—"Thou shalt make a rampart around the sanctuary a hundred
cubits wide, which will separate the holy sanctuary from the city."

30. 51:8-10 ולוא ישקצו את נפשותמה בכול אשר הבדלתי להמה לטמאה והיו קדושים—
"They shall not make their lives abominable with anything which I have
set apart for them as defiling, (then) they shall be holy."

to dwell (לשכן)

31. See no. 17 above.

32. See no. 22 above.

33. See no. 20 above.

34. 60:12-14 וכי יבוא הלוי . . . אל המקום אשר אבחר לשכן שמי—"If a levite shall

come . . . to the place which I shall choose to cause My name to dwell.''

to rejoice (לשוש, לשמוח)

35. See no. 7 above.

36. See no. 8 above.

37. 25:9 [עב[ודה]‎ תשמחו ביום הזה לוא תעשה בו כול מלאכת—"Ye shall rejoice on this day. Thou shalt not do any work on it.''

38. 59:12–13 ופדיתים והרביתים וששתי עליהמה והייתי להמה לאלוהים והמה יהיו לי לעם—"I shall redeem them, I shall make them numerous, and I shall rejoice on their account. I shall be their God and they shall be My people.''

39. See no. 2 above.

A glance at these and similar lines of the fragments will reveal the author's aims and concerns. The fear that the Israelites would backslide into idolatry and other pagan practices, so basic a theme in the biblical tradition, is reiterated throughout the fragments. The author accentuates the anxiety about טומאה (impurity) even beyond the strong emphasis found in similar levitical passages. Impurity involves not only coming into contact with corpses or lepers, as in the canonical Torah, but any serious breach of the Law. A judge who accepts a bribe pollutes the house in which such a violation occurs.[55] Impurity results as well from תערובת, a mixing of diverse classes or different people from higher and lower stations. The priests must be kept apart from the Israelites,[56] and the high priest and his vicar from the lower ecclesiastical authorities.[57] Remarkably, חטא (sin) and its cognate עוון (iniquity), as well as their converse סלח (forgiving), are relatively absent, being absorbed under the categories טמא (impurity) and טהור (purity). A breach in any of the commandments results, in the biblical tradition, in sinfulness, in the fragments, it results in impurity as well.

The goal in observing the commandments is the reverse, טהרה (purity), which seems to be a prerequisite for קדושה (sanctity). The prescribed cleansings and ablutions as well as the sprinkling of the ashes remove impurities caused by contact with sources of contamination, but purification from breaches of the law can only come from כפרה, a term that defies definition but seems to mean the observance of the divine prescriptions. Although *kapparah* still retains the traditional meaning of atonement or ransom, it also signifies a recognition for performing God's command.[58] The usual meaning that God will forgive for the wine or the oil seems inappropriate.[59] Does *kapparah* here mean a reward for fulfilling the prescribed ritual concerning the wine and the oil? What is beyond doubt in 11Q Torah is the ultimate reward: God promises to dwell (שכן) in Israel. This verb appears nearly a dozen times, almost always in places original to the author. On the other hand, the promise to prosper (יטב) is absent, except in lines transcribed from Deuteronomy.

Reward and punishment, so typically Deuteronomic, do not appear to play a role in the author's theology.[60] Certainly, in spite of the many passages reproducing sections of Deuteronomy, especially in the last part of the work, it is the priestly passages, with the emphasis on holiness, which permeate the work. 11Q Torah repeatedly states that the ritual serves to bring joy;[61] thus the author adds a new note of rejoicing to the biblical text.[62] However, the author does not merely reproduce Pentateuchal ideas; his main goal appears to be the creation of conditions of holiness that will result in a renewal of the covenant between Israel and God so that God will fulfill His promise of the ultimate redemption of Israel. This idea appears not only in scattered passages but also in col. 2 dealing with the covenant, and is clearly articulated in cols. 29 and 59. Before examining these columns in greater detail, it is worth noting that the author's theology is not only spelled out in the ergative passages but is mirrored in the book's architecture.

Composition

The book's organization gives glimpses into the motivations of its composer. As pointed out by Yadin, the introductory lines of col. 1 apparently contained Moses' ascent to Mount Sinai, where he received the tablets of the covenant as recorded in Exodus 24 and 34, a theme continued in the extant lines of col. 2. What follows is a version of the Torah (Jub. 1:26 refers to it as the "last Torah") which records the conditions of the covenant.[63] The author's central concern was the construction of a sanctuary, which, although containing furnishings similar to those of the wilderness tabernacle, in essence bore no resemblance to the central shrines recorded in Scripture.[64] Cols. 3–13, as will be pointed out in the next chapter, drew their inspiration from Exodus 25–30, but must be regarded as presenting the outlines of a temple unknown in the scriptural tradition. Although seemingly a repetition of Exodus 25, in fact, these columns contain a version that diverges from the tabernacle of the wilderness. 11Q Torah prescribes characteristics of a sanctuary never recorded in the biblical tradition, such as square dimensions, a terrace,[65] a rampart,[66] storehouses,[67] and three courtyards, each with gilded gates on all four sides.[68] All of these features contain dimensions which have no scriptural precedent. Devoting the next sixteen columns to a restatement of the sacrificial calendar of the temple, the author superficially copies the related passages in Leviticus 23 and Numbers 28–29, but in fact reasserts ecclesiastical supremacy in Israel. The coronation of the high priest,[69] the seasons of the new wine[70] and new oil,[71] as well as the six days of the wood-offering festival,[72] extend the priestly and levitical privileges far beyond what is prescribed in the Mosaic source.[73] What characterizes these innovations, however, is the treatment of Israel at the wilderness camp at Sinai, in which the twelve tribes assist in the priestly reign.

After describing the square sanctuary and its ritual, the author restates the measurements of three structures which were mentioned in cols. 4–6, but whose dimensions and functions are given in cols. 30–35: the בית מסבה (staircase), the בית כיור (house of the laver), and what was evidently called the פרור (storehouse).[74] These buildings, together with the altar of stones recorded in 12:11[75] and the *heykal* (main sanctuary), are designated the *kodeš kodašym*.[76] This term, as attested in Exod. 29:37 and 30:29, assigns a supreme sanctity to the items listed in 11Q Torah 35:8–9. Of lesser sanctity was the porch made of pillars, located north of the *parwar,* which served as stalls for the sacrificial animals.[77] The area designated the holy of holies was distinguished from the other buildings of the temple by the fact that only unblemished priests wearing the sacred garments could enter.

What follows in the next ten columns is a description of the three courtyards, each encompassing the other. The inner courtyard, which contained the holy of holies, was reserved entirely for the priests who were officiating; the middle courtyard was for Israelites of twenty years or over who paid the half-shekel; and the outer courtyard admitted converts and apparently women.[78] The author devotes considerable space to the twelve gates. Each bearing the name of one of the sons of Jacob, they were to be constructed with meticulous care. The dimensions of the buildings and the gates were apparently intended to stress the number fourteen, which, in addition to the septimal symbolism found in the fourteen *šelemym* offerings, stood for the sacred community consisting of twelve tribes plus the priests and the levites. Each group within the community, like various structures in the temple precinct, had its own level in the hierarchy of sanctity. The temple precinct was separated by thirty *ris*[79] from the city (Jerusalem is not mentioned by name), which was kept apart from the surrounding country by an area of 3,000 cubits.[80]

The last third of the fragments is devoted to diverse themes,[81] mainly the laws of purity,[82] clean and unclean animals,[83] vows,[84] false prophets and idolatry,[85] obedience to the priest,[86] and a charter for the king making him subordinate to the priesthood.[87] Column 60, which contains the rules governing the division of war spoils and the perquisites of the king, priests, and levites, appears to be an appendix to the royal charter treated in the preceding four columns. The remainder of the book, beginning with the end of col. 60, consists of a plethora of subjects: the false prophet, the rules of evidence, warfare, atonement for a slain body, the captive woman, the favorite co-wife, the rebellious son, the traitor who denounced his people to the pagans, restoration of lost animals, garments, a bird's nest, a parapet for a roof, slander and seduction, and the rape of a virgin. The final topic, which ends col. 66 and was intended to continue in the next column, lists the prohibited marriages.

Ignoring minor subjects, the overall organization of the Temple Scroll seems to follow the Pentateuchal order[88]:

Building of the temple	cols. 1–13	Exodus 25–40
Sacrificial rites	cols. 13–29	Leviticus, Numbers
Resumption of the account of the temple structure and its courts	cols. 30–46	Exodus 25–40
Laws of defilement and purity	cols. 47–54	Leviticus, Numbers
Deuteronomic laws	cols. 54–66	Deuteronomy

What this architecture seems to reveal is that the author's imagination was first of all captured by subject-matter relating to the second half of Exodus and then by matters related to Leviticus and Numbers. He apparently found the Book of Deuteronomy the least interesting of the five Mosaic books.[89] This apparent lack of interest in Deuteronomy may account for two phenomena. First, that the amount of material dependent upon Deuteronomy is limited. Second, in spite of the amplification of Deuteronomic themes, such as the royal charter and the captive woman, the fifth book of Moses has by and large escaped the radical transformation allotted to the subjects of the preceding three Mosaic books. Beginning with 11Q Torah 52:7, the changes from the Mosaic version are minor. With the exception of the royal charter, the wording tends to closely follow the Mosaic text, even though Numbers 30 is included. 11Q Torah 60:12–66 exemplifies the close correlation of the scroll and Deuteronomy. Only here and there, as in the case of the purity of the captive wife (11Q Torah 63:10–15) and of hanging on a tree (11Q Torah 64:6–13),[90] is the text substantially modified. Since copying requires less effort and thought than the composition of new material, the author appears to have invested most of his effort in subject-matter that interested him. Thus the laws of ritual impurity and ecclesiastical perquisites form the core of the Temple Scroll.

The book's economy seems to suggest that the essence of 11Q Torah lies not in the passage taken more or less directly from the Mosaic *Vorlage,* but in the sections which the author either rewrote or formulated anew. The work is not to be characterized, as Yadin does,[91] by editorship, but by authorship.

Yadin has rightly emphasized the centrality of the sanctuary in the scroll. Except for the sixteen columns dealing with the daily and festive rituals, the first forty-six columns are devoted almost exclusively to the design and furnishings of the sanctuary. It would be erroneous, however, to assume that the author had an abiding interest in architectural design. His central concern seems to have been in properly separating the various degrees of sanctity of the major groups in the community.[92] Whether he is describing the functions and dimensions of the buildings, the nature of the sacrificial calendar, or even the king's army, the central theme of properly placing the priests, levites, and tribal groups is never far removed from the author's mind. It is easy to get lost in the diverse topics and subtopics of the various prescriptions and to forget that a single theme governs the entire scroll: to reproduce in the holy land the sacred camp in Israel as it stood before the Lord at Mount Sinai. The attainment of the highest degree of *kedušah* (sanctity) was necessary to prepare the community for the impending epiphany.[93]

Before proceeding to a discussion of some of the central features of this dominant theme, a digression is necessary to consider the possibility of multiple authorship.

Unity

The hypothesis of a single work with a central purpose underlies the discussion thus far. However, is there an alternative possibility? Is there evidence that the sixty-seven columns in fact contain the works of two or more writers?[94] The book contains some apparent contradictions. The passage relating to the king would seem to indicate the prohibition of bigamy and divorce.[95] On the other hand, the admonition that the heirs of the hated wife are to share in the inheritance equally with the offspring of the beloved wife appears to sanction bigamy.[96] Furthermore the divorcee (*gerušah*) is specifically mentioned in 54:4. Several passages—for example, those dealing with impurity[97] and the eating of the blood of slaughtered animals,[98] as well as sections relating to the "false prophet"[99]—are duplicated for no apparent reason. One might argue that the section beginning with 53:14, which deals with the absolution of the wife's vows, and continuing to the end of the book differs sharply in some basic characteristics from the preceding fifty-two columns. In the major part of the book, the fragments contain relatively few passages that reproduce large sections of the Mosaic books without significant rewriting or additions. However, this second section, commencing with the vows, represents a copy of Num. 30:3-10 and goes on to duplicate in a more or less systematic way large blocks of Deuteronomy. Can these and other non-coherent sections support a hypothesis which would assume a composite work drafted by two or more authors?

The answer to this question is an emphatic negative. It is not necessary to presume a contradiction between the prohibition of divorce and bigamy in 56:18 and the supposition of such institutions in other sections. The prohibition refers to the king, presumably to the high priest, and possibly to the priests and levites, whose state of purity had to be exemplary.[100] Nowhere, however, does 11Q Torah outlaw bigamy or divorce as such for Israel as a whole.

In spite of the apparently dissimilar methods of composition in cols. 2–52 and 53–66, a close analysis of the document would seem to point to a conclusion against multiple authorship. What is before us certainly contains a greater unity than the Pentateuch, a text that evolved for centuries. To be sure, the selections from Deuteronomy in the second section lack the independence of composition found in the first part of the fragments, but even cols. 53–66 seem to have undergone much editing by a pen similar to the one which wrote the more original material. Although 56:12–21 virtually reproduces Deut. 17:14–18, the additions in cols. 57–58 and some lines in 59 make sense only if composed by the same hand that wrote the first part of the book. The same compositional unity is evident from col. 60. 11Q Torah prescribes the death penalty for traitors, an ordinance not recorded in Scripture.[101] The last lines of the preserved text prohibit marriage with a niece, also without any biblical precedent. As was shown above, the tendency to edit the Mosaic passages from the third person into the first and second persons is less frequent in the last dozen columns, but this method of rewriting retains its dominance throughout the entire manuscript, strongly indicating an editorial as well as a compositional unity. It is ironic that the author of the fragments, who, according to Yadin, aimed to conflate the Mosaic texts into a harmonious unity, was himself duplicating passages.[102] But this phenomenon of redundancy may only show that the achievement of literary harmony was not one of the author's chief aims. Another possible explanation may be found in the observation that the duplications as well as the relatively small number of editorial alterations appear only in the last dozen columns. For some reason, the author did not revise this part of the book with the same thoroughness as he did the earlier sections. Although one may grant all this, the alterations that were made at the very end of the extant scroll seem to attest to an editorial unity, even if not executed with equal vigor. The fragments' apparent contradictions, duplications, and editorial diversity pale into insignificance in comparison to the scroll's singularity of thought and radicalism of ideas. There is no reason to doubt that 11Q Torah emanates from a single author.

"Torah"

The thematic and syntactic unity of the book, as well as its claim for authority, are manifest in the use of the term "Torah," a word of paramount significance in the scriptural tradition. "Torah" may refer to divine teachings in general, or to a specific set of rules given by God. But scholars differ as to when the term came to designate Mosaic Law or the Pentateuch as a whole. Some think that passages such as the following presupposed the attribution of a great part or the entirety of the five books of Moses: "This is the law which Moses set before the children of Israel; these are the testimonies, the statutes, and the ordinances, which Moses spoke to the children of Israel when they came out of Egypt" (Deut. 4:44–45); "when Moses commanded us a law, as a possession for the assembly of Jacob" (Deut. 33:4).[103] Others maintain that the name *nomos* (law), referring to the Pentateuch, originated only in post-exilic times and is to be found first in passages such as Neh. 8:1: "they told Ezra the scribe to bring the book of the Law of Moses which the Lord had given to Israel."[104] The existence of a canonical Torah finds clear expression in the prologue to Ben Sira, where the threefold division of the *Tanak* is already quite apparent: "reading of the law and the prophets and the other books of our father." Whatever the evolution of the meaning of "Torah," there is no question that by the time of our author the term had acquired the meaning which it has in Greek, *nomos* (law) of Moses, i.e., the entire Mosaic Pentateuch.[105]

"Torah" appears in 11Q Torah in several passages.

1. After prescribing the ordinances of the sacrifices that pertain to the festive cycles in eighteen columns, col. 29 summarizes the main points: that they are to be presented "in the house which I shall make My name dwell upon it . . . burnt offerings . . . daily in accordance with תורת המשפט הזה." The latter phrase is untranslatable into English, since "Torah" is usually rendered as *nomos* (law) in the Septuagint and here *mišpaṭ* certainly means law.[106] The basic meaning of the phrase is nevertheless clear—rules or legal teachings of the Torah. In paraphrase, the whole line may be understood as "in accordance with the Torah's rules for the perpetual sacrifices." Although it is true that "Torah" sometimes designates ritual,[107] *mišpaṭ* can also have this meaning.[108] The conjunction of the two is intended to give this phrase additional authority. "Torah" here refers not only to the law of God but also to the section pertaining to sacrifices which begins with col. 13. If there be any doubt as to the authoritativeness of this Torah, the remainder of col. 29 and presumably parts of the next column make the covenant between God and Israel conditional upon the observance of this Torah, i.e., 11Q Torah. Although the term *torat hammišpaṭ* may seem to designate merely a specific section of 11Q Torah or to reflect a term equivalent to what the rabbis call *halakah,* there is every reason to regard it as the author's title for the whole book. In other words, 11Q Torah is presented as an alternative to the canonized Torah.[109]

2. Further evidence that the author wished to present this work as the Torah is found in 50:5–7: "A person who in the field touches a bone from a human corpse or a body slain by the sword or a corpse or blood from a dead man or an open grave, he shall be cleansed in accordance with the norms of this rule, and if he is not purified *kemišpaṭ hattorah hazzoʾt,* he shall remain in a state of impurity." It is clear that this Torah adds the authoritativeness which this technical term invokes to *mišpaṭ.* "This Torah" could refer only to the title of the work as a whole. It has the same meaning as וכתורה יעשה (in accordance

with the Torah, it shall be done) or כתוב בתורה (as recorded in the Torah), meaning the formal name of the Mosaic Pentateuch.[110] The same claim is repeated a few lines further in this column in 50:17; "In accordance with this *mišpaṭ hattorah* you shall do them." In the concluding lines of this section on impurities, the author makes crystal clear that his Torah was delivered by God: "And they shall not be polluted by these things (i.e., the corpses, etc.) which I tell you on this mount. They shall not be polluted, for I am the Lord dwelling in the midst of the Israelites, and you shall sanctify them and they shall be holy."[111]

3. The first part of col. 56 (lines 1–9) reproduces with slight paraphrase Deut. 17:8–11, a selection that prescribes how the local judges are to proceed in difficult cases of law. They should request a judgment from the current priest or judge in the central city, who shall instruct them in accordance with the Torah, and whose verdict shall be final. The anonymous author, however, seems to have significantly transformed the text:

Deut. 17:10	*11Q Torah 56:3–4*
ועשית על־פי הדבר אשר יגידו לך מן המקום. . . .	ועשיתה על פי התורה אשר יגידו לכה ועל פי הדבר אשר יואמרו לכה מספר התורה ויגידו לכה באמת מן המקום. . . .
"And you shall do in accordance with the word that they shall tell you from the place. . . ."	"And thou shalt do in accordance with the Torah which they shall tell to thee, the word that they will say to thee, from the Book of the Torah, which they will tell thee in truth from the place. . . ."

Yadin believes that the Qumran writer's alteration here introduces a polemical tone against the Pharisaic exegesis which interprets *dabar* as alluding to the authoritativeness of the halakah; i.e., only the written, not the oral exegesis is to be the basis of the priest's decision.[112] Yadin's interpretation of the intent of the variant would be likely if one accepts his reading of the anonymous work as a response to the traditional halakah. But even if one accepts such an intent, and I certainly do not,[113] the thrust of the Qumranic version seems to be part of the author's claim for the equality, and perhaps even the superiority, of his version of the Torah to the canonical text. But whether or not this author wished to make an invidious comparison with the authoritativeness of the old text, it would seem that "Torah," repeated three times in this section,[114] refers to the very work whose fragments are before us.

4. More than three columns of the text[115] are devoted to the constitution of the king, the rules which he must observe to retain his office.[116] This section

has two parts, one reiterating the substance of Deut. 17:14–20, and the other consisting of norms not found in Mosaic Scripture. Lines 56:20–21 read: "And they shall write him this Torah" instead of "he shall write for himself this *Mišneh Torah,*" as in Deut. 17:18. The ancients interpreted *Mišneh Torah* in one of two ways, either as a copy of the Torah (Targums) or as a second Torah (LXX).[117] Yadin supposes that the omission of *Mišneh* in the fragments was intended to mean that the king need not record the entire Book of Deuteronomy but only "this Torah," i.e., the section of royal rules.[118] But it is equally reasonable to account for the omission of the "Second" (*Mišneh*) with the suggestion that the anonymous writer is emphasizing "this Torah," i.e., his version of the Pentateuch. But even if we grant that the king was to keep only the rules pertaining to the royal office, this constitution must certainly embrace both the section taken from Deut. 17:14–20 and the parts added by our author.

If there is any doubt remaining concerning the use of "Torah" in this scroll, its appearance in 57:1 and 57:14 adds clarity: "This is the Torah . . . on the day when they crown him." Whether or not Yadin's interpolation from Deut. 17:18 is correct, "This is the Torah [which they will write for him from that of the priests]," one need not question that "Torah" refers here to the text of 11Q Torah. In this section, which is without a model in Deuteronomy, the author prescribes a council of thirty-six members divided equally among the priests, levites, and Israelites. The members of this council "will deliberate together with him concerning *mišpaṭ* and Torah."[119] The appearance of these terms in this passage can only mean that the author wished to give the impression that his work has the same normative sovereignty as the canonical Torah. Continuing with the same theme, col. 59 fuses into the constitution of the king some of the curses of Leviticus 26 and Deuteronomy 27–28. The author uses this fusion, it would seem, to condemn the historical monarchs of Israel, who as a consequence of their backsliding received their retribution. The list of the violations committed by the kings concludes:

> And I shall hide My face from them and they shall be as food, as prey, and as spoil, with no one to save them, because of their evil, when they violated My covenant and despised My Torah when (or until) they were guilty of all manner of guilt. Afterwards they will return to Me with all their heart and with all their soul in accordance with the words of this Torah; then will I save them from their enemies' power and redeem them from their adversaries. I will bring them to the land of their fathers, I will redeem them, I will cause them to multipy, and I will rejoice on their account. I will be their God and they shall be My people.[120]

This passage seems pivotal. It condemns the past kings of Israel, including the Davidic monarchs, for violating בריתי (My covenant) and despising תורתי (My Torah), and suggests that the redemption will to come to Israel only when the king observes the royal charter in this Torah, i.e., 11Q Torah.[121] Certainly the *beryt* here alludes to cols. 1 and 2, which quote Exod. 34:10: "Behold I am making a covenant with you today," a theme repeated in 29:10: "in accordance with the covenant which I made with Jacob at Bethel." This *beryt*, introduced at the beginning of this work and first made with Jacob, attempts to convey the author's view of the relationship between Israel and the Divine Sovereign. This covenant, while found in the Mosaic source, has a new meaning in 11Q Torah. The author alleges that Israel's misfortune took place because of its failure to observe the prescriptions of this Torah, but he brings hope that the ultimate acceptance of this Torah will, as stated in col. 29, redeem Israel unto eternity. Torah and its synonym *beryt,* although they do not exclude the prescriptions found in the Mosaic books, necessarily embrace the prescriptions of the Temple Scroll. Put more simply, the Mosaic books are "a Torah" and this scroll is *"the* Torah." The observance of "the Torah" is the precondition for God's שכן (dwelling) or placing His name in the midst of Israel, a claim persistently reiterated in the scroll.[122]

Until now in this chapter, I have frequently followed Yadin's proposal to call the longest scroll found at Qumran מגלת המקדש (the Temple Scroll). The fact that cols. 2–12 and 30–43 prescribe the erection of a *miqdaš* (temple), coupled with the prescription of the sacrificial rites in cols. 13–29, lends plausibility to Yadin's title. Upon closer analysis, however, the name מגלת המקדש is unacceptable. What about the second half of the book, which deals with matters other than the sanctuary and its rites? Ancient as it is, the first word of the title *megillah* (scroll) reflects a modern, archaeological concept which is reinforced by the word *miqdaš.* Together these two stress the architectural ordinances of the Lord's house. But the main objection to the title lies elsewhere: it contravenes the wishes of the author. After all, he refers again and again to his work as *Torah* or *Seper Torah.* It is this title which permeates the entire work, including those sections which prescribe the erection of a sanctuary. The title "Temple Scroll" is both inappropriate and misleading. 11Q Torah or simply the Qumranic Torah, an intentional contrast to the canonical Pentateuch, is a more fitting title for this sectarian text.[123] It corresponds to the name given to the book by its author as well as to the book's content and purpose.

The Future Sanctuary (Column 29)

Two related questions arise in regard to col. 29. The first is concerned with semantics: what specifically did the author mean by the numerous phrases containing שכן, "in which I shall make My name dwell"?[124] Secondly, the problem of time must be addressed: When will this epiphany implied in the whole book take place? These questions go to the heart of resolving the enigma of the book's purpose. I believe that 29:3–10 presents the key:

In the house which I shall make My name dwell upon it . . . burnt offerings
. . . daily in accordance with this *torat hammišpaṭ, tamyd* offerings from the
Israelites alone, from their free-will offerings for each one who presents it,
for all their vows[125] and for all their gifts which they bring to Me for their
acceptance. I shall accept them that they may be My people and I may be
theirs forever; I shall dwell with them forever and shall sanctify My sanctuary with My glory when I make My glory dwell upon it during[126] the day
of blessing,[127] when I shall create My sanctuary to establish it for Myself for
all time, in accordance with the covenant which I made with Jacob at
Bethel.

This passage presents the author's epilogue to the section dealing with the festive offerings that began on 13:8, but it may in fact have served as a concluding explanation for cols. 3–29:2, which include the orders to construct the
sanctuary. Clearly 29:3–4, "in the house in which I shall make My name
[dwell]," refers to 3:4, "house to place My name upon it." After summarizing
the prescribed offerings the text gives the purpose of these sacrifices in 29:7–8,
"And I shall accept them (i.e., the offerings), that they may be My people and I
may be theirs forever." In other words, the offerings in cols. 13–29:2 are a
condition of the *beryt* mentioned in cols. 1–2. If Israel will observe its part of
the covenant, so will God. The text goes on to confirm this: "I shall dwell with
them forever and shall sanctify My sanctuary with My glory when I make My
glory dwell upon it during the day of the blessing, when I shall create My
sanctuary to establish it for myself for all time, in accordance with the covenant I made with Jacob at Bethel." A number of clauses in these lines require
special attention.[128] The problematic phrases will be dealt with in turn.

The meaning of the preposition *ʿad* in 29:9 is of crucial importance. The
meaning and purpose of this scroll, no less than the sectarian perception of
the eschatological sanctuary, are affected by it. Yadin and Maier differ as to its
exact reference but agree that it here means "until." Yadin summarizes these
lines as follows: "The author of the scroll stresses that all the aforementioned
sacrifices shall be offered in the temple constructed by the Israelites, where
God will make His name dwell. This temple will stand only until the 'day of
blessing' (i.e., the end of days), when God will build the temple Himself."[129]
In other words, this passage deals with two temples: one is the current building, which ought to be restructured in accordance with the ordinances prescribed in this scroll; and the other will be created by God Himself in the end
of days.[130] Yadin speculates that the author assumed the eschatological temple
would perhaps resemble the accounts of the sanctuary found in Ezekiel 40–47.
On the other hand, this passage could support the conception that the sectarians foresaw a spiritual temple replacing the physical structure, a view
recorded in Rev. 21:22–23: "And I saw no temple in the city, for its temple is
the Lord God, the Almighty. . . . the city has no need of sun or moon to shine
upon it, for the glory of God is its light."

Johann Maier conjectures[131] that 29:8–9 refers to the Second Temple, which 11Q Torah depicts in a utopian form. Then the eschatological sanctuary is announced by the author, beginning with the words *yom habberakah,* to which Maier would add the words *meḥadaš* (newly). According to this view, the prescriptions in these fragments present a glorified version of the sanctuary of the Second Temple.[132] These prescriptions, Maier adds, may have served as a basis for Herod's renovation of Zerubbabel's structure.[133]

Neither of these views appears to have a justification. Certainly, the prescriptions for the construction of the sanctuary and its ritual must be regarded as ordained for an entirely new temple, not a mere glorification or refurbishing of the extant structure. In spite of the apparent dependence on the wilderness tabernacle and the modeling of the community of Israel after the camp at Sinai, the author prescribes at great length the building of a sanctuary that has only a superficial relationship to any of the historical structures. If there is anything that is reiterated repeatedly in 11Q Torah it is that the prescriptions of the temple and its rites are to be eternal.[134] These statements, repeated again and again, stressing the observance of the prescriptions in the scroll for eternity ought not to be regarded as mere summary clauses taken from the Mosaic exemplar, since they appear in passages original to our author.[135] Note that nowhere does the canonical Torah ordain that the measurements of the tabernacle are to have eternal validity. The same is true of the accounts of the Solomonic temple in the books of Kings and Chronicles. It seems quite inconceivable, after the author's repeated insistence on its eternity, that the sanctuary was to be merely ephemeral. It will not do to argue, as Jacob Milgrom does, that ושכנתי אתמה לעולם ועד (and I shall dwell with them forever and ever) does not mean what is says, but refers only to the time up to the eschaton, when the structure so amply elaborated in our text will disappear to make way for a house erected by the Lord Himself.[136] After all, the "end of days" hoped for by the sectarians did not refer to the distant future but rather to immediate events. It is curious that elsewhere in the extant fragments, extensive as they are, the author seems to be absolutely silent concerning this messianic temple which God Himself will allegedly create in a period after eternity, as perceived by Yadin and Maier. Thus Yadin's explanation that 29:8–9 refers to two epochs—the period of the existence of the temple prescribed at the time of the author, and the age when God will create a new sanctuary—is textually inconsistent with the remainder of 11Q Torah, as well as logically faulty.

In fact, 29:8–9, which seemingly sets up an eschatological age following the erection of the book's temple, appears contradictory. How could God have promised to dwell in a newly designed sanctuary "forever" (לעולם) and in the next clause limit His dwelling there merely "until" (עד) the day of the blessing? Syntax and the general contents of the scroll compel us to presume here that the preposition *ʿad* does not have its usual definition "until," but rather, as noted in biblical and rabbinic lexica, means "during" or "while."[137]

It is worth noting that the problem of ʿad also appears in Jub. 1:29.[138] After announcing the coming of the new heaven and the new earth, the author concludes: "until the sanctuary of the Lord shall be made in Jerusalem." He could not have meant that after renewing the heavens and the earth, this process of rebirth would be halted, for he continues the phrase quoted above "and all the luminaries be renewed. . . ." Obviously ʿad, which lies behind Charles's translation of "until," actually means "when" in this text. Otherwise, the text would refer to two periods: first, when the heavens and earth will be renewed, and second, when a new sanctuary will be built. It is clear, however, that the phrase "the luminaries be renewed" refers to a single eschaton. Furthermore, "the sanctuary of the Lord shall be made in Jerusalem" refers to a human construction. Certainly Jub. 1:26–29, which correlates the new temple with the new heaven and earth, knows of only one eschaton.

If the preceding explanation is correct, 11Q Torah 29:2–10, which begins with "these you shall perform" with reference to the festive calendar of sacrifices, and which concludes with the allusion to the covenant of Jacob, applies entirely to the rite that will be instituted in the temple of the future. Furthermore, what animates these lines is also implied in all the ergative terms and clauses that contain promises of atonement or God's ransom (לכפר) as well as pledges of His presence (לשכן) among the Israelites.[139] Presumably, the prologue and epilogue of this book, which have perished, made this clear, but they must now be reconstructed on the basis of col. 29 and similar passages. Likewise, the phrase *torat hammišpaṭ hazzeh* (this Torah of the rule),[140] whose antecedent includes the prescriptions to make a sanctuary and introduce the proper rite, serves as a precondition of what God expects Israel to fulfill in eschatological times. In other words, the entire document makes sense only if understood as a presentation by God to Moses of the Torah of the eschaton.

Yadin cogently notes the author's attempts to harmonize incoherent and inconsistent passages by conflation or elucidation. But harmonization of the Mosaic Scriptures was only a byproduct of the author's main purpose. Nowhere does the author of 11Q Torah define the relationship between his Torah and its Mosaic archetype. Frequent allusions throughout this text, particularly 29:3–10, which advance the claim that this text is to be another Torah would seem to imply that the author wished the people to believe that the Mosaic books constituted the Torah of the past. And since we need not suppose that our author wished to be understood as denying the divine origin of the Pentateuch, it can only mean that God had in fact presented Moses with two *torot,* both given at Sinai.[141]

Why did God give Moses two Torahs? The extant fragments do not deal with this problem directly, although, as will be shown below, the question is discussed extensively in the Qumran literature.[142] It would seem, however, that col. 59—and perhaps other passages—does imply a response to this crucial problem. After adding nearly two columns to the royal charter which is reproduced from Deut. 17:14-20, the author of 11Q Torah inserts a stringent admonition to the king exhorting him to observe the prescribed charter. At first sight, col. 59, which continues at the top of col. 60, seems to contain nothing new. It is a précis of the dire curses found in Deuteronomy 28 and to some extent in Leviticus 26.[143] In the Mosaic source these admonitions are addressed to all of Israel; here, however, they are revised so as to address the king specifically. The apparent explanation for attaching the admonishments of Deuteronomy 28 to the king's charter seems to be Deut. 28:36: "The Lord shall carry you and your king. . . ," as well as Deut. 28:68, which, with a slight paraphrase, repeats the words in the king's charter as quoted in 11Q Torah 56:16-18: "He shall not make the people return to Egypt for warfare in order to increase his horses, silver, and gold. I have said to you, 'Never return this way again.'" In reality, however, it would seem that the author only uses the Deuteronomic curses as a means of shifting to the concluding section of Leviticus 26, which, in contrast to its counterpart, ends with God's promise of redemption: "For their sake, I shall remember the covenant with the first ones (i.e., the patriarchs), when I brought them out of the land of Egypt before the eyes of the nations, to be their God, I am the Lord."[144]

It would be a serious mistake to regard 59:7 ff. as a mere conflation of the two sets of curses in Deuteronomy and Leviticus plus a redemptive peroration, though it is this as well. In the course of the apparent paraphrase and harmonization the author presents a new perspective, shifting the account from the past to eschatological times. In the Mosaic passages the period of backsliding is in the future, when Israel will be settled in the land. In 11Q Torah it is the period when Israel has already backslid, calling for a renovation of the covenant.[145]

Lev. 26:14-15	*11Q Torah 59:8-9*
If you will not listen to Me, if you will not do all these commandments, if you spurn My statutes and you despise My ordinances, so as to not do all My commandments, to violate My covenant . . .	When they violated My covenant and despised My Torah, until they will have been punished . . .

That which is still hypothetical in Leviticus has already taken place, as far as the author of the scroll is concerned. That some other passages still preserve the old form is not very significant. As noted in the parallel columns, 11Q Torah paraphrases the first section of Lev. 26:14-39. But instead of repeating the consolation in Lev. 26:42, "But I will remember My covenant with Jacob, as well as My covenant with Isaac, and also My covenant with Abraham I will remember," an apparent reference to the post-exilic restoration of Israel's remnant, 59:9–10 makes the redemption dependent on "when they will turn to Me with all their heart and with all their soul in accordance with the words of this Torah." Redemption will not come here, as in Lev. 26:42–45, merely by the merits of the patriarchs, but through Israel's repentance and their resolve to follow this Torah with all their heart and all their soul.[146] Furthermore, this will not include a mere remnant. The author foresees a full redemption of all Israel, a complete, absolute, and eternal reconciliation between God and His people, as stated in succeeding lines and culminating in line 13: "And I shall be their God and they shall be My people."

If 59:9–10 is understood as a call for the author's contemporaries to repent, as it seemingly must, then the preceding lines in col. 59 ought to be interpreted as the author's condemnation of Israel's past. In other words, this passage responds to the question: Why, in view of God's promise to Israel, is Israel's historical situation so desperate while that of the idolaters is propitious? Except for brief, occasional moments of exaltation, such as the Maccabean triumph in 164 B.C.E., this question was a constant which every generation of Jewish teachers had to confront. By appending col. 59 to the two sections of the royal charter, the first reproducing Deut. 17:14–20 and the second adding a long series of provisions, the author implicitly, perhaps explicitly in the missing lines at the top of the column, castigates the former kings of Israel for the people's sufferings in the past as well as the present. As the author could have amply documented from the books of Kings and Chronicles as well as the prophetic writings, the kings of Judah and Ephraim, with occasional exceptions, were the first to introduce pagan practices. In post-exilic times, to be sure, the monarchy was not renewed and a resurgence of Torah observance did take place. Still, there was no amelioration of Israel's position among the nations. As the author saw it, pagan practices continued to penetrate into what was regarded as the Jewish way of life. In what seems to be a reference to Zedekiah, the king of Judah taken captive by Nebuchadnezzar, 59:13–15 says: "And the king who . . . shall have no successor on the throne of his fathers forever, for I shall eternally cut off his seed."[147] The author's call for repentance is clearly addressed to his contemporaries, but also includes his judgment on the historical period of the monarchy.

The pivotal point in 11Q Torah is not that Israel had backslid from the covenant with God, but that God had foreseen the impiety and prescribed a redemptive Torah. That is to say, on Mount Sinai God had entrusted to Moses and Israel the Ten Commandments and the rest of the Law. Some of these provisions were to apply immediately while others were to be carried out upon entering into the holy land. But God foresaw that after the death of Moses and Joshua the people would disregard the numerous warnings about the worship of idols, many of which are reproduced in the Qumranic Torah.

He therefore entrusted to Moses another Torah, which would be revealed when Israel had learned from bitter experience the consequences of their evil ways.[148] The author claims to have found this second Torah which God had prepared for Israel to accept after having received retribution for backsliding. This seems to be the force of the word אחר (afterwards),[149] which is intended to mark a new epoch in Israel's history. After they have received their due punishment, they would become aware of the second Torah presented to Israel in this scroll: "Afterwards they shall repent with all their heart and with all their soul in accordance with the words of this Torah"; i.e., the Qumranic Torah. The results of Israel's acceptance of *this* Torah are clearly stated: "And I shall save them from their enemies, I shall redeem them from their antagonists, I shall bring them to the land of their fathers, I shall redeem them and I shall multiply them. I shall rejoice over them, and I shall be their God and they shall be My people."[150]

The promise of redemption in 59:11–13 was probably stated more explicitly at the beginning or end of the book, but it must be interpreted in light of 29:2–10, which in the extant fragments optimally expresses the book's professed purpose. However, in order for the reader to fully perceive the author's claim for the acceptance of his Torah, the final three lines of col. 29 must be analyzed more closely: "And I shall accept them that they may be My people and I may be theirs forever; I shall dwell with them forever and shall sanctify My sanctuary with My glory when I make My glory dwell upon it during the day of the blessing, when I shall create My sanctuary to establish it for Myself for all time (literally—all the days), in accordance with the covenant which I made with Jacob at Bethel." The sanctuary in this passage, as has been explained above, refers to none other than the one prescribed in this book by God to Moses on Mount Sinai.[151] The clause "and they shall be My people and I shall be theirs forever" is virtually identical to 59:13, and both must be perceived in the light of 3:4, which contains the initial commandment to erect the sanctuary of the future.

Lines 29:9–10 appear paradoxical. After revealing the divine prescriptions for the erection of the sanctuary and the observance of its ritual, injunctions given to Moses, the author says in 29:9 that God Himself shall create it. How can this promise be reconciled with the multitude of details recorded in the book's commandments? I have no answer to this question, except to presume that the writer, if confronted with this query, might have responded that the absolute observance of the Torah's commandments is but a condition for God's own creation of His dwelling place. The immense effort required and the countless talents of gold represent the human expression of man's devotion to God. All these labors, however, are but ephemeral. God alone can build His sanctuary; and He will, if Israel will obey what has been prescribed in the scroll.

The final clause in 29:10 reveals that the promise for this eschatological sanctuary did not begin with Moses on Mount Sinai but went back to the time of the partriarchs: "in accordance with the covenant that I had established with Jacob at Bethel." Although the patriarchs are alluded to elsewhere in the surviving fragments, only Jacob is mentioned by name.[152] Where does Scripture, the question arises, record this covenant? Of course, it is possible to cite here, as Yadin correctly does, chaps. 31–32 of Jubilees, which go to great lengths to elaborate on God's promise to consecrate His son Levi and to establish an eternal sanctuary.[153] To regard Jubilees 31–32 as the author's source, however, would mean that the Book of Jubilees antedates these fragments, an issue that will be discussed in the next chapter.[154]

The exclusive naming of Jacob from among the patriarchs may be accounted for on the basis of the contents of the scroll itself, and need not be dependent on Jubilees. The basic symbolism which characterizes the architecture of the sanctuary, the sacrificial rites, and the king's council, is the number twelve, for the twelve sons of Jacob. Moreover, as in Scripture, the words *Beney Yiśra'el* never lose their primary meaning as a synonym for Jacob. The author may have intended to stress the linkage of Jacob-Israel in the last two extant words of the column—"at Bethel"; evidently he is alluding to God's appearance upon the return of the patriarch to Bethel[155] rather than to Jacob's dream and the ladder.[156] It is here that Jacob builds an altar and removes idolatry.[157] This is the only specific allusion to the Book of Genesis and its patriarchal lore, as well as to a geographical location other than the holy land or Egypt. It was at Bethel that God told Jacob his name would henceforth be Israel. On account of the missing lines at the top of col. 30, the full scope of the clause "in accordance with the covenant that I established with Jacob at Bethel" remains obscure; however, the basic point is that the covenant on Sinai constitutes but a renewal of the relationship established between God and Jacob at Bethel.

It is ironic that the figure who, aside from the Lawgiver Himself, appears in almost every line of the fragments may escape the reader's notice. As has been explained above, it seems quite likely that the book's introductory section, now missing, identified the subject, who in the fragments appears exclusively as "thou" (i.e., Moses). Such phrases as "thou shalt make," "as I have spoken to thee," and "thy brother Aaron," disclose the identity of the second-person singular. Any hesitation vanishes in light of the words "on this mountain" (i.e., Sinai),[158] which state the focus of the revelation that the author attributes to 11Q Torah. Although the patriarch Jacob and his sons, as well as Aaron, are mentioned by name, the law-receiver is not, since Moses is the addressee of the entire scroll. No figure posterior to him, not even the sons of Aaron, has his appelation recorded. What is true of the prosopography of the fragments also applies to their geography. Only Egypt, a country where the Israelites dwelt in the past, and the seven nations of Canaan, where they will settle in the future, are mentioned. The Mosaic books refer to quite a multitude of other nations. The author of 11Q Torah carefully refrained from anachronistic allusions. Even in passages directly reproduced from Deuteronomy, as in large sections following col. 48, the author seems to consciously avoid pericopes that contain Amalekites, Ammonites, and Moabites.[159]

Without directly mentioning him in the extant remnants, the author of 11Q Torah succeeds in raising the figure of Moses to hitherto unheard-of dimensions. In the five books bearing his name, Moses serves as messenger to Pharaoh, as the teacher of the divine law to Israel, as the builder of the tabernacle, and as the guide of Israel in the wilderness. Exilic and post-exilic writings ascribe the Torah to him. The Pharisaic and rabbinic traditions additionally credit him with providing midrashic and halakic amplifications. Rarely, however, does Moses appear, as he does in a late Palestinian Targum, as the associate of the Messiah.[160]

If we focus solely on the work at hand, we see that these fragments elevate Moses from a mere legislator of the past to an anointed lawgiver of the future. The nature of this elevation becomes discernible in the new dimension which God reveals to Moses in our text. The canonical Mosaic books contain three dimensions of time: from the creation of the world to the Exodus is the past; from the Exodus to the death of Moses in the land of Moab is the present; and from the crossing of the Jordan to the conquest of Canaan is the future. Surprisingly, however, the Pentateuchal narrative contains quite a number of passages which in a conditional form tell us what will happen after the conquest; namely, the backsliding of the people and the divine retribution. There is little in the Mosaic books that temporally goes beyond the format of "if you follow . . ." or "but if you do not turn away . . . ." Only Lev. 26:44–45 does so: "But even then, during their stay in the land of their enemies I will not have despised them. . . . But I shall remember the covenant." Passages such as this are rare, since they seem to allude to exilic and post-exilic times. Whenever the final composition of the Pentateuch took place, the epoch of אחרית הימים (the latter days), which fills the prophetic books, is absent in the Mosaic Torah.[161]

What is rare, if not entirely absent, in the Mosaic archetype becomes the chief theme of the scroll. The epoch of the eschaton fills most of its columns; those few passages dealing with the period of the foreseen backsliding serve to bring the future era into relief. At the very beginning of the work, the period of Israel's backsliding, which was presumably included in the missing lines at the bottom of col. 2 and the top of col. 3, was bridged to the succeeding period that commenced with the erection of the eschatological temple.[162] The conclusion of almost every subsection reiterates the eternal validity of the prescriptions in this book. Although there are many such examples in the Mosaic Torah, there are equally numerous passages where such endings are entirely absent. The constant presence of concluding lines implying the perpetuity of the commandments listed in 11Q Torah may have been intended to draw a

contrast with the ephemeral standing of the Mosaic Pentateuch.[163] Certainly
the sanctuary prescribed in the scroll was to be sufficiently distinct to utterly
eclipse the preceding sanctuaries described in the historical prophetic
accounts. The unique features of this eschatological temple—its square
dimensions, fantastic gilding, lofty two-storied structures, suggestive numerology, triple courtyards, and highly decorated gates—were evidently intended
to call attention to the sharp contrast between the sanctuaries of the past and
that one which, as stated in 29:8–10, God Himself would ultimately create.[164]
In a way, therefore, 11 Q Torah may have been intended to supersede not only
the canonical Pentateuch but the other books of the Hebrew Scriptures as
well.

Conclusion

In this study, the proposition accounting for the main aim of the scroll differs
substantially from that advanced by Yadin, as well as by Maier and Milgrom.
As proposed by Yadin in his extensive introduction and commentary, the
author's purpose was twofold. Inasmuch as the fragments reproduce and conflate the scriptural passages, the author acted as an exegete, wishing to produce a harmonious Torah free of incoherence and duplication. The other aim,
according to Yadin, was polemical. Many of the additional laws, not found in
the biblical tradition, must be understood as indirect arguments against the
current observances of the Torah, especially those advocated by the Pharisees.
The scroll was for Qumran what Midrash Halakah was for the rabbis. Histori-
cally speaking, the temple of the scroll resembles that of Mishnah Middot, the
differences being primarily formal or sectarian. The rabbis used the scholastic
mode of presentation, the Qumran author the more authoritative mode
found in the Apocrypha. In a word, according to Yadin the Qumranic Torah
fuses and supplements the scriptural accounts in an attempt to make the tradition more meaningful to its author's generation, but the author never consciously attempts to rival or to depart from the Mosaic Law.

This study proposes an alternative postulate. Although it is true that some
passages in the scroll were built by fusing diverse lines from its Mosaic source,
and that some of the views expressed in the scroll may have resulted from reactions to current normative practice, while others reflect archetypes containing
textual traditions which vary from the Masoretic text,[165] the author's main
interest lies elsewhere. His purpose in composing this work is not to be sought
in the passages that reproduce or conflate biblical texts, but in the lengthy sections that present radical innovations allegedly ordained by God to Moses.
Nowhere in the canonical Torah does God ordain pentecostal feasts celebrating the first wine and the first oil, which are to be concluded with a season of
six days of the offering of woods. The Hebrew Scriptures contain several
lengthy accounts which detail the dimensions of several sanctuaries. None of

these account for the square dimensions prescribed in the fragments. What characterizes the scroll is not 56:12–21, but cols. 57–60, which formulate an utterly new royal charter, one that has almost no basis in Scripture. In spite of the apparent indebtedness to the Mosaic Torah, the fragments can be properly perceived only as presenting a new and superior Torah that reveals, its author claimed, what was still unrecorded in the Mosaic books.

The author employed a deliberate vocabulary, syntax, and organization to boldly advance his claims for the divine origin of his work and for its superiority to the canonical Pentateuch. Except for a few passages, such as the Decalogue or the ordinances of the tabernacle, the Law was transmitted to Israel not by God Himself but through Moses. The scroll, the author seems to claim, reproduces the words of God as delivered directly to Moses on Mount Sinai. Even quotations from Deuteronomy appear here as if given directly from God. The account of God's covenant with Israel begins this book, which then continues with prescriptions for the eschatological temple, whose design and dimensions emphasized holiness more strongly than had the tabernacle of the wilderness. The stringent rules against any defilement as well as against idolatry have as their central purpose the perpetuation of Sinai, whose state of purity was prescribed in Exodus 19, as Israel was making itself ready to hear the voice of God. Thematically and formally, the author composed a work that recreated the essence of the Mosaic Torah.

In contrast to the Mosaic Torah, which records Israel's experience up to the death of the lawgiver, 11Q Torah deals exclusively with the future. The scroll responds to a central question: Why has God turned away from Israel? The answer seems to be that, as foreseen by God, the experience of Sinai was of but a fleeting duration. In spite of all the efforts of Moses, the forty years of wandering in the wilderness proved of no avail, since soon after the entry into Canaan, the people failed to observe the Law as they had promised to do in the covenant. But rather than destroy them or treat Israel like any pagan nation, God had entrusted to Moses a second Torah giving Israel another chance. Whereas the first Torah was, on account of Israel's violations, ephemeral, the second would last eternally. The tabernacle of the wilderness had been prescribed for only forty years; the First and Second Temples, according to the author, apparently lacked divine authority, having incorporated many features from the surrounding nations. Only if Israel will renew the covenant, then construct a new sanctuary and inaugurate a new rite, will God come down from heaven to dwell forever in Israel's midst.

All indications are that the author called his book *Seper Torah* or *Torah,* a title that implied an invidious comparison with the Mosaic Pentateuch. If this is correct, the name *Megillat Hammiqdaš* given to this work in the editio princeps is both inappropriate and misleading. On the other hand, "Qumranic Torah" seems to be a fitting and proper title for a book that was claimed to have been given to Moses on Mount Sinai. Such a title was intended to reinforce the book's claim not only for equality with its Mosaic counterpart, but for superiority to it. The author's attitude to the traditional Torah was perhaps similar to that found in Matt. 5:17, which in paraphrase may be rendered: "I have not come to diminish the law of Moses, but to complete it."[166]

Chapter 2

The Sectarian Torah in Qumranic Literature

The preceding chapter advances the hypothesis that the Qumranic Torah presented itself as a copy of a Torah which God had ordained to Moses on Mount Sinai. The text would be revealed to Israel only at the time of the eschaton, when the messianic epoch would be inaugurated. 11Q Torah arrogates to itself not merely equality to the traditional Pentateuch, but superiority to the Mosaic Law.

This proposition heightens the enigma of the Qumranic Torah: Who authored this book, when did he live, and how seriously was he taken by his contemporaries? A basic fact is known about the provenance of 11Q Torah. It and remnants of two or three other copies were part of the library of the Commune (*Yaḥad*) recovered from the caves of the Judaean wilderness. Was its author then, as some scholars have contended, a member of the Qumran commune; or, as argued by others, was he an outsider whose writings were reproduced by a Qumranic scribe? The questions of authorship and date will be examined in the succeeding chapters. In this section, however, we deal with the literature that in one way or another seems related to the text of 11Q Torah. The Book of Daniel, a treatise that did not receive its present form prior to 165 B.C.E. but was included in the Hebrew canon, may perhaps be counted among the works that are related to the scroll. Certain Graeco-Jewish writings also show some kinship to the contents of the Qumranic Torah. But here we deal primarily either with writings which show some affinity to the Qumranic Torah, such as the Book of Jubilees, or with strictly sectarian writings, such as the War Rule and the Community Rule. Assuming, for example, that sections of the books of Enoch or Jubilees display an affinity with 11Q Torah, it will be our task to respond to these questions: Is there an interdependence between Jubilees and 11Q Torah, or do the two pieces follow a work now lost? If truly interdependent, which is the original and which its revision? The related literary works which preceded or followed the sectarian Torah will provide a relative chronology for the most important Qumranic works. This analysis will also provide the key to an appreciation of the scroll's significance for the history of the sect.

Enoch

The only writings outside of the Bible that may have influenced the Qumranic Torah are sections of what is now known as the Book of Enoch, which has survived in its entirety only in the Ethiopic version of the Old Testament.[1] The antiquity of parts of the Book of Enoch need not be doubted. Remnants of an Enochite library were discovered at Qumran, and according to Milik they are contemporaneous with the time of the composition of Gen. 5:21–24.[2] Without necessarily accepting Milik's dating of the Aramaic Enoch, we contend that these fragments cannot be later than the third century B.C.E. Already in this period, two qualities were ascribed to Enoch that were associated with his name: he was the first mortal to become one of the heavenly beings and he revealed the making of the calendar. As pointed out by Milik, the fact that he lived 365 years can only mean that the discovery of the length of the solar year was ascribed to him.[3]

The Book of Enoch, probably composed originally in Aramaic, is a composite of elements written over centuries. But its earliest parts may go back to the fourth century B.C.E., if not earlier. It is not only that Pseudo-Eupolemus, who flourished around 200 B.C.E.,[4] and the author of Jubilees, writing circa 170 B.C.E, cite Enoch as the discoverer of astronomy,[5] but significant fragments of the Aramaic original found at Qumran indicate a late Persian or early Hellenistic date of composition.[6] In view of the existence of Aramaic literary works such as Ahikar at Elephantine,[7] the prevalence of astronomical treatises among the Jews may be presumed. According to Milik, an independent Aramaic Astronomical Enoch, in part paraphrased or used in the Ethiopic Enoch's chapters 72–82, goes back to the fifth century B.C.E.[8] Whatever the exact date of composition, it forms an important strand in the making of the Book of Jubilees which was titled by its author, "This is the history of the division of the days of the law and of the testimony, of the events of the years, of their (year) weeks, of their Jubilees throughout all the years of the world."[9] For the formation of his angelology as well as for his solar calendar, the author seems to have been indebted to the Astronomical Enoch, whose full title was: "The book of the revolutions of the lights of heaven, each as it is, according to their classes, according to their (period of) rule and their times, according to their names and their places of origin, and according to their months."[10]

Fragments of the four copies of 4Q Enastr give us the flavor of what must have been an extensive treatise on astronomy. The author describes the movement of the moon thus:

> [1. . . . . And it (sc. the moon) shines during the rest of this night with three seventh (parts); 2. and it waxes during this day up to four sevenths and a half. And then it sets and enters (the same gate as before), and it is covered, the rest] of this day, to [two 3. sevenths [and a half. And in night] twenty-[four] of this (month) it is covered by four sevenths and a half; and there is subtracted from its light 4. [four sevenths and a half]. And then it emerges (from the same gate) and shines during the rest of this night with two

sevenths and a half; it waxes 5. [during] this day up to five sevenths. And then it sets and enters (the same gate) and it is covered, the rest of this day, to two sevenths (of its light).

6. And at the (beginning of) night twenty-five of this (month, the moon) is covered to five seventh (parts of its light, i.e.) five seventh (parts) are subtracted from its light. 7. And then it emerges (from the same gate as on the preceding days) and shines during the rest of this night with two seventh (parts of its light); and it waxes during this day up to five sevenths and a half (of its light). 8. And then it sets [and] enters the second gate and it is covered during the rest of this day to one seventh (part) and a half (of its light).[11]

Fragments like this copy continue in the same manner. Features that typify these fragments are also found in Ethiopic Enoch: (a) the redundancy of the formulation, (b) the stress on the divisibility by seven, and (c) the role assigned to the gates of the heavens (תרעא).[12]

Some fragments are significant for establishing a concrete link with extant sections of the Ethiopic Enoch, as well as with elements of the Qumranic Torah:

3. . . . and three (gates) after those on the north, [and three after those on the west. 4. And through four of these come forth winds which] are for the healing of the earth, and for its revival. And [through eight of these come forth harmful winds; when they are spent, they destroy all the earth] and the waters and all that is in them which grows and flourishes and creeps [in the waters and on the dry land, and all (men) who live in it. 5. And first of all,] the east wind comes through the first gate which is in [the east, and it inclines to the south; and from it comes destruction, drought, heat, and desolation.] . . . 14. And the twelve gates of the four quarters of heaven are completely (described); their complete explanation I have shown [to you, my son Methuselah].[13]

The dependence of Enoch 72–82 on the astronomical fragments published by Milik is clear. The following citation shows the indebtedness of the Ethiopic Enoch to the Astronomical Enoch:

3. . . . And three (are) towards the north, and the three after these on the left (are) towards the south, and three (are) in the west. 4. Through four of them come winds of blessing and peace, and from those eight come winds of punishment; when they are sent, they bring devastation to the whole earth, and to the water which (is) on it, and to all those who dwell upon it, and to everything which is in the water and on the dry ground. 5. And the first wind from those gates, called the east (wind), comes out through the first gate which (is) towards the east, (the one) which inclines to the south; from it come devastation, drought, and heat, and destruction . . . 14. And

(thus) the twelve gates of the four quarters of heaven are complete. And all their laws, and all their punishments, and all their benefits I have shown to you, my son Methuselah.[14]

11Q Torah 30–46, which describes the four sides of the sanctuary square, its gates, courtyards, and architecture, is clearly in accordance with Enoch's description of the universe.

The major portion of what has survived of the Aramaic original of the Astronomical Enoch deals with the movement or rotation of the moon through the portals of the heavens.[15] Some of the lost portions of that book can probably be recovered by comparing its fragments with the description of the movement of the sun in chap. 72 of the Ethiopic Enoch. The following passage is a representative section of that chapter:

> 8. When the sun rises in the heaven, it goes out through that fourth gate for thirty days, and exactly in the fourth gate in the west of the heaven it goes down. 9. And in those days the day grows daily longer, and the night grows nightly shorter, until the thirtieth morning. 10. And on that day the day becomes longer than the night by a double (part), and the day amounts to exactly ten parts, and the night amounts to eight parts. 11. And the sun rises from that fourth gate, and sets in the fourth gate, and returns to the fifth gate in the east for thirty mornings; and it rises from it, and sets in the fifth gate. 12. And then the day becomes longer by two parts, and the day amounts to eleven parts, and the night becomes shorter and amounts to seven parts. 13. And the sun returns to the east, and comes to the sixth gate, and rises and sets in the sixth gate for thirty-one mornings because of its sign. 14. On that day the day becomes longer than the night, and the day becomes double the night; and the day amounts to twelve parts, and the night becomes shorter and amounts to six parts.[16]

This passage is cited here for two reasons. First, it would seem there is a resemblance in the morphology of the sanctuary in 11Q Torah and of the universe in Enoch. The second reason for bringing in this passage is to shed light on the original Aramaic Enoch, for though the Ethiopic Enoch lacks a detailed account of the lunar movements, this reflects an editorial peculiarity of the latter document. The Aramaic account contains portions of a most detailed description of the lunar rotation. What characterizes both accounts is the repetition of every movement; in the Ethiopic Enoch, of the sun; in the Aramaic, of the moon.

Ethiopic Enoch's account of the movements of the moon contrasts sharply with what must have been a lengthy description in its Aramaic source. In the passage quoted earlier, as well as the following lines,[17] the attention to detail exhibited in this day-by-day account of lunar activity is most striking:

1. [And (the moon) shines in night eight of] this (month) with four sevenths. And then it sets and enters (the same gate as before). During this night the sun 2. completes the passage (across) all the sections of the first gate, and it begins again to go and to come out through these sections (i.e., of the first gate). [And then the moon] 3. sets and enters (the same gate). And it wanes (during) the rest of this night by three sevenths. And it waxes during this day up to four sevenths and [a half. And then] 4. it emerges (from the same gate as before) and it keeps during the rest of this day two seventh (parts of its light) and a half.

And it shines during night nine of this (month) with four 5. [sevenths] and a half. And then it sets and enters (the gate).

The contrast between this work and its successor becomes clear when we turn to some of the lines describing lunar movement in the Ethiopic text:

3. And every month its rising and its setting change, and its days (are) as the days of the sun, and when its light is uniformly (full), it is a seventh part of the light of the sun. . . . 6. And on the day it receives a seventh part and a half of its light, its light amounts to a seventh-and-seventh part and a half. 7. It sets with the sun, and when the sun rises, the moon rises with it and receives a half of one part of light; and on that night at the beginning of its morning, at the beginning of the moon's day, the moon sets with the sun, and is dark on that night in six and seven parts and a half. 8. And it rises on that day with exactly a seventh part, and goes out, and recedes from the rising of the sun, and becomes bright on the remainder of its days in (the other) six and seven parts. . . . 74:6. It goes out for seven days, and turns back, and returns again to the gate from which the sun rises; and in that (gate) it makes all its light full, and it recedes from the sun, and comes in eight days to the sixth gate from which the sun rises. 7. And when the sun rises from the fourth gate, (the moon) goes out for seven days until it rises from the fifth (gate); and again it returns in seven days to the fourth gate, and makes its light full, and recedes, and comes to the first gate in eight days. 8. And again it returns in seven days to the fourth gate from which the sun rises. . . .[18]

Long as this passage is, it constitutes only a précis of the elaborate description attested in the Aramaic citations from its astronomical antecedent. The fact that Ethiopic Enoch describes the solar movement (most likely also included in the Astronomical Enoch) in some detail, however redundant, whereas it merely summarizes the lunar movements, may be of significance. This brevity may reflect a progressive diminution of the moon's role in the astronomical lore, a decrease that becomes so prominent in the advocacy by Jubilees of a calendar that is absolutely solar.[19]

The Qumranic fragments of the Astronomical Enoch leave no doubt that what lies behind the Ethiopic version is an account of the movements of both the sun and the moon. Thus the belief that Enoch presumes a solar reckoning like that in Jub. 6:23–38 rests on error.[20] It could be argued that the Aramaic text contained only a solar calendar, and that the lunar calendar and inter-calary month are peculiar to the Ethiopic Enoch. This view is unacceptable, since, if anything, the Ethiopic version is less lunar and more solar in char-acter than its Aramaic archetype. Furthermore, the lunisolar character of Enoch has its foundation in the very structure of the astronomical book. Both 4Q Enastr and the Ethiopic version form part of a work intended to illumine Gen. 1:16: "God made the two great luminaries, the big luminary to rule during the day and the small luminary to rule at night." From Gen. 1:14 we know that it is prescribed that "They shall be for signs and *mo'adym* (seasons), for *yamym* (days) and *šanym* (years)." Enoch, like the rabbis, understood this as referring to the festivals and the years. For the Enochite writer, the year and its festivals were to be reckoned according to the two great luminaries. There is no reason to question the originality of the 354-day lunar year mentioned in the Ethiopic Enoch.

A number of elements in the sectarian Torah makes sense only if a strong influence of the Astronomical Enoch is presumed. The number seven, which appears again and again in the various measurements of the buildings and the gates, is basic to the dimensions of the sanctuary described in the Qumranic Torah. The stairwell is seven cubits from the sanctuary,[21] the height of the gates of the laver is seven cubits,[22] the wall of another building is seven cubits from the wall of the laver,[23] the width of the wall of the inner court gate is seven cubits,[24] the thickness of the outer court's wall is seven cubits,[25] and the gates stick out from the outer court's wall seven cubits.[26] The frequent use of the multiples of seven accentuates the septimal theme of this work. Fourteen finds frequent mention: the gate of the inner court has a width of fourteen cubits,[27] the beams of the gate of the inner court are fourteen cubits above the top doorsill,[28] the width of the doors of the outer court is fourteen cubits,[29] and the width of the terrace around the outer court is fourteen cubits.[30] The laver in the scroll is twenty-one cubits square,[31] another employment of the septimal theme. Frequent references to twenty-eight also appear: twenty-eight cubits square is mentioned in the initial description of the sanctuary,[32] the gate of the inner court has a height of twenty-eight cubits,[33] the height of the wall around the middle court is twenty-eight cubits,[34] the total width of the gates in the middle court is twenty-eight cubits,[35] and the height of the doors of the gate of the outer court is twenty-eight cubits.[36] Finally, the height of the gates of the outer court is seventy cubits.[37] While very frequent in 11Q Torah's design, these measurements are absent in the older designs of the sanctuaries of the wilderness and of Jerusalem, whether in the account of Kings, Chronicles, or Ezekiel.[38] The Astronomical Enoch, however, does not

tire of emphasizing the significance of the septimal number, no doubt wishing
to link the cosmic movements with the Sabbath.[39] The dimensions of the eternal sanctuary incorporate this sabbatical architecture of the universe. To be
sure, it could be argued that the sabbatical numbers appear frequently in
Pentateuchal or other biblical texts. Nevertheless, only in the two versions of
the Astronomical Enoch no less than in the sectarian Torah is this number
extended to matters other than temporal. Before Enoch, the number seven
gained great significance, but it did not assume the paramount role it was to
have in the books of Enoch and in the sectarian Torah.

Squareness is another outstanding characteristic of both Ethiopic Enoch
and the scroll. In Enoch 76:1–4, the heavens are described as follows:

> 1. And at the ends of the earth I saw twelve gates open to all winds, from
> which the winds come out and blow over the earth. 2. Three of them (are)
> open in the front of heaven, and three in the west, and three on the right of
> heaven, and three on the left. . . . 4. Through four of them come winds of
> blessing and peace, and from those eight come winds of punishment. . . .[40]

As with much of Enoch 76, the concluding verse of this chapter is also found
in the Aramaic fragments: ושלמו תרי עשר תרעי ארבע רוחי שמ]יא "And the twelve
gates of the four sides of heaven are complete."

In the Qumranic Torah likewise, some structures, such as the laver and the
middle courtyard, have four sides,[41] which in the words of its fragments are
רוחות. The twelve gates, three on each side, receive paramount emphasis in
Enoch's construction of the universe. The Qumranic Torah equally stresses
the twelve gates in the middle courtyard, where each side is taken up by three
of the twelve tribes of Jacob: "The names of the gates for this court will be the
names of the sons of Israel: Simeon, Levi, and Judah on the east; Reuben,
Joseph, and Benjamin to the south; Issachar, Zebulon, and Gad to the west;
and Dan, Naphtali, and Asher to the north."[42] The outer courtyard has a
similar arrangement: "Three gates are in the east and three in the south, three
to the west and three to the north."[43] The names of the twelve tribes are then
listed again in the same order. The author of the sectarian Torah apparently
fused the theme of the sons of Jacob with his prescriptions for the festive
calendar of sacrifices, assigning to the twelve tribes a prominent role absent in
the scriptural tradition.[44]

Another puzzling aspect of the scroll may be explained on the basis of the
Astronomical Enoch. The author of the Qumranic Torah asserts that each of
the structures and gates consists of a main floor and a second story of smaller
dimensions;[45] both are described at length and are to be covered with pure
gold, a feature without precedent in the biblical accounts.[46] Can it be that the
greater and lesser stories correspond to the greater and lesser luminaries
whose movements are depicted at great length in Enoch 72–73?

On the basis of fragments from the Qumran library, Milik has presented a

seemingly convincing case for an Aramaic version of the Astronomical Enoch
dating back to the Persian period.[47] He interpolates lacunae in lines of the
Aramaic fragments on the basis of the Ethiopic Enoch, on the assumption that
the latter was dependent upon the former, a supposition based on the relative
antiquity of the Aramaic manuscripts and their more detailed descriptions of
the celestial movements. Thus, the Astronomical Enoch may have begun as
the Ethiopic Enoch did, with a revelation by the angel Uriel (light of God) to
Enoch. This Aramaic work may also have served as a model for the introduction of the angel Penuel at the beginning of Jubilees.[48] The evidence
assembled suggests a clear relationship between the Astronomical Enoch, the
Ethiopic Enoch, and the Qumranic Torah. Certainly the Ethiopic Enoch is
posterior to its astronomical archetype. Also apparent is the dependence of
the sectarian Torah on this lore. But what needs further clarification is
whether 11Q Torah used both the Astronomical and the Ethiopic Enoch, or
only one—and if the latter, which of the two?

The epiphany at Sinai, as depicted in Deuteronomy 33, where it is linked
with the blessing of the twelve sons of Jacob and with the creation of the universe, may have served as the inspiration for linking the Enochite astronomical lore with the prescriptions in the Qumranic Torah. Enoch's descriptions of
the movements of the sun and the moon and 11Q Torah's design of the ritual
both portray events at the time of the new creation.[49] Thus the future sanctuary prescribed in the scroll seems to have been designed to correspond to
the renewal of the heaven and the earth at the end of days. The Enochite
astronomical lore forms part and parcel of 11Q Torah and is the only non-
canonical work which we can be sure decisively influenced the composition of
the Qumranic Torah.

In addition to the books of Enoch, most of them dating to the third century
B.C.E., there is the work entitled דברי המאורות (Words of the Luminaries).[50] The
Qumranic parchments have been paleographically dated to 150 B.C.E. and
may in fact have been composed in the third century. As Baillet and Vermes
point out,[51] the title "Words of the Luminaries" seems mysterious for a book
containing hymns and prayers. The remnants of seven columns contain liturgical sections clearly marked for Wednesday and the Sabbath,[52] suggesting
that the remainder of the work was intended for other days of the week. The
last paragraph of M. Tamid lists Psalms assigned to each day of the week,[53] but
the Qumran psalter gives different listings. The "Words of the Luminaries"
appropriately contain supplications to be recited at sunrise, as suggested by
the title (cf. Gen. 44:3), and may be equivalent to the *šaḥaryt* (morning
prayers), which were recited at the rise of the morning star. There is nothing,
however, in the "Words of the Luminaries," to suggest that this work formed
part of the sectarian literature, and it need not be considered here, except to
note that the putative assumption that the pseudepigraphic writings necessarily emanate from the second century onward ought to be revised.[54]

The Book of Jubilees

Composed originally in Hebrew, the Book of Jubilees survives now in an Ethiopic translation, along with some Greek and Hebrew fragments.[55] Its content is of paramount significance for understanding the history of Qumran as well as the sectarian Torah. The existence of a close connection between its author and the Qumran community has been recognized, since the Damascus Document cites Jubilees by its full Hebrew title and because fragments of this book have been discovered in the Qumran caves.[56] Due to alleged references to John Hyrcanus (134–104 B.C.E.), Charles argued that the author of Jubilees wrote during his high-priesthood.[57] VanderKam, however, redates the book, arguing for its composition during the high-priesthood of Jonathan (152–142 B.C.E.) or Simon (142–134 B.C.E.).[58]

VanderKam's dating of Jubilees needs to be modified. The following indices are the basis for his dating: (a) He says that Jubilees' account of the war between the sons of Jacob and the seven Amorite kings is modeled after the account of Judah Maccabee's warfare in 164–160 B.C.E.;[59] (b) the same is said to apply to the war between Jacob and Esau;[60] (c) the passages in Jubilees stressing the significance of the observance of circumcision are taken to be reactions to Antiochus IV's persecution of Judaism in 167–164 B.C.E.;[61] and (d) the attack on public nudity in Jubilees is directed to the athletes who performed in the gymnasium which Jason had constructed while he was high priest.[62] VanderKam, therefore, concludes that the Book of Jubilees was composed in the middle of the second century B.C.E.[63]

A close study of the accounts of patriarchal warfare in Jubilees does not necessarily bear out VanderKam's contentions. To be sure, a number of place-names in the account of Judah Maccabee's battles and in the embellishment of Genesis in Jubilees do coincide, and others might be hypothesized. But some of these place-names linking patriarchal and Maccabean warfare are sheer conjectures.[64] Others may be ascribed to mere coincidence.[65] Contrary to VanderKam, not even one example exists which could be regarded as necessitating the assumption that the account of patriarchal warfare in Jubilees was influenced by the Maccabean wars. The warfare in Jubilees can be more adequately accounted for by postulating that the author used the description of the battle between the four and five nations[66] than by assuming he was influenced by the strategy ascribed to Judah in 1 and 2 Maccabees.

The denunciation of nakedness in Jubilees and the stress on the rite of circumcision have been taken as indications of the book's post-Maccabean origins. These two issues need to be discussed separately. It was natural for the author of Jubilees to stress the rite of circumcision, as it forms an integral part of the Book of Genesis. It would have been more surprising had he decided to omit all mention of its observance. The discussion of nakedness is taken as an allusion to the presence of a Greek gymnasium in Jerusalem.[67] Since 1 Mac.

1:14–15 and 2 Mac. 4:9–15 record the establishment of this institution at the beginning of Antiochus IV's reign prior to the Maccabean revolt, the reference to nakedness cannot be considered decisive evidence for the book's post-Maccabean origins. Furthermore, the problem of nakedness could have originated with the penetration of Hellenism into certain segments of Judaean society, such as the Tobiads, during the early decades of the second century B.C.E.. It is worth noting that the writer of Jubilees made no mention of the persecution of Antiochus IV in his work, as could be expected of an author writing in the aftermath of such momentous events. In contrast to the Book of Daniel, which is replete with references to Antiochus IV's persecution of the Jewish religion, Jubilees contains no reference to this monarch. In spite of the arguments of Charles and VanderKam, there are no compelling reasons for setting the date of Jubilees after the Maccabean revolt in 167 B.C.E.[68]

The Book of Jubilees contains no discernible borrowings from the Book of Daniel. It does record that Enoch married Edni, the daughter of Daniel.[69] If the reference is to the alleged author of the biblical book, then Jubilees is post-Danielic. But it is more plausible to assume that the marriage of Enoch to the daughter of Daniel in Jub. 4:20 refers to the figure of the righteous pagan Daniel, who is listed together with Noah and Job in Ezekiel.[70] If so, the author of Jubilees was not aware of the Jewish Daniel, the author of the canonical book.

The historiographical indices in Jubilees place the work in the tradition of ancient Jewish Enochite literature, a corpus that possibly goes back to the Persian period but certainly to the third century B.C.E.[71] Yadin's commentary on the Qumranic Torah, citing parallels between many of its provisions and those found only in the Book of Jubilees, has amply demonstrated an interdependence between these two works.[72] The problem, however, is the exact nature of this relationship. Does the scroll depend on Jubilees, or vice versa, or do both follow a lost work? Because of the complexity of the question, it requires a detailed answer, which will be found under the following headings:

Introduction
Legal lore
Calendar
Heavenly tablets
Jacob's dream

Introduction

The loss of col. 1 and the top of col. 2 raises the question, How did 11Q Torah begin? Yadin's reconstruction of the surviving lines in col. 2 is as follows:

1. [For it is an awesome thing that] I will d[o with you.

2. [Behold, I shall drive out from before you] the Amori[tes, the Canaan-
   ites,]

3. [the Hittites, the Girgashi]tes, the Per[izzites, the Hivites,]

4. [and the Jebusites. Be]ware lest thou makest a cove[nant with the inhabitants of the land]

5. [when thou] comest to them, lest they be a lu[re in thy midst. But]

6. [their alta]rs ye shall break down, their pil[lars ye shall shatter,]

7. [their ash]erim ye shall cut off, and the idols of their [gods ye shall burn]

8. [with fire. No]r shall ye desire gold and silver in wh[ich thou wilt become
   ensnared, for it is an abomination]

9. [to me. Nor] shalt thou take from it and thou shalt not br[ing an abomination to thy house,]

10. [so that thou shalt] be under a ban like it. Thou shalt surely dete[st it and
    thou shalt surely abhor it]

11. [for] it is a banned thing, and thou shalt not worship anot[her God, for
    the Lord is jealous,]

12. [His name] is God, he is jealous. Beware lest thou makest a [covenant
    with the inhabitants of the land,]

13. [and they go wantonly] after [their go]ds, sacrificing to [their gods and
    they call to thee,]

14. [and thou shalt eat from their sacrifices, and ta]ke [from their daughters
    for thy sons,]

15. [and thy daughters shall go wantonly after their go]ds, and they shall
    make [thy sons go wantonly after. . . .][73]

The general topic of these remnants is clear enough, since it contains a slight
paraphrase of Exod. 34:10–16, along with some additions from Deuteronomy
7, as pointed out by Yadin. What follows are the extant lines from col. 3,
which introduce the instructions for the erection of the temple. Two questions
arise: What is the purpose of col. 2? How could it help in the reconstruction
of col. 1, which has perished, since both cols. 1 and 2 must have served as a
proem to the Qumranic Torah? According to Yadin, the author based col. 2,
and presumably col. 1, upon Exod. 34:10–16 and Deuteronomy 7. These two
columns relate to the sectarian Torah as its parallel, the covenant in Exod.
34:10–16, does to Exodus 35, both serving as introductions to the construction of a sanctuary. Even Deuteronomy 7 serves as a prelude to the building of
the sanctuary, according to Yadin.[74] One may question, however, whether the
covenant either in Exodus 34 or Deuteronomy 7 is in fact introductory to the
description of the sanctuary. Col. 3 seems to follow Exodus 25 rather than
Exodus 35.[75] Furthermore, it seems doubtful that cols. 1 and 2 served as an
opening only to the account of the temple; more likely they were a prologue
to the entire book. Certainly the covenant, the destruction of idolatry, and the

warnings against intermarriage, major themes in these lines, harmonize with the concluding columns as well as they do with the section relating to the sanctuary. Col. 2, therefore, seems to be introductory not only to the description of the temple but to the entire work. Elsewhere in the fragments the author reiterates again and again the purpose of his work. It may be presumed that he did the same in the two prefatory columns.

Can some of the content of these lost lines be recovered? Since 11Q Torah 2:1 ff. reproduces Exod. 34:10 ff., we may presume that the preceding lines (01–06?) and some twenty-two lines of col. 1 repeated, in addition to anything else they may have contained, the substance of Exod. 34:1–9.

> 1. The Lord said to Moses, "Cut two tables of stone like the first; and I will write upon the tables the words that were on the first tables, which you broke.
> 2. Be ready in the morning, and come up in the morning to Mount Sinai, and present yourself there to Me on the top of the mountain.
> 3. No man shall come up with you, and let no man be seen throughout all the mountain; let no flocks or herds feed before that mountain."
> 4. So Moses cut two tables of stone like the first; and he rose early in the morning and went up on Mount Sinai, as the Lord had commanded him, and took in his hand two tables of stone.
> 5. And the Lord descended in the cloud and stood with him there, and proclaimed the name of the Lord.
> 6. The Lord passed before him, and proclaimed, "The Lord, the Lord, a God merciful and gracious, slow to anger, and abounding in steadfast love and faithfulness,
> 7. keeping steadfast love for thousands, forgiving iniquity and transgression and sin, but who will by no means clear the guilty, visiting the iniquity of the fathers upon the children and the children's children, to the third and the fourth generation."
> 8. And Moses made haste to bow his head toward the earth, and worshipped.
> 9. And he said, "If now I have found favor in thy sight, O Lord, let the Lord, I pray Thee, go in the midst of us, although it is a stiff-necked people; and pardon our iniquity and our sin, and take us for Thy inheritance."[76]

The tablets, then, and their covenant were the main subjects of the prologue. Combining this preliminary material with what has survived of col. 2, we see that it contains an account of Moses' ascent to Mount Sinai to receive the tablets of the law which, according to Exod. 34:10 and Deuteronomy 7, form part of the covenant.

A comparison of Jubilees 1 with Exodus 34 will shed further light on parts of the lost prologue of 11Q Torah. After giving the date and the title of his comparison, as well as the account of Moses' ascent to Mount Sinai in Exod. 24:12–18, the author of Jubilees immediately begins to paraphrase Exodus 34.[77]

Placing an outline of Exodus 34 side by side with that of Jubilees 1 will reveal a complex relationship between the two. The author of Jubilees apparently follows closely the scheme of Exodus 34; nevertheless, the contents of Jubilees 1 frequently seem unrelated to its real source. The relationship between Jubilees 1 and Exodus 34 is apparent, in spite of the failure of the critics to see the connection. Even Charles, with his masterful understanding of biblical literature, saw no link between them.[78] The existence of a link, however, seems certain:

1. Moses' ascent to Sinai	Jub. 1:1–4	Exod. 24:12–18; 34:1–5
2. God's first address to Moses	Jub. 1:5–18	Exod. 34:6–7
3. Moses' intercession for Israel	Jub. 1:19–21	Exod. 34:8–9
4. God's second address to Moses	Jub. 1:22–26	Exod. 34:10–26
5. God's command to the angel of presence	Jub. 1:27–28	

The author of Jubilees begins by fusing Exod. 24:12–18 with Exod. 34:1–28, but continues only with the latter. Perhaps because Exod. 24:12–18 makes the description of Moses' ascent appear more glorious or, as seems more likely, since it contains the key terms "the Law and the commandment" (התורה והמצוה)—which is how he usually defines Scripture—the author chose to begin his work with Exod. 24:12. Nevertheless, even here the use of Exod. 34:1–5 is a postulate crucial for the understanding of Jub. 1:1–4, for it alone contains the paraphrase "two tablets of stone." This image becomes the central theme of both the prefatory section and the remainder of Jubilees 1.

The fascinating reinterpretation in Jubilees of the exchange between God and Moses[79] adds features entirely absent in the source. Instead of God's depiction of His own characteristics delivered in the third person, in Jubilees the Lord predicts in the first person what will befall Israel as a consequence of abandoning His "Law and commandment" from the present until the post-exilic times,[80] i.e., roughly to the days of the composition of Jubilees. The plea by Moses that God not destroy Israel in spite of its stiff-neckedness[81] is transformed into a supplication very apropos to the situation in Judaea at the beginning of the second century B.C.E.[82]

The divine response to Moses' prayer is even more radical than God's first words.[83] Moses, the text implies, misunderstood God's concluding statement in Jub. 1:15–18 as referring to the rededication of the sanctuary following the rebuilding of the temple by Zerubbabel (516 B.C.E.). Moses was dissatisfied, for in spite of the reestablished sacrificial rites, Israel remained essentially idolatrous; hence his pleas in Jub. 1:19–21.[84] In God's second address to Moses He clarifies what the allusions to Israel's complete repentance and the erection of the temple meant in the first speech. Contrary to the way Moses understood it, God had not referred to the Jerusalem sanctuary of the Second Temple, but to another temple that would be built in the messianic age when Israel will indeed have repented and God will dwell in their midst forever. God's final sentence to Moses and his command to the angel of presence sums up the purpose of this address:

> 26. "And do thou write down for thyself all these words which I declare unto thee on this mountain, the first and the last, which shall come to pass in all the divisions of the days in the law and in the testimony and in the weeks and the jubilees unto eternity, until I descend and dwell with them throughout eternity." 27. And He said to the angel of the presence: "Write for Moses from the beginning of creation till My sanctuary has been built among them for all eternity. 28. And the Lord will appear to the eyes of all, and all will know that I am the God of Israel and the Father of all the children of Jacob, and King on Mount Zion for all eternity. And Zion and Jerusalem will be holy."[85]

In other words, Jub. 1:26b–29, which has no parallel in Exod. 34:10–28, presents something entirely new.[86] Moses, the author of Jubilees seems to say, has hitherto misunderstood the significance of the tables of the law and the commandment, having perceived them as referring merely to the canonical Pentateuch. Jub. 1:26b explains that the canonical Pentateuch was only the "first table," and he is now being instructed to write down the "last table," which would serve as Israel's constitution at the time of the future temple, that sanctuary erected at the end of days. Reinforcement of God's command to Moses comes with the addition of the injunction given to the angel of presence: "Write for Moses from the beginning of creation till My sanctuary has been built among them for all eternity."

If this perception of Jubilees 1 is correct, its central thesis rests on the premise that the divine promise of the covenant mentioned in Exodus 34 is necessarily preliminary to the new temple that will be built when God descends to the earth forever, not to the temple of Zerubbabel still standing in Jerusalem. However, its author could not have been dependent only on the Pentateuchal passage for his interpretation. Since Jub. 1:26–29 has no basis in this source, the question arises, What authority does the author of Jubilees have for proposing a sanctuary other than the existing one in Jerusalem? As far as we know, there exists no canonical text detailing the construction of a novel sanctuary and introducing it with Moses' ascent to Mount Sinai to receive the two tablets. Jubilees' source for this is presumably 11Q Torah, for it alone, as far as we know, could have served as the basis for Jub. 1:26–29. If so, Jubilees understood the sectarian Torah as referring to a sanctuary that would be built in the future, rather than to a refurbishing of the Second Temple. This perception of 11Q Torah contrasts sharply with Yadin's argument that the scroll called for extensive modifications in the current sanctuary.[87] Even if we presume that the author of the Qumranic Torah is here dependent on Jubilees, the conclusion would still be the same, since it cannot be supposed that the sanctuary in Jub. 1:29 differs from that of 11Q Torah 3:4. It will not do to argue that Jub. 1:29 refers to a utopian temple allegedly mentioned in 11Q Torah 29:8–10 in contrast to the structure prescribed in 11Q Torah 3, since the author of Jubilees, like the writer of the scroll, links the prescriptions for the sanctuary with Exodus 34. We must suppose that the sanctuary which the author of Jubilees had in mind is none other than the one depicted at great length in the newly found sectarian scroll.

The interpretation that the future sanctuary of Jubilees 1 refers to the commandments related to the eschatological sanctuary spelled out in 11Q Torah may help clarify the reference in Jub. 1:26: "And do thou write down for thyself all these words which I declare unto thee on this mountain, the first and the last . . ." What does this last phrase mean? If the words "the first and the last" were only to be found here it would be a minor problem.[88] But the prevalence of similar statements contrasting the earlier and the latter laws in Qumran writings[89] necessitates the presumption that "the first and the last" in Jub. 1:26 in fact means the first Torah and the second Torah. In other words, God gave to Moses two sets of the Law. The question is, What are these two *Torot?* The origin of two *Torot* appears to rest on an interpretation of Exod. 34:1, "the two tablets of stone," which was understood as indicating that God had entrusted to Moses two sets of the Law, the first and the last. The first is the canonical Pentateuch and the last is 11Q Torah. Conceivably Jubilees refers again and again to these two *Torot* in the phrase "the heavenly tablets."[90]

Since Jubilees 1, in its utilization of Exodus 34, is apparently indebted to cols. 1–3 of the sectarian Torah, a work which frequently embellishes the biblical account, the question arises, How much of this radical reinterpretation is also dependent on 11Q Torah? It is quite likely that the Qumranic Torah contained the phrase "two tablets of stone."[91] It is also conceivable that the scroll actually began not with Exod. 34:1–10 but with Exodus 24's account of Moses' ascent of Mount Sinai. Surely there is enough space in the lost parchment to justify the consideration of such a possibility. If this is so, some other lines in Jub. 1:27–29, not contained in Exodus 34, may come directly from the lost sections of cols. 1 and 2. Thus, a comparison between the reconstructed prologue in the Qumranic Torah and chap. 1 of Jubilees may enhance our

understanding of both pieces of literature. Jubilees 1 presents us with some of
the lost lines of cols. 1 and 2 of the sectarian Torah, while the latter furnishes
us with a deeper understanding of the prologue to Jubilees.

Legal Lore

Prior to the discoveries in the Judaean desert, and to a lesser extent even
thereafter, the legal lore in the Book of Jubilees has been puzzling. Though
many of the provisions are copied from Pentateuchal passages, quite a number of them have no such exemplars. A few have been found to correspond
with the legal lore in sectarian documents at Qumran.[92] The formulation in
Jubilees, however, differs essentially from the terminology used in the Community Rule.[93] The recovery of the extensive fragments of the Qumranic
Torah may resolve this problem. To determine this relationship, we will proceed with an examination of the legal material in the Book of Jubilees and its
relationship to 11Q Torah.

1. Jub. 2:17–33 embellishes Gen. 2:1–3 with a homiletical and legal digression. Some of these clauses have been shown to echo the Sabbath laws in CD
10:14. Others become clear only with the discovery of 11Q Torah.

"Behold, I shall separate unto Myself a people from among all the
peoples"[94] is a phrase that seems to have been included in 11Q Torah 3 as an
introduction to the account of the building of the sanctuary, in 11Q Torah 29
in connection with the ritual, and in 11Q Torah 59 in the section on the blessings and curses. The prominence of Jacob among the patriarchs, an idea
found in Jubilees 32, may be connected with 11Q Torah 29:10 as well. Like
the scroll, Jubilees never tires of reiterating the sacrificial requirements of the
ritual, "And he caused His commands to ascend as a sweet savour acceptable
before Him all the days."[95] In other words, the author of Jubilees ascribes to
the patriarchs a ritual whose full significance will only be realized in the
future. Nothing in Jub. 2:17–33 would seem to compel us to conclude that
Jubilees is citing directly from the sectarian Torah, which, as far as we know,
did not contain the laws of the Sabbath.[96] However, it seems that the scroll is
precisely what Jubilees alludes to in 2:24: "And to this (Jacob and his seed) it
was granted that they should always be the blessed and holy ones of the first
testimony and law, even as He has sanctified and blessed the Sabbath day on
the seventh day." This term, "the first testimony," makes no sense unless it is
in contrast to the "latter," which will be shown to refer to the Qumranic
Torah. In other words, Jubilees is pointing out that the laws of the Sabbath
are to be found in the first law only, i.e., the traditional Mosaic books. The
author of Jubilees returns to the subject of the Sabbath in his concluding
chapters with a renewed emphasis on the sanctuary and its ritual. He presents
a defense for the ritual of the offering of sacrifices on the Sabbath, this act
being an exception to the universal prohibition against any labor on the
Sabbath:

. . . they should . . . rest thereon from all labour which belongs to the labour of the children of men, save burning frankincense and bringing oblations and sacrifices before the Lord for days and for Sabbaths. This work alone shall be done on the Sabbath days in the sanctuary of the Lord your God; that they may atone for Israel with sacrifice continually from day to day for a memorial well-pleasing before the Lord and that He may receive them always from day to day according as thou hast been commanded.[97]

A striking similarity is to be observed in the wording of the previous lines and the prescriptions for the various sacrifices in 11Q Torah:

14:10–11 כול מלאכת ע[ב]חדה לוא תעשו ועשיתמה שעיר עזים לחטאת] לבד הוא יעשה לכפ]ר עליכמה—"Any lab[or not shall ye do. Ye shall take a he-goat for a sin-offering,] it alone will be done to make ato[nement for you."

16:10 [ע]ולה הוא אשה ריח ניחוח ל[פני יהוה]—"[A burnt] offering is, a fire of pleasing odor be[fore the Lord]."

25:13–14 שעיר עזים אחד לחטאת לבד מחטאת הכפורים—"one he-goat for a sin-offering apart from the sin-offering of the atonement."

27:5–6 פעם אחת בשנה יהיה היום הז]ה ל[המה לזכרון ולוא יעשו בו כול מלאכה—"one time in the year [this] day shall be for them a memorial. They shall not do any labor in it."

To be sure, passages relating to offerings on the Sabbath go back to Num. 28:9–10, but the particular stress on sacrifices as well as the wording of Jubilees makes more sense if they are related to the sectarian Torah.

Scholars have pointed out that Qumranic texts did not sanction the daily offering (*Tamyd*) on Saturdays.[98] Both the Qumranic Torah and Jubilees go out of their way to require the sacrificial offering even on the Sabbath. Damascus Document 11:17–18 states: אל יעל איש למזבח בשבת כי אם עולת השבת כי כן כתוב מלבד שבתותיכם—"Let no man offer on the altar on the Sabbath except the burnt offering of the Sabbath; for thus it is written, 'apart from your Sabbath-offerings.'" Yadin says that the author of the scroll likewise prohibited the *Tamyd* offering on the Sabbath.[99] When Yadin sets up the calendar, therefore, he does not count the Sabbath as one of the days of a feast lasting six or seven days, such as the offering of woods or the feast of Passover. Jub. 50:10–11, however, makes it clear that bringing the daily or additional festal offerings does not constitute a desecration of the Sabbath: "save burning frankincense and bringing oblations and sacrifices before the Lord for days and for Sabbaths." Does it follow, then, that there is a divergence between 11Q Torah and Jubilees? Perhaps it does not. 11Q Torah 14:13 prescribes a sacrifice on the first day of the month. מלבד, though partly conjectural, seems quite cogent: "in addition to" the normal offering on the new moon.[100] These indications, though not specifically mentioning the Sabbath, suggest that the author of the Qumranic Torah, like the writer of Jubilees, did not diverge here from Numbers 28–29 with regard to the daily or additional sacrifices on the Sabbath. In 11Q Torah 13:17 is found the Sabbath offering as it is listed in Num. 28:9. While the defective column does not permit an examination of the total account, it does add confirmation of the scroll's reliance on Numbers 28 for these prescriptions. There is no reason, then, to presume an alteration in the sacrificial calendar on account of Saturdays in the sectarian Torah.

This does not necessarily mean that CD 11:18, which apparently restricts the sacrifices to the burnt offerings, diverges from the fragments and from Jubilees. Scholars take the phrase עולת השבת (the burnt offering of the Sabbath) as limiting the offerings specifically ordained for the Sabbath by prohibiting the daily and festal burnt offering. But this interpretation is clearly contradicted by the proof-text, Lev. 23:38, which says מלבד.[101] This citation makes sense only if the *oʾlat haššabbat* does embrace the daily and festive offerings prescribed in Lev. 23:38 which Scripture again and again mandates,[102] i.e., the three sets of burnt offerings when a feast day falls on the Sabbath. It seems that CD 11:17–18 is not inconsistent with Jubilees and 11Q Torah. *Oʾlat haššabbat* in CD 11:18 necessarily embraces all of these requirements, but is intended to exclude merely what the rabbis call *ḥagygot* (festive offerings) and the sectarian Torah *šelamym* (well-being offerings), brought when the feast fell on a weekday.[103] Thus the Damascus Document points out that these offerings may be brought only when the feasts do not coincide with the Sabbath. When they do, such as on the fourth day of Passover and Sukkot in the sectarian calendar, sacrifices not designated for the Sabbath are banned. The Qumranic Torah, moreover, seems to have required that all free offerings be brought on the feasts during the seasons of *bikkurym* (first fruits).[104] As Jubilees says, "This work alone shall be done on the Sabbath-days."

2. Jubilees 49 contains a lengthy discourse on the details of the offering of the paschal lamb, some of which seemingly differ from talmudic exegesis. M. Zebahim 5:8 says that the paschal lamb is to be slaughtered in the temple but that it may be eaten within the confines of Jerusalem's walls. Jubilees, however, repeatedly requires that it be eaten in the courtyard of the sanctuary.[105] 11Q Torah 17:8–9 says, "And they shall eat it in the evening in the courtyards of the sanctuary." The significance of the word בחצרות (in the courtyards) becomes clear only in the context of the architecture described in the sectarian Torah. Throughout the fragments, the author prescribes what should be eaten in each of the three courtyards. 11Q Torah 17:8–9 seems to sanction its consumption in all three of the courtyards, with various segments assigned to each court. Jubilees 49 also follows 11Q Torah 17 in other details relating to the paschal lamb. According to M. Pesahim 5:1, the presentation of the paschal sacrifice follows that of the Tamid offering, complying with the principle that what is frequent precedes the less frequent. 11Q Torah 17:7, however, ordains that "they shall slaughter the paschal offering prior to the

afternoon offering." Jub. 49:10–12 stresses this point with a digression as to the meaning of *beyn haʿarbayim* (at twilight).[106] While Exodus 12 does not prescribe an age requirement for participants in the offering of the paschal lamb, 11Q Torah 17:8 and Jub. 49:17 mandate "from twenty years old and upward."[107] According to Yadin, the Qumranic Torah and Jubilees permit the eating of the paschal lamb during the whole evening while M. Pesahim 10:9 restricts it to midnight: "After midnight the Passover-offering renders the hands unclean." But this view fails to take account of several tannaitic passages which sanction the eating of the paschal lamb until morning and which declare that the restriction of midnight is only part of the "hedge around the law."[108] In all these instances Jubilees concords with 11Q Torah, but diverges from the halakah.

3. Jub. 3:10. As stated above, if there is any theme that pervades the sectarian Torah it is defilement of all sorts, including an allusion to the seven and thirty-three days or to the fourteen and sixty-six days of waiting after childbirth, which find mention in Jubilees.[109] Jubilees points out that Eve's entrance into the Garden of Eden was postponed eighty days on account of her uncleanness: fourteen plus sixty-six days for a total of eighty days. Jubilees also gives uncleanness as one of the three reasons for the flood, the other two being fornication and iniquity.[110]

4. Jub. 3:31. The covering of shame and the injunction regarding circumcision[111] are two items in Jubilees which, as far as we know, were not included in the Qumranic Torah. Another commandment the author of Jubilees mentions as inscribed in the heavenly tablets, but found in neither the Mosaic books nor the scroll, is that no one should give the younger daughter in marriage before the elder one.[112]

5. Jub. 4:31–32. According to Jubilees, "At the close of this jubilee Cain was killed after him in the same year; for his house fell upon him and he died in the midst of his house, and he was killed by its stones; for with a stone he had killed Abel, and by a stone was he killed in righteous judgment. For this reason it was ordained on the heavenly tablets: 'With the instrument with which a man kills his neighbor with the same shall he be killed; after the manner that he wounded him, in like manner shall they deal with him.'" This legislation corresponds to 11Q Torah 61:11–12, where the author does not soften the stringency of this law. Both Jubilees and the sectarian Torah invoke capital punishment for all kinds of transgressions. The scroll applies it to priests who do not wear the proper garments,[113] corrupt judges who accept bribes,[114] those who engage in idolatry,[115] the Israelite who betrays his people to the nations,[116] those who commit a capital crime and flee,[117] and the man who lies with a betrothed virgin.[118] Jubilees reflects a similar stringency, tending to invoke capital punishment for a variety of violations: neglecting circumcision,[119] incest,[120] fornication,[121] marriage of a Hebrew girl with a Gen-

tile, which is fused with the prescriptions against adultery,[122] and lying with
the father's wife.[123] The last item is of particular significance since it also
appears in the last column of the scroll.[124] Again, the concordance of 11Q
Torah and Jubilees is apparent.

6. Jubilees 7. The author of Jubilees again and again links the shedding of
blood with the eating of the flesh of any animal.[125] This is the abomination
that provoked the Lord to cause the flood, according to Jub. 7:23–26. Most of
the covenant with Noah is devoted to the pledge that the Israelites will not eat
flesh with blood in it.[126] Leviticus does prohibit the eating of blood,[127] but the
aversion to blood is stressed even more vigorously in Deuteronomy.[128] As in
that biblical work, the Qumranic Torah prohibits the use of any blood: רק הדם
לוא תואכל על הארץ תשופכנו כמים וכסיתו בעפר—"only the blood thou shalt not eat.
Upon the earth, thou shalt pour it as water and thou shalt cover it with
dust."[129] Its author also incorporates the prohibition against blood into his
architecture. 11Q Torah 34:5–8 requires that in slaughtering the animals even
the blood of the sacrifices must be carefully gathered together and disposed of
entirely. The waters of the laver are not to be touched because there is blood
in them: "where the waters will be poured and they will go into it and they
will disappear into the earth. No man may touch them, for the blood of the
burnt offering is mixed in them."[130]

7. Jub. 7:36. Apparently alluding to Lev. 19:23–24, which lists the fruit of
trees of the fourth year as קדש הלולים, a phrase that may be rendered "dedicated for praise," Jub. 7:36 says: "in the fourth year its fruit will be accounted
holy [and they will offer the first-fruits] . . . . Let them offer in abundance the
first of the wine and oil (as) first-fruits on the altar of the Lord. . . ." Similarly,
11Q Torah 60:3–4 proclaims, "All their sacred things which they sanctify to
me, together with [all their things dedicated] for praise. . . ," listing it among
the things consecrated to the temple, such as the first-born animals as well as
the *kodeš hylulym.* As Yadin notes, this view that the fruit of the fourth year is to
be dedicated diverges from the rabbinic tradition, which understands it to
mean that the fruit is to be eaten in Jerusalem, since it belongs to the category
of second tithe.[131]

Unique to the sectarian Torah are the pentecostal seasons of the new fruit
described in cols. 18–23.[132] As if this lengthy account did not sufficiently
emphasize these innovative features of the ritual calendar, the author incorporates the consumption of the three staples, grain, wine, and oil, into the
structure of the sanctuary, alluding to them again and again with reference to
the courtyards and the priestly perquisites. What seems to have inspired the
author of the scroll in this emphasis are the laws of first fruits and tithing
which, as he understood them, applied only to grain, wine, and oil.[133] Thus
the separation of *terumah* (priest's portion) applied to all animals and fishes,[134]
though a share of the produce was apparently restricted to wine, wheat, and

oil.[135] Moreover, all the first-born animals are to be brought on the feasts of the first fruits. Thus these three pentecostal seasons became central to the sacrificial offerings of Israel, a view that departs radically from the Mosaic archetype.

The author of Jubilees similarly attaches paramount significance to the tithing of grain, wine, and oil. Whenever he discusses tithing, he lists these three staples.[136] It is a sign of acute distress when Jacob goes down to Egypt and must celebrate the festival of first fruits with old grain, since there is no new.[137] The feast of Shavuot (Weeks), Jubilees says, bears a double name, making it central to the book's calendar.[138] This use of the double name is also apparent in the Qumranic Torah.[139] Thus the morrow of the Feast of Weeks, on the sixteenth of the third month, is the date when God reveals the Book of Jubilees to Moses.[140] This day, the same one on which the covenant with Noah was made,[141] is also celebrated by the patriarch Abraham when the Lord appears to him and they make a covenant.[142]

Not to be forgotten is Jub. 21:12–14, which presents a detailed prescription for the wood-offering: "And as regards the wood of the sacrifices, beware lest thou bring (other) wood for the altar in addition to these: . . . And of these kinds of wood lay upon the altar under the sacrifice, such as have been tested as to their appearance, and do not lay (thereon) any split or dark wood, (but) hard and clean, without fault, a sound and new growth; and do not lay (thereon) old wood, . . . for there is no longer fragrance in it as before." This seems to be a reference to the six-day feast of the wood-offerings prescribed in 11Q Torah 23:1–25:1, which unfortunately is quite defective.[143]

Even if there were no other connections between these two books, the peculiar characteristic of the first fruits in the Qumranic Torah and Jubilees places these works in a unique relationship that contrasts sharply with the traditional Pentateuch. Since coincidence is to be excluded and indebtedness to a third source is most unlikely, the interdependence of the Book of Jubilees and the sectarian Torah must be presumed. What is even more significant is that, as was shown above, the author of the scroll made the three seasons of first fruits an integral part of the temple's architecture and ritual. The author of Jubilees, however, takes this design for granted but exploits it for the formulation of a radical solar calendar. In other words, Jubilees sides with the Qumranic Torah against the traditional Pentateuch but goes further by dating events in the Book of Genesis during the Feast of Weeks.

The Calendar

A study of the calendar advocated by the author of Jubilees displays a complicated relationship between this work and the Qumranic Torah. Yadin presumes that the calendar underlying the festive seasons in 11Q Torah takes for granted the sectarian mode of reckoning as recorded in Jub. 6:20–38 and other Qumranic parchments.[144] This calendar had a solar year of 364 days divided into twelve months, eight of which reckoned 30 days and four had 31.[145] The four exceptional months were the third, the sixth, the ninth, and the twelfth. Each period reckoned 91 days and each of these seasons began on a Wednesday and ended on a Tuesday. Accordingly, the festive seasons always fell on the same day of the week. The first days of Passover, Rosh Hashanah, and Sukkot all fell on Wednesday, the days of the Omer, Shavuot, and the other seasons of the first fruits on a Sunday, and the Day of Atonement on a Friday.[146]

If this calendar, first recorded in Jubilees, is superimposed on the fragments, the festivals and seasons in cols. 13–29 fall as follows:[147]

New Year	I:1	Wednesday
Seven Days of Consecration	I:1–7	Wednesday–Tuesday
Paschal Lamb	I:14	Tuesday
Feast of Unleavened Bread	I:15–21	Wednesday–Tuesday
Waving of the Omer	I:26	Sunday
First Fruits of Wheat	III:15	Sunday
First Fruits of Wine	V:3	Sunday
First Fruits of Oil	VI:22	Sunday
Offering of Woods—6 days	VI:23–28	Monday—Saturday
Blowing of the Shofar	VII:1	Wednesday
Sukkot	VII:15–21	Wednesday-Tuesday
Azeret	VII:22	Wednesday

Two questions arise. What is the evidence that this revolutionary calendar is presumed in the scroll?[148] How did this radical calendar come into being? Since Yadin views the extant literature of the sect as part of a unified system, the sectarian calendar reproduced in the Book of Jubilees and other Qumran fragments necessarily forms the basis of the yearly festal cycle in the scroll.[149] However, this study argues that the Qumranic Torah is antecedent to the Book of Jubilees and that much of the legal lore in the latter is directly dependent on the former. Furthermore, it will be shown that 11Q Torah bears traces of neither the calendrical phenomena found in Jubilees nor the advocacy of a solar recokoning.

In both Jubilees and 11Q Torah 14:9, the first day of the first month is a festive day receiving a significance absent from Leviticus 23 and Numbers 28–29, the passages which form the basis of the festal calendar. As suggested by Yadin's interpolation, 14:9 reproduces Exod. 12:2 in part or as a whole: "This month shall be the first of the months of the year," a line whose insertion into the list of the feasts indicates the presumption of a lunar or lunisolar rather than a strictly solar reckoning.[150] To be sure, Jubilees does employ the term *ḥodesh,* but it rejects a lunar reckoning. As in the Julian calendar, "month," in spite of its etymology, is no longer linked to a lunar calendar. But החדש הזה (this new moon), especially if it is interpolated into a paraphrase of Numbers 28, an account of the festive seasons, would make sense only if the author wishes to emphasize the lunar aspects of reckoning, a calendar that is vehemently rejected in Jubilees.

The passage that may conceivably be taken as introducing the sectarian calendar similar to the one found in Jub. 6:32 is 11Q Torah 18:10, repeated in 19:11, 13 as well as in 21:12: וספרתה (And thou shalt reckon). The emphasis on ממוחרת השבת (on the morrow of the Sabbath) can only mean Sunday, not the day after the feast of unleavened bread on the fifteenth of the first month as interpreted by the sages. Contrary to Yadin, however, I find nothing novel in 11Q Torah that does not already apply to Lev. 23:15–16 as well.[151] Thus it must be taken for granted that, according to 11Q Torah, the day of the waving of the Omer and the seasons of first grain, new wine, and new oil all fell in successive pentecontal reckonings on Sunday. What need not be supposed, in fact seems unlikely, is Yadin's postulate that the day of the Omer fell, as in the Jubilees calendar, on the twenty-sixth of the first month, and the feast of Shavuot on the fifteenth of the third month. To be sure, the surviving lines where such a dating would be expected are too sparse to state absolutely that none of the lists of the feasts of new fruits contained the day of the month. But all that does remain tends to favor the presumption that for the author of 11Q Torah, in contrast to the author of Jubilees, the festal seasons of first fruits did not have a set day in the month, only a set day in the week, i.e., Sunday. In other words, 11Q Torah would set the waving of the Omer on a Sunday following the feast of unleavened bread. As in the Karaite calendar, the day of the Omer would fall sometime between the seventeenth of the first month, if the first of the month fell on a Friday, and the twenty-second of the first month, if the first of the month occurred on a Sunday. As in Lev. 23:9–21, the feast of first fruits remained flexible. One must conclude that the lunisolar reckoning, which had apparently prevailed in post-exilic times, remained unaltered by the author of the Qumranic Torah.

On the other hand, it is absolutely necessary to presume that the solar calendar in Jubilees depends on the Qumranic Torah. Two points receive particular emphasis in Jubilees 6, which records the covenant God made with Noah upon his departure from the ark on the first of the third month. The writer stresses the prohibition of eating meat with its blood (7–17) and the reliance upon a solar calendar (23–38). After having expounded at length on the abomination of blood, Jub. 6:20–21 continues: "And do thou command the children of Israel to observe this festival in all their generations for a commandment unto them: one day in the year in this month they shall celebrate the festival. For it is the feast of weeks and the feast of first fruits: this feast is twofold and of a double nature; according to what is written and engraven concerning it, celebrate it." The view that Shavuot is "of a double nature"— "the feast of weeks and the feast of new fruits"—could be derived from the relevant passages in the Mosaic Torah, such as Exod. 34:18-20, Lev. 23:15-21, Num. 28:26, and Deut. 16:9-10; but it finds explicit expression only in 11Q Torah 19:9: "It is the Feast of Weeks and the Feast of First Fruits."[152] Jubilees' repeated insistence on the paramount importance of the Feast of Weeks, which receives its first mention in 1:1, makes sense only if its author used the sectarian Torah, where the Feast of Weeks is celebrated not once, as ordained in the Mosaic Torah, but in three successive pentecontal periods: new grain, new wine, and new oil. As if these calendrical additions did not suffice to stress the significance of the feasts, 11Q Torah reiterates their mode of observance in sections which deal with the architecture of the sanctuary.[153] Jub. 6:21 similarly adds special significance to this feast by invoking God's own words: "according to what is written and engraven." But the author of Jubilees wished to make certain that his readers did not presume that the Feast of Weeks was found in the "latter law," i.e., the Qumranic Torah as defined in Jub. 1:4. Jub. 6:22 therefore points out what is found in the Mosaic Torah as well: "in accordance with what I (i.e., God) have written in the first law." In other words, Jub. 6:20-22, which serves to introduce the author's solar reckoning, ascribes scriptural authority to both the first and the last Torah.

After invoking the two Torahs, the author of Jubilees records something which, as far as can be determined, is only found in part in either the Mosaic Torah or the sectarian Torah. In Jub. 6:23 we read: "And on the new moon of the first month, and on the new moon of the fourth month, and on the new moon of the seventh month, and on the new moon of the tenth month are the days of remembrance, and the days of the seasons in the four divisions of the year." 11Q Torah, as stated in Jub. 6:20-21, does ordain the celebration of the first day of the first and seventh months,[154] but it definitely does not mention a festive season for the summer and winter solstices. Neither does the Qumranic Torah lend support to the claimed quadrennial division of the year, each part of which counted thirteen weeks, or 91 days, for a total of 364 days for the entire year.

Since the calendar advocated by Jubilees does not seem to rest on the Qumranic Torah, the question arises, What is the authority which Jub. 6:29-32 invokes as its witness for a 364-day year? The answer is to be found, as indicated above, in the Astronomical Enoch, fragments of which have been edited by Milik, who dates it to the Persian period.[155] Only a few remnants have survived from the Aramaic composition, but a great deal has come down in Enoch 72-82, which in essence paraphrases the lost Astronomical Enoch.[156]

Enoch 72 begins with Uriel revealing to Enoch "the book of the revolutions of the lights of heaven, each as it is, according to their classes, according to their (period of) rule and their times, according to their names and their places of origin." This lengthy title gives a glimpse into the book, which, as far as we can tell, was restricted to the celestial lore of the time from when God created the world "until the new creation shall be made which will last forever."[157] Chapter 72 then records the movements of the sun through the twelve portals of heaven and chap. 73, the movements of the moon. The calendrical corollaries of these revolutions are given in 74:10–75:2, a passage which, despite its length, deserves to be cited:

> 10. And (if) five years are added together, the sun has an excess of thirty days; but all the days (which) accrue to it for one year of those five years, when they are complete, amount to three hundred and sixty-four days. 11. And the excess of the sun and the stars comes to six days; in five years, six (days) each (year) they have an excess of thirty days, and the moon falls behind the sun and the stars by thirty days. 12. And the moon conducts the years exactly, all of them according to their eternal positions; they are neither early nor late even by one day, but change the year . . . in exactly three hundred and sixty-four days. 13. In three years [there are] one thousand and ninety-two days, and in five years one thousand eight hundred and twenty days, so that in eight years there are two thousand nine hundred and twelve days. 14. For the moon alone the days in three years come to one thousand and sixty-two days and in five years it is fifty days behind . . . 15. And there are one thousand seven hundred and seventy days in five years so that for the moon the days in eight years amount to two thousand eight hundred and thirty-two days. 16. For the difference in eight years (is) eighty days, all the days which (the moon) is behind in eight years (are) eighty days. 17. And the year is completed exactly in accordance with their positions and the positions of the sun, in that (sun and moon) rise from the gates from which (the sun) rises and sets for thirty days. 75:1. And the leaders of the heads of thousands who (are) in charge of the whole creation and in charge of all the stars (have to do) also with the four (days) which are added, and are not separated from their position, according to the whole reckoning of the year. And these serve on the four days which are not counted in the reckoning of the year. 2. And because of them men go wrong in them, for these lights really serve in the stations of the world, one in the first gate, and one in the third gate, and one in the fourth gate, and one in the sixth gate; and the exact harmony of the (course of the) world is completed in the separate three hundred and sixty-four stations of the world.[158]

This passage apparently presents two variations of a lunisolar calendar.[159]

The first assumes a lunar year of 354 days, six months of 29 days each and another six months of 30 days. To reconcile the lunar orbit with the revolution of the sun, an embolistic month of 30 days is added every five years. Enoch fails to mention, in 74:10, that four days are added each year to make it total 364 days. The second calendar likewise begins with a 354-day lunar year, but adds an embolistic month every three years for a similar total of a mean year of 364 days.[160] Both systems assume, of course, the solar year of 364 days in contrast to the Egyptian year, which has 360 plus 5 days, or the Julian calendar, according to which the year is composed of $365\frac{1}{4}$ days. The additional days in the third month of the quadrennial cycle are intrinsic to the revolution of the sun, according to Enoch 75:1-2. Thus Enoch 72-82 supposes that in the majority of the years, whether the embolistic month is a triennial or a quintennial phenomenon, the standard reckoning is lunar. Thus the often-repeated presumption that the Enochite calendar, no less than that of Jubilees, was heliacal cannot be substantiated in the sources. It may not be argued that the solar aspects of the calendar are peculiar to the Ethiopic version but absent from its Aramaic archetype. It was shown above at length that, if anything, the Qumranic fragments of the Astronomical Enoch reflect a more stringent lunisolar calendation than that represented in the Ethiopic version. Thus the Enochite calendar could not have served as the model for Jubilees without elemental revisions. The author of Jubilees, though clearly indebted to the Enochite astronomy of a lunisolar year which uses 354 days, proposed an invariable year of 364 days, thus creating a calendar that ignores the moon completely. It is also behind a truly solar calendar by $1\frac{1}{4}$ days. The sun alone becomes the basis of the festive cycles. Jub. 6:22-38 castigates as impious those who use the lunar month, i.e., the lunisolar reckoning.

This is not all that Jubilees seems to have added to the Enochite calendar. The lunisolar cycle of Enoch assumed a variable year; most years consisted of 354 days, but every third or fifth year would have an embolistic month. The years in Jubilees are completely identical. Each and every year in the Jubilees calendar consists of 364 days. The author of Jubilees introduced two radical changes: first, the invariable year of 364 days; second, the Sabbath was made an integral part of the solar reckoning. Unlike Enoch, which has an embolistic month of 30 days[161] disturbing the septimal order, Jubilees has no provision for intercalation whatsoever. Since every year consisted of 364 days, full advantage was taken of its divisibility by seven so that the festive seasons would invariably fall on the same day of the week. The setting of a festive season whose day of the week never changes gave the calendar's designer an option as to the day on which he wished to set its beginning. Once set it could not be altered, since the calendar would be unaffected by the apparent movements of the sun. As the library at Qumran tells us,[162] the author of the calendar determined that the first day of the first month is to fall on a Wednesday. Why that

selection in preference to any other day of the week? Scholars cite Gen.
1:14–19; since the greater and lesser luminaries had been created on Wednesday,[163] it seems appropriate that the first day of the first month should come
on that day. This reason may or may not have been a factor in the choice; but
what seems to have been more decisive is that the author, having rejected a
year of a variable length, also spurned a calendar which did not have a fixed
day of the month for one of its major feasts, Shavuot. Since the pilgrimage
festivals fall in the middle of the month, on the fifteenth day of the first and
seventh months, he also set Shavuot, which falls in the third month, on the
fifteenth day. Now according to Lev. 23:15, Shavuot is to fall *mimmoḥorat
haššabbat* (i.e., on Sunday); thus the fifteenth day of the third month had to fall
on Sunday. From this date the rest of the festive calendar followed. The first
day of the third month had to fall on a Sunday as well, the first day of the
second month on a Friday, and the first day of the first month on a Wednesday. Thus the first day of the quadrennial cycle always fell on a Wednesday.
The lengthening of the month, according to the chart of the Astronomical
Enoch, had to take place on the third month of the quadrennial cycle: the
third, sixth, ninth and twelfth months. Thus calendrical rather than exegetical
considerations played a primary role in determining the weekly days of the
sectarian calendar.

As was pointed out above, the author of the Qumranic Torah seems to have
made the design of the sanctuary follow the heavenly movements of Enochite
astronomy.[164] This shows a dependence either on the Astronomical Enoch or
on its successor in Enoch 72–82. Whatever the source and whatever the solar
astronomy, in most years the calendar in Enoch remained lunar and was
adjusted by the embolistic month. It is not necessary, therefore, that the sacrificial cycle in the Qumranic Torah refer to a solar calendar. Only in the Book
of Jubilees, which calls those who insist on the visibility of the new moon
pagan, is the calendar strictly solar.

An interesting question arises: Was the author of Jubilees himself the inven-
tor of the Qumran calendar, or does someone else before him deserve the
credit for its creation? No definite answer is possible, except that Jubilees, in
the chapter in which the calendar is outlined, states: "For I know and from
henceforth will I declare it unto thee, and *it is not of my own devising; for the book
(lies) written before me,* and on the heavenly tablets the division of days is
ordained, lest they forget the feasts of the covenant and walk according to the
feasts of the Gentiles after their error and after their ignorance."[165] If a book
advocating a strict solar reckoning indeed lay before the author of Jubilees, as
he claims, it is necessary to suppose the existence of a work that is posterior to
the scroll but was available to the author of Jubilees.

A summary of the literary tradition discussed so far yields the following
chronological sequence:

1. The Astronomical Enoch (fragments of which were in the Qumran library)
2. "The book of the courses of the luminaries . . . ." (Enoch 72–82)
3. The Qumranic Torah
4. The calendrical work used by the author of Jubilees (cf. Jub. 6:35)
5. The Book of Jubilees—"This is the history of the division of the days of the law and of the testimony, of the events of the years, of their (year) weeks, of their Jubilees throughout all the years of the world"

Heavenly Tablets

The Book of Jubilees consists of amplifications and embellishments of the canonical Genesis. But the author of Jubilees never tires of reiterating the claim that his book was based on authoritative sources, especially the inscrutable "heavenly tablets." Charles has pointed out that the citation of the heavenly tablets as a source appears in other pseudepigraphic works as well, such as the Book of Enoch and the Testament of Levi, not only in matters relating to law but also to bolster predictive claims.[166] These citations from books other than Jubilees need not concern us here since they are evidently secondary, being an imitation of the Jubilees formula.[167] It is necessary, however, to distinguish between the references to this source by Jubilees in matters of law and its citation in other subject-matter. By combining all such allusions into a single unit, Charles has obscured the problem.

In Jubilees, the invocation of the heavenly tablets appears to be wholly bound to the covenant or its provisions. Charles, assuming that the law referred to in such citations could only have been the canonical Torah, was confronted by many references which could not be located therein. But now, with the discovery of the sectarian Torah and the awareness that the author of Jubilees regarded it as authoritative, there is no difficulty.[168] As was pointed out above, Jubilees invokes the heavenly tablets with unusual frequency in passages containing statutes that either received emphasis in the Qumranic Torah or had particular meaning in its own day. The sacrificial calendar,[169] the blood of the animals,[170] and the Feast of Weeks[171] are among the themes taken from the scroll.

The formula "heavenly tablets" in the Book of Jubilees was possibly derived from cols. 1 and 2 of 11Q Torah, in which God would have ordained Moses on Sinai to inscribe two stone tablets.[172] The two tablets mentioned in Exod. 34:1 and cited in Jub. 1:1 no longer meant the two tablets of the Decalogue, but the tablet given to Moses "first" at Sinai on the fifteenth day of the third month[173] in the presence of Israel, and the "later" tablet, the Qumranic Torah, which was entrusted to Moses alone at Mount Sinai on the sixteenth day of the third month[174] and would be uncovered at the end of days. Thus the heavenly tablets in Jubilees have a technical meaning which is not reproduced in works dependent upon it, such as the Testament of Levi and sections of Enoch.[175] It was the author of Jubilees who first used the term.

Jacob's Dream

In 11Q Torah 29:10, God tells Moses that He will create a new temple in accordance with the covenant established with Jacob at Bethel. The problem arises, Which of Jacob's two encounters with God is meant?[176] Jubilees reproduces these two visits of Jacob to Bethel, but in the light of 11Q Torah 29:10, the author dates the covenant during the second journey, which he goes on to describe at great length.[177] Apparently understanding 11Q Torah 29:10 as an allusion to Exod. 19:3, where God tells Moses to speak to the house of Jacob, the author of Jubilees embellishes the biblical account of the patriarch's second journey to Bethel as a model of what was to come later at Sinai. Jacob prepares his household by ordaining the cleansing of idolatry.[178] The consecration of Levi and the building of an altar ensue; then God speaks, changing Jacob's name to Israel. This account concludes with the vision of the seven tablets.[179] What was meant by the seven tablets is puzzling, since throughout the book we have heard of only two tablets. Perhaps the answer is that the two tablets may be divided into seven books: the Five Books of Moses, the Qumranic Torah, and another book, possibly Enoch or even the Book of Jubilees itself.

The preceding discussion will suffice to indicate the interdependence of the sectarian Torah and Jubilees on a number of points. It also makes unlikely any hypothesis which would make the author of the scroll dependent on the Book of Jubilees. To be sure, the presumed relationship of Jubilees 1 to the section lost from the beginning of 11Q Torah does not tell us which of these texts served as the archetype of the other. Yet the content of Jubilees 1, with its emphasis on a new sanctuary that will be eternal, makes sense only if its author was alluding to the sanctuary prescribed in 11Q Torah. It cannot be said that the author of Jubilees shaped the ritual of the sacrifices and feasts in the Qumranic Torah. Such a supposition could not account for other material in the scroll which has no counterpart in the Book of Jubilees. The latter had no legal standing. On the other hand, 11Q Torah was regarded as authoritative by a segment of Jewry. Most, if not all, of the departures of the Book of Jubilees from the canonical Torah can be reasonably accounted for by a dependence on 11Q Torah. Furthermore, material dealing with such subjects as the blood, sacrifices, and the paschal lamb forms the core of the scroll, whereas in Jubilees it serves as embellishment. Of course, it is possible to argue that the authors of both Jubilees and the sectarian Torah were dependent on another source now lost, but such a hypothesis is unacceptable since it posits a work for which there is no evidence. The thesis of this chapter finds further support in Jubilees' use of the first and last Law, which can now be explained as references to the canonical and the sectarian Torahs, respectively. "First and last Law" supposes two Torahs which, prior to the discovery of 11Q Torah, found no satisfactory explanation. Further proof for the posterity of Jubilees is its delineation of the sectarian calendar. The author of 11Q Torah, to the extent which can be determined, still used a traditional lunisolar calendar, vigorously attacked by Jubilees. Since the calendar of Jubilees is known to have become standard in the sect, its apparent observance in 11Q Torah can be ascribed to that work which postdates its composition. This phenomenon finds its best explanation in the supposition that the composition of 11Q Torah antedates that of Jubilees. Not all the arguments presented thus far are of equal weight, but in combination the evidence is clear-cut. There is nothing to indicate (a) that 11Q Torah was dependent on Jubilees, or (b) that both of these works borrowed from a third exemplar. The simplest explanation is that the author of Jubilees was profoundly indebted to the Qumranic Torah. Thus the numerous allusions to the Law in Little Genesis presumably embrace subject-matter taken either from the canonical Torah or the Second Torah, i.e., 11Q Torah.

If the preceding analysis is correct, the author of Jubilees not only used the sectarian Torah, but made it a pillar of his own work. Beginning with Jub. 1:1, which stresses the centrality of the Feast of Weeks, the author goes on to cite at great length numerous portions of the scroll, which receive recognition equal to, if not greater than, the traditional Pentateuch. The two tablets of stone mentioned in Exodus 34 lose their original reference to the Decalogue and become the first and the last Law. This change in meaning would explain Jubilees' embellishments of Genesis with sacrificial passages that are attributed to the ante- and post-diluvian patriarchs. Not only is Jubilees deeply indebted to the Qumranic Torah, but its author made it his task to propogate the book as a revelation of God at Sinai—comparable, if not superior, to the Mosaic Torah. Thus many aspects of Jubilees, which have continued to puzzle scholars, find their solution in the paramount influence of 11Q Torah.

Eupolemus

The extant fragments of Eupolemus may furnish evidence of the sectarian Torah's existence prior to the time of this Judaeo-Greek writer. Eupolemus authored a history of the Jews from the beginning until at least the post-exilic period, if not up to his own time.[180] This work is lost, but Alexander Polyhistor, who flourished in the first half of the first century B.C.E., excerpted Eupolemus' book for his own massive account of the Jews, which he evidently prepared for Pompey.[181] This account has also perished, but citations from Eupolemus survive in the works of Clement of Alexandria and especially Eusebius of Caesarea (Palestine). Although his identity has long been disputed, there seems no valid reason to presume that the historian named Eupolemus is anyone other than "Eupolemus son of John, son of Accos," who served as Judah Maccabee's ambassador.[182] For the dating of Eupolemus it is worth remembering that, according to 2. Mac. 4:11, his father, John, was the chief negotiator with Antiochus III when the Seleucid troops occupied Jerusalem circa 198 B.C.E. A chronological fragment, preserved by Clement, possibly indicates that Eupolemus reckoned the date of the Exodus from the vantage point of 157 B.C.E.[183]

To give the reader an idea of the flavor and quality of this historian's fragments, I reproduce here Eupolemus' entire description of the temple, as quoted by Eusebius from Alexander Polyhistor's history of the Jews:

> 4. And he (i.e. Solomon) began to build the temple of God at the age of thirteen. And the work was done by the above-mentioned nations; and the twelve Jewish tribes supplied the 160,000 with all their needs, one tribe each month.
>
> He laid the foundations of the temple of God, sixty cubits its length and sixty cubits its width, but the width of the building and of the foundation was ten cubits. Thus he was commanded by Nathan, the prophet of God. 5. He built alternately a course of stone and a layer of cypress wood, bonding the two courses together with bronze clamps of a talent weight. Having built it thus he boarded the inside wall with cedar and cypress wood so that the stone walls were not visible. He overlaid the *naos* with gold on the inside by casting golden bricks row by row, five cubits long, fastening them to the walls with silver nails, weighing a talent, in the shape of a breast, four in number. 6. Thus he covered it with gold from the floor to the ceiling; and the ceiling he made of gold; but the roof he made of bronze tiles, having smelted the bronze and cast it into molds.
>
> He made two pillars of bronze and covered them with pure gold, a finger thick. 7. The pillars were of the same height as the temple, the width of each pillar was ten cubits in circumference; and he set one of the pillars on the right side of the house, the other on the left. He also made ten lampstands of gold, each weighing ten talents, having taken as a model the lampstand made by Moses in the tent of the testimony. 8. He placed some of the lampstands at the right of the shrine, others at the left. He also made seventy lamps of gold, so that each lampstand had seven lamps. He also built the gates of the temple, adorning them with gold and silver, and he paneled them with cedar and cypress wood. 9. He also made, in the northern portion of the temple, a porch, and he supported it with forty-eight pillars of brass.
>
> He also built a bronze laver, twenty cubits long, twenty cubits wide and five cubits high, extending a brim around the base a cubit long, projecting to the outside, so that the priests may stand upon it when they dip their feet

and wash their hands. He also made the twelve legs of the laver of cast oxen, the height of a man, and he attached them to the lower part of the laver, at the right of the altar.

10. He made a bronze platform, two cubits high around the laver, so that the king may stand upon it when praying, that he would be seen by the Jewish people. He also built an altar twenty-five cubits by twenty cubits and twelve cubits high.

11. He made two bronze ringlike lattices, and he set them upon contrivances, which rose above the temple twenty cubits, and they cast a shadow over the entire sanctuary. Upon each network he hung four hundred bronze bells of a talent weight. He made all the networks so that the bells would toll and frighten away the birds, that none would settle upon the temple nor nest in the panels of the gates and porches nor pollute the temple with their dung. 12. He surrounded the city of Jerusalem with walls, towers and trenches. He also built a palace for himself.

13. The shrine was first called the Temple of Solomon, but later, because of the Temple, the city was falsely called Jerusalem, but by the Greeks it was called Hierosolyma. 14. When he had completed the Temple and the walls of the city, he went to Selom and offered a sacrifice to God, a burnt offering of 1,000 oxen. Then he took the tabernacle and the altar and the vessels, which Moses had made, and he carried them to Jerusalem and he placed them in the house. 15. The ark, the golden altar, the lampstand, the table and the other vessels he also placed there, just as the prophet had commanded him. 16. There he offered a myriad offering to God; 2,000 sheep, 3,500 oxen.

The total weight of gold expended on the two pillars and the Temple was 4,600,000 talents; silver for the nails and the other furnishings 1,232 talents; bronze for the columns, the laver and the porch, 18,050 talents.[184]

A basic problem confronting the reader of Eupolemus is determining the sources he used for the description of the Solomonic temple. Freudenthal says that Eupolemus based his account primarily on the version of Solomon's sanctuary in 2 Chronicles 3–5.[185] It has been shown, however, that quite a number of details given in Eupolemus cannot be traced to any of the known biblical sources.[186] Since the books of Kings and Chronicles were presumably available to this Graeco-Jewish writer, on what basis did he depart from the scriptural sources, giving dimensions for which there seems to be no biblical authority?

The recovery of extensive remnants from a lengthy account of the dimensions of a temple enables us to examine the possibility that Eupolemus was dependent on the work found at Qumran. The passages that may indicate an interdependence between the two sources will be examined in turn in the following sections.

(1)

Eupolemus (P.E. 9:34:4)	*11Q Torah 4:7–10*

θεμελιῶσαί τε τὸν ναὸν τοῦ θεοῦ,
μῆκος πηχῶν ξ', πλάτος πηχῶν
ξ',τὸ δὲ πλάτος τῆς οἰκοδομῆς καὶ
τῶν θεμελίων πηχῶν ι'.

7. ... ה הרחב וקומת הק
8. ... א[מה ובאתה את האולם ...
9. ... ב עשר באמה וקירות ...
10. ... וגובה ששים באמ]ה ...

He laid the foundations of the temple of God, sixty cubits its length and sixty cubits its width, but the width of the building and of the foundation was ten cubits.

7. ... the width and height of . . .[187]
8. ... cub]its and thou enterest the porch . . .
9. ... ten cubits and the walls . . .
10. ... and the height of sixty cubi[ts . . .

What is puzzling in Eupolemus is that his dimensions diverge from those given in 1 Kgs. 6:2 and 2 Chr. 3:3, which say that the length of the house was sixty cubits, its width twenty cubits, and its height thirty cubits. To be sure, Ezra 6:3 assigns sixty cubits to its height, but the dimensions of the width and length of Zerubbabel's sanctuary, described in Ezra, are not recorded.[188] Eupolemus, on the other hand, does not give the height of Solomon's temple. What is most puzzling in Eupolemus is not the divergence in the measurements, but the fact that he makes Solomon's temple a square, perhaps even a cube, of sixty cubits, whereas all other sources—the Bible, Ezekiel, Josephus, and the sages—insist it was rectangular.[189] Did Eupolemus himself, who frequently embellishes his sources, invent the square shape? Or was he dependent on a source such as the scroll?

Unfortunately, only isolated letters of the words in col. 4, where the Qumranic Torah presumably prescribed the dimensions of the future sanctuary, have come down to us. Several words of the relevant lines, however, do remain, and these may point to some similarities with the dimensions given by Eupolemus. As Yadin understands it, 4:7–10 gives the dimensions of both the main sanctuary (*heykal*) and the porch. In 4:7, "the height of haq[. . .]," he restores haqq[odeš]; "the width and height of the holy," referring to the sanctuary.[190] But since nothing remains of the measurements of this "holy," Yadin suggests that this line, or perhaps even the end of the preceding one, reproduced the dimensions of the Solomonic temple found in 1 Kgs. 6:2: sixty cubits long, twenty wide, and thirty high.[191] As to line 4:8, whose words ובאתה

את האולם do not make sense, Yadin proposed they mean ובניתה את האולם (and thou shalt build the porch). In line 9, Yadin suggests the word ending in *beyt* was *roḥab*; thus the line reads: "the width ten cubits." Combining lines 8–10, Yadin presumes that the text assigns to the porch a width of ten cubits (line 9) and a height of sixty cubits (line 10).

Except as a desperate attempt somehow to find mention of the main sanctuary,[192] it is difficult to see on what basis the last two remaining letters of 4:7 *haq* could be read as *haqqodeš* (the holy), meaning the *heykal* (sanctuary). This term is not used in any of the traditional descriptions of the building of the temple, neither is it found in the remnants of the scroll. The reconstruction הרוחב וקומת הקירות (the width and the height of the walls) seems more plausible.[193] Given the incompleteness of the text, it is impossible to conjecture to which structure these walls refer. The reading of ובניתה את האולם (and thou shalt build the porch) in line 8 instead of ובאתה is unacceptable, since this form is not found in the scroll and runs counter to its usage;[194] one would expect ועשיתה (and thou shalt make), a formula normally adhered to in the work.[195] If one has to emend the remnants of line 8, the more plausible change would be the reading of *ʾel* in the place of *ʾet*, i.e., "and thou shalt come to the porch." This seems to refer to a discussion of the gates or doors leading to the porch and the temple, possibly from the terrace mentioned in the preceding lines of this column.

Even less acceptable than Yadin's notes on lines 7 and 8 is his conceptual reconstruction of the temple's dimensions in the scroll's ordinances; i.e., its width and length correspond to those of the Solomonic structure.[196] This supposition seems implausible for two reasons. First, none of the details mentioned in the scroll's temple have dimensions that resemble the account of the Solomonic sanctuary in the account of 1 Kings and 2 Chronicles. If there is a central idea underlying the design of the structures in 11Q Torah, it is the squareness of the shrine's building.[197] According to Yadin, however, the rectangular shapes of the *heykal* and the *ʾulam* were exceptions, a view that violates the principal idea of the author. As the lengthy account of the outer courtyard suggests, the author's insistence on the evenness of the width and length is based on the symbolic link between these dimensions and the tribal organization of Israel.[198] Each of the four sides was shared by three tribes, hence, the twelve gates even in the outer courtyard, the seemingly least sacred of the temple's network of buildings. The presence of similar symbolism in all the structures whose dimensions have survived in the scroll necessitates the supposition that this also characterizes the *heykal*. If the *heykal* was in fact square, the question arises, What were the dimensions of the structure? 11Q Torah 4:9–10 apparently is the remnant of ordinances that prescribed the *heykal*. Since 4:5–6 dealt with the terrace, 4:7 with the width of the walls or perhaps the gates that separated the terraces from the main structure, and 4:8 with the entrance to the porch, then 4:9–10 presumably described the measurements of the sanctuary. The ten cubits in 4:9 seemingly refers to the measurement of the foundations, and the height of sixty cubits (4:10) to the walls of the main structure. Nothing remains, however, of the *heykal*'s width and length.

When only sketchy information was available concerning the newly discovered scroll, I wrote:

> There is no doubt, however, that, according to Eupolemus, the Temple's height was twenty cubits. This is so not because, as Freudenthal says, he followed the Scriptural tradition, but because this is the height of the network which Eupolemus says covered the *naos*. Incidentally, of some interest to our subject is a Temple Scroll in the Qumran texts recently discovered by Yigael Yadin, envisioning an eschatological Temple with "three courts, each an exact square, one inside the other."[199]

Now, unfortunately, the poor state of the relevant passage does not yield much new information, except that 4:10 makes the conjecture of a cube for the shape of the main structure seem more plausible. The network of twenty cubits may refer to dimensions of twenty cubits above the height of the sanctuary. Up to the publication of the sectarian Torah, there existed no authority for these dimensions. Does it follow, then, that Eupolemus ascribed dimensions to Solomon's temple which he had derived from these fragments? Furthermore, was Eupolemus' claim that Solomon's temple was a square of sixty cubits equally based on the same source? If the answer to these questions is yes, then the Greek fragments of Eupolemus may be helpful for the restoration of some of the lacunae in col. 4.

---

(2)

Eupolemus (P.E. 9:34:8)

οἰκοδομῆσαι δὲ καὶ τὰς πύλας τοῦ ἱεροῦ καὶ κατακοσμῆσαι χρυσίῳ καὶ ἀργυρίῳ καὶ καταστεγάσαι φατνώμασι κεδρίνοις καὶ κυπαρισσίνοις.

He also built the gates of the temple, adorning them with gold and silver, and he paneled them with cedar and cypress wood.

11Q Torah 5:8–11

8. ... יכה וארבעה שערים [לעליה לארבע] ...
9. ... השער שתים עשרה ...
10. ... באמה וכול הכיו]ר ... צלתותיו ...
11. התח[תון והכול מצופה [זהב טהור] ...

8. ... and four gates [of the roof chamber for the four] ...

9. ... twelve gates ...

10. ... cubits and all of the la[ver ... its doors ...

11. the lo]wer and all are inlaid with [pure gold] ...

Quite a number of biblical passages emphasize the importance of the temple's gates, especially in Ezekiel, who devotes considerable space to them.[200] But only these Qumran fragments repeatedly describe the dimensions of the gates of each of the temple's structures, invariably concluding that they were overlaid with gold.[201] The question arises whether Eupolemus' mention of the gates and their adornments was influenced by the sectarian Torah, which as far as is known, is the only text that noted the requirement that the gates be gilded. The mention of silver and of wood paneling of cedar and cypress, which is found in Eupolemus, is not found in the surviving fragments of the Qumran text, but may have been mandated in the scroll.

---

(3)

Eupolemus (P.E. 9:34:10)	*11Q Torah 12:8–13*
οἰκοδομῆσαι δὲ καὶ τὸ θυσιαστήριον πηχῶν κε΄ ἐπὶ πήχεις κ΄, τὸ δὲ ὕψος πηχῶν δώδεκα.	8. [. . . .]ל מדותיו יהיו 9. [. . . .]רים[. . .]נה[. . .]פנה ואמה 10. [. . . .]ם בנוי כולו 11. א[בנ]ים . . . ת[עשה כול 12. שורות ב[. . .]ו 13. וקרנותיו ופנ[ו]תיו . . . תע[שה לו
He also made an altar twenty-five cubits by twenty cubits and twelve cubits high.	8. . . .]its measurements will be 9. tw]enty [. . .] corner, and cubit 10. . . .]built all 11. s]tone[s . . . thou] shalt make all 12. lines [. . . 13. its horns and its cor[ners . . . thou] shalt make it

---

The dimensions of the altar that are prescribed in the remnants are uncertain; only the last three letters of the word *ʿeśrym* (twenty) have been preserved. The same is true of the account found in the description of the New Jerusalem, which does contain the word *ʿeśrym*,[202] but it is impossible to say whether it had an additional digit following the number twenty. It appears that the stone altar, in contrast to the altar of bronze mentioned in col. 3:15, must have been a square of twenty cubits, corresponding to the measurements found in 2 Chr. 4:1 and in the report by Hecataeus of Abdera.[203] If this is so, the report in Eupolemus that the altar was a rectangle of twenty-five by twenty cubits and was twelve cubits high has no parallel. It has been frequently suggested, however, that "five" is a dittograph and that the altar in Eupolemus was also square.[204] It is important to remember that with respect to all the other dimensions given in the scroll, there is not even one that corresponds to those given in the historical accounts of Kings-Chronicles. There is, then, a possibility that, as in the case of the *naos,* the dimensions of the stone altar in the scroll served as a model for Eupolemus' account of the Solomonic sanctuary; both Eupolemus and 11Q Torah prescribed a square altar of twenty cubits.

---

(4)

Eupolemus (P.E. 9:34:6–7)	*11Q Torah 13:1–7*

ποιῆσαι δὲ δύο στύλους χαλκοῦς καὶ καταχρυσῶσαι αὐτοὺς χρυσίῳ ἀδόλῳ, δακτύλου τὸ πάχος. εἶναι δὲ τοὺς στύλους τῷ ναῷ ἰσομεγέθεις, τὸ δὲ πλάτος κύκλῳ ἕκαστον κίονα πηχῶν δέκα στῆσαι δὲ αὐτοὺς τοῦ οἴκου ὅν μὲν ἐκ δεξιῶν, ὅν δὲ ἐξ εὐωνύμων.

1. ‏למען‎ ...
2. ‏[ו]עשר א[מות]‎ ...
3. ‏תעשה‎ ...
4. ‏ודלתו[תיו]‎ ...
5. ‏אחד ... לימין ואחד ל[שמאול]‎ ...
6. ‏מצופים‎ ...
7. ‏לו שער כ‎ ...

He made two pillars of bronze and covered them with pure gold a finger thick. The pillars were of the same height as the temple, the width of each pillar was ten cubits in circumference; and he set one of the pillars on the right side of the house, the other on the left.

1. in order that . . .
2. [and] ten cub[its] . . .
3. thou shalt make . . .
4. and its do[ors] . . .
5. one . . . to the right and one to the [left] . . .
6. overlaid . . .
7. for it a gate . . .

The feature common to Eupolemus and the scroll is the measurement of ten cubits[205] and the pillars' being set on either side of the structure.[206] It is by no means certain that the two accounts are genuine parallels. While Eupolemus describes the Jachin and Boaz, the two pillars mentioned in 2 Chr. 3:15–17, the structure described in 11Q Torah 13:1–7 remains uncertain. Yadin conjectures that it refers to an edifice adjoining the altar described in 12:7–16, an additional building to the ones listed in the structures of the inner court: *heykal,* altar, laver, slaughterhouse(?) and *parwar.*[207] Possibly, Yadin says, these lines describe the *beyt-ḥallypot,* used for keeping the knives. It is clear, however, that this section does not deal with the building, but with the pillars.[208] In the Solomonic temple the pillars dominated the sky.[209] Eupolemus likewise makes the pillars a principal part of the architecture. The scroll differs from the biblical accounts, which place these pillars in front of the house, and instead situates them before the altar. It seems that in the view of the scroll, the sanctity of the altar equaled, or perhaps even surpassed, that of the main structure. In the list of the structures that embrace the holy of holies, according to 35:8–9, the altar precedes the *heykal*.

(5)

Eupolemus (P.E. 9:34:9)

κατασκευάσαι δὲ καὶ λουτῆρα
χαλκοῦν, μῆκος πηχῶν κ' καὶ
πλάτος πηχῶν κ', τὸ δὲ ὕψος πηχῶν
ε'. ποιῆσαι δὲ ἐπ' αὐτῷ στεφάνην
πρὸς τὴν βάσιν ἔξω ὑπερέχουσαν
πῆχυν ἕνα πρὸς τὸ τοὺς ἱερεῖς τούς
τε πόδας προσκλύζεσθαι καὶ τὰς
χεῖρας νίπτεσθαι ἐπιβαίνοντας
ποιῆσαι δὲ καὶ τὰς βάσεις τοῦ
λουτῆρος τορευτὰς χωνευτὰς
δώδεκα καὶ τῷ ὕψει ἀνδρομήκεις καὶ
στῆσαι ἐξ ὑστέρου μέρους ὑπὸ τὸν
λουτῆρα, ἐκ δεξιῶν τοῦ θυσιασ-
τηρίου. ποιῆσαι δὲ καὶ βάσιν
χαλκῆν τῷ ὕψει πηχῶν δυοῖν κατὰ
τὸν λουτῆρα, ἵν' ἐφεστήκῃ ἐπ'
αὐτῆς ὁ βασιλεύς, ὅταν προσε-
ύχηται, ὅπως ὀπτάνηται τῷ λαῷ
τῶν Ἰουδαίων.

He also built a bronze laver, twenty cubits long, twenty cubits wide, and five cubits high, extending a brim around the base a cubit long, projecting to the outside, so that the priests may stand upon it when they dip their feet and wash their hands. He also made the twelve legs of the laver of cast oxen, the height of a man, and he attached them to the lower part of the laver, at the right of the altar. He also made a bronze platform, two cubits high around the laver, so that the king may stand upon it when praying, that he would be seen by the Jewish people.

11Q Torah 31:10–13

10. ועשיתה בית לכיור נגב מזרח מרובע
לכול רוחותיו אחת ועשרים
11. אמה רחוק מהמזבח חמשים אמה ורחב
ה[ק]יר שלוש אמות וגבה
12. [ע]שרים אמה ... ושערים עשו לה
מהמזרח ומהצפון
13. ומהמערב ורוחב השערים ארבע אמות
וגובהמה שבע

10. And you shall make a house for the laver southeast, a square with all its sides twenty-one
11. cubits, away from the altar fifty cubits, the thickness of the [wa]ll is three cubits, and its height
12. [tw]enty cubits ... and gates attached to it from the east and from the north
13. and from the west. The width of the gates is four cubits and their height seven.

The possibility, even likelihood, of an interdependence between these descriptions of the wash basin of the temple emerges from a comparison of Eupolemus and 11Q Torah with the biblical tradition concerning the *kyyor*. Exod. 30:17–21 ordains the making of a *kyyor* and its stand for the tabernacle, without specifying any of its measurements. The account of the Solomonic temple mentions a *kyyor*, but the reference is clearly to a platform rather than to a washbasin.[210] Instead, 1 Kings records the *yam* (sea), whose diameter was ten cubits, the circumference thirty (thirty-three in LXX), and the height five.[211] There is nothing in 11Q Torah 31:10–13 to indicate any dependence on the Solomonic "sea." On the contrary, in spite of Yadin's speculation, the author of the scroll makes it manifest that the future temple's *kyyor* will bear no resemblance to the Solomonic work, perhaps regarding the latter as idolatrous.[212] On the other hand, the author of the sectarian Torah expanded the Mosaic *kyyor* into the measurements of his own futuristic temple.[213] The words "square in all of its sides,"[214] i.e., a cube, contrast sharply with the circular shape of the "sea," the laver in the Solomonic sanctuary.[215] Unless it be presumed that the author of the fragments was completely unaware of the books of Kings and Chronicles, the contrast is intentional; i.e., the scroll regards the circular "sea" standing on cast oxen as a detail that was not to be reproduced in the eternal temple.[216] The contrasting shapes of the *kyyor*, which in 1 Kings was a round sea whereas in the futuristic temple it was to be a square basin, symbolize 11Q Torah's rejection of the sanctity of the Solomonic temple. Of course, the author of 11Q Torah attempts, by retrojecting his account back to Moses, to suggest that this rejection took place long before the Solomonic structure was erected. On the other hand, the measurements of this laver found in the scroll are not intended merely to harmonize and supplement the Mosaic commands in Exod. 30:17. The *kyyor* was to be a cube of twenty-one cubits, a multiple of seven, that measurement which was elemental in the design of the future temple.[217]

Eupolemus, who was undoubtedly aware of the Pentateuch and historical versions of the laver, ascribes to Solomon a laver that seems to have no model in the biblical sources.[218] On what basis does the Judaeo-Greek historian ascribe to Solomon a laver whose base was twenty by twenty cubits plus a stand of one cubit around it, making it a square of twenty-one cubits, or twenty-two if both sides are counted?[219] Ought one to ascribe the fact that 11Q Torah's ordinance and Eupolemus' statement both contain a base of twenty-one cubits to mere coincidence or to interdependence? The latter seems quite possible. On the other hand, Eupolemus' use of 1 Kings and 2 Chronicles need not be doubted, as is indicated by his ascription of a height of five cubits, which corresponds to the height of Solomon's sea.[220] In other words, Eupolemus seems to present a conflation of the Qumranic Torah, 1 Kgs. 7:23, and 2 Chr. 4:2.

(6)

Eupolemus (P.E. 9:34:9)	*11 Q Torah 34:2–6, 15; 35:8–9*

ποιῆσαι δὲ καὶ κατὰ τὸ πρὸς
βορρᾶν μέρος τοῦ ἱεροῦ στοὰν καὶ
στύλους αὐτῇ ὑποστῆσαι χαλκοῦς
μή.

2. ... ובין העמוד לע[מוד]
3. ... אשר בין העמדים
4. ... הפרים אל בין הגלג[ל]ים
5. ... י]ם וסוגרים את הגלגלים וא[חר]
6. ואוסרים את קרני הפרים אל הטבעות ...
בטבעות

He also made, in the northern portion of the temple, a porch and he
supported it with forty-eight pillars of brass.

2. ... and between the pillar[s]
3. ... that is between the pillars
4. ... bulls between the wheel[s
5. ... They ope]n and they close
the wheels af[ter]
6. And they bind the horns of the
bulls to the rings ... in the rings

15. ועשיתה שלשלות יורדות מן מקרת שני
עשר העמודים

15. Thou shalt make chains hanging from the beams of the twelve
pillars.

8. וקדשת[מ]ה את ס[בי]ב למזבח ולהיכל
ולכיור
9. ולפרור ...

35:8 ... [Ye] shall sanctify aro[und]
the altar, the sanctuary, the laver
9. and the *parwar* ...

It is apparent that Eupolemus records here a structure that has no walls,
standing upon forty-eight pillars of bronze.[221] Since no such building is
recorded in the biblical accounts of the Solomonic temple, the question arises
whether Eupolemus himself invented it or whether, as is evident in other
instances, he wove into his description of the Solomonic sanctuary items from
non-biblical sources.[222] Two passages concerning the temple complex recorded in the remains come under consideration. Beginning on top of col. 34, the
scroll devotes almost the entire column to a building labeled by Yadin as *beyt
hammiṭbaḥayim* (the slaughterhouse), serving as a place where the animals
were slaughtered in preparation for the offering on the altar.[223] As Yadin sees
it, this structure had no walls but consisted of twelve pillars, to which chains

were attached for securing the victims. The question arises whether Eupolemus refers to a similar structure that had no walls, a stoa of forty-eight pillars. The basic difference between the two is that whereas Eupolemus mentions a porch of forty-eight pillars, the scroll records only twelve. Unfortunately, the meaning of the number twelve in 34:15 is unclear because of the loss of the remainder of the line. Possibly, the statement concerning the twelve pillars refers to one side only. If so, it might be that they were to be repeated on each of the four sides of the complex, bringing the total number of pillars to forty-eight. Then, the number of pillars in Eupolemus would be identical to that in 11Q Torah.

On the other hand, the unwalled stoa mentioned by Eupolemus may refer to the building mentioned in 11Q Torah 35:10–15. As Yadin understands 35:10, the text ordains the building of a *parwar* of vertical pillars.[224] A close reading of these lines, however, indicates that it refers to a structure other than a *parwar*: "And thou shalt make a place on the west of the sanctuary (*heykal*) around (*sabyb*) the *parwar* of standing pillars for sin and guilt offerings. They shall be separate from one another, the sin offering of the priests and the he-goat from the sin offerings of the people and their guilt offerings. None of these shall be mixed with one another, for their locations shall be separate. . . ." 11Q Torah 35:11–15 might mean that, within the structure of pillars, the sacrifices of the priests ought to be kept apart from those of the people, in keeping with the scroll's insistence on the hierarchy of sanctity. It is more likely, however, that the "place . . . for the sin and guilt offerings" refers to the structure wherein only the sacrifices of the people were to be brought, whereas the sacrifices of the priests were alluded to in a preceding section. This would mean that the structure mentioned in col. 34, whose name is missing in the scroll and which Yadin labeled as "the slaughterhouse," in fact was named *parwar*. Lines 8–9 provide proof that the *parwar* mentioned in 35:10 had already been ordained: "And thou shalt sanctify around the altar, the sanctuary, the laver, and the *parwar*." This list, which defines the "holy of holies," necessarily refers to the complex of buildings that have been mentioned previously, not, as Yadin presumes, to the *parwar* that follows in 35:10.[225] As explained above, this line ordains an annex to the *parwar* of col. 34. In fact it may be supposed that both buildings, the house of the *kyyor* and the *parwar*, are the structures that had been mentioned before, as were the altar and *heykal*, in the introductory columns of the Qumranic Torah.

It might be asked whether there is any relationship between the account of a stoa in the fragments of Eupolemus and the annex that consisted of pillars. To be sure, Eupolemus places this porch on the northern side of the sanctuary, whereas the scroll says that the pillars were located to the west of the *heykal*; and while Eupolemus says that the total number of pillars was forty-eight, the fragments give no definite number. But 11Q Torah does assign a definite purpose to this structure, which Eupolemus does not. If an interdependence between Eupolemus and the scroll is presumed, they may complement each other. Then the porch of forty-eight pillars in Eupolemus was intended to serve the same purpose as the *parwar* and its annex in the Qumran text: to keep the sacrificial animals in preparation for their presentation on the altar. The total number of pillars, either in the building described in col. 34 or the one in 35:10–15, or perhaps both together, numbered forty-eight.

(7)

Eupolemus (P.E. 9:34:11)

ποιῆσαι δὲ καὶ δακτυλίους δύο
χαλκοῦς ἀλυσιδωτοὺς καὶ στῆσαι
αὐτοὺς ἐπὶ μηχανημάτων ὑπερ-
εχόντων τῷ ὕψει τὸν ναὸν πήχεις κ´
καὶ σκιάξειν ἐπάνω παντὸς τοῦ
ἱεροῦ. καὶ προσκρεμάσαι ἑκάστῃ
δίκτυϊ κώδωνας χαλκοῦς ταλαν-
τιαίους τετρακοσίους. καὶ ποιῆσαι
ὅλας τὰς δίκτυας πρὸς τὸ ψοφεῖν
τοὺς κώδωνας καὶ ἀποσοβεῖν τὰ
ὄρνεα, ὅπως μὴ καθίξῃ ἐπὶ τοῦ ἱεροῦ
μηδὲ νοσσεύῃ ἐπὶ τοῖς φατνώμασι
τῶν πυλῶν καὶ στοῶν καὶ μολύνῃ
τοῖς ἀποπατήμασι τὸ ἱερόν.

He made two bronze ringlike lattices, and he set them upon contrivances, which rose above the
temple twenty cubits, and they cast a
shadow over the entire sanctuary.
Upon each network he hung four
hundred bronze bells of a talent
weight; he made all the networks so
that the bells would toll and
frighten away the birds, that none
would settle upon the temple nor
nest in the panels of the gates and
porches nor pollute the temple with
their dung.

11Q Torah 46:1–3

1. [לו]א יעוף [כול]
2. עוף טמא על מקד[שי...].[גגי השערים
[אשר]
3. לחצר החיצונה...

1. [no]t shall fly [any]
2. unclean bird upon my sanct-
[uary . . . upon] the roofs of
the gates [that are]
3. for the outer court . . .

The problematic state of 46:1-2 deprives the reader of a clear statement concerning a matter that was of paramount concern to the ancient writers, both Greek and Jewish. Josephus describes a scarecrow on top of the Herodian sanctuary.[226] Eupolemus and, apparently, M. Middot 4:6 affix this device onto the Solomonic structure as well, although they seem to differ as to the mechanism which protected the temple from the birds' droppings.[227] Yadin presumes, and he may well be right, that 46:1-3 is evidence of the existence of a similar device.[228] This presumption, however, is by no means certain. If the reconstruction of 46:1-2 is correct: "any unclean bird shall not fly upon my sanctuary," the prohibition is directed only to the unclean birds, thus presuming a device that could distinguish between the droppings of the clean and unclean birds. The solution may lie, according to 11Q Torah and some rabbinic commentators, in the observance of the prohibition by the unclean birds themselves, who would not approach even the outermost gates of the sanctuary.[229] If this is the case, it is similar to one of the wonders listed in Abot 5:5, where "no fly ever appeared in the slaughterhouse" of the temple. Eupolemus, however, like Yadin, may have understood 11Q Torah 46:1-3 to refer to the existence of an actual scarecrow.

Aside from these passages in the Judaeo-Greek historian (1-7 above) that may suggest a literary dependence, there seems to be also a more general relationship between Eupolemus and the sectarian Torah. The dependence manifests itself in both form and content, in spite of the fact that Eupolemus describes what he says was the sanctuary erected by Solomon, while the scroll prescribes the design of the future sanctuary. Another difference between these versions of the temple is that 11Q Torah devotes some twenty-five columns to the subject, whereas a bare paragraph treats the same theme in the Greek fragments. The following outline of Eupolemus' account of the Solomonic temple shows how the much more extensive description found at Qumran seems akin to it:

Eupolemus (P.E. 9:30:1-34:18)	*11Q Torah*
i. material for the temple (gold, silver); 30:6-8	col. 3
ii. the sanctuary; 34:4	cols. 4-6
iii. the gilding of the temple; 34:5-6	cols. 4-6, etc.
iv. gilded pillars; 34:6-7	col. 13
v. the lamps and lampstands of gold; 34:7-8	col. 9
vi. the gilded gates; 34:8	cols. 5, 36

vii. the porch of 48 pillars; 34:9	cols. 34–35
viii. the bronze laver; 34:9	col. 31
ix. the twelve oxen; 34:9	?
x. the bronze stand; 34:10	?
xi. the altar; 34:10	col. 12
xii. the bronze lattices for a scarecrow; 34:11	col. 46

Several items in Eupolemus' account of the Solomonic temple may be ascribed to his dependence on the historical account in 1 Kings and especially 2 Chronicles. Indeed, Freudenthal, who has contributed significantly to the understanding of Judaeo-Greek historiography, believed that Eupolemus' account tended to differ from that of 1 Kings but was in harmony with the Chronicler's.[230] It was shown, however, that there is no reason to presume that Eupolemus gave greater credence to the later biblical tradition than to that of the author of Kings, but that both the Graeco-Jewish historian and the Chronicler show an awareness of the desert tabernacle, a structure largely ignored in 1 Kings. With the discovery of the extensive remnants of this messianic temple, the presumption of Eupolemus' dependence on the Chronicler needs to be modified, if not rejected altogther. Eupolemus' assertion that Solomon's coronation was inaugurated in the presence of the high priest Eli and the twelve tribal heads seems puzzling, since no such event is recorded in the biblical tradition.[231] The prominence given to the high priest as well as to the tribal chiefs in the fragments, although not entirely solving the problem, makes it less enigmatic. The tribal leaders, according to 11Q Torah, led in the celebration of the thanksgiving feasts and constituted the lay members of the king's council.[232] The characteristic formula used by Eupolemus to introduce an item in the building of the temple is *kai poiein* (and he made). This was originally thought to have been borrowed from the Hebrew *wayya'aś*, employed in the Chronicler's account of the Solomonic temple. Now, however, with the apparent dependence of Eupolemus on the account of the tabernacle in Exodus 25–40 as well as on the scroll, the *kai poiein* in the Greek fragments seems to be more adequately explained as a paraphrase of *we'aśy-tah*.

Enough evidence has been presented to necessitate a supposition that there exists an interdependence between Eupolemus' account of the Solomonic temple and the sanctuary portrayed by the author of the scroll. The possibility that both Eupolemus and the scroll follow some common source that is now lost need not be entirely excluded. But, as long as no inkling of the existence of such a common ancestor is found, it can be safely ignored. On the other hand, if the question arises whether the author of the scroll used Eupolemus' history of Solomon or vice versa, the answer is clear-cut. There is not even a shred of evidence that the author of 11Q Torah used Greek sources. However, Eupolemus' dependence on Hebrew sources, including some texts now lost, need not be questioned. The possibility exists, therefore, that Eupolemus was indebted to the account of the sanctuary in 11Q Torah. Such an assumption, however, may have far-reaching implications for Eupolemus himself. What was it that impelled the Graeco-Jewish writer, a servant of Judah Maccabee, to use unauthorized versions of the Mosaic Pentateuch, attaching them to an account of the Solomonic sanctuary? More obvious are the implications of this thesis for the dating of the Qumranic Torah. If Eupolemus used 11Q Torah, then Yadin's dating of this work to 125–75 B.C.E. is clearly unacceptable. Its date of composition must antedate 157 B.C.E., the time when Eupolemus completed his work.[233]

The War Rule

A lengthy section earlier in this chapter assembles overwhelming evidence not only for the posteriority of the Book of Jubilees to the Qumranic Torah, but also for numerous indications that the author of Jubilees cited this work on a par with the Mosaic Pentateuch, regarding them both as documents of what God had revealed to Moses on Mount Sinai. The question arises, however, whether we can only postulate that Jubilees is one of the many books that regarded the scroll as a Mosaic work or whether we can also say that it was the first to have done so. If the second alternative can be demonstrated as true or probably true, then Jubilees antedates the bulk of the Qumranic works. If this is so, then the question arises, Which of the writings found at Qumran may be said to be posterior to Jubilees but anterior to what has become characteristic of the sectarian literature?

Before endeavoring to answer this question, it is necessary to say a word concerning the temporal relationship between the Book of Jubilees and the Book of Daniel. Written in 165 or 164 B.C.E., Daniel is the last work that became part of the authoritative Hebrew Scriptures, evidently at the initiative of Judah Maccabee, whose interest in such matters is well attested.[234] Scholars have long recognized the indebtedness of the sectarian writings at Qumran to the Book of Daniel.[235] Were the Qumranic Torah and the Book of Jubilees equally dependent on Daniel?

There exists nothing in the published fragments of the sectarian Torah to suggest an awareness by its author of a work such as Daniel.[236] This fact by itself does not support the argument that the scroll is anterior to the work that fathered the apocalyptic movement: the reason for denying 11Q Torah's indebtedness to Daniel is that the author of the scroll seems to have avoided the use of scriptural books other than the Mosaic source, such as Kings, Isaiah, or the Psalms. Only the fragments of Eupolemus, who wrote circa 160

B.C.E. and whose dependence on the Qumranic Torah has been demonstrated,[237] support the postulate of the priority of the scroll to the Book of Daniel. What seems to be true of the Book of Daniel and the sectarian Torah may apply to Jubilees as well. As was pointed out above, in spite of Charles's arguments for setting Jubilees during the high-priesthood of John Hyrcanus, or VanderKam's dating of it in the middle of the second century B.C.E., a cogent case can be made that Jubilees was composed prior to Antiochus IV's persecution of Judaism.[238] Both the sectarian Torah and the Book of Jubilees seem to antedate, or at least were not affected by, the events that shook Judaea in the 160's B.C.E.

Is there, then, a work which seems to be posterior to the Qumranic Torah, Daniel, and Jubilees, but evidently antedates the known writings at Qumran? I believe such a composition is the so-called War Between the Children of Light and the Children of Darkness, in short the War Rule.[239] Its nineteen columns depict the forty-year war between the camp of light, i.e., Israel led by the angels Michael, Gabriel, Sariel, and Raphael, and the camp of darkness, i.e., the Kittim and other pagan nations who were joined by some renegades of Judah and Benjamin and led by the rebellious angels, such as Mastema. The entire camp of Israel will make war with the Kittim for six years, but only sections of the camp will fight during the twenty-nine years of battle with Israel's other enemies. No war shall take place in the five sabbatical years, which are periods of respite. In one respect the War Rule diverges from the sectarian Torah and the Book of Jubilees. In spite of the occasional use of Ezekiel's vision of the future sanctuary, the Qumranic Torah, as was pointed out above, reflects an independent attitude toward the non-Torah books of the Hebrew Scriptures.[240] It depicts a temple that is minimally, if at all, related to the historical accounts of the Solomonic sanctuary in 1 Kings and 2 Chronicles. In the extant fragments of sixty-six columns there is not a single line that can be said to have been taken from a book other than the Torah, a work which the scroll constantly reproduces.[241] The Book of Jubilees, likewise, seems to be minimally dependent on scriptural books other than the Pentateuch. The Jubilean chronology of the world ends with the Israelites crossing the Jordan. The War Rule, on the other hand, which sets out to describe the forty years of the encampment as a prelude to the resettlement in the eternal city, constantly paraphrases lines from Isaiah, Psalms, and other biblical books. It is difficult, however, to assess the significance of the War Rule's use of scriptural books, whether it forms a part of the trend in the pesherite writings which recognizes the authoritativeness of the *Tanak* as a whole, or whether its author broke new ground in the schismatic movement.

There exists overwhelming evidence for the War Rule's indebtedness to the sectarian Torah. In his commentary, Yigael Yadin has discussed many passages common to these two works, a list which could be extended. A few examples will suffice: the משנה (vicar) of the chief priest;[242] the decimal organization of the camp or temple into units of thousands, hundreds, fifties, and tens;[243] mention of the sons of Levi;[244] the use of the word נצחו as a verb for victory,[245] which finds its closest parallel in 1QM 4:13; and leaders are permitted to be up to the age of sixty.[246] 1QM 1:9, "unto all appointed times of [eternity] for peace and blessing, glory and joy,"[247] as well as 17:7–8, shows a remarkable similarity to 11Q Torah 29:9–10 and to other leading phrases which were mentioned in Chapter 1 of this work as indicative of the purpose of the scroll.[248] It is implausible to argue that the author of the scroll utilized the War Rule in these and other instances. Many phrases are common to both writings: "blue and purple,"[249] "in the gates of the holy,"[250] and the list of sacrifices.[251] These are sui generis to the scroll, necessitating the postulate of the dependence of the War Rule on the Qumranic Torah.

The structure of the War Rule, as well, indicates the author's indebtedness to the sectarian Torah. In the historical books of Scripture and even in the Pentateuch, Manasseh and Ephraim replace Joseph in tribal listings. The Qumranic Torah, however, as well as the War Rule, ignores this, listing Joseph as one of the twelve tribes. The War Rule makes this point by the repetition of כתולדותם (according to their birth), indicating that Joseph was included in the roster.[252] In the scroll, Joseph is included with the other sons of Jacob in the order of the sacrifices[253] and in the names of the gates of the middle court.[254] This is in contrast to Num. 1:32–35 where, in the account of the census of the wilderness, he is listed merely as the father of the tribes of Ephraim and Manasseh.

The rules of purity and the prohibition of defilement, much emphasized in the Qumranic Torah, are reiterated in the War Rule. Women and children are barred from the war camp,[255] just as they are not permitted into the middle and inner courts of the temple.[256] In the same way that the blind man is not permitted to go out to battle,[257] he is also not permitted to enter even the outer court of the temple.[258] As noted by Yadin, these blemishes, all of which were probably included in the sectarian Torah, apply only to the priests in the biblical tradition.[259] Furthermore, the War Rule says that any man "who is not pure with regard to his sexual organs on the day of battle shall not join them in battle."[260] Similarly, the Qumranic Torah does not permit him to enter even the city of the temple until he has been cleansed from that impurity.[261] In this last comparison, it is worth noting that both works base their prohibition on the presence of the holy: "holy angels" in the War Rule, and the place "that I shall cause My name to dwell in it" in the Qumranic Torah. According to 11Q Torah, ritual uncleanness is strictly guarded against in the army of the king.[262]

It is remarkable that the War Rule insists on the punctilious observance of the sacrificial rites even in the midst of the battle. Even more significant is the sacrificial system presented here, which corresponds to that of the sectarian Torah: the chief priest and his vicar;[263] the gates of the temple;[264] and the sacrifices "for the festivals, for their new moons, for the sabbaths and for all the days of the year."[265] The order designated for the drinking of the new wine in 11Q Torah 21:4–7 appears to agree with the hierarchy of service in 1QM 1:17–2:3. Since these elements appear extrinsic to the book's main theme, their inclusion in a war book can only be accounted for by the influence of the Qumranic Torah.

The royal charter in 11Q Torah 56–60, which prescribes a council of thirty-six members, shows a remarkable similarity to the structure of service in the War Rule:

1QM 1:17–2:2	*11Q Torah 57:11–15*
heads of the tribes	twelve princes of the people
twelve chiefs of the priests	twelve priests
twelve levites	twelve levites

In the War Rule the king is not necessarily of Davidic lineage. The sectarian Torah also warns the king of the extinction of his posterity.[266] There are some differences, however. In the scroll, the high priest is called the כוהן גדול (high priest), while in the War Rule his epithet is כוהן ראש (chief priest). An explanation of this distinction may be that the high priest was not supposed to leave the temple, so another term had to be given to the ecclesiastical general to permit this figure to lead a holy war.

The theme of the forty years in the War Rule appears in itself to be a complement to 11Q Torah. The latter describes the sanctuary of the future when the sacred city and the precinct of the temple will forever resemble the position of the tribes at Sinai.[267] There is nothing in the work that describes any of the events which would precede the establishment of such a permanent Sinai. The author of the War Rule apparently made it his task to fill the record, extending what 11Q Torah 3:3 says, "[rest from all] your enemies round [about]." What will be the fate of these enemies and how long will the war last? From this perspective, the War Rule represents a large-scale embellishment of the Qumranic Torah.[268]

The War Rule is clearly dependent upon the book of Daniel. Words or phrases common to both of them include the following: עמוקות (deep things);[269] צבא מאורות (hosts of the luminaries) and צבא השמים (hosts of the heavens) or כוכבים (stars);[270] ברוך אל ישראל השומר חסד לבריתו (blessed be the God of Israel who preserveth mercy for His covenant)[271] and האל . . . שמר הברית והחסד לאהביו (God . . . who preserveth the covenant and mercy with those who love Him);[272] [בי]נה משכילי בי[נה] (those enlightened with underst[anding])[273] and להשכילך בינה (to enlighten you with understanding);[274] קץ מלחמה (epochs of war).[275] The angel Gabriel is found in the Hebrew Scriptures only in Dan. 8:16 and 9:21, and Michael is recorded in Dan. 10:21. The War Rule includes them with the four angels in 9:15–16. Furthermore, God sends help through Michael both to Daniel and to the children of light.[276] The rest of Daniel 10 contains an account of Michael's relating to Daniel what is to happen in the end of days. Such a role is ascribed to the same angel in 1QM 17:6–9. Finally, the emphasis on the sanctified people of the covenant finds expression in both writings: in the War Rule—עם קדושי ברית (sanctified people of the covenant)[277] and עם קדושים (sanctified people);[278] in Daniel—עם קדושים (sanctified people)[279] and ברית קדש (sanctified covenant).[280]

The posteriority of the War Rule to Jubilees need not be questioned. The author goes out of his way to list twenty-six *mišmarot* who serviced the sanctuary,[281] not twenty-four as in 1 Chronicles.[282] He also includes fifty-two fathers of the congregation.[283] Both of these numbers correspond to the solar calendar advocated in Jubilees 6 and neither is found in the Qumranic Torah, nor even in the astronomical Enoch, which does deal with the calendar, though it does not consist of a strictly solar mode of reckoning.[284] The author of Jubilees and, apparently, the author of the War Rule may be said to have advocated this radical departure from the traditional division of measuring time. Yadin has shown many parallels between Jubilees and the War Rule,[285] of which some can be traced to the Qumranic Torah, but others can only be accounted for if the author of the War Rule was dependent on Jubilees. The division into four groups of three tribes each, also found in Numbers 2 and the sectarian Torah, is a major feature of the military organization in 1QM 3:13. This arrangement is similar to the pattern used by the sons of Jacob as they go to battle against their enemies in the account found in Jub. 38:5–8. Jub. 1:29 describes the future when "all the luminaries [shall] be renewed for healing and for peace and for blessing for all the elect of Israel, and that thus it may be from that day and unto all the days of the earth." In a remarkably similar vein, 1QM 1:8–9 says, "At the appointed time of God, His lofty majesty shall shine unto all appointed times of [eternity] for peace and blessing, glory and joy, and long life for all the Sons of Light." Just as Jub. 50:4 speaks of "yet forty years to come," so the outline of the War Scroll is based on a forty-year time period.[286] The progression of this war is interrupted every seven years by a sabbatical year, a stipulation which is outlined in Jub. 50:1–4. Much more evidence could be cited to show the numerous ways in which the author of the War Scroll reveals his knowledge of Jubilees.

The nature of the dualism presented in this stylized description of the impending conflict likewise demonstrates the War Rule's posteriority to the Book of Jubilees. The biblical tradition is replete with antithetical passages,

beginning with Genesis and Deuteronomy and continuing through the
prophecies of Isaiah and the Psalms, where light is contrasted with darkness,
life with death, and Israel with the pagans. What may be called dualism,
however, first appears in the biblical tradition only in the Book of Daniel. But
even Daniel is not truly dualistic, for it manages to retain a concreteness referring to the rise and fall of empires, as well as to those who acted righteously
and wickedly in the face of persecution. The War Rule does have a fully developed concept of dualism.[287] By contrast, the Qumranic Torah and the Book
of Jubilees,[288] like the traditional Pentateuch, lack a developed dualism.
Hitherto, the contrast between light and darkness reflected only an aspect of
Judaism. In the War Rule this contrast becomes the focal point. Although
there is some question as to whether Daniel is dualistic, there is no doubt as to
the War Rule.

The dualistic epithets in the War Rule belong to a different category than
those in Daniel and other biblical writings. Not only are there angels such as
Michael, Gabriel, and Raphael, but there is also a host of angels of destruction giving power to the forces of evil. During the war, the armies of Israel and
the armies of the Kittim will each be successful three times. This portrayal of a
dualistic balance is summarized in the phrase, "the children of light and the
children of darkness," which forms the title of the book. In prior literature we
find something like this only with Jannes and his brother, who balance the
scales against Moses and Aaron.[289]

The legacy of the sectarian Torah is quite evident in the subsequent literature. The forty years of Israel's wandering in the wilderness, which become in
the War Rule the period of struggle against the forces of darkness, are used in
the communitarian literature to explain the period of the sect's persecution.
The principle that the chronology of the past foreshadows the future is thus
taken for granted in the War Rule. The epithets "children of light" and "children of darkness" multiply into the "ways of light" and "ways of darkness,"
"spirits of light" and "spirits of darkness," and so forth. What requires
emphasis is that the composition of the War Rule antedates the writing of the
bulk of Qumranic literature. The various elements of this literature, whether
the peshers, the Community Rule, the Damascus Document, or other numerous fragments, have one thing in common; they portray a community apart
from the rest of Israel. Its adherents identify themselves either as *Yaḥad* or
"Zadokites" or "people of the covenant," all sectarian terms. None of these
terms are to be found in the excessively wordy War Rule. Significantly, the
term *Yaḥad* does appear in the War Rule seven times, although always adver-
bial in meaning, and in no way presuming the existence of a commune by
such a designation. A telling example of this is in 1QM 13:11–12: "All the
spirits of his lot, the angels of destruction, walk in the boundaries of darkness,
and unto it shall be their desire all together (*yaḥad*)." Unless it is suggested that

there existed a parallel commune comprising the powers of darkness, for which there is absolutely no indication, the use of *Yaḥad* with regard to the evil angels lends telling proof that the War Rule's author was not aware of any community with such an appellation. The community in the War Rule is the encampment consisting of twelve tribes with their standards and priestly divisions, not the "true" Israel, which designates a sectarian group within that society. What marks the War Rule in distinction to the Qumranic Torah and Jubilees is the introduction of categorical dualism.

The Literature of the Commune (Yaḥad)

Josephus reports that the Essenes were prolific writers.[290] Whether or not one identifies the Qumranites with the sect mentioned in Josephus, they do seem to have had a compulsion to record everything on parchment or papyrus. Aside from reproducing biblical and Enochite texts, which were not necessarily sectarian, the Qumranites created the following genres which were intended for internal use:

a. peshers-biblical commentaries, so-called on account of the characteristic opening of their exegesis with the term *pišro* (its interpretation is)—some peshers fuse a number of biblical verses under a single theme, others present a line-by-line exegesis of entire biblical books
b. legal lore—in addition to the rules of the sect, this also embraces paraphrases of biblical texts, calendars, and descriptions of the future Jerusalem and the sanctuary
c. liturgical pieces
d. histories of the group[291]

These genres are not always kept separate. Thus the Community Rule, which is mainly devoted to regulations for its members, concludes with a liturgical section. The Damascus Document is a miscellaneous collection which includes a historical account.

What permeates all this literature is the presumption that Israel is divided into two groups: the faithful, the "true Israel" who live in accordance with the laws of purity (*tohorah*), and those of Israel who "defile" the divine commandments. The question arises, How do these varied genres, in which sectarianism is a prominent feature, relate to the literary lineage whose sequence has been described above, in which the group still identifies itself as part of Israel? Can it be shown that the communal texts necessarily depend on works such as the Qumranic Torah, Daniel and the War Rule? It is beyond the scope of this study to analyze all the scraps of sectarian texts in the Qumran library, but let us see what answers emerge from a review of some of the major sectarian works:[292]

Community Rule
Hodayot (Thanksgivings)
Pesherite texts
Pesherite references to the Second Torah
The Copper Scroll and New Jerusalem

סרך היחד *(Community Rule)*

First published by Burrows, the Community Rule is the most partisan work
of the Qumran literature, defining the conditions and rules of membership in
the *Yahad,* the name given to the Commune.[293] One of the most radical
requirements for membership was the abandonment of private property;
everything belonged to the collective.[294] Scholars have assiduously endeavored
to define the organization and purpose of the Commune.[295] It is not my intention here to give a detailed explication of the Community Rule; nevertheless,
it will be necessary to touch on the nature of its composition in order to determine the aim and purpose of the sect.

Fortunately, the treatise's repetitiveness, which frequently goes beyond the
redundancies usually found in Qumranic writings, presents a clue as to its original composition. The work begins with an apparent title, "the Book of the
Community Rule,"[296] and goes on to define its ideological purpose before
proceeding to the ordinances. This formula, with some variation, appears
again in the following passages: "This is the rule for the men of the Commune";[297] "This is the rule for the public assembly";[298] "These are the ordinances by which they will judge them";[299] "These are the ordinances which
the men of perfect holiness will follow";[300] "These are the statutes for the
master to walk in";[301] "These are the rules of conduct for the master in those
times";[302] "And this is the rule for all the congrgation of Israel in the latter
days";[303] "This is the rule for all the hosts of the congregation, for every
native of Israel."[304] These introductory formulas usually contain the name
Yahad which, in addition to being the name of the Commune, underscores the
collective ownership of property and the group's public morality. It is only
after such a preliminary statement that the ordinances are spelled out. It
seems likely that the core of the treatise consists of a collection of minutes of
sessions of the מושב הרבים (the public assembly, literally "sitting of the
many").[305] Evidence for the argument that the treatise reproduces, in essence,
summaries of the Commune's sessions is threefold: (a) the preliminary formulas just mentioned, which in essence serve as the group's rallying cry, (b) the
ordinances in the various sections which have no apparent sequence (as one
would expect in real authorship) but which do manifest a variability that proceeds towards greater stringency, and (c) a statement in 9:10 which refers to
earlier sections as if they were minutes of former sessions. The common denominator of these summaries is the preliminary formulas whose apparent aim
was to remind the members of the community's ideology.

The basic question is, What was the goal of this *Yaḥad*? Scholars have identified it as the attempt to live a life of separation and purity, a foreshadowing of the monastic life.[306] But surely monasticism, or even purity and perfection, were not the goals of the sect. These served only as a means for something else. What was that? In other words, what inspired the members to give up their possessions and renounce their families and roots to join the Commune?

I believe the Qumranic Torah provides a clue for answering this and other questions. Significant aspects of the ceremonies prescribed in this treatise make sense if traced to 11Q Torah. The feasts of new bread (לחם) and wine (תירוש) could not be accounted for before its discovery.[307] 11Q Torah 18–25 now gives us seven columns devoted to the pentecostal seasons of new fruits to be celebrated "year by year,"[308] thus illuminating the background of the bread and wine ordinances in 1QS. There are, of course, basic differences which will be explained shortly. The insistence on the priestly perquisites, as well as the divisions among the priests, levites, and Israelites representing the *Yaḥad*'s leadership, are apparently modeled after a similar system in the sectarian Torah. The Community Rule restricts membership to those of the age of twenty and over, even prohibiting marriage before that age.[309] Though these requirements could be traced to the Pentateuch, their listing in this treatise can best be explained by the emphasis given to them in the scroll.[310] קודש הקודשים (the holy of holies), mentioned explicitly four times in 1QS,[311] and alluded to elsewhere, must refer to the altar, the sanctuary, the laver, and the storehouse—all the items included in this designation by 11Q Torah 35:8–9. There is also the emphasis on defilement. The importance of the themes of defilement and purity in the Qumranic Torah have already been discussed in Chapter 1. טומאה (defilement) is a matter of grave concern in the Community Rule as well. In addition to statements that the property of all those outside the covenant is defiled[312] and that defilement is part of the way of falsehood,[313] we also find that "Defiled is everyone who transgresses his word."[314] Similarly, "Defiled, defiled he shall be for as long as he scorns the ordinances of God."[315] Whereas in the biblical and rabbinic traditions defilement and impurity form two categories, only occasionally blurred, this distinction disappears almost completely in the Qumranic Torah; all come under the rubric of defilement. The Community Rule follows the sectarian Torah in placing sinfulness under impurity.

One of the terms which signifies participation in the very core of the sect seems to be טהרה (purity).[316] In the Pentateuch, purity forms a basic constituent of the camp of Israel. But it is only in the sectarian Torah that טהרה dominates all other ordinances.[317] Deut. 21:13 prescribes the conditions before an Israelite may cohabit with a captive woman. After reproducing this passage, 11Q Torah 63:14–15 adds: "She may not touch your טהרה for seven years." This word becomes almost synonymous with participation in the *Yaḥad*.

Many of the ordinances of the Commune can only be understood if they are presumed to have been modeled after the Qumranic Torah. In addition to the evidence cited above, this relationship is also apparent in the construction, "by thousands, hundreds, fifties, and tens," a prominent phrase in the Community Rule as well as 11Q Torah.[318] Thus in the Commune we find reflected an attempt to reproduce the camp at Sinai—via the sectarian Torah.

All this does not by itself show the Communty Rule's dependency on the sectarian Torah. Theoretically, one might argue that the Qumranic Torah reflects the religiosity and vocabulary of the Community Rule, but combined with the evidence cited above, in which it was shown that the Qumranic Torah knows nothing of the existence of a Commune, it is quite reasonable to presume that the features found in the sectarian Torah are duplicated in the Community Rule. Thus the indebtedness of the latter to the former need not be questioned.

The Community Rule's indebtedness to Jubilees is evident in chap. 10. As Dupont-Sommer has noted, this passage affirms the solar calendar of 364 days.[319] The use of תקופה here,[320] as well as in rabbinic literature,[321] refers to the vernal and autumnal equinoxes and the summer and winter solstices.[322] The mention of the sabbatical and jubilee years in 10:8 cannot but be a direct allusion to the Book of Jubilees.

As has been indicated, there are also differences between the prescriptions of the Qumranic Torah and the rules of the Commune. Whereas in the former there are three pentecostal seasons, the latter records only a single annual event.[323] The basic divergence between the two, however, appears to be in the sacrificial rites. Obviously the Commune had no altar for animal slaughtering, a basic requirement of the scroll.[324] At first sight, this would suggest a sharp distinction between the two works. Whereas 11Q Torah makes the sacrificial ritual the pivotal point of religious observance, the Community Rule does not prescribe the practice of sacrificial offerings. Many students of Qumran have therefore argued that the Commune rejected animal offerings and understood them metaphorically or spiritually. If their view is correct, this would indeed be a radical departure from the spirit that dominates the Qumranic Torah.

What initially appears as a divergence is in fact complementary. In at least eight instances, 1QS employs לכפר as atonement for sins in a form that is standard in the sectarian Torah, i.e., referring to sacrificial atonement. These passages cannot be explained away as merely metaphorical, although many scholars have done this. These references to atonement in 1QS are of two types: (a) ephemeral atonement while the Commune is still functioning prior to the eschaton[325] and (b) the ideal atonement after the erection of the sanctum sanctorum under the direction of the Aaronides.[326] Column 9 and, in a somewhat abbreviated form, col. 8 distinguish between these periods, referring to three epochs: (a) the period of the formation of the sect, (b) the time when the *Yaḥad* has been fully established, and (c) the end of days, when God will dwell in the sanctuary of the Commune. "When these things take place in Israel according to all these precepts, they shall establish the holy spirit of truth forever. They shall make atonement for the guilt of transgression and faithless sin, that being more acceptable for the sake of the land than the flesh of burnt offerings and the fat of sacrifice. The offering of lips for justice shall be as a pleasing righteousness and a perfect way, as a pleasing free-will offering."[327] In this section the opening phrase, בהיות אלה בישראל (When these things take place in Israel), indicates the beginning of the second epoch, i.e., after the *Yaḥad* has been established. Subsequently, בעת ההיאה (at that time) refers to the activity which will take place at the end of days. "*At that time,* the men of the Commune shall set apart a house of holiness for Aaron, to be together a holy of holies and a communal house for Israel, for those who walk in perfection. The sons of Aaron alone shall have authority in matters of justice and property."[328] Similarly in 1QS 8:4–10:

> In the inauguration of the epoch, when these things will be in Israel, the council of the Commune will be established in truth, an eternal planting, a house of holiness for Israel and an assembly of the holy of holies for Aaron, witnesses to truth for the sake of justice, the chosen who are acceptable to make atonement on behalf of the land . . . the dwelling of the holy of holies for Aaron with all knowledge for the covenant of justice, to present a pleasing odor and a perfect and true house in Israel that they may establish a covenant according to the statutes forever. They will be acceptable to make atonement for the land.

As in the previous passage, *ʿet* (time or epoch), which appears at the beginning of this selection, designates the future time, the age-to-come. Contrary to some scholars, these passages cannot but mean that the Community Rule prescribes the building of a sanctuary centered around sacrificial rites.[329] Before the discovery of 11Q Torah, the meaning of these passages was obscure, seeming on the one hand to disassociate the Commune from the current sanctuary, and on the other to make the Commune embrace a sacrificial system not dissimilar to the one then practiced in Jerusalem. Now with the Qumranic Torah before us, this apparent incoherency is cleared up. At the time of the composition of the Community Rule, the sect had no sanctuary, having spurned God's house in Jerusalem as idolatrous. But the Commune certainly looked forward to the building of a sanctuary like the one prescribed in 11Q Torah. The holy of holies found in 1QS 8:8 most certainly refers to 11Q Torah 35. In other words, whereas other Jews regarded Jerusalem's temple as the center of Judaism, the Qumran sect for all practical purposes did not have a current temple, but rather waited for an eschatological one.[330]

The numerous references to time here and elsewhere link the Community Rule to the books of Daniel and Jubilees. קץ, מועד, and אחרית הימים are basic to

Daniel's technical terminology, always referring to the eschaton, as they do in
1QS. Evidently, as understood in these passages, the temporal references in
Qumranic texts point to the eschatological sanctuary prescribed in 11Q
Torah. It may be presumed, therefore, that the main purpose of the *Yaḥad* was
to prepare the members of the Commune for God's eternal house.

Hodayot

Sukenik and others have published much of the Commune's liturgy.[331] Not
only does the rather lengthy scroll of 1QH contain columns of forty lines, but
numerous fragments of other texts of this type have been uncovered. In fact,
the last two columns of the Community Rule, as has been frequently noted,
belong to the genre of the sect's supplications.[332] Modeled after certain
Psalms, these prayers are those of an individual, never of a collective.[333] The
basic structure consists of lines using *ʾany* (I) and *ʾattah* (thou), contrasting the
weakness and insignificance of the petitioner with the infinite potency of the
Deity. Since the standard opening word of the extant prayers is almost invariably *ʾodeh* (I shall give thanks) and since neither the first-person plural nor the
plural imperative ever appears in the body of the petitions, it would seem the
Commune did not have sessions of public prayer.[334] If this is true, the reason
seems to be that neither the Mosaic Torah nor 11Q Torah ordained communal supplication. With the exception of the Psalms, personal petition seems
to characterize prayer in Scripture.

Despite the extreme individualism that permeates the liturgical pieces, their
sectarian nature never disappears for long. The petitioner does not tire of
expressing gratitude to God for making him part of the true Israel and for
divine protection from the enemies of the collective. This Qumranic dualism
finds expression throughout the scroll. A few examples follow: "I thank thee,
O Lord, for Thine eye watches over me. Thou hast delivered me from the zeal
of the interpreters of falsehood and from the congregation of the teachers of
emptiness";[335] "For Thou hast created the just and the wicked";[336] "Thou
hast closed up the mouth of the young lions whose teeth are like a sharp spear,
the venom of serpents . . . Thou, O God, hast protected me from the sons of
men and Thy Torah Thou hast hidden in me until the time when Thou
shouldst reveal Thy salvation to me."[337] The concluding clause refers to the
hidden law that will become operative in the eschaton, apparently an allusion
to the Qumranic Torah. The epithets concentrating on the contrasts between
light and darkness,[338] life and death,[339] the moist and the dry,[340] the good and
the evil,[341] the true and the false,[342] as well as the righteous and the wicked,[343]
often give these petitions a high pitch of religious fervor. The language seems
to rely on the imagery of the desert, whose horizon is undistubed by human
works and where the contrast between the potency of the heavens and the
frailty of the earth is so sharp. The *Hodayot* always thank God for making the

petitioner a member of the Commune; this leaves no doubt that these prayers were composed by the collective's members, not borrowed from outside the group. The ever-present communal dualism gives assurance that the composition of the *Hodayot* is contemporary with the recording of the Community Rule. The composition of the *Hodayot*, then, belongs to a later period than the Qumranic Torah, the Book of Jubilees, and the War Rule.

It has frequently been noted that the personage of the *Hodayot* seems to have been the Teacher of Righteousness who authored them.[344] As long as no date existed for the *Moreh Ṣedeq* and as long as it was presumed that he flourished at the time when the Commune (*Yaḥad*) was in full bloom, such conjectures were not out of line. According to the scheme followed in this book, however, in which we shall date the *Moreh Ṣedeq* a generation or two prior to the formation of the Commune, such speculation becomes untenable. Certainly the *Hodayot* do contain allusions to the then-existing Commune and its fully developed theology. These could not, therefore, in their present form have been penned by him at the time of the movement's birth.[345]

Pesherite Commentaries

The pesherite commentaries on Scripture relate to the Commune's house of study as the *Hodayot* do to its worship. Study and learning occupied a prominent role in the Commune; at least a third of each evening was devoted to such efforts.[346] Although the Commune's members recited their prayers individually, they studied collectively. The Teacher of Righteousness presided over a group of twelve instructors who taught the membership-at-large, which was seated by rank.[347] As the Community Rule records, the instructors, who were the superior officers of the Commune, were experts in the sect's lore. The main subject of study consisted of the Holy Writ or Torah as explicated by means of *peyruš* and *midraš*,[348] terms whose exact meaning at Qumran remains obscure, though both refer to the teachings of Scripture.[349] Scripture embraced the Torah, which sometimes is called *nigleh*,[350] the Prophets, and the *hagu*. That the Book of Jubilees was included in the sect's sacred writings is indicated in 1QS 10:3–8.

The surviving commentary on the first two chapters of Habakkuk and the numerous fragments which bear the name *pešer* present the modern reader with the material that was taught in the Commune's study sessions. Unlike some other terms, the exact connotations of *pešer* are clear. The term meant not only the explication of scriptural words or clauses, but an exegesis that would account for the present or future flow of events. In other words, the pesherite commentaries, in distinction to the *peyruš* or the midrash or the less formal "as written" (אשר כתוב or אשר אמר), were restricted to messianic exegesis.[351] There existed no clause in the entire prophecy of the obscure prophetic book of Habakkuk which did not, according to the Qumranic exegetes, refer to the present and future life of the movement. It goes without saying that the Commune's purpose was to prepare for the eschaton, and the understanding of the current events served as a prelude to the "end of days." There frequently exists a correlation between the contents of the scriptural line and its pesherite meaning. Thus when Habakkuk speaks of the righteous and the wicked he allegedly refers to the Teacher of Righteousness who is to be persecuted by the Wicked Priest.[352] Habakkuk's Chaldeans are said to refer to the contemporary Kittim.[353] Only exceptionally do passages occur where there is little connection between the scriptural clause and its pesher. Thus the pesherite writer finds in Habakkuk, without any basis, proof that the Teacher of Righteousness would be persecuted on the Day of Atonement.[354] As argued below, however, the Qumran commentary on Habakkuk is not typical of the pesherite texts since it probably antedates the existence of the Commune and seems to reflect the earlier days of the movement.[355] As such, it may be regarded as a prototype of the pesherite genre.

Scripture relates to pesher as does a dream to its interpretation. The resemblance between the two may be close, or the relationship may be merely suggestive. What is prerequisite, however, is that the interpreter be a man able to discern God's will. The reader will recognize a likeness between the pesherite genre and the resolution of dreams in Daniel. The relative dating of the pesherite genre may be viewed in two ways. On the one hand, it may be considered to be of post-Danielic origin in accordance with the following argument. Daniel 9 presents a lengthy account which may be taken as the origin of the Qumran commentary. The chapter begins with an account of Daniel's tribulation over Jeremiah's promise that Jerusalem would be humiliated for seventy years,[356] an allusion which the author perceived as referring, not to the reconstruction of the Temple, but to the "end of days." It was only after a period of trepidation in which the author could neither eat nor drink that Gabriel imparted to him the prophet's true meaning.[357] Here we find what appears to be a model of the pesherite commentary, which always finds that a scriptural passage embraces an eschatological nuance, regardless of its original intent. Thus not only the name *pešer* but also the form and nature of the genre may be Danielic.

On the other hand, it is conceivable that the pesherite literature originated before Daniel. The term *pešer* may be ascribed to the Aramaic form of Joseph's interpretation of Pharaoh's dream.[358] The author of Daniel may have been influenced by the writing of the pesherist on Habakkuk. Whether one regards the pesher texts as having originated before or after Daniel will then depend upon the date of Pesher Habakkuk. It is argued below in Chapter 5 that the commentary on Habakkuk found at Qumran predates the persecution of Judaism by Antiochus IV[359] and therefore precedes the final composition of the Book of Daniel. Students of Qumran have rightly pointed out that the pesherite commentator paid little attention to the wording of the biblical text, feeling free to interpret it as referring to present or future events, regardless of what was said in Scripture. This pesherite characteristic, however, as stated below, is absent in the Qumranic commentary on Habakkuk.[360] Here the text and commentary fuse to illustrate the disappointment that followed the failure of the Teacher of Righteousness to be crowned in Jerusalem. Presumably, therefore, the pesherite genre at its inception did pay close attention to the text being interpreted. It was only in a subsequent state that the commentary completely overshadowed the scriptural passage. Most of the pesherite fragments seem to be post-Danielic, forming an integral part of the communal teachings. Thus the Pesher on Nahum mentions Demetrius[361] and Antiochus[362] and attacks "those who seek smooth things, whose evil deeds shall be uncovered to all Israel at the end of time."[363] This certainly belongs to a time when the pesherite genre had been fully developed and was used as instruction in the sessions of the *Yahad*. It is here that pesher seems to fuse with related terms such as *midraš* and *peyruš*, all intended to serve as the sect's instructional material.

Pesherite References to the Second Torah

Some pesherite texts allude to 11Q Torah in a manner which clearly indicates that it was considered a primary text for communal teaching. It was argued above that the author of 11Q Torah put forth a claim that his work had been revealed by God to Moses on Mount Sinai as a second Torah, the first being the Pentateuch. It was also said that one of the main goals of the Book of Jubilees was to propagate the authoritativeness of the so-called Temple Scroll as the "last Law" in contrast to the "first Law," both together being the two heavenly tablets that God had revealed to Moses. There are four fragments that likewise mention the "second" or "last" Torah, whose referent seems to be 11Q Torah or a Torah like it.

a) 4Q 171, 4:7–9 (Pesher on Psalm 37):

7. צופה רשע לצדיק ומבקש [להמיתו יה]וה [לוא יעזבנו בידו ולוא י]רשיענו בהשפטו

8. פשרו על [הכו]הן הרשע אשר צ[ופ]ה הצד[יק ומבקש] להמיתו [. . .] והתורה

9. אשר שלח אליו

"(7) The wicked looks for the righteous one and seeks [to kill him. Yah]weh [will not desert him into his hand and will not co]ndemn him with his judgment." (8) Its interpretation concerns the wicked [pries]t who l[ook]s for the right[eous one and seeks] to kill him . . . and the Law (9) which he sent to him.[364]

The wicked wish to kill the righteous on account of the Torah God had sent through the righteous one. Then the passage goes on to refer to the eschaton, when the wicked will be destroyed.[365] In 2:2–3 of this same work, we read, "Its interpretation concerns all those who turn to the Torah, who will not turn away from evil." It is significant that this text regarding the Torah precedes a discussion of the destruction of the wicked at the end of the forty years prior to the end of days.[366] It is quite possible that "Torah" in line 2 is a reference to 11Q Torah. If so, the Qumranic Torah would also find mention in 2:14 and 22, where the observers of the Torah will be upheld by God.

b) 4Q 177, 1:12–16 (Catena):

12. ו[עתה הנה הכול כתוב בלוחות אשר . . . ל ויודיעהו את מספר . . . ת וינח[ל]
13. ל[ו] ולזרעו [עד] עולם ויקום משמה ללכת . . . מן אדם . . . תקעו שופר בגבעה השופר הואה ספר]
14. הו[אה ספר התורה שנית אשר . . . מאסו כ[ול א]נשי עצתו וידברו עליו סרה וישלח[ן]
15. או[תות (על?) גדולות על ה . . . ויעקוב עומד על הגתנות ושמח על רדת . . .
16. נבחרה אפת[. . .].ל אנשי עצתו המה החרב ואשר אמר]

"(12) Now, behold, everything is written on tablets which . . . and he taught him the number of . . . and caused to inher[it] . . . (13) to [him] and to his seed [for]ever. And he arose from there to go . . . from man . . . "Blow the horn in Gibeah"; "the horn" is the book of [. . . (14) i]t is the book of the Second Law which [. . . all the m]en of his council despised, but they spoke rebelliously against him and sent . . . (15) great [si]gns upon . . . and Jacob shall stand upon the winepresses and rejoice over the flowing down . . . (16) tested is . . . the men of his council, they are "the sword"; and it says . . . "[367]

The redemption described in these lines will happen in the latter days, as attested in lines 5 and 10–11. Then line 12 makes mention of the *luḥot* (tablets) upon which "everything is written." This reference appears in the context of the *seper hattorah šenyt* (book of the Second Law) in line 14,[368] mentioned frequently in Jubilees and probably alluding to Exod. 34:1, which mentions two stone tablets. As was noted above, Exod. 34:1 forms the cornerstone of chap. 1 of Jubilees and probably of cols. 1–2 of 11Q Torah as well.[369] The link between the second Torah and the Qumranic Torah has already been recognized by Yadin.[370] This association with Jubilees and the scroll finds confirmation with the mention of Jacob in line 15. As noted previously, the covenant of Jacob in 11Q Torah 29:10 is a central concept, and Jacob's dream becomes the occasion for the choice of Levi and the building of the future temple in Jubilees.[371] Although fragmentary, this passage does link the tablets, Jacob, and the Second Torah, thereby probably alluding to 11Q Torah.

c) 4QPBless 3–6:

3. עד בוא משיח הצדק צמח
4. דויד כי לו ולזרעו נתנה ברית מלכות עמו עד דורות עולם אשר
5. שמרה . . . התורה עם אנשי היחד כי
6. . . . . היא כנסת אנשי

(3) . . . until the Messiah of righteousness comes, a plant (4) of David; for to him and to his seed is given the covenant of the kingship of his people forever, (5) that he keeps it . . . the Law with the men of the Commune. For (6) . . . it is the assembly of the men of. . . .[372]

In an interpretation of Gen. 49:10, "Torah" also finds mention. 4QPBless establishes that the future Messiah will be of the branch of David. The partial nature of this reference does not permit a precise understanding of the relationship between "the Torah with the men of the Commune" and this future Messiah, even though שמרה (observing) appears to be a part of it.[373]

d) The final reference to "Torah" in these fragments appears in the material designated 4Q174 (Florilegium), I:1–13:[374]

1. [ולוא יוסי]ף בן עולה [לענות] ו כאשר בראישונה ולמן היום אשר

2. [צויתי שופטים] על עמי ישראל הואה הבית אשר . . . ל . . . באחרית הימים כאשר כתוב בספר

3. . . . מקדש אדוני כ]וננו ידיכה יהוה ימלוך עולם ועד הואה הבית אשר לוא יבוא שמה

4. [. . . עד] עולם ועמוני ומואבי וממזר ובן נכר וגר עד עולם כיא קדושי שם

5. יהיו [עד ל]עולם תמיד עליו יראה ולוא ישמוהו עוד זרים כאשר השמו בראישונה

6. את מקד[ש י]שראל בחטאתמה ויואמר לבנות לוא מקדש אדם להיות מקטירים בוא לוא

7. לפניו מעשי תודה ואשר אמר לדויד ו[הניחו]תי לכה מכול אויביכה. . . .

10. [וה]גיד לכה יהוה כיא בית יבנה לכה והקימותי את זרעכה אחריכה והכינותי את כסא ממלכתו

11. [לעו]לם אני אהיה לוא לאב והוא יהיה לי לבן. . . .

12. . . . [ב]אחרית הימים כאשר כתוב והקימותי את סוכת דויד הנופלת הואה סוכת

13. דויד הנופל[ת א]שר יעמד להושיע את ישראל

(1) And the son of wickedness [will not increase] his [affliction] as at the first, from the day that (2) [I set judges] over My people, Israel. It is the house which [he will build for them in] the last days, as it is written in the book, (3)[375] ["The sanctuary which] Thy hands have established, O Lord, Yahweh will rule forever and ever." It is the house into which never shall enter (4) [. . .] the Ammonite or the Moabite . . . for My holy ones (5) [will be there] forever. He will be seen upon it, and strangers shall not again lay it waste, as they formerly laid waste (6) the sanctua[ry of I]srael on account of their sin. And He said[376] they should build a sanctuary to Him that they could make sacrifices of deeds of thanks (7) before Him in it. As He said to David, "I will give you rest from all your enemies." . . . (10) "The Lord declares to you that He will build a house for you." "I will raise up your seed after you." "I will establish the throne of His kingdom (11) forever." "I will be his father and he will be my son." . . . (12) in the latter days as it is written "I will raise up the tent of David which is fallen. It is the fallen tent of (13) David which will arise to save Israel."

I would agree with David Flusser that the reference here is to the sanctuary of the future.[377] 11Q Torah 29:9–10, where it is stated that God Himself will build the sanctuary as promised, here finds expression in the pesherite citation from Exod. 15:17–18, where it is said that God Himself will build the temple wherein He shall dwell forever. One of the assurances given to David and quoted by the Qumran writer is that "I will be his father and he will be my son," an apparent reference to Solomon. It would appear that the author had 11Q Torah 59:13 in mind as he wrote, "I will be their God and they will be My people," the promise given to those who turn to the covenant. In other words, this so-called Florilegium gives the Mosaic archetype for 11Q Torah 29, combining it with the prophet's promise of the Davidic restoration. In fact, the expectation of building the house of God was the raison d'être of the Commune.

These four passages, drawn from the communal literature, apparently reiterate the views first stated in Jubilees 1 linking the eschatological sanctuary with the text of 11Q Torah. Although very fragmentary and replete with terms still not fully understood, these passages leave no doubt as to the paramount role of 11Q Torah among the members of the Commune. In fact, the expectation of building the house of God in accordance with 11Q Torah was the primary concern of the sect.

The Copper Scroll and New Jerusalem

1. The contents of two other puzzling texts likewise point to the pivotal role of the sectarian Torah in the development of the Qumranic writings. In a literature full of problems, the so-called Copper Scroll has been one of the most enigmatic finds.[378] Engraved in copper, its columns list the locations of fantastic amounts of gold and silver that are hidden in caves whose locations are revealed in the text:

> 1:1–4: "At Horebah, situated in the valley of Achor, under the steps which go to the east forty cubits: a chest of silver, whose total weight is seventy talents."[379]

The Copper Scroll raises two basic questions. First, are these lists on the whole or at least in part historical, or are they an imaginary composition? Regardless of the answer to this question, the second remains, How do the contents of the Copper Scroll relate to the life of the Commune and its literature? In Qumranic writings the gathering of *hon* (property or possessions) was regarded as a mortal sin.[380] The renunciation of the acquisition of goods was a prerequisite for admission into the collective. The pesherite commentators do not tire of denouncing the enemies of the *Yaḥad* for their indulgence in wealth, whether on account of the alleged despoiling of the Kittim or their collections from the poor. With the possible exception of the Book of Psalms, the communal writings present the most ancient idealization of poverty. All this appears to be in contrast to a text that, imaginary or real, goes on to itemize the locations of vast sums of treasures which seem to exceed the holdings of the ancient world.

The contents of the Qumranic Torah may perhaps provide a satisfactory resolution to the problem of the need for precious metals in Qumran. In its ordinances for the construction of God's house, 11Q Torah characteristically reiterates the requirement that virtually all of the surfaces of the temple's precinct be overlaid with "pure gold." A few examples will suffice: "gold and copper for all . . .";[381] "all its vessels will be made of pure gold";[382] "All this staircase is covered with gold";[383] "The ceiling is to be panelled with cedar covered with pure gold and its doors are covered with good gold."[384] "Pure" here points to the quality of the metal, an interpretation differing from that of Lehmann, who argues that it refers to defilement.[385] After all, ritual purity was not restricted to the precious metal. The members of the Commune no doubt contributed the half or entire shekel required in accordance with Exod. 30:13 and 11Q Torah 39:8-9. In joining the collective, a person not only renounced private possessions but donated whatever he had owned to the Commune. The money which the ordinary Jew would contribute for the upkeep of the temple provided another source of income for the Commune, since its members refrained from dispatching gifts to Jerusalem.[386] It is reasonable to postulate that the Commune did not utilize this income to raise the standard of living of its members, whose modest lifestyle required minimal expenditures. On the other hand, 1QS 9:6-7, as well as other texts, did obligate the members of the Commune to prepare themselves for the erection of the house of the Lord wherein He will dwell eternally, which, as prescribed in the sectarian Torah, would require enormous amounts of gold, not only for specifically prescribed ordinances, but also for the "blue and purple,"[387] the cedar wood, and the precious stones and marble. Was the Copper Scroll, whether actual or imaginary, a preparatory element in the fulfillment of the construction of the future sanctuary? If the answer is yes, the treasures listed in the Copper Scroll become less puzzling.

2. Caves 1, 2, 4, 5, and 11 of Qumran contained copies of an Aramaic work now called "The New Jerusalem," extensive fragments of which have been recovered.[388] Written in Aramaic, this text provided the measurements of the rebuilt Jerusalem, its walls, gates and towers: "base of the column . . . above the column";[389] "two columns";[390] "all . . . the wheel . . . for the wheel";[391] ". . . ten. The fourth row . . . walls of white stone . . . the others from the outside, twenty . . . to make expiation by it upon . . . and it is not withheld any more, every day . . . the court, and he caused me to see . . ."[392] Since this was written before 70 C.E., "New Jerusalem" must have been in contrast to the extant holy city which the author spurned, evidently regarding it as defiled. As

pointed out by Yadin, quite a number of measurements in accounts of the New Jerusalem correspond so closely to those listed in 11Q Torah that it is sometimes possible to interpolate some defective lines in either work from the dimensions provided in the fragments of the other.[393] In other words, since coincidence between the corresponding standards is to be excluded, an interdependence between the accounts of the future sanctuary in 11Q Torah and in the fragments of the New Jerusalem seems certain. Can it be that the author of the Qumran Torah borrowed from the measurements of the New Jerusalem? This question might be answered in the positive: "New Jerusalem" is a major apocalypse that probably antedates both Qumran and the sectarian Torah.[394] If so, this apocalypse served as a major source for the author of the Qumranic Torah. This seems quite unlikely.

Although it is conceivable that the author's main interest was the sanctuary, the extant fragments do not relate to it but to the holy city which housed the temple. The extant fragments present the eschatological Jerusalem that would contain the House of the Lord, presumably constructed along the lines prescribed in the sectarian Torah. Everything that is known from the ancient tradition maintains that Jerusalem's claim for sanctity was derived from its having the *sanctum sanctorum* in its midst, not vice versa. It is necessary to postulate that the author of the New Jerusalem modeled his Aramaic version of the holy city after the dimensions of the sanctuary in 11Q Torah, a work that provides minimal information concerning the city in which the eternal sanctuary will be located.[395] In fact, it does not even mention Jerusalem by name. "New Jerusalem" assures the reader that the future temple at the end of days will be located nowhere else except in the chosen city and that the dimensions of both will correspond to a similar architectural design. The fact that the temple in the sectarian Torah was prescribed by God to Moses served as an inspiration to the author of the New Jerusalem.

In sum, our study argues that sectarian works from the Book of Jubilees and the War Rule down to Qumranic writings such as the Community Rule and the pesherite commentaries show an unmistakable development from 11Q Torah. The sectarian Torah was apparently known to the author of Jubilees as the "last tablet" and to the pesherite writers as the "Second Torah," in contrast to the "first tablet" which referred to the Pentateuch. In other words, for the author of Jubilees, 11Q Torah was not a mere conflation or précis of the Mosaic Torah, as maintained by Yadin, but a divine work equal, if not superior, to the authority of the Five Books of Moses. Many passages in Jubilees, including its introductory chapter, become more intelligible if read as propagating the authoritativeness of 11Q Torah. On the other hand, aside from clear dependence on Scripture, the author of the so-called Temple Scroll used what may be labeled as the Enochite astronomical texts, whose beginnings seem to antedate the composition of the Book of Genesis. The War Rule recognized the authoritativeness of the sectarian Torah and Jubilees, but was written prior to the time when clear identification of a group which assumed several appellations, but was chiefly known as the *Yaḥad* (Commune), is discernible. The chart appended here presents the relative chronology of these writings in a tabular form.

A principle dogma in the minds of the founders of the Commune was that both the Solomonic sanctuary and its post-exilic successor lacked the appropriate sanctity which God had reserved for the eternal structure, thus branding these temples as defiled. The authority for this doctrine, it has become clear, rested on 11Q Torah. From the Book of Jubilees came the revolutionary idea that the lunisolar calendar be suspended, to be replaced by a reckoning independent of the moon's visibility, i.e., a pure solar calendar. Aspects of dualism have always been a part of the Jewish tradition, but its absolute form in the imagery of light and darkness appeared first in the War Rule. In the communal literature, this dualism, which referred to the children of light as Israel and the children of darkness as the pagans, was transferred to the true Israel and the defiled (שחת) Israel. Thus the eschaton would bring the destruction not only of paganism but also of the wicked of Israel. In its literature, the Commune utilized the pesherite form to insist that the eschaton, as had been foretold, was not only inevitable but would come about out of the persecution experienced recently under Antiochus IV. Members of the Commune, as well as the Teacher of Righteousness, or the *maśkyl,* by mastering the proper meaning of the Holy Writ, could unravel the mysteries of the end of days. The pesherite commentaries attempted to account for the events of the current scene in the light of the impending eschaton. But the ultimate raison d'être of the Commune was to prepare for the day designated since creation (called *qeṣ* or *moʿed*) when God would come down, as He had at Sinai, and dwell in their midst forever.

The emphasis on the wine and oil in Jubilees,[396] the Community Rule,[397] and the *Hodayot* provides additional evidence that the sectaries at Qumran regarded this scroll as the Torah. That Qumranic liturgy considered this scroll to be the Torah is confirmed by its mention of the series of festivals which are described only in the sectarian Torah: "plenty of *dagan* (new grain), *tyroś* (new wine), and *yiṣhar* (new oil)."[398] The role of new wine in the Community Rule, where it is equal to the first bread (*leḥem*), which finds no support in the canonical Pentateuch, does find its authority in the sectarian Torah. The final lines of 11Q Torah, forbidding the marriage of a niece and branding it an abomination, are the subject of exegesis in CD 4:19–5:11.[399] A discussion of this passage and other examples of the substantial use of the sectarian Torah can be found in the succeeding chapters. We shall see that it is not only that the author of 11Q Torah presented it as a work revealed at Sinai, but that the Qumran writers accepted it as authoritative and cited it as such in polemical discussions.

The Temple Scroll: Anterior and Posterior Writings

Anterior:

    Enochite Literature:

        Astronomical Enoch (in Aramaic)   Persian period?

        Enoch 72–82 (preserved in Ethiopic)

        Genesis Apocryphon (in Aramaic)

Qumranic Torah

Posterior:

        Solar Calendar (known only from Jub. 6:21 ff.)

        The Book of Jubilees (composed in Hebrew but preserved in Ethiopic)

        Book of War Rule (known only from 1QM)

    Communal Literature

        Community Rule

        Hodayot (Thanksgivings)

        Pesher commentaries

    Works whose relationship to the Communal writings is unknown:

        Copper Scroll

        New Jerusalem

Chapter 3

Who Is Zadok? 11Q Torah and the Teacher of Righteousness

The name Zadok looms large in Qumranic writings:

1. The Copper Scroll describes the burial place of a certain Zadok where the sect's treasures were allegedly concealed.
2. CD 5:4 says that a scroll of the Torah was hidden in a sealed ark until the rise of Zadok.
3. The *sons* of Zadok are prominent in the Qumranic writings. Kuhn's concordance lists twelve occurrences of this title in sectarian literature. It sometimes appears to signify a privileged group within the sect, but at other times it is synonymous with the Commune.
4. A number of passages contrast the reign of *Malky-ṣedeq* with that of *Malky-rešaᶜ*.
5. The *Moreh Ṣedeq* (Teacher of Righteousness), whose paramount role is described at great length in the Commune's literature, seems to be a paranomasia on the name Zadok.

It is curious that in spite of the prolific Qumranic scholarship, the issue of the identity of Zadok has been treated only casually, without any presentation of the massive evidence available. Solomon Schechter did entitle the treatise which he had discovered in the Cairo Genizah the "Zadokite Fragments," thus making this name fundamental to the sect,[1] but the problem of identifying Zadok, whose name becomes virtually synonymous with the sect itself, has been neglected. It is this issue which constitutes the subject of this chapter. We have here assembled various hints from the Qumran library as to the possibility of identifying this enigmatic figure. Chapter 4 will do the same for rabbinic, Karaite, and Greek writings.

The Copper Scroll

As noted earlier, the Copper Scroll is one of the most baffling texts of the Qumran library.[2] A central question involves whether it ought to be classified as a sectarian document, as Dupont-Sommer and others propose,[3] or whether it belongs to some other group, possibly recording the burial of the treasures of the temple.[4] References to the "Reservoir ('Canal')[5] of Solomon" may suggest a fictive construction of the fabulous treasure associated with the son of

David. Vermes argues against the latter thesis,[6] which has been advanced most vigorously by Milik.[7] Among the many treasures engraved in this document for perpetuity is the description of the tomb of Zadok, recorded in 11:2–7:[8]

בתכן אצלם
מתחת פנת האסטאן הדרומית
בקבר צדוק תחת עמוד האכסדרן
כלי דמע סוח דמע סנה ותכן אצלם
בהבסה אש הסלע הצופא מערב
נגד גנת צדוק תחת המסמא ה
גדולא שבשילוחו חרם

> Nearby, below the southern corner of the portico, at the tomb of Zadok, under the pillar of the vestibule: a vase of fir balsam, (a vase of) senna perfume. And nearby, in a garden (situated) on top of the rock, facing west towards the courtyard (of the tomb) of Zadok, under the large flat stone found in the water channel: anathema.

The absence of any further identification of Zadok suggests that both of the geographical indices of this burial place were presumed to be known to the searchers for the treasure. The absence of the customary gentilic gives the impression that Zadok was regarded as one of the most important personalities of the group. This view is strengthened by the allusion to a sepulcher which seems almost royal. "The southern stoa" indicates that the sepulcher perhaps had other stoas. There is also the mention of the exedra and the "garden" or "orchard" of Zadok. Significantly, the list of treasures of the Copper Scroll identifies only one other grave wherein the sect's wealth was reputedly hidden: "the burial place of the sons of העבט הירחי."[9] As pointed out by Milik, neither the name nor the gentilic of this family is known. The burial place refers, however, to a family sepulcher. Only Zadok has a grave designed for himself. Even with the allusions to Solomon mentioned above, the question still remains why only Zadok, not even Solomon himself, is said to have been memorialized with exedras and stoas. Although the matter is far from certain, the most cogent argument is that the unique monument described in 3Q 15, 11:2–7 records a fictive memorial to the founder of Qumran. Not only would the father of the sect have an exquisite sepulcher, but it would be located in proximity to Mount Zion, where the fabulous treasures were allegedly concealed. In brief, although the uncertainties surrounding the comprehension of the Copper Scroll are sufficiently serious as to preclude citing this text as support for our identification of Zadok, the evidence for Zadok as the founder of the sect in other texts which are discussed below does lend validity to the hypothesis that the Copper Scroll was engraved by a sectarian craftsman.

The Damascus Document

The key to the identity of Zadok is found in the Damascus Document. Since it is an important reservoir of information for the history of Qumran, it will be necessary to present first the methodology adopted to wrest this history from its source. Scholars have long recognized the significance of the treatise since, even in summary accounts and brief reconstructions of the history of the sect, they devote considerable space to its contents.[10] In spite of the considerable attention it has received, its basic structure and the date of composition of the extraordinary story it relates have remained to a large extent hidden.

The Zadokite Fragments or, as now used, the Damascus Document, are apparently not a single composition. The legal lore on pages 15–16 and 9–14, together with some of the Qumran fragments found by Milik and Baillet, originally comprised another work and was apparently not connected with pages 1–8.[11] Page 20 in Rabin's edition, which is identical to pages 19–20 in Zeitlin's photographic reproduction, belongs neither to pages 1–8 nor to the legal material of 15–16 and 9–14. It may have come from a third source. Fortunately, as attested by Milik, pages 1–8 have proven to be relatively well-preserved in Mss. A and B of Schechter's Genizah documents. The Genizah document, then, consists of three compositions:

I   Pages 1–8, which will be discussed more fully in the following section.
II Pages 15–16 and 9–14, comprising legal material and belonging to the same literary genre as the Community Rule and the *Hodayot*.
III Page 20, which will require further investigation to determine whether it is part of II or of still another treatise, as seems more likely.

At least forty years separate page 20 from pages 1–8. The following analysis will show it to be a literary unit independent of I.

Most scholars now postulate that page 20, a continuation of Genizah Ms. B, forms part of the original treatise. This opinion readily concedes that the legal texts form part of another treatise which was originally longer, as the fragments published by Baillet and Milik now attest. Page 20, however, which begins with the *moreh hayyaḥyd* (unique teacher or teacher of the Commune) and ends with a reminder of the foundation of the sect, *beryt ri'šonym* (covenant of the founders), according to the putative view, formed an integral part of the treatise.[12]

An analysis of the technical vocabulary, content, and spirit of page 20 does not bear out the validity of this view.[13] In fact, the new section begins at 19:34, where material not present in Ms. A at the end of page 8 is found. A line-by-line commentary will demonstrate a lack of correspondence between page 20 and pages 1–8 of this work, thus casting suspicion on their being part of the same treatise. For the sake of clarity, we differentiate here between what had formed part of the treatise composed during the lifetime of the *Moreh Ṣedeq* as attested on page 8 of Ms. A up to 19:34a and the supplement added following his death (19:34b ff.):

The original text in
Ms. A—to the end of page 8

The original text in
Ms. B.—to 19:34a

Supplement only in Ms. B—19:34b–20:34

20:1 —"from the day of the gathering in of the Teacher of the Commune."

20:13—"from the day of the gathering in of the Teacher of the Commune."

20:1. מורה היחיד (Teacher of the Commune). Any reference to the *Yaḥad* is not to be found in CD 1–8.[14] It appears here in 20:14 and 20:32 as well.

עמוד משיח (establishment of an anointed). The establishment of both the Teacher of Righteousness and the preacher of lies is described in part I with the word עמוד. This word also is used to designate Zadok in 5:5.

המשפט (the ordinance). This term refers not to the Torah but to the laws of the Commune. While the few references on pages 1–8 play only a minor role in that description of the development of the sect, the use of this word is frequent and central in the Community Rule.[15]

20:2. עדה (congregation). This word appears five times in CD 1–8. Whether the term is used in a positive or negative sense, it invariably refers to all of Israel.[16] Here it clearly refers to the sectarians, who have chosen to follow the perfect path. This term is frequently used in the Messianic Rule as the name of the sect and the term also appears in the Community Rule, in the *Hodayot,* and in various pesherim for the same purpose. It is employed as a name for the sect in CD 9–14 as well.

אנשי תמים הקדש (men of perfect holiness). In addition to two other places in this column, this formula appears only in 1QS 8:20.

20:3. בהופע מעשיו ישלח מעדה (when his deeds become apparent, he shall be expelled from the congregation). Expulsion from the group is never mentioned in part I. This phrase could only refer to the Commune, to which there is no allusion in pages 1–8 but which forms the core of the Community Rule and related texts.

20:4. גורלו (his lot). A common word in many other Qumran documents, it is not included in section I.[17] Alluding to the Commune, it is prominent in the Community Rule.

יוכיחוהו (they shall reprove him). This term's use in part I is confined to one biblical quotation,[18] while its use here as well as in other communitarian literature is substantive.

20:6. מדרש התורה (searching the law). This is also found in 1QS 8:15. The Community Rule uses *midraš* in other places as well. It is generally used to signify instruction in the communal way of life.

20:7. בהון (concerning possessions). While here this word refers to the control of wealth in the Commune, as it does in the Community Rule, the reference to *hon* in CD 4:17, though obscure, apparently concerns tithes and temple tax and possibly exploitation of the poor.[19]

20:8. אררוהו (they have cursed him). Absent in part I, this word is common in the Community Rule.

20:8–9. בראשונים ובאחרונים (the former and the latter). This phrase acquires a meaning different from its use in part I, and from its use in Jubilees.[20] The meaning here is similar to that in the Community Rule, where the two terms signify different stages of the new covenant.[21]

20:9–10. בשרירות לבם (in the stubbornness of their heart). It is members of the sect who walk "in the stubbornness of their heart," i.e., are backsliders, rather than Israel in former times.[22]

20:12. אמנה (covenant). The "compact" appears elswhere in the work only at CD 13:16. The term was adopted from Neh. 10:1.

אשר קימו בארץ דמשק (which they established in the land of Damascus). There are references to the exile in Damascus in CD 1–8; however, there the term is used differently. Whereas in 1–8 the exile is a contemporary event, here it is historical, referring to a time prior to the foundation of the Commune, whose existence is presumed in this column.

והוא ברית חדשה (it is the new covenant). In context, the phrase here refers to a past event, whereas in CD 1–8 the discussion concerns the actual making of the covenant.

20:13. משפחותיהם (their families). The word "families" is used in describing the faithful in the War Rule and the Messianic Rule[23] but not in CD 1–8, where they seem to be without families due to the exile.

20:13–14. ומיום האסף מורה היחיד (and from the day when the Teacher of the Commune was gathered in). This is the second reference to the death of the Teacher of Righteousness (or Teacher of the Commune), this event having first found mention in CD 19:35–20:1. The niphal perfect tense makes this a clear reference to a past occurrence. Since it follows immediately after the mention of the covenant of Damascus as a previous event in the history of the sect, this can be accepted as additional evidence that the migration to Damascus took place in the past.

יחיד is a reference to יחד which, as already pointed out, is not found in CD 1–8.

20:15. שנים ארבעים (forty years). A period of forty years is not mentioned in section I. This must be added to the 390 plus 20 years of CD 1:1–12; however, it need not follow in a consecutive manner.[24]

20:22. בית פלג (house of division).[25] This phrase is a reference to the division which had taken place in the past, when the exiles went to Damascus. These lines paraphrase what occurred at that time.

20:22, בית פלג—20:25, הקדש (the holy). These lines refer to the three stages of the formation of the sect: the abandonment of Jerusalem, where the group first originated, through their exile in Damascus, to the formation of the council of the holy, a synonym for *Yaḥad*.[26]

20:23. בקץ מעל ישראל (in the epoch when Israel sinned). The author here had in mind the period of 390 years mentioned in CD 1:5–6.[27]

20:24–25. בעצת הקדש (in the council of the holy). The council is a dominant feature of the Community Rule. It finds mention in CD 5:17, however, only as part of a quotation from Deut. 32:28. On page 20, it has the same communitarian use as it does in its frequent manifestations in the Community Rule.[28]

20:27–28. וכל מחזיקים במשפטים האלה לצאת ולבוא על פי התורה (and all who hold fast to these statutes, going out and coming in in accordance with the Law). "To go out and come in" in accordance with the rules of the Commune is also ordained in 1QS 10:13.

20:28–29. כי אנו רשענו גם אנחנו גם אבותינו בלכתנו קרי בחקי הברית (For we acted wickedly, both we and our fathers by going against the ordinances of the covenant). As in 1QS 1:24–26, sin and unfaithfulness to the covenant are adopted as explanations for the continuing bad fortune of the sect. This statement attempts to account for the failure of the eschaton to arrive at the end of twenty years.[29]

20:29–30. צדק ואמת משפטיך בנו (just and true are your judgments upon us). This phraseology appears frequently in the Community Rule.[30] The similarity of the previous line to 1QS 1:24–26 has been noted. Both texts follow the discussion of unfaithfulness with the phrase quoted here.[31]

20:31. והתיסרו במשפטים הראשונים אשר נשפטו בם אנשי היחיד (They were instructed in the former statutes by which the men of the Commune were judged). This statement refers to earlier rules of the sect, rather than to the patriarchs of Israel, as it does in part I.[32]

Several lines in this column indicate that its author considered the exile to Damascus to be a past event. The leaving of the house of Peleg, when the sect established the new covenant referred to in CD 6:5 and 6:19, is part of its former history. This section also speaks twice of the death of the *Moreh Ṣedeq*.[33] Furthermore, there is an allusion in line 23 to CD 1:3–6, i.e., to the opening discussion where the "epoch" of Israel's "transgression" is considered to be 390 years. Thus the vocabulary, which does in part resemble CD 1–8, reflects an indebtedness to that earlier composition. Aside from this fact, the terminology as well as the specific reference to the expulsion of recalcitrant members, makes this page part of the genre which falls under the communal rules. The liturgical references also show some relationship to the *Hodayot*. All in all, page 20 attempts to explain why the prediction in CD 1–8 had not been fulfilled, ascribing it to the lack of faithfulness to the covenant. This section, therefore, may be considered either a peroration to the legal material which preceded it in cols. 15–16 and 9–14—thus part of the Damascus Document, Ms. A—or as a portion of a treatise, otherwise lost, which had become attached to this work because of its mention of Damascus in the archetype of Ms. B. The Damascus Document referred to in the following discussion is restricted to cols. 1–8, which presumably represent the oldest element of what is now combined under the title "Damascus Document."

The Structure and Date of the Damascus Document

It is not the intention of this study to enter into literary analysis, but it is precisely such an investigation which is necessary in order for the reader to appreciate the information that the Damascus Document seems to contain. Although Milik states that the treatise may have been lacking its original beginning, in its present form pages 1–8 form a single unit that seems to have been divided into two parts:

Part 1. Introduction
Part 2. The body of the treatise

This latter unit, in turn, consists of three sections:[34]

A. Reasons for abandoning the Jerusalem sanctuary (4:12–6:11)
    a. The new planting in Damascus (6:1–11)
B. The new covenant in the region of Damascus (6:1–7:9)
    a. Introduction to the new covenant (6:1–11)
C. The predictions of the prophets on the Damascus Covenant (7:9–8:21)

Introduction: 391–410 after the Exile   The author's introduction seems to have consisted of three similarly constructed forewords.

a. 1:1 begins with "And now hearken, all who know righteousness," and concludes with 2:1, "to make known to the latter generations that which he would do to the last generation, the congregation of the faithless."
b. 2:2, "And now hearken to me, all who have entered the covenant," to 2:13, "and in the listing of their names; and those whom He (God) hated—He caused to stray."
c. 2:14, "And now, children, hearken to me and I shall open your eyes," and concludes with 4:12, "The wall is built, the fence is removed."

Not only do the three prefatory sections have similar beginnings, but also their contents, form, and ideology contain a remarkable similarity and perhaps even synonymity. In spite of their similarity, however, each preface contains information not present in the other two sections. In other words, in spite of the apparent redundancies, each preface serves to interpret the others.[35] The following outline will demonstrate the inner relationship of these three prefaces. Significant phrases common to two or all three are italicized.

1:1–2:1	*2:2–2:13*	*2:14–4:12*
a. 1:1. *And now hearken,* all knowers of righteousness.	2:2. *And now hearken* to me, all comers into the covenant.	2:14. *And now* children, *hearken* to me,
b. 1:1–2. and *consider the deeds of God.*	2:2–3. and I *shall uncover your ears* concerning the ways of the wicked.	2:14–15. and I *shall uncover your eyes* to see and *consider the deeds of God.*
c. 1:2–3. For he hath a controversy with all flesh, and *He will execute judgment upon all His despisers.*	2:3–7. God loves discernment; wisdom and counsel He has set up before Him. Patience and much forgiveness are with Him toward those who turn from transgression, but *power, might, and great wrath with flames of fire by the hand of all angels of destruction toward those* who backslide from the way, and those *who abhor the precept,* so that there shall be no remnant or survivor among them.	2:15–16. to choose that in which He delights and *to despise that which He hates,* to walk perfectly in all His ways and not to follow after thoughts of the guilty inclination and the eyes of lust.
d.	2:7–8. For God did not choose them prior to the world, and *before they were established, He knew their deeds.*	2:17–3:1. When they *walked in the stubbornness of their hearts,* the watchers of heaven fell. By it they were caught, for *they did not keep the commandments of God.* Their sons were as tall as high cedars and their bodies were like mountains when they fell. All flesh that was on dry land perished, and as if they had not been because they did their own will and *did not keep the commandments of their Maker,* until His anger was kindled against them. Because of this, the sons of Noah and their families went astray, because of this they were cut off.

e. 1:3–4. For with their sins when they forsook Him *He hid his face from Israel,* and from His sanctuary, and *He gave them up to the sword.*
1:5–6. During *the epoch of wrath,* 390 years after giving them into the hands of Nebuchadnezzar, king of Babylon.
f. 1:4–5. When He *remembered the covenant* of the forefathers, He *caused a remnant* of Israel to remain and did not give them up to destruction.

2:8–9. He abhorred the generations *because of blood,* and *He hid his face from the land until they were consumed.*

2:11–12. In all of them, He raised up for Himself *men called by a name* to leave *a remnant* for the land and to fill the face of the earth with their seed.

3:4–12. The sons of Jacob went astray through them and *were punished for their error.* Their sons in Egypt walked in the stubbornness of their hearts, conspiring against the commandments of God and each man doing what was right in his own eyes. They *ate the blood* . . .

3:2–4. Abraham did not walk in it and he was reckoned a friend, through his keeping of the commandments of God and not following his own desire. He handed this down to Isaac and Jacob and they observed and were written down as *friends of God* and as *possessors of the covenant* forever.

3:12–16. But with them that held fast to the commandments of God, those who remained of them, God *established His covenant* with Israel forever in *revealing to them hidden things* in which all Israel had erred. His holy sabbaths and festivals in His honor . . .

g. 1:7–8. *He visited them;* and He *caused to spring* forth from Israel and Aaron a *blooming root* to possess His land and to grow fat on the goodness of His earth.
1:10–12. God considered their deeds, for with a whole heart they sought Him, and He *raised for them a Teacher of Righteousness* to guide them in His way *to make known* to the latter generations what he would do to the last generation, the congregation of the faithless.

2:12–13. *He made known to them* by means of *His anointed* His holy spirit and the seers of truth, and in the listing of His name (?) and their names,

3:18–4:12. God . . . built for them *a sure house* in Israel . . . *Those that hold fast* to it . . . The *sons of Zadok* are the *chosen of Israel,* called by a name, who rise up in the latter days . . . To do according to the statement of the Law, which was accepted by the forefathers . . . Like the covenant which God established with the forefathers to atone for their iniquities, thus God will make atonement on their behalf . . .

3:17–18. They *defiled themselves with the impiety of man* and with ways of uncleanness, and they said, "Because it belongs to us."

h. 1:8–9. They *considered their iniquity* and they *knew they were guilty men.* They were like the blind and those who grope their way, for twenty years.

1:13–21. They are *the turners
from the way,* this is the time
about which it is
written,*"like a backsliding
heifer* thus did Israel slide
back," when there arose a
scoffer who preached to
Israel from the waters of
falsehood . . .

The recognition that the three prefatory sections have equivalent elements is of paramount significance for the understanding not only of the introductory material but of the entire treatise, as well as the early history of the sect. Design and meaning fuse to illumine some basic sectarian concepts. An essential problem is the time implied in 1:11, "And he established for them a *Moreh Ṣedeq* (Teacher of Righteousness)." This epithet appears again as *yoreh ṣedeq* in CD 6:11 in the interpretation of the digger of the well, an exegesis of Num. 21:18, as well as in CD 20:11, where it refers to the forty years after his death. The chronological problem is particularly acute with regard to his role in 1:11, in the face of the preceding reckoning. Beginning with 1:5, the author dates the growth of the new planting at 390 years after the exile to Babylonia, following which there is a period of twenty years of groping in the darkness.[36] Thereupon the text continues, "And God considered their deeds, for with a whole heart they sought him; and he established for them a Teacher of Righteousness to guide them. . . ." The question arises whether the establishment of the Teacher of Righteousness is to be understood as a synonym for the Aaronide planting (1:7) which the author says will begin to flourish during the twenty years, i.e., from 390 to 410 after the era of the exile, or whether he will appear at the end of the 410 years after the exile. A scholarly consensus maintains the latter view, namely that the Teacher of Righteousness will function during a new epoch which will begin at the end of the twenty years. His period of activity will last for a generation, about forty years, which will be followed by the forty-year period after his death mentioned in CD 20:15; so that the eschaton will take place 490 years (390 + 20 + 40 + 40) after the exile.[37]

This view seems unacceptable. Note that CD 1:1–12 contains no allusions to one or two cycles of forty years and that this portion of the chronological sequence is adapted from page 20. As was shown above, the forty years is part of a treatise distinct from CD 1–8, which attempts to explain why salvation had not come at the end of twenty years. The rise of the Teacher of Righteousness necessarily antedates the forty years. The assertion that there is an additional interval of forty years between 1:11 and 20:15 rests on imagination. Bruce and others take it for granted that the chronology of the Damascus

Document is ultimately a borrowing from Daniel.[38] But as will be shown below, CD 1–8 does not seem to contain any borrowings from Daniel;[39] thus there is no reason to assume that the 490 years is taken from that source. Certainly the numbers 390 and 20 are not Danielic.[40]

According to the commonly held view, the twenty years is the period of groping in the dark prior to the coming of the *Moreh Ṣedeq,* but the question arises, Why does 1:11 fail to give the forty years thereafter? The author, who had such a specific chronology up to this point, neglects to assert a crucial date. This becomes particularly problematic in light of the third preface when it refers to הקץ השנים האלה (epoch of these years) in 4:9, למספר השנים האלה (number of these years) in 4:10–11, and ובכול השנים האלה (and during all these years) in 4:12, clauses which evidently refer to specifically defined times.[41] The author of this treatise seems to be precise in his chronology and nothing can be attributed to him which he fails to state. In the context of pages 1–8, the chronological indicators can only mean that the *Moreh Ṣedeq* will arise at the beginning of the twenty years, set in contrast to the 390 years which preceded them. It is during these twenty years that Israel will be groping in the darkness and will be like a rebellious cow. It is in these years that the *Moreh Ṣedeq* will preside over the exiles while the scoffing priest shall rule in Israel. There might be some doubt as to the epoch mentioned here in the first preface since it could be interpreted as referring to three epochs, but the two other prefaces, particularly preface three, which is lengthy and very explicit, contains only two reckonings. In light of this section, the first epoch is the end of the 390 years and the second is the end of the 20 years, which is described as follows: "And when the epoch is completed according to the number of these years, they shall not still be united with the house of Judah, but rather a man will stand upon his watchtower. 'The wall is built, the ordinance is extended.'"[42] Then the reign of the lying priest will end and the holy city will be entrusted into the hands of the Teacher of Righteousness.

The evidence that both the "blooming root" which "He caused to spring forth from Israel and from Aaron"[43] and the *Moreh Ṣedeq* which "He established for them"[44] refer to the same person necessitates the postulate that the planting and the Teacher of Righteousness are synonymous. According to this treatise, therefore, the appearance of the Teacher of Righteousness marks the beginning of the movement. Before the time of creation, the role of this planting had been determined.

The treatise emphasizes the place of the *Moreh Ṣedeq* by using a number of sobriquets to designate his paramount role:

2:12—anointed one, holy spirit, and seer of truth[45]
2:13—his name
3:19—sure house
6:4—staff

6:6—searcher of the Law and the staff
6:11—Teacher (*yoreh*) of Righteousness
7:18—star and searcher of the Law
7:19—scepter
7:20—prince of all the congregation, shepherd and friend
7:21—anointed one of Aaron and Israel.

If our interpretation is correct, these references reveal the significant role of the Teacher of Righteousness in the foundation of the sect. The threefold preface is used to emphasize the one who was to be regarded as the father of the movement. He is an Aaronide, the interpreter of the Law; he is the one whom prophets predicted of old; he is the *Moreh Ṣedeq,* the one who will lead the group. Another way of perceiving this figure is in contrast to the lying priest, described as "the scoffer who preaches to Israel from the waters of falsehood";[46] "Belial";[47] "fear and the pit and the snare";[48] and "Zaw, the preacher."[49] Unlike the subsequent literature, where there is a leadership group, here there is only one supreme figure, the Teacher of Righteousness who founded the sect from those who had left Jerusalem for Damascus in 390–410 of the era of the exile. The *Yaḥad* of page 20, mentioned frequently in some pesherite texts and the Community Rule, is still unknown to the author of this treatise.

The Body of the Treatise. Following the introductory material devoted essentially to the cosmic significance of the Teacher of Righteousness, the body of the treatise as is outlined above begins with line 4:12, which gives an account of why the *Moreh Ṣedeq* left the holy city for a profane land, Damascus. This explanation begins by citing Levi the son of Jacob, who interprets Isaiah's alliterative terms, פחד ופחת ופח (terror, the pit, and the snare), and ends with the prediction that the *yoreh ṣedeq* is the digger of the well foretold in Numbers. The citation of Levi has been taken to be a quotation now missing in the Testament of Levi, a part of the Testaments of the Twelve Patriarchs.[20] This conclusion seems unlikely, and the citation may be explained more satisfactorily by looking at the role of Levi in Jub. 30:15–16 and 21–22, where, upon his special consecration, the abomination of Israel and its unworthiness in the end of days is presaged.[51] In the Damascus Document, then, Levi the son of Jacob, serves as a commentator for Isa. 24:17. It seems fitting that this section concludes with the *yoreh ṣedeq,* who, as explained above, is a descendant of Levi arising at the end of the 390–410 years after the *Ḥurban.*[52]

Levi not only gives an interpretation, but he does so using the term *pišro.* Noting this usage, scholars have considered this document to belong to the pesherite genre, but this is not necessarily the case.[53] It is worth noting that although this treatise expounds on many biblical passages, this is the only occurrence of the term. The explanation seems to be that this use of *pešer* precedes what became in subsequent Qumran writing a mechanical term for textual hermeneutics. In the Damascus Document, *pešer* still retains the original meaning of the word, found in texts as early as Genesis or Daniel, where it provides the key to an enigma as to the meaning of a dream or a biblical text. This usage of the term is distinct from and may have inspired the subsequent use of *pešer* as a technical term for a line-by-line biblical commentary. *Pišro* here serves the same purpose as the introduction of Levi son of Jacob: to provide authoritativeness for the exegesis that follows. Both the attribution to Levi and *pišro* serve to stress that the three sins mentioned by Isaiah are of central importance for the treatise. In short, this section describes the raison d'être of the movement, distinguishing it from the rest of Israel led by Belial.

Section II contains the platform of the covenant with a codicil making it a temporary covenant which will not necessarily be valid after the sectaries leave Damascus and settle in camps.[54] It is this platform which is called the ברית חדשה (new covenant) made in the land of Damascus. After they return, this covenant is called the ברית (covenant) in the subsequent literature.[55] This is the covenant which will ultimately become a pivotal text of the Commune.

The last section of the body of this treatise itemizes a number of prophecies beginning again with Isaiah and also including Moses, Ezekiel, Amos, Zechariah, and Hosea.[56] Each of these prophets, the author argues, reveals a specific aspect of the group's humiliation, which was that they, God's righteous, were on defiled soil while the scoffing priest and preacher of lies ruled in the holy city. The original treatise had ended with a reference to the platform, which is found in the last lines of page 8 in Ms. A, "All the men that have entered into the new covenant in the land of Damascus." The peroration, beginning with 8:16, reiterates the essential elements of the treatise's introduction: the fulfillment of the promise for those who would repent. At this point both manuscripts inserted material from other sources, Ms. A using legal material included in CD 15–16 and 9–14,[57] Ms. B incorporating different materials which seem to belong to the genre of the *serek* literature, beginning at CD 19:34.[58] Subsequent events necessitated a revision of the expectation found in the original treatise of Damascus which had foreseen a speedy victory for the *Moreh Ṣedeq*. When these predictions did not come true, the treatise was revised, not by altering the original text, but by adding supplements, Ms. A attaching legal lore and Ms. B affixing subsequent history. Thus the entire Damascus Document contains three elements: pages 1–8, dating prior to 410 after the *Ḥurban*; pages 19–20, which were written some time after the death of the *Moreh Ṣedeq*; and the legal lore of pages 9–16, which comes from the time when the *Yaḥad* had been fully established. In any case, the revisions go back to Qumran and need not be attributed to medieval scribes. CD 1–8 describes the movement prior to the foundation of the Commune, of which there is no awareness in the text.

"Until the Rise of Zadok"

The name Zadok appears in the Qumranic writings, especially in the Damascus Document and in Pesher Habakkuk, in three forms: (1) simply as Zadok; (2) as the father or ancestor of the so-called *Beney Ṣadoq*; and (3) in paronomasia, such as *Moreh Ṣedeq* (Teacher of Righteousness) or *ʾanšey Ṣedeq* (righteous people). Aside from the attestation of Zadok's sepulcher in 11:2–7 of the Copper Scroll, which has been discussed above,[59] the name Zadok appears without any other identification only in 5:5 of the Damascus Document in the highly pregnant clause עד עמוד צדוק (until the rise of Zadok). The passage in which this clause appears has many complexities, but the most baffling problem is the identity of Zadok.

The discussion above has shown the wide range of epithets given to the *Moreh Ṣedeq* as well as his paramount role. Much of Qumran scholarship has been focused on the question of the identity of the Teacher of Righteousness. Can it be that the Zadok of CD 5:2–7 is identical to the figure whose quasi-royal sepulcher is alluded to in the Copper Scroll, and that both references are to none other than the *Moreh Ṣedeq?* The question must be asked once again: Who is the Zadok in the clause "until the rise of Zadok"? This clause forms part of an apology for David, who, according to our author, sinned by having more than one wife. David's straying, however, the author claims, was unwitting since the ספר תורה (the Scroll of the Law), which allegedly contained the prohibition against polygamy, remained concealed in a sealed ark "until the rise of Zadok." Schechter's interpretation of this clause, expressed some seven decades ago, has on the whole remained unchallenged: "It is to a Zadok to which the Sect ascribes the merit of having rediscovered the Law, in which act he is favourably contrasted with David, who was ignorant of it. . . . Who this Zadok was, of the many persons bearing this name in the Bible, it is impossible to say. At any rate, the impression is that he was a Biblical personage."[60] What has split the commentators is whether, as held by Dupont-Sommer and others, Zadok is to be identified with the chief priest in the days of David and Solomon, from whom Jerusalem's priesthood traced its lineage;[61] or whether, as argued by Ginzberg and others, the word בן (son of) had preceded the word Zadok, the reference then being to Hilkiah the grandson of Zadok, who found what modern commentators consider the Book of Deuteronomy hidden in the sanctuary.[62]

The identification of Zadok with either David's priest or with the grandfather of Hilkiah cannot stand close scrutiny.[63] The customary translations of the phrase עד עמוד צדוק into English, "until Zadok arose"; into French, "jusqu'a' l'avènement de Sadoq"; and into German, "bis zum Auftreten Zadoqs" fail to express the meaning of עמוד. The author of CD derived it from cognates in Num. 27:19 and 21, where the word והעמדת (cause to stand) refers to Joshua's accession to leadership upon the death of Moses. Dan. 11:4, וכעמדו תשבר מלכותו, must be rendered as "and upon his (i.e., the king's) assumption (of office) his kingdom shall be broken up."[64] In other words, the Hebrew usage requires a paraphrase which includes a precise time, namely, the very beginning of the subject's assumption of leadership, not the indefiniteness of time in the English "rise," which can extend to a relatively long period. This is precisely the connotation of the phrase as used in Ezra 2:63 and Neh. 7:65: ויאמר התרשתא להם אשר לא־יאכלו מקדש הקדשים עד עמד כהן לאורים ולתמים. "And the governor said to them that they were not to partake of the holy food until the establishment of a priest in charge of the Urim and Thummim." The context of this passage refers to priests whose pedigree was unblemished and whose status would be clarified by the oracular instruments of the Urim and Thummim. It is evident that the returning exiles felt deprived of this mode of divination which they expected to be reestablished with the advent of the priest, i.e., the divinely preordained priest. It is taken for granted that as soon as the Urim and Thummim would become available, the status of the blemished priest would be determined one way or another. The very beginning is also meant in Ezra and Nehemiah—as soon as the priest is established to consult the Urim and Thummim. In fact, the usages of עד עמוד in CD 5:5 cannot but compel its rendition as "until the time when Zadok will assume office," i.e., the beginning of his leadership. This cannot apply to Hilkiah, the chief priest, whose discovery of the lost sacred book occurred long after his accession to ecclesiastical office. The identification with Hilkiah is, of course, objectionable for other reasons as well. First, it requires an emendation of the text to בן צדוק (son of Zadok), a phrase which is then taken to refer to the priest's grandfather, who, except for a genealogical reference in 1 Chr. 5:38, is not recorded in Scripture. Why would one identify the known Hilkiah by his obscure grandfather? I also find it hard to believe that the ancients perceived 2 Kings 22 as a reference to the loss of the Mosaic book for a period extending from Joshua to King Josiah, as many modern scholars do;[65] rather, they must have had in mind the neglect of God's word during the sinful reign of Manasseh.[66] However long ago the loss had taken place, it seems inconceivable that in the view of the author of the Damascus Document, it extended back to the days of David, who was regarded as a righteous king.

The putative consensus that CD 5:5 refers to Zadok, the chief priest under David and Solomon, is equally unacceptable.[67] This would mean that Zadok discovered the lost book of the Law. As shown in the examination of עד עמוד צדוק, this would further suggest that he had found the sealed book at the time of his assumption of the ecclesiastical office, i.e., at the same time that David became king.[68] If this were the case, the hidden book ought to have been known to David as well. Why then did this king not refrain from practicing polygamy? It will not do to interpret *ʿamod* as the time that Zadok's co-priest was eliminated with Solomon's accession to the throne and Zadok was put in the place of Abiathar,[69] for then the question with regard to David's polygamy can still be applied to Solomon, whose harem was certainly no less modest than his father's.

There is an even more powerful reason why this clause could not allude to any biblical figure. As in Daniel 11:4 and Ezra 2:63, the clause עד עמד in the Damascus Document refers not to Israel's past but to the אחרית הימים (end of days) when the messianic era will have begun: "the Sons of Zadok are the elect of Israel, 'the men called by name,' who shall arise in the end of days";[70] "and without which they shall not grasp (instruction) until there shall arise he who teaches righteousness in the end of days";[71] "the Scepter is the prince of all the congregation, and when he arises he shall strike violently all sons of Seth."[72] The use of this phrase to designate a future, and possibly messianic, time can be found already in Ezra 2:63: "They were not to partake of the holy food until the establishment of a priest in charge of the Urim and Thummim." Similarly this was most likely the original phrase in 1 Mac. 4:46: "and stored the stones in a fitting place on the temple hill, until a prophet should arise who could be consulted about them" (NEB). Thus Zadok's assumption of office in CD 5:5 could only refer to a person who had lived at the time of the sect's foundation or who would live in the eschatological epoch. But since the author of the Damascus Document claims intimate knowledge of the sealed Torah, the possibility that this Zadok will function in the future is excluded. Thus in the usage of this author, עד עמד צדוק could only refer to Zadok's assumption of office within the period of the existence of the sect, or very near it.[73]

This view may seem to require further substantiation. Can it not be that in this instance the author of the Damascus Document departed from custom, referring here indeed to a biblical figure— or at least to a figure of the remote past? A glance at the indices of time in the treatise up to this point necessitates the assumption that the temporal reference in 5:5 is to the beginning of the eschaton, which occurred when the sect was formed. Addressing the men of righteousness, 1:4–9 sets the time when God planted a new seed: the beginning of the "end of days," 390 years following the era of the exile to be followed by a period of twenty years of groping in the dark.[74] In other words, the truly sincere repentance took place in year 390 after the exile, and the new planting began to flourish in 391–410. The author then identifies the new planting with the coming of the *Moreh Ṣedeq*,[75] who, the text goes on to say, will for two decades (391–410) contend with the scoffer and his adherents.[76] Lest the reader fail to grasp the significance of a new era which had begun in year 391 after the exile, the author reviews the chronology twice more, first beginning at 2:1 and then with 2:14.[77] Apparently using the Book of Jubilees as his source, the writer in CD 2:2-14 claims that God had set the new era, i.e., the establishment of the Teacher of Righteousness, as part of the world's order even prior to its creation.[78] Translated into plain language, the author says that even before time was created, God had listed the names of both the Teacher of Righteousness and the scoffing priest.[79]

In spite of having stated his chronological framework twice, first in 1:1-2:1 and then in 2:2-13, the author of the treatise was not convinced that he had made his main point quite explicit. He restated his historical review for the third time, adding more details,[80] beginning once again with the introductory word, ועתה (and now). As he did in the first two sections, so in the third section he likewise divides the history of the world into two epochs— prior to and after the establishment of the covenant with the new planting, i.e., in year 391 after the exile. As CD 2:14-3:12 narrates the first epoch, i.e., from creation until the beginning of the eschaton, the covenant was observed only by certain notable individuals such as Noah, Abraham, Isaac and Jacob. However, the descendants of these and other patriarchs violated it, especially the prohibition of eating blood.[81] Noteworthy here is the author's universality, making hardly any distinction between the Noachite and the Israelite. Certain elect individuals in both groups observed the covenant, but the masses did not. Hence the Israelite progeny was destroyed. Beginning with 3:12, the author starts to relate the story of the Teacher of Righteousness and his followers. In a simplified form, CD 3:12-4:12 relates that in year 391, in accordance with the covenant of the patriarchs, God will establish a new house: a new leader, to whom the hidden precepts of the observance of the Sabbath and the seasons, which Israel has failed to follow, will be revealed. On the other hand, there will be those who will despise this new house and his Torah, i.e., the hidden precepts which he will reveal.

The key to understanding the framework of the treatise (and of Qumran literature as a whole) is its use of the proof-text from Ezek. 44:15: "'And the priests and the levites and the sons of Zadok who kept charge of My sanctuary, when the sons of Israel strayed from Me, shall bring to Me fat and blood.' The priests are the repenters of Israel, who left the land of Judah, and those who joined with them. The sons of Zadok are the chosen of Israel, called by the name, who will arise in the latter days."[82] Beginning with Schechter, scholars have failed to grasp the meaning of this exegesis.[83] As universally perceived, in these lines the treatise claims that the new sectaries are to be identified with the "sons of Zadok," who, in the words of the prophet, have the right to serve at God's altar. Thus the sectaries presume to appropriate an appellation that goes back to David and Solomon. For example, Cothenet states that "with the introduction of 'and' between 'priests,' 'Levites' and 'sons of Zadok,' our author transposes onto the text the situation of his own time when a distinction was made between the Zadok lineage (from which the high priests were appointed), the other priestly families, and finally the levites."[84] Thus the author of the Damascus Document associates himself with Ezekiel 43–44, as well as with Ben Sira 51:12 (Hebrew), which likewise assigns a special role to the sons of Zadok in the temple priesthood. In this argument, "Sons of Zadok" here refers to descendants of Zadok, the high priest who officiated during the erection of the Solomonic temple. This understanding, however, seems to diverge from, and perhaps contradict, the thesis outlined above. In a perceptive essay, J. Liver has shown that the view which understands בני צדוק (Sons of Zadok) in the Qumran literature as a claim for ancient ecclesiastical lineage is erroneous.[85] The author of the Damascus Document appears to claim that Israel, especially its priesthood, has been guilty of all kinds of abominations. How then do the Sons of Zadok, the Aaronide aristocracy condemned throughout the treatise, serve as a model for God's chosen planting? To be sure, the writer concedes that certain individuals, such as Noah and the patriarchs, were among the few righteous who had kept the covenant against the eating of blood. But it seems quite unlikely that the author of the Damascus Document would have included the Zadokite line of priests among those uniquely called קריאי השם (God's chosen). After all, they are part of the defiled priesthood against whom this diatribe is directed and who are held responsible for Israel's sinfulness. Moreover, a careful reading of 4:2–12, in which the author makes a strenuous effort to complete a complicated hermeneutical task, reveals an attempt to relate the Sons of Zadok in Ezekiel to the new house, not vice versa, i.e., the sectaries to the prophet's בני צדוק.[86] In other words, what the pesher tells us is the converse of the putative understanding: do not associate Ezekiel's "Sons of Zadok" with their namesake in the days of David and Solomon, but with the "true" Zadok and his sons to whom God has revealed the secrets of His Torah and whose name is explicitly stated פרוש שמו שמותיהם. The hermeneutics of this passage resembles that of the Gospels, in which Isaiah's prophecy concerning the virgin birth of Emmanual is identified not with the birth of Hezekiah, who is really irrelevant, but with Mary and Jesus.[87] The Qumran commentator claims that the monopoly given to Zadok and his sons to serve in the sanctuary was not really given to the priests who had served David and Solomon in what was in fact a "bloody sanctuary," but to Zadok and his sons of the future, in the year 391 after the exile. When Ezekiel says בני צדוק, according to this pesher, he means the Teacher of Righteousness, named Zadok, and his sons.

What may seem only implicit in 4:1–9 becomes explicit in 4:12b and 5:4. After interpreting Ezekiel's statement concerning the sons of Zadok as applicable to the sectaries, the author foresees the end of time which will mark the actual messianic epoch.[88] In 4:12b, however, the treatise reverts to the epoch of 391–410: "and during these years Belial will still reign in Israel." Proof for this statement is found in Isa. 24:17, "Fear, pit, and a snare are upon you, inhabitant of the land." From this verse the three sins that will afflict the people who would resist the *Moreh Ṣedeq* and his followers are interpreted as fornication, wealth, and defilement of the sanctuary.[89] Attempting to document the charge of fornication against the sectaries, the author of the Damascus Document cites the practice of bigamy "they take two wives while they are alive."[90] Lines 4:21–5:2 present three arguments for the case that Scripture in fact prohibits the marriage of a second wife while the first is alive: (a) God created only pairs, not threes or more; (b) they entered into the ark in twos; and (c) concerning the king it is said, "he shall not have many wives."[91] The author, however, seems to be aware that unlike the first two proofs, which seem obvious, the third requires elaboration. The source of its weakness is that it is possible to retort that Deut. 17:17 does not in fact prohibit bigamy but only an excessive number of wives, and fearful lest the opponents of the sect will cite the case of David, who did have many wives, CD 5:2–4 responds, "David had not read in the sealed Book of the Law which was located in an ark, for it (i.e., an ark) had not been opened in Israel since the day of the death of Eleazar, Joshua, and the elders; for they (Israel) worshipped the Ashtarot."

It is lines 4–5 that have baffled the commentators: ויטמון נגלה עד עמוד צדוק. It is necessary to deal with the phrase ויטמון נגלה, which seems to be gibberish. The first word may be rendered as an active, "and he hid," or as a passive, "and it was hidden." But if the former reading is adopted, who is the subject? Who had hidden the Book of the Torah? The answer seems to be Eleazar the priest, apparently with the assistance of Joshua and the elders. Referrring to Judg. 2:10, the author charges that the Torah, which contained the prohibition against polygamy, was stored in a sealed ark and was not available to David for perusal, for had he known about such a prohibition, he would not knowingly have violated it. Scholars have proposed two solutions to the problematic word *nigleh* or *niglah*. One solution proposes to insert the negative ולוא (and not) between the words ויטמון and נגלה, reading ולוא נגלה (and it was not revealed) "until the appointment of Zadok."[92] Other scholars dispense with the emendation by making the word נגלה a technical term, a synonym for Torah.[93] According to this interpretation, the phrase ויטמון נגלה may be rendered as "and he (Eleazar) hid the *nigleh,*" or if passive, "the *nigleh* (i.e., the Torah) was hidden." Whether one inserts a negative into this phrase or attempts to understand it without an emendation has little effect upon the next phrase, עד עמוד צדוק, which may be rendered as "until the assumption of office by Zadok." This clause alleges that from the time of Eleazar's priesthood until Zadok's assumption of office, the *Seper Torah,* which contains the prohibition against bigamy, had been concealed in the ark.

The central question is, Who is this Zadok? The seal of the ark was broken, according to the putative exegesis, by Zadok; some claim that this happened after the death of David, while others maintain that the author had in mind the grandson of a certain Zadok, Hilkiah, who was high priest during the reign of Josiah and found the Book of the Law of the Lord in the temple in 622 B.C.E.[94]

Such an exegesis of this crucial passage is entirely unacceptable, for as has been shown above, neither the patronymic of the *Beney Ṣadoq* nor the personage in whose days the Book of the Law was found refers to either of the proposed biblical figures. But if not to the biblical Zadok, to whom do they refer? Can it be that the figure called Zadok does not indicate any of the biblical personages with such a name but rather points to a contemporary, or near-contemporary, of the author of the Damascus Document?[95] I shall argue that the answer is positive. "Until the assumption of office by Zadok" means that Zadok had discovered the Book of the Law which had allegedly been sealed in the ark ever since the days of Joshua. Furthermore, it is this Zadok who was both the founder of the sect and the *Moreh Ṣedeq* mentioned in the Damascus Document and Pesher Habakkuk.[96] It is this Zadok to whom the various epithets, such as lawgiver, staff, sure house, and searcher of the law, are applied.[97] These and similar epithets were not intended as mere idle verbiage, but were phrases of reverence for the founder of the sect. It was this Zadok who announced that the end of days had come at this time, i.e., in 390 of the era of the *Ḥurban*. If this interpretation is correct, every word in the Damascus Document has a pointed meaning, referring either to the *Moreh Ṣedeq* sent by God or to his opponent, the scoffing priest of Jerusalem who represents the reign of Belial. CD 5:5 contains a startling piece of information: it identifies the extraordinary figure who launched a movement known to us from the library of Qumran. According to the Damascus Document, it is this Zadok to whom the *Beney Ṣadoq* of Ezek. 44:15 point. The text also points to a temporal fact of paramount significance: the assumption of office by Zadok marks the beginning of the new cosmic era ordained at creation.

When did this era begin? Scholars seem to have understood the twenty-year period, which is described as a time in which the members of the sect "were like the blind and like them that grope their way,"[98] as merely parenthetical. Furthermore, they assume that the treatise's new epoch refers to a period of forty years following the 410 years. But as is shown above, the epoch depicted in this treatise is that of the period of twenty years. From the days of Eleazar's death until Zadok's assumption of the office of Teacher of Righteousness marks the time, according to the author, of Israel's worship of idolatry. With Zadok's unsealing of the ark in which the Torah had been hidden, a new era commences, of which 4:12–13 states: "and during these years Belial will be sent to Israel." In other words, both the Teacher of Righteousness named Zadok and the unnamed Belial, i.e., the scoffing priest, began their reigns at about the same time: in year 391 after the *Ḥurban,* according to CD 1:5–6. Put in another way, our hypothesis postulates that the "new planting"[99] begins twenty years of struggle between the *Moreh Ṣedeq* (Teacher of Righteousness) and איש הלצון (the scoffer).

The figure of Zadok in CD 5:5 is of maximal significance for the origin of the Qumranic sect. We have already discussed the five lines inscribed into the Copper Scroll which allude to the sepulcher of an otherwise unidentified Zadok.[100] Unfortunately, the enigmatic nature of the reference in that work hampers our comprehension. What gives this description of the splendor of Zadok's grave some credibility is the identification of Zadok with both the Teacher of Righteousness, the founder of the sect and with the person who had unsealed the Book of the Law placed by Eleazar and Joshua in an ark.

Israel's Three Sins and the Qumranic Torah

If our hypothesis is valid, the author of the Damascus Document claims that the prohibition of polygamy was not explicitly known from the time of Joshua until Zadok, the Teacher of Righteousness, discovered it in the concealed Scroll of the Law; the explicit ban on polygamy was not contained in the canonical Law but was in the concealed Torah. That is to say, up to the time of Joshua there existed another Torah aside from the Pentateuch. What was this other Torah? There could be no answer to this puzzle before Yadin's publication of 11Q Torah. With this work before us, the question now is whether the "sealed Scroll of the Law" in CD 5:5 is the Qumranic Torah or whether a still unknown book was meant.[101] Assuming that the sectarian Torah is intended, the question arises whether Zadok is to be regarded merely as its finder, or as its author as well.

An examination of CD 4:12–8:21 may help to resolve this problem. In this section the author charges the opponents of the sect with three violations, an accusation repeated three times. Aside from historical digressions, these charges form the core of the treatise. As was indicated above, these three sins are: (1) fornication; (2) acquisitiveness; and (3) defilement of the temple. The author stresses the seriousness of the charges by introducing them with a pesher of Isa. 24:17: "Fear, the pit, and the snare are upon you, inhabitant of the land"; and by attributing this exegesis to none other than Levi son of Jacob. But he does not do so before having already given an exegesis of Ezek. 44:15: that the "sons of Zadok" in the prophetic text presage the new house, evidently Zadok and his progeny, which will appear in year 391 after the exile.[102] It seems apparent that in the author's mind there was a close link between the prophecies of the two seers. Just as Ezek. 44:15, according to the commentator, foretold the coming of Zadok, so Isa. 24:17 predicted the threefold sins stressed in the Zadokite text. Commetators on the Damascus Document have never dealt with the question of why the author specifies these

sins and not others.[103] But the postulate assumed in this study does offer a
rationale for the listing of these three sins: that they are conceptually, as well
as in their particularity, derived from 11Q Torah. This connection becomes
clear in the following presentation, which links the accusations in the Damascus Document with their apparent references in 11Q Torah:

---

1. Whoredom

Damascus Document

1. 4:20–21 (see also 7:1–2 and
8:5). הם ניתפשים בשתים בזנות לקחת
שתי נשים בחייהם. "They are caught in
two manners of whoredom: by
marrying two women in their lifetime."

2. 5:7–8. ולוקחים איש את בת אחיהו
ואת בת אחותו. "(one of their transgressions is that) a man marries the
daughter of his brother or the
daughter of his sister."

3. 7:1 (see also 8:6). ולא ימעל איש
בשאר בשרו. "A man shall not profane the kin of his flesh."

Qumranic Torah

56:18. ולוא ירבה לו נשים. "He shall
not multiply wives for himself."

57:17–18. ולוא יקח עליה אשה אחרת כי
היאה לבדה תהיה עמו כול ימי חייה. "He
shall not acquire another wife in
addition to her, for she alone shall
be with him all the days of her life."

66:15–17. לוא יקח איש את בת אחיהו
או בת אחותו כי תועבה היא. "A man shall
not marry the daughter of his
brother or the daughter of his sister
for it is an abomination.

66:11–14. לא יקח איש את אשת אביהו
ולוא יגלה כנף אביה לא יקח איש את אשת
אחיהו ולוא יגלה כנף אחיהו בן אביה או בן
אמו כי נדה היא לוא יקח איש את אחותו בת
אביהו או בת אמו תועבה היא. "A man
shall not marry the wife of his
father, he shall not uncover the skirt
of his father. A man shall not marry
the wife of his brother, he shall not
uncover the skirt of his brother, the
son of his father or the son of his
mother, for it is an impurity. A man
shall not marry his sister, the
daughter of his father or the
daughter of his mother, it is an
abomination."

2. Acquisitiveness (*hon*)

1. 6:15–17.   ולהנזר מהון הרשעה הטמא
בנדר ובחרם ובהון המקדש ולגזול את עניי עמו
להיות אלמ[נו]ת שללם ואת יתומים ירצחו.
"To separate themselves from evil possessions which are defiled in the vow, the dedication, and the wealth of the temple; to not rob from the poor of his people, make the widow their prey or murder the orphan."

6:21.   ולהחזיק ביד עני ואביון וגר.   "to strengthen the hand of the poor, the needy, and the stranger."

57:20–21.   ולוא יקח שוחד להטות משפט
צדק ולוא יחמוד שדה וכרם וכל הון ובית וכול
חמוד בישראל וגזל ...   "He shall not take a bribe to pervert righteous judgment, he shall not covet a field or vineyard, or any property or house. Any coveting in Israel, or robbery ..." (Note that the last word of the column is גזל [robbery]. See also the discussions of the vow: 53:9–54:7; and of the ban: 55:6–11; 60:5; 62:13–15. See as well 43:2–17 on the second tithe.)

3. Defiling the Sanctuary

1. 5:6–7.   וגם מטמאים הם את המקדש
אשר אין הם מבדיל כתורה.   "Also they profane the sanctuary by not distinguishing according to the Torah."

16:10–12.   [בשר הפר] ואת עורו עם
פרשו ישרופו מחוץ ל[עיר המקדש] במקום
[מובדל לחטאות שמה ישר[ופו אותו.]   "[The flesh of the ox] and its skin with its dung they shall burn with wood outside the [city of the temple.] In a place separated for the sin offerings, there they shall bu[rn it.]"

35:10–14.   ועשיתה מקום למערב ההיכל
סביב פרור עמדים עומדים לחטאת ולאשם
מובדלים זה מזה לחטאת הכוהנים ולשעירים
ולחטאות העם ולאשמותמה ולוא יהיו
מערבים כולו אלה באלה כי מובדלים יהיו
מקומותמה זה מזה למען לוא ישוגו הכוהנים
בכול חטאת העם. ...   "Thou shalt make a place to the west of the sanctuary around the *parwar,* standing columns for the sin offering and the guilt offering. Separated from one another shall be (the place for) the sin-offering of the priests and (the place for) the goats and sin-offerings of the people and for their guilt-offerings. These shall not mingle with one another; their

places shall be separated in order that the priests shall not err with any sin-offering of the people. . . ."

46:16–18. ‏ועשיתה שלושה מקומות‎
‏למזרח העיר מובדלים זה מזה אשר יהיו באים‎
‏המצורעים והזבים והאנשים אשר יהיה להמה‎
‏מקרה‎ "Thou shalt make three places east of the city, separate from one another, where the lepers, those with a flow, and men who have had a (nocturnal) emission will go."

51:8–10. ‏ולוא ישקצו את נפשוותמה בכול‎
‏אשר הבדלתי להמה לטמאה והיו קדושים‎
"They shall not make themselves detestable with any of those things which I have separated from them as polluted; and they shall be holy."

2. 5:7. ‏ושוכבים עם הרואה את דם זובה‎.
(They defile the sanctuary when) "they lie with a woman who sees the blood of her flux."

46:16–18 (already quoted in previous listing).

48:14–17. ‏ובכול עיר ועיר תעשו מקומות‎
‏למנוגעים בצרעת ובנגע ובנתק אשר לוא‎
‏יבואו לעריכמה וטמאום וגם לזבים ולנשים‎
‏בהיותמה בנדת טמאתמה ובלדתמה אשר לוא‎
‏יטמאו בתוכם בנדת טמאתם‎. "In every city, ye shall make places for those stricken with leprosy, a wound, or a scab, so that they do not enter your cities and defile them, and also for those who have a flux and for women in their menstrual impurity or when they give birth, that they shall not be a (source of) defilement in their midst with their menstrual uncleanness."

3. 6:17 (see also 5:7 and 7:3). ‏ולהבדיל בין הטמא לטהור‎. "To distinguish between the clean and the unclean."

45:4. ‏יצא הרישון מימ[י]ן ולוא [יהי]ו‎
‏מתערבים אלה באלה‎. "The first shall leave from the right side, and they shall not intermingle with one another."

45:11–14. ‏ואיש כיא ישכב עם אשתו‎
‏שכבת זרע לוא יבוא אל כול עיר המקדש אשר‎

אשכין שמי בה שלושת ימים כול איש עור
לוא יבואו לה כול ימיהמה ולוא יטמאו את
העיר אשר אני שוכן בתוכה. "If a man
lies with his wife in intercourse, he
shall not enter any of the city of the
temple wherein I cause My name to
dwell for three days. No blind person shall enter into it all his days.
They shall not defile the city wherein I dwell." (Other references
include 16:5; 47:3–7; 50:17–19;
51:6–8.)

4. 6:17–18.   ולהודיע בין הקודש לחול.
"to make known the difference
between the holy and the common."

51:5–10.   והזהרתמה את בני ישראל מכול
הטמאות ולוא יטמאו בהמה אשר אני מגיד
לכה בהר הזה ולוא יטמאו כי אני יהוה שוכן
בתוך בני ישראל וקדשתמה והיו קדושים ולוא
ישקצו את נפשותמה בכול אשר הבדלתי
להמה לטמאה והיו קדושים "Ye shall keep
apart the children of Israel from all
impurities. They do not defile
themselves with the things which I
have told thee on this mount. They
shall not be defiled, for I am the
Lord, dwelling in the midst of the
Israelites. Thou shalt sanctify them
and they shall be sanctified. They
shall not make themselves detestable with any of those things which
I have separated for them as polluted; let them be holy."
(Other references include the following: 16:5; 27:8–9; 47:3–7.)

5. 6:18.   ולשמור את יום השבת כפרושה.
"to keep the Sabbath according to
its requirements."

27:5–6 (with reference to the Day of
Atonement).   פעם אחת בשנה יהיה היום
הזה ל[ה]מה לזכרון ולוא יעשו בו כול מלאכה
כי שבת שבתון יהיה [לה]מה. "One time
in the year this day shall be [for]
them a memorial; they shall not
perform any labor on it, for it shall
be a sabbath of solemn rest [for
th]em." (See also 8:8–11. The Sab-

bath was probably the subject of discussion in the missing lines at the bottom of col. 13 and the top of col. 14.)

6. 6:18. ואת המועדות "(to keep) the festivals."   17:6–29:2.

7. 6:19. ואת יום התענית "the fast-day" (i.e., the Day of Atonement).   25:10–27:10.

8. 6:20. להרים את הקדשים כפירושיהם "to raise the holy offerings according to their requirements."   13:8–29:2; 43; 52:7–9; 60:6–9.

The allegation that Zadok, evidently the Teacher of Righteousness, had unsealed an ark in which a Book of the Law had been hidden for twelve hundred years may seem unprecedented. In fact it is not, for, as has been alluded to above, 2 Kings 22 relates a similar incident during the eighteenth year of Josiah's reign. Many scholars postulate that Hilkiah found what is known as the Book of Deuternomoy.[104] What is the "Book of the Law" allegedly discovered by Zadok, the Teacher of Righteousness? Can this Sefer Torah be identified with the fragments of 11Q Torah, which Yigael Yadin has published under the title *The Temple Scroll?*

As has been shown, unlike the finding of the sacred scroll during the reign of Josiah, the discovery of the sealed Torah was not a sheer accident resulting from the cleansing of the sanctuary. The thrust of the Damascus Document is that the time for this disclosure had been foretold even before creation.[105] For this was an event that was to change the fate of Israel and the world: the revelation of the eternal Torah! The discovery was part of the beginning of the eschaton, according to the author of Jub. 1:4–29, a work used in the Damascus Document. If the attribution of the scroll's discovery was to Zadok, then he would have been the messenger who was to announce the new epoch.

It was demonstrated above that many of the passages in the Damascus Document harmonize with the newly discovered scroll. This, however, does not clear up the matter entirely since it might be argued that the canonical Torah contains similar passages against fornication, improper acquisition and pollution of the sanctuary. Further review of the evidence will necessitate the conclusion that in CD 5:1–5, the lost book is not the traditional Mosaic book but a sectarian *Seper Torah*. The author's phrase, "And (perhaps—"even") concerning the prince (i.e., king), it is written 'He shall not multiply wives for himself,'" may be taken as a citation of Deut. 17:17, which does have such a statement. Although cogent, the relationship remains problematic. The sectaries accuse their opponents of misinterpreting Deut. 17:17 as banning only a multiplicity of wives, when according to our author, לא ירבה לו נשים in fact prohibits polygamy altogether. The polemicist uses three proofs that Scripture bans the practice of polygamy: (1) God created only two humans, Adam and Eve; (2) the animals entered the ark in pairs; (3) לא ירבה לו נשים (he shall not multiply wives for himself). The first two proofs are precedents, but they are not apodictic commands. The citation from Deut. 17:17 belongs to another category of evidence. The strength of this citation rests on the fact that it is an outright prohibition. Yet the context makes it problematic, as the prohibition against many wives is joined together with the ban against the multiplicity of horses and gold. Surely the accompanying prohibitions in Deuteronomy against the multiplicity of horses and silver, using the same wording as with regard to wives, do not mean that the king may only own a single horse or a single piece of silver.

The author of the Damascus Document, here citing the Mosaic passage Deut. 17:17, is at the same time arguing that this phrase must be understood in the light of 11Q Torah 56:18, where this verse is repeated and then interpreted in the succeeding columns. The first two proofs support the practice of monogamy but do not necessarily support the author's other contention prohibiting divorce, i.e., one may not remarry while one's former wife is alive. CD 4:20–21, "whoredom, taking two wives during their lifetime" (בחייהם), apparently bans not only bigamy but divorce as well. Certainly, as has frequently been pointed out, the canonical passage does not lend support to the word בחייהם. In fact, if the reference is to the traditional Pentateuch, none of these proofs substantiates the prohibition of marrying another woman while the preceding wife is alive, a conclusion that prompted Ginzberg and Rabin to argue that CD 4:21 was intended to prohibit only polygamy, not divorce.[106] However, there can be no question as to the meaning of CD 4:20–21, when the wording of 11Q Torah concerning the King is taken into account: ולוא יקח עליה אשה אחרת כי היאה לבדה תהיה עמו כול ימי חייה (He shall not marry another wife in addition to her, for she alone will be with him all the days of her life.)[107] The linking of לא ירבה לו נשים (he shall not multiply wives for himself)[108] with בחייהם in the Qumranic Torah sheds new light on the use of Deut. 17:17 in the Damascus Document. What the author says is that both the canonical and sectarian *Torot* contain the prohibition against the multiplicity of wives but King David's misunderstanding of Deut. 17:17 was due to the unavailability of the sealed *Seper Torah*. Thus the apology for David not having the *Seper Torah* must not refer to the alleged loss of Deuteronomy but to the temporary absence of the sectarian Law. The author of CD 4:21–5:5 is really saying that 11Q Torah was buried by Eleazar and the elders and was not available until the establishment of Zadok. If it is postulated that the writer here actually has 11Q Torah 56:18–57:18 in mind, the argument embodied in the Damascene treatise becomes clear. The Qumranic Torah does explicitly and repeatedly prohibit bigamy as well as divorce.

This is not all, for there is other evidence that the accusations in the Damascus Document originate from the Qumranic Torah. In addition to charging its opponents with bigamous practices under the category of whoredom, CD 5:6–11 contains the accusation of another abomination: וגם מטמאים הם את המקדש אשר אין הם מבדיל כתורה (Moreover they defile the sanctuary by not making distinctions in accordance with the Law.)[109] Here again the Damascus Document's polemic against mainstream Judaism revolves around the relationship between the canonical Pentateuch and 11Q Torah. To illustrate the defilement which he mentioned, a charge of violating 11Q Torah 66:16–17 is leveled against his opponents by the writer of this document: ולוקחים איש את בת אחיהו ואת בת אחותו (a man marries the daughter of his brother or the daughter of his sister).[110] Should his opponents not accept this charge of defilement, for it is taken from a sectarian document, the exegete goes on to say that it is based on a biblical text: ומשה אמר אל אחות אמך לא תקרב שאר אמך היא ומשפט העריות לזכרים הוא כתוב וכהם הנשים ואם תגלה בת האח את ערות אחי אביה והיא שאר (But Moses said, "You shall not approach the sister of your mother, she is your mother's kin").[111] The author of the Damascus Document argues that, though not explicitly stated, the Hebrew syntax of the canonical Torah requires that this passage be interpreted as prohibiting the marriage of a niece.[112] Lev. 18:13, which lists marriage with the sister of one's mother as incestuous, prohibits the woman from being married to her nephew. How could it be, the author of the Damascus Document asks, that the woman is prohibited from marrying her nephew while the man is allowed to marry his niece since the sect says that the prohibitions in Scripture, though grammatically masculine, actually refer to both sexes? The citation from Moses (ומשה אמר) makes it evident that the reference is to the canonical Torah which is accepted by the opponents of the sectaries. Nevertheless, it is clear that the author's argument rests not only on sheer hermeneutics, but also on the authority of 11Q Torah 66:17–18, which bans marriage to a niece, calling it an abomination. In other words, the passage concerning the dispute about the incestuousness of marrying the niece is a continuation of the argument about the sealed Book of the Law mentioned in CD 5:2–3. Thus 11Q Torah 66:17 is basic for understanding the polemical passage in CD 5:6–11. All in all, pages four and five in the Damascus Document ultimately depend on the divine authority of the *Seper Torah* found by Zadok.

Scholars have noted that the citation of Deut. 17:17 or 11Q Torah 56:18 refers only to the king, while the author of the Damascus Document apparently argues that polygamy and perhaps divorce are to be prohibited for all of Israel, not only for the king.[113] The Damascus Document seems to take note of this fact in its use of the phrase על הנשיא (concerning the prince, i.e., king), but fails to resolve the problem. Another question raised by this text is why, of all the differences between the sect and current halakah that the Qumran writer might have invoked, marriage to a niece is cited and dealt with at length in our treatise, a point made by Al-Muqammiz and cited by the Karaite Al-Qirqisani.[114] The resolution of these puzzles can be found in the consideration that the accusation, though leveled against all of Israel, may have been directed against a specific target, the current high priest called the "liar" in CD 1:15 or the "wicked priest" in Pesher Habakkuk.[115] Could it be that the antagonist of the *Moreh Ṣedeq* had in fact divorced his wife or married his niece?

Additional details concerning the arguments regarding the authenticity of the Book of the Law found by Zadok are provided by the author, who goes so far as to actually quote the opponents: פתחו פה על חוקי ברית אל לאמר לא נכונו (They have opened their mouth against the precepts of the covenant of God, saying "They are not true").[116] The opponents of the sect blasphemed what was apparently the Qumran Torah as לא נכונו, evidently referring to the preceding polemic on whoredom as well as to the other contents of this scroll. It is against this charge that our author addresses his vituperative reply, berating his accusers as blasphemous. In other words, he considers the sectarian Torah just as divine as the traditional Pentateuch.

As if these railings were not sufficient, 5:15–21 cites two incidents from the past which, like the current arguments of the opposition, gave power to the forces of evil. First, Belial marshaled his angelic power by establishing Jannes and his brother to oppose Moses and Aaron. Here the concluding statement is missing in which the author would blame the hiding of the second Torah on the forces of the angels of Mastema. In 5:2–5 the author had dated the hiding of the Torah in the period after Eleazar's death. Here he says that Belial retained his strength even during the lifetime of Moses and Aaron, but became dominant only after the death of Joshua and the elders. In other words, the blasphemy against the Qumranic Torah cited above, according to the author of the Damascus Document, parallels Belial's use of the magicians against Moses and Aaron. Second, the author explains why the revelation of the sealed Torah had to wait until recent times and did not take place following the destruction of the Solomonic temple: ובקץ חרבן הארץ עמדו מסיגי הגבול ויתעו את ישראל ותישם הארץ כי דברו סרה על מצות אל ביד משה (And in the epoch of the desolation of the land, removers of the boundary arose and led Israel astray. The land was ravaged for they spoke rebellion against the commandments of God [given] by the hand of Moses.)[117] The question arises, What compelled the author to apologize for the failure to reveal the Torah at the time of the temple's destruction? If the underlying argument concerns the sanctity of 11Q Torah, the author's defensiveness on the question of why the lost Torah was not revealed at the time of the exile is quite understandable. After all, much of 11Q Torah is devoted to the dimensions of a sanctuary that contrasted sharply with the current, and for that matter the Solomonic, structure; both were quite unacceptable to the sectaries. The question seems to have arisen, Why did God, having destroyed the Solomonic temple, allow its substantial rebuilding instead of revealing at that time the dimensions of the new sanctuary which will remain eternally? The author in 5:20–21 concedes the cogency of the challenge and responds that this was indeed the proper time for the revelation of the sealed Torah. However, the מסיגי הגבול (removers of the boundary) arose again, evidently powered by the angels of חבלה (destruction).[118] These two lines, incidentally, explain why the author dates the appearance of the new planting, i.e., the *Moreh Ṣedeq,* according to the era of the *Ḥurban.* Yes, the author says, the eternal sanctuary was not built following the exile because of people who, like the present-day opponents, had rejected God: these idolaters necessitated the concealment of the scroll containing the Law of the end of days.

The implicit question this text answers is, How does the present situation differ from that of the era of the *Ḥurban?* If redemption had not come at the time of the exile, what proof was there that it is coming now? CD 6:1–11 provides the answer:[119]

> . . . They prophesied falsehood to cause Israel to turn away from God. God remembered the covenant with the forefathers, and He established men of understanding from Aaron and sages from Israel. He caused them to hearken and they dug the well: "the well which the princes dug, which the nobles of the people dug with the staff." The well is the Law and those that dug it are the repentent[120] of Israel who went out from the land of Judah and sojourned in the land of Damascus, where God called all of them princes for they sought Him, and their renown was not rejected by anyone. The staff is the searcher of the Law of whom Isaiah said, "who brings forth a tool for his work." The nobles of the people are those who come to dig the well with the staves which the staff established to walk in them throughout all the epoch of wickedness, for without them they shall not succeed until the establishment of the Teacher of Righteousness at the end of days.

Translated into plain language, this is what our author is saying: in the recent past there have also been similar scoffers who have rejected the anointed,[121] but the situation is quite different from that at the time of the *Ḥurban,* for God has remembered the covenant he established with the patriarchs (ראשונים). In other words, he could no longer wait for the complete redemption; the prescribed time has arrived. What proof is there that this is indeed so? God has given rise to the men of understanding from Aaron and to wise men from Israel; וישמיעם (and He let them know) that they have found the ground of the well. In other words, the descendants of Aaron now know the truth, for God has revealed it to them through the מחוקק (staff) and the well.[122] It would seem that the lawgiver refers to Zadok and that the well is the Torah, alluding to the sectarian Torah.[123] The forces of Belial, however, attempt to fill up the well since it was dug by the lawgiver. These evil forces will exist until the rise of the *yoreh haṣṣedeq*,[124] whose coming is described as עד עמוד יורה הצדק, paralleling עד, עמוד צדוק in CD 5:5. In this argument, the *ṣedeq* in both *Moreh Ṣedeq* and *yoreh ṣedeq* refers to none other than Zadok, listed in 5:5 as Zadok and in 4:1 as the progenitor of the *Beney Ṣadoq*. The members are *yodʿey* (those who know) *ṣedeq*.[125]

The single word *ṣedeq* summarizes the contrast between Jerusalem under the rule of the scoffer and the group which was led by the Teacher of Righteousness in Damascus. What is unique to the Damascus Document is the satirical use of *ṣedeq*. As was already pointed out, the members of the movement are referred to as *yodʿey ṣedeq* and its leader is the *Moreh* or *yoreh ṣedeq*, all of which designate Zadok, the founder of the group. The writer points out, however, that even Belial, wicked as the priestly liar is, cannot abstain from referring to the three abominations practiced under his rule by the appellation used for the leader of the sect: ויתנם פניהם לשלושת מיני הצדק (He [Belial] made them appear as three kinds of righteousness).[126] According to the author of the Damascus Document, it was not so much the practice of the three abominations, namely whoredom, acquisitiveness, and the defilement of the temple, that angered the pious, but rather Belial's claim that these observances came under the category of righteousness (*ṣedeq*), when it was clear that they were exactly the opposite.

The author of the Damascus Document expressed his deep disappointment that, confronted with the choice to follow the "staff" or the "scoffer," the large majority of the people preferred the latter. In addition, many of those who had affirmed their belief in the מחוקק stayed back, failing to join the migration to Damascus. This does not, the composer of this work tells us, entirely surprise him, for the "staff" is not unique in this respect. Even Moses and Aaron, whom everyone grants served as God's messengers, were confronted by Jannes and his brother, set up by Belial to strengthen the sinners. Now too, the author says, only the truly righteous actually reached Damascus. The tarriers were promptly put to the sword by the scoffer or joined him.

The New Covenant in Damascus

Students of Qumran have either ignored or interpreted metaphorically a key passage in the Damascus Document. It deserves close attention, for it comes the closest to what may be labeled the covenant of the immigrants to Damascus, who ultimately became what is now known as the Qumranic sect. After describing the paramount role of the Aaronide *meḥoqeq-doreš hattorah-yoreh ṣedeq* as the chief of the "well diggers," CD 6:11–14 reproduces the preamble to the covenant of the group: "All those who have been brought into the covenant (pledge) not to enter the temple for the purpose of kindling the altar in vain—they shall become shutters of the door . . . unless they follow according to the explication of the Torah (i.e., the sectarian Torah) for the evil epoch."[127] This statement obligates the covenanters to figuratively lock up (i.e., have no contact with) the current sanctuary in Jerusalem, and also mandates the construction of a sanctuary in accordance with its Torah, allegedly discovered by Zadok. The Qumranic Torah, as well, frequently calls itself Torah and is similarly named Torah in Qumranic texts, as discussed in the previous pages. A statement in *AJ* 18:19 concerning the Essenes may find its parallel in this passage: "they are barred from those precincts of the temple that are frequented by all the people and perform their rites by themselves."[128] There is nothing in this passage banning animal sacrifices; it only reflects an attempt to separate the faithful from the multitude, apparently the same separation as that required in the sectarian Torah for the sake of the temple's sanctity. The first clause even suggests that the very structure of the temple was contrary to God's will, "They shall become shutters of the door." Though this statement echoes Mal. 1:10, the pledge here is more emphatic in its rejection of Jerusalem's current sanctuary.

11Q Torah prescribes a sanctuary that diverges radically from any known historical structure that served as the House of the Lord, be it the tabernacle of the wilderness or the temple of Solomon or Zerubbabel.[129] Even the observance of the feasts, and presumably of the Sabbath offerings, departs from what had been assumed to represent the traditional practice. The author of the Book of Jubilees, it was argued above, claimed that both the "first" tablet of stone, i.e., the traditional Torah, and the "last" Torah, i.e., the Qumranic Torah, were equal in authoritativeness and divine origin.[130] However, CD 6:11–14 appears to assert the superior authority of 11Q Torah over its Mosaic archetype "at the time when the rule of evil" would be ending, namely, at the age of eschaton. With the first Torah to be observed in the time of sinfulness and the other in the messianic age, there was no doubt as to which has priority. The closing up of Zerubbabel's sanctuary, which to a large extent was modeled after the Solomonic one, seemed to be a prerequisite for the eschaton. Viewed in this light, CD 6:11–14 assumes a literal meaning: כפרוש התורה means in accordance with what is explicitly stated in the Torah (i.e., 11Q Torah).

The clause that gave rise to the foundation of the sect in Damascus seems to be CD 6:14–16, ולהבדל מבני השחת ולהנזר מהון הרשעה הטמא בנדר ובחרם ובהון המקדש (and to separate themselves from the sons of hell and to set themselves apart from evil possessions which are defiled with the vow, the dedication, and the wealth of the temple). What before the publication of the Qumranic Torah had been mere words now finds explanation in that work. להבדל (to be separate), a common term in the Damascus Document, is one of the words employed by the Qumranic Torah to express its dominant theme of separation and purity: "For their location shall be separate from one another, so that the priests shall not sin inadvertently in the entire sin offering for the people";[131] "They shall not make themselves abominable by anything which I have set apart for them as defiling."[132] The reference to *hon,* stated in 11Q Torah in relationship to the king, applies *a fortiori* to ordinary people: "He (the king) shall not desire a field, vineyard, or any material wealth, any house or any desirable object in Israel, and he shall not steal."[133] Furthermore, it should be noted that the sectarian Torah repeatedly records both the vow[134] and the dedication.[135]

It is difficult to pinpoint the specific passage in 11Q Torah which is referred to in the Damascus Document's charge that the established authorities in Jerusalem robbed the orphans and oppressed the widows. Possibly 11Q Torah 43:2–17, which elaborates on what the rabbis called the מעשר עני (tithe of the poor), may be what the author of the Damascus Document had in mind. Certainly the requirement להבדיל בין הטמא לטהור ולהודיע בין הקדש לחול (to distinguish between the defiled and the clean and to declare [the difference] between the sacred and the common) finds numerous paradigms in the Qumranic Torah:[136] "a holy convocation this day shall be for you, and you shall sanctify it for a remembrance";[137] "The city which I shall sanctify to cause My name and [My s]anctuary to dwell [within it] shall be holy and pure."[138]

Interesting is the avowal: לשמור את יום השבת כפרושה ואת המועדות ואת יום התענית כמצאת באי הברית החדשה בארץ דמשק (to observe the day of the Sabbath in accordance with its elaboration and the festive seasons and the day of fast [i.e., Day of Atonement] in accordance with the finding of those entering into the new covenant in the region of Damascus).[139] These stipulations find their best elucidation in light of the provisions found in the Qumranic Torah. Unfortunately, the ordinances relating to the observance of the Sabbath's offerings, except perhaps for the placement of the shewbread,[140] are lost in the surviving fragments of that document. The Sabbath offerings are apparently the subject of the bottom of col. 13 and the top of 14.[141] 11Q Torah does supply ample evidence of the profound gulf that separated the "last Torah" from its Mosaic archetype with regard to the מועדות (festive seasons).[142] It is, after all, concerning the observance of the pentecostal seasons of first fruits that 11Q Torah departs most radically from the traditional Law.[143] What was true of the divergence between the sectaries and the traditionalists with regard to the observance of the seasons of the first fruits applies, even if to a lesser extent, to the observance of the Day of Atonement.[144] There are not enough differences between the two sources on the latter passage alone to postulate that the requirement to observe the "day of the fast" actually alludes to the sectarian mode of reckoning found in the Book of Jubilees and in other Qumranic texts. On the other hand, ואת יום התענית כמצאת באי הברית החדשה (day of the fast according to the finding of those who come into the new covenant) may signal the inauguration of the sectarian calendar recorded in the Book of Jubilees.[145] One need not exclude the possibility that it was at Damascus that the solar calendar replaced the traditional lunisolar mode of reckoning.[146] The postulate that the alteration in the calendar took place at the time when the sectaries formulated their platform would explain the statement in 6:19, "in accordance with the finding of the comers into the new covenant in the region of Damascus." Since nowhere else in this covenant is such phrasing to be found, can it be that this passage stresses that the introduction of the new calendar was based on views first formulated during the period of the Damascus exile, unlike the other provisions, which could be backed up with the citations from 11Q Torah?[147]

The pledge להרים את הקדשים כפירושיהם (to contribute the heave offerings according to their specifications)[148] is one of the clauses that hardly made sense prior to the publication of the Qumranic Torah. The bringing of *terumah* is greatly emphasized in 11Q Torah, differing sharply from the ordinances spelled out in the traditional Torah. It must also have been disparate with the current practice. This seems to be the burden of the term כפירושיהם (in accordance with their specifications), i.e., in the Qumranic Torah. This word no doubt refers in part to the diversity of the kinds of *terumah* required. But the primary reference seems to be, as elsewhere in this covenant, to the sectarian understanding of the priestly and levitical perquisites of 11Q Torah. Certainly the requirement to bring all the *bikkurym* on the feasts of the first fruits[149] and the first-born to the temple illustrates this difference: "And in the days of the first fruits of new grain, new [wine, and new oil, and on the festival of the offering] of wood, on these days he eats (it in the temple), and he does not ke[ep it from one year] to the next, for in this manner they shall eat it";[150] "Any firstling that is born in your herd or in your flock that is a male, you shall dedicate to Me. You shall not labor with the first-born of your ox and you shall not shear the firstling in your flock. Before Me you shall eat it year by year in the place which I shall choose."[151]

The following pledges introduce a new topic: לאהוב איש את אחיהו כמהו ולהחזיק ביד עני ואביון וגר ולדרוש איש את שלום אחיהו (That each man love his brother like himself, to lend support to the poor, and destitute, and proselyte,[152] and that each person inquire concerning the peace of his neighbor).[153] These lines do not have clear references in the surviving fragments of the Qumranic Torah. As indicated above with regard to the avowal that the opposition violates the rights of the orphans and widows, this passage may also refer to the tithe of the poor, which is differently defined in 11Q Torah 43. In the main, however, there is no reason to search for the source of these clauses elsewhere since the pledge of mutual support and love is a basic ingredient in the formation of a new movement and may be intended to add current meaning to the known sectarian source.

After having elaborated on matters relating to what the author of the Damascus Document calls *hon* (possessions) in the last two lines,[154] he goes on in 7:1 to define what is called "fornication": ולא ימעל איש את בשאר בשרו להזיר מן הזונות (No one shall profane the kin of his flesh, [i.e.,] keep apart from fornication). CD 4:20–5:11, discussed above, provides an extensive commentary on these terse words, explaining the first phrase as a prohibition against marrying one's niece, and the other clause as a pledge against the practice of bigamy and perhaps even against divorce.[155]

The text then continues with the fraternal obligations of the sect: להוכיח איש את אחיהו כמצוה ולוא לנטור מיום ליום (That each man chastise his neighbor in accordance with the commandment and not keep a grudge from day to day).[156] Like the pledges to lend support to other members of the sect and to love, this line forms a basic element in sectarian self-preservation. The source for these avowals is, as has often been pointed out, Lev. 19:17–18.[157] Interestingly, only the pledges relating to mutual help seem to have been based on sources other than the Qumranic Torah.

Observe the summary lines of the platform: ולהבדל מכל הטמאות כמשפטם ולא ישקץ איש את רוח קדשיו כאשר הבדיל אל להם כל המתהלכים באלה בתמים קדש על פי כל יסורי ברית אל נאמנות להם . . . אלף דור (To keep apart from any defilement according to their commandment, and not to abhor his holy spirit, as God had set them apart. All those who follow [or pledge] these things with holy perfection according to all the instructions of the covenant of God, being a trust for them . . . for a thousand generations).[158] If there is a single motive that permeates the sectarian Torah, it is to keep apart the holy from the profane, as stated in the following examples:[159] "in a place set apart for the sin offerings";[160] "You shall sanctify the area around the altar, the sanctuary, the laver, and the storehouse, and it shall be a holy of holies forever";[161] "They shall be separate from one another, the sin-offering of the priests and the he-goat from the sin-offerings of the people and their guilt-offerings. None of these shall be mixed with one another, for their location shall be separate from one another";[162] "Thou shalt sanctify them and they shall be holy. They shall not make themselves abominable with anything which I have set apart for them as a defilement, and they shall be holy."[163]

The concluding lines of the covenant of Damascus, like its beginning, pledge the members of the sect to live in accordance with the most stringent laws of טהרה (cleanliness). What was the point of keeping themselves apart from the Jerusalem sanctuary if not to separate the defiled from the sacred? The promise that God will protect the members of the covenant for a thousand generations concludes the Damascus covenant.[164] Except for the clauses relating to mutual help and to the assistance of the destitute, virtually all the other avowals in the Damascus program seem to bear a close relationship to the distinct legislation spelled out in the remnants of 11Q Torah. As the author of the Damascus Document understands this covenant it falls under

three categories, though not in the same order: זנות (fornication), הון (possessions), and טמא המקדש (defilement of the sanctuary). Clearly, all of the avowals
in the covenant fall under one of these rubrics, and virtually all are found in
the text of the Qumranic Torah.

The covenant has a codicil, which may shed new light on the entire code:
ואם מחנות ישבו כסרך הארץ [אשר היה מקדם] ולקחו נשים [כמנהג התורה] והולידו בנים ויתהלכו
על פי התורה וכמשפט האסרים כסרך התורה כאשר אמר בין איש לאשתו ובין אב לבנו (But if
they live in camps according to the custom of the land . . .[165] they shall take
wives [in accordance with the practice of the Torah,] they shall bear children
and shall walk according to the Torah and according to the requirement of the
vow in accordance with the Torah, as it is said, "between a man and his wife
and between a father and his son").[166] The conditional "and if they live in
camps" seems to imply that they had not done so up to the time of writing.
This codicil appears to suggest that the members of the new covenant had
pledged to stay in Damascus as a group, without attempting to settle in private
life as families.[167] Students of Qumran have cited this passage as testimony
that members of the *Yaḥad* lived outside the settlement of the sect.[168] Whether
or not this is correct with respect to the Commune, this passage cannot be
used in support of that hypothesis. As argued above, this document as a whole
(CD 1–8) antedates the formation of the Commune. The reference to camps
shows the provisions for the return to the land of Israel, but that is still in the
future.

Nehemiah 10 seems to have served as the model for this covenant. In that
biblical work the covenant is called an אמנה (trust) or אלה (oath). The specific
pledges in the Damascus Document diverge from those listed in Nehemiah
10; nevertheless the imprint of that chapter on the Qumranic work is unmistakable. Those who accepted the covenant are called מחזיקים (those who
hold fast), a term frequently used to refer to the Damascus covenanters.[169] The
Sabbath, the holy days, and the offering of tithes are listed in both.[170] Common to the two works is the jussive use of the *lamed* for the specific pledges.[171]
Incidentally, the influence of this passage on the Qumranic Torah can be seen
in the listing of the wheat, the wine, and the oil, all prominently featured in
that work.[172] Only Neh. 10:35 and 13:31 provide a biblical source for the
offering of woods, which 11Q Torah elaborates at length.[173] Apparently the
migrants took Ezra and Nehemiah as their forerunners. To their minds, they,
rather than the current priesthood in Jerusalem, were carrying on the tradition.

All in all, the Damascus Document may be read as a defensive work. CD 1–8
simply attempts to account for the fact that these migrants who made up the
founding fathers of the sect were living in exile rather than in the holy city.
After all, the members of the new covenant had presumably been among the
leading functionaries of the sanctuary, and their presence outside the holy

city, and even more so on foreign soil, had to be explained. In other words, the charges expressed in the covenant against the present state of the sanctuary and its sacrificial rites served as an apology. Why was it that the *Moreh Ṣedeq* and his faithful had to flee the holy land while the priestly scoffer and those who despised the wrath of God occupied the sacred soil? The answer given was that the exile was only ephemeral, and even though it dragged on, it could not last more than twenty years. CD 7:4–6 emphasizes the point that in the minds of the sect's founders, they were only temporarily a tiny segment of Israel.[174] In the near future they would be triumphantly welcomed into the holy city as its saviors. There is nothing in this covenant, or for that matter in pages 1–8, to indicate that the founders had intended to organize a distinct sect.[175] They merely wished to serve as forerunners of the impending eschaton, to prepare for the construction of the eternal sanctuary as had been prescribed at Mount Sinai on a stone tablet we know as the Qumranic Torah.

CD 1:1–7:19 seems to have been intended to serve a purpose similar to the Book of Jubilees, to propagate the idea that 11Q Torah has equal, if not superior, authority to the traditional Pentateuch. The difference between the two is that Jubilees restricts itself to the context of the text, whereas the Damascus Document elaborates on the time of discovery, concentrating on the finder of the Torah and his followers. The author uses "Torah" ten times, apparently always referring to the law of 11Q Torah. He seems to employ precise terminology, "Torah" referring to the scroll, and "Moses" indicating the canonical law. The traditional texts of the Five Books of Moses and the Qumranic Torah here possess equal authority, except in the case of the main themes of the treatise, such as material laws, tithing, and defilement of the temple, where 11Q Torah is paramount. The pledges of the new covenant formed the basis for a movement which expected soon to become supreme in Jerusalem, at the latest in twenty years. Thus Damascus Document 1–8 relates the origin of the sect from God's election of the Teacher of Righteousness, which found expression in his discovery of the lost Mosaic Torah, to the formulation of the platform in Damascus, a period of twenty years, which began 390 years after the destruction of the temple.

The Moreh Ṣedeq *and the* Beney Ṣadoq *in the Texts of the Commune*

So far, this study's postulate that *Moreh Ṣedeq* and its congruents refer to a certain Zadok, the leader of a migration to Damascus where the new covenant launched a movement, rests almost entirely on evidence from a single treatise, the Damascus Docment, and then merely on cols. 1–8. Since the term Teacher of Righteousness occurs often in the pesherite texts, one must ask, Does the supposed meaning of *Moreh Ṣedeq* fit these passages as well? Another unexpected problem is the exact designation of *Beney Ṣadoq*. The Damascus

Document does not employ this term except when citing Ezekiel's prophecy, but other Qumranic writings, especially the Community Rule and the pesherite fragments, do use it frequently. As in the case of Ezek. 44:15, it has been taken for granted that *Beney Ṣadoq* is to be rendered as the Zadokite priests, the alleged descendants of David's chief priest who, since Solomonic times, officiated in Jerusalem's sanctuary.[176] The problem with this rendition has been that the title of Jerusalem's ecclesiastical party was *Saddukaioi,* so designated by Josephus and the New Testament, and by the talmudic tradition as *Ṣadduqym* or *Ṣedoqym.*[177] Is it not puzzling that the Commune, which was ideologically far apart from the Sadducees, would refer to its adherents with a designation identical to that of a group which it detested? The scholarly literature has attempted to obviate this question by shunning the name "Zadokite Fragments" given to the treatise in its editio princeps in order to maintain a sharp distinction between Sadducees and Zadokites.[178] The hypothesis of this study, however, removes the enigma altogether, for it is no longer necessary to suppose that *Beney Ṣadoq* in Qumranic writings refers, as in the case of the *Saddukaioi* or *Ṣedoqim,* to the "sons of Zadok," the Solomonic priest in Ezek. 44:15, but that "sons of Zadok" may in fact designate the physical descendants of Zadok, the Teacher of Righteousness. It was shown above that at least in CD 3:21's exegesis of Ezek. 44:15, the prophetic phrase *Beney Ṣadoq* is taken to foretell the advent of Zadok, the Teacher of Righteousness. This means, in fact, that the biblical use of the term is of secondary significance to the Qumranic writers, the primary designation being the founder of the movement. The question then arises whether *Beney Ṣadoq,* as used in the sectarian writings, retains the biblical meaning found in Ezekiel or whether, as in CD 3:21–5:12, the "sons of Zadok" means the descendants of Zadok.[179]

Omitting occurrences of *Moreh Ṣedeq* where the context is lost, the following discussion lists published passages from the Qumranic literature which contain this term:

(i) 1QpHab 1:13, "[Interpreted, the wicked is the wicked priest and the righteous] is the Teacher of Righteousness."

(ii) 1QpHab 2:1–2, "[Its interpretation concerns] the treacherous ones with the liar, who did not [hearken to the words of] the Teacher of Righteousness."

(iii) 1QpHab 5:9–11, "Interpreted, this concerns the house of Absalom and the men of their council who were silent during the reproof of the Teacher of Righteousness and did not help him against the liar."

(iv) 1QpHab 7:4–5, "Its interpretation concerns the Teacher of Righteousness to whom God made known all the mysteries of the words of His servants, the prophets."

(v) 1QpHab 8:1–3, "Its interpretation concerns all who do the law in the house of Judah, whom God will deliver from the house of judgement because of their suffering and because of their faith in the Teacher of Righteousness."

(vi) 1QpHab 9:9–10, "Its interpretation concerns the wicked priest who, on account of the iniquity of the Teacher of Righteousness and his council, God put him into the hands of his enemies."

(vii) 1QpHab 11:4–6, "Its interpretation concerns the wicked priest who pursued the Teacher of Righteousness to the house of his exile in order to consume him in the heat of his rage."

(viii) CD 19:35–20:1, "They shall not be entered in their book from the day the Teacher of the Commune is gathered in until the establishment of the anointed from Aaron and from Israel."

(ix) CD 20:13–15, "From the day when the Teacher of the Commune is gathered in, until the end of all the men of war who returned with the liar is about forty years."

(x) CD 20:27–28, "to go and to come according to the law and to hearken to the voice of the teacher."

(xi) CD 20:32–33, "Those who listened to the voice of the Teacher of Righteousness and did not despise the precepts of righteousness."

(xii) 1Q 14, 10:5 (Pesher on Micah), "[Its interpretation concerns] the Teacher of Righteousness, who [taught the Torah to his council] and to all who pledged to join the elect of [God]."[180]

(xiii) 4Q 171, 3:15–19 (Pesher on Psalm 37), "Its interpretation concerns the priest, the Teacher of [Righteousness, whom] God commanded (or chose) to appoint for He designated him to build [His] congregation . . . [and] His [wa]ys he directed towards His truth . . . [the interpretation] of the matter concerns the Teacher [of Righteousness]."[181]

(xiv) 4QPBless 3, "For the staff is the covenant of the kingship, the thousands of Israel are the feet, until the Messiah of righteousness comes, the branch of David."[182]

It is worth noting that the pesherite texts, like the Damascus Document, are replete with references to the Teacher of Righteousness, while other documents such as the Community Rule and the Thanksgivings do not contain a single reference to him. How is this phenomenon to be explained? Aside from the allusions to the invasion of the Kittim, Pesher Habakkuk's main theme consists of the polarity between the priestly scoffer and the Teacher of Righteousness, mentioned in this treatise seven times.[183] The *Moreh Ṣedeq* is here associated mostly with suffering and persecution. This portrayal contrasts sharply with the *Moreh Ṣedeq* found in CD 1–8, who is the interpreter of Scripture and the anointed redeemer of the Lord, sent at the time of the eschaton. As will be shown below, this diversity requires no explanation other than the shifts in the fate of the master. The accounts of Zadok in the Damascus Document depict the mood of exaltation at a time when he, together with his early followers, left the holy city for the region of Damascus, which they regarded as a temporary exile just prior to the triumphant reentry into a newly consecrated Jerusalem. The failure of these hopes to materialize and major debacles in which the master's life hung by a thread seem to be reflected in the Habakkuk commentary. The anonymous pesherist regards the *Moreh Ṣedeq*'s suffering as atonement for his minor peccadilloes, just before the ultimate fall of the wicked priest and the vindication of the anointed Aaronide.[184]

In contrast to Pesher Habakkuk, which speaks of the persecution of the *Moreh Ṣedeq* by the scoffer, or the other pesherite fragments which seem to attempt to link the Teacher of Righteousness with the Commune, the fragment that became attached to the Damascus Document is the only Qumran text which mentions the master's death. Calling him *moreh hayyaḥyd* (the unique teacher), which some read as *yaḥad* (Commune), the last line of col. 19 and the top of 20 reads: "And from the day of the ingathering of the teacher of the unique (of the Commune) until the establishment of the anointed from Aaron and from Israel." CD 20:13–15 repeats perhaps a similar occurrence: "and from the days of the death of the unique teacher (of the Commune) until the end of all the men of war who had returned with the liar is about forty years." These lines suggest that this fragment is a remnant of a work written later than Pesher Habakkuk, which speaks of the master as still being alive, and certainly much later than CD 1–8, a text describing the initial organization of the movement in the region of Damascus. The death of the master and founder of the movement must have endangered the existence of the covenanters, but the group had gained enough strength to outlive its dependence on the *Moreh Ṣedeq*. CD 20:14–15 expresses the hope that salvation would come forty years after the *Moreh Ṣedeq*'s death, attesting that the *Yaḥad* (Commune) was already in full existence during the early decades after his death. There is a subsequent reference to the anointed after the forty years, when in a reinterpretation of the sect's ideology, the *Moreh Ṣedeq* again becomes a messianic figure. The references to the *Moreh Ṣedeq* in the pesherite texts other than Habakkuk also contain allusions to his return.[185] Like CD 20, 4QpPs 37, 3:15–19 apparently alludes to the *Moreh Ṣedeq* as a historical personality after his death. Whereas the latter seems to have been written within forty years after his demise, this pesher depicts the role of the *Moreh Ṣedeq* and his descendants for the Commune as a whole. Although *Ṣedeq* here is a textual restoration, one need not doubt that this is a necessary interpolation since the passage refers to his group as עצת אביונים (congregation of the destitute) or עצת בחירו (congregation of the chosen), and the opposing party is made up of the princes of evil. As I understand this passage, it transforms Zadok from a historical to a messianic figure. Like 4QpPs 37, Pesher Micah 8–10:6 also deals with the *Moreh Ṣedeq* as a messianic figure who opposed the "Spouter of Lies," whoever he may be. This messianic deliverer apparently leads "those who shall be saved on the day. . . ." In brief, *Moreh Ṣedeq* in all texts refers to Zadok, who alone bore this title. In CD 1–8 and in Pesher Habakkuk, the reference is to him while alive; in CD 20 and in other pesherite fragments, Zadok is portrayed as dead and there is an expectation of his return. A number of fragments published since 1965 may provide further evidence of the apotheosis of Zadok. In these fragments, the figure of *Malky-ṣedeq*, who makes his first appearance in Genesis 14, reappears as the leader of the angelic hosts against those of *Malky-reša*ᶜ. It is possible that *Malky-ṣedeq*, in these passages, too, alludes to the discoverer of the lost *Seper Torah* mentioned in CD 5:5. If so, these texts supply the first evidence of the deification of a mortal at Qumran.

Who took over the leadership after the death of the *Moreh Ṣedeq?* The frequent references to the *mošab harrabbym* and to the twelve-member council indicate that no one fully inherited the mantle worn by the *Moreh Ṣedeq*. On the other hand, quite a number of passages allude to the leadership position of the *Beney Ṣadoq* in the Commune:

1QS 3:20, "By the prince of light are governed all the Sons of Zadok, who shall walk in the ways of light."

1QS 3:21–22, "The angel of darkness leads all the Sons of Zadok astray."

1QS 5:1–2, "They shall separate from the congregation of the men of injustice and be joined together with respect to the law and possessions, and they shall submit to the Sons of Zadok, the priests, who keep the covenant."

1QS 5:8–9, "He (the convert) shall undertake by a binding oath to turn to the Law of Moses in accordance with all he commanded with all his heart and soul, to all which is revealed of it to the Sons of Zadok, the priests, who keep the covenant and interpret his will."

1QSa 1:1–2, "This is the rule for all the congregation of Israel in the latter days, when they shall be [joined to the Commune to walk] according to the judgment of the Sons of Zadok, the priests, and their covenant."

1QSa 1:24, "under the authority of the Sons of Zadok, the priests."

1QSa 2:2–3, "All the [sages] of the congregation, the learned, those who know the way of perfection, the men of might . . . and all their judges . . . are members of the council of the Commune in Israel before the Sons of Zadok, the priests."

1QSb 3:22–23, "Words of blessing for the man of wisdom to bless the Sons of Zadok, the priests, whom God has chosen to strengthen his covenant."

4Q 174, 1:17 (Florilegium), "They are the Sons of Zadok and the men of their council, the pursuers of righteousness that come after them."[186]

In a valuable study, Jacob Liver comments on the above-mentioned references to the sons of Zadok in Qumran literature: "These texts testify . . . that the words 'Sons of Zadok' . . . are directed to the priests who had in the sect a

position of authority and leadership.''[187] Having observed that they are called
the keepers of the covenant and that all of the council is under their authority,
he notes that there is no mention of their cultic functions; they are, rather,
given a special role in the training of new members. While documenting the
unique place of these members in the sect, he also holds that the phrase "Sons
of Zadok" designates a genealogical relationship rather than a party affilia-
tion. Liver then joins those many other scholars who maintain that this Zadok
is the priest of David and Solomon from former times. As Liver puts it, all the
mentions of *Beney Ṣadoq* in the Qumran literature are to be understood literally as the sons or grandsons of the founder of the sect, who retained moral, if
not factual, leadership of the Commune. However, with the identification of
Zadok as the actual founder of the sect, Liver's explanation that the *Beney
Ṣadoq* retained the leadership of the Commune assumes a new meaning. *Beney
Ṣadoq* are those of direct lineage, the sons or grandsons of Zadok, the founder
of the sect.[188]

Zadok in the Qumran texts, except perhaps when these works cite Ezekiel, is
not a biblical figure, but is either the *Moreh Ṣedeq* or the patronymic of the elite
in the Commune. Even in later periods, the memory of the *Moreh Ṣedeq* was
perpetuated by the belief that he would return in the eschaton. Alive or dead,
he remained the undisputed master of the Commune. The elaborate memorial erected at the place where Zadok's physical remains were buried, recorded
in the Copper Scroll, may also display his abiding influence at Qumran. It is
even conceivable that the members of the sect turned him into the leader of
the hosts of Yahweh (*Malky-ṣedeq*), doing battle with the forces of Satan (*Malky-
reša'*).

Chapter 4

Zadok in Talmudic and Karaite Writings

Zadok and Baethus, the Disciples of Antigonus of Soko

Both talmudic and Karaite sources mention a certain Zadok and his companion Baethus; each, it is said, was the founder of a heretical movement during the period of the Second Temple. Zadok and Baethus, according to Abot de-Rabbi Nathan, studied under the master Antigonus of Soko, himself a disciple of Simon the Just, one of Jerusalem's high priests during the third century B.C.E.[1] Depending on one's understanding of the relevant passage, Zadok and Baethus, either because they misunderstood Antigonus' instructions or because they were disaffected with his teachings, departed from the mainstream of Pharisaic Judaism by launching two heretical movements which are frequently mentioned in the Mishnah and Tosefta, the *Ṣadduqym* or *Ṣedoqym* (Grk. Σαδδυκαιοι) and the Baethusians or Boethusians.[2] Putative rabbinic scholarship unanimously agrees that the priestly party, known as Sadducees in the writings of Josephus and the New Testament, originated with the disciples of Antigonus of Soko.[3] As to the *Baytusym* (Baethusians), it was said that they were a variant from or a segment of the aristocratic Sadducees. Abraham Geiger challenged the historicity of the talmudic account by claiming that the Sadducees were so named because they traced their ecclesiastical lineage to Zadok, the priest of David and Solomon.[4] According to this theory, the *Beney Ṣadoq* of Ezekiel 44 and Ben Sira 51:12 retained their identification with this high priest.[5] Twentieth-century scholarship tends to agree with this view, dismissing the talmudic and Karaite anecdotes concerning Zadok and Baethus as legends that originated during the Middle Ages.[6]

The hypothesis in this study that a certain Zadok was the founder of the sect which ultimately settled at Qumran necessitates a reexamination of ARNA 5. Is the Zadok mentioned in this passage identical with the Zadok who "found" the Qumranic Torah, or are they two different personages? Can it be that the obscure references to the two disciples of Antigonus refer not to the Sadducees but rather to the *Beney Ṣadoq,* the descendants of the founder of the Qumranic sect? Can it be that *Ṣedoqym* in the talmudic sources does not always allude to Jerusalem's aristocratic party but rather to the *Beney Ṣadoq* of the Judaean scrolls?

To clarify the sources, a word needs to be said concerning the provenance of
the talmudic references to Zadok and Baethus. ARNA 5 and ARNB 10 relate
the anecdotes concerning the origin of the Zadokite and Baethusian sects as
part of an exposition of Antigonus' saying, adding a conclusion not found in
M. Abot 1:3. It is possible that the Mishnah used by the author of Abot de-
Rabbi Nathan differed at this point from the putative text of M. Abot.[7]

As to the date of M. Abot, it must be regarded as one of the treatises that
assumed their present form after the Mishnah as a whole had been published
circa 200 C.E.[8] Chapter 1 of Abot clearly presumes that the Mishnah had
already been edited and that Rabbi Judah Ha-Nasi, the editor of the Mishnah, was no longer alive. As for Abot de-Rabbi Nathan, its title suggests that
it is a commentary on the Mishnah, claiming to be the Tosefta to the older
tannaitic treatise. Be this as it may, there is no reason to assume that Abot de-
Rabbi Nathan assumed its present form prior to the seventh or eighth century,
and it seems that version B was composed even later.[9] The relative lateness of
the sources that preserve traditions concerning Antigonus and his disciples
has magnified the problem of determining their provenance and historicity.
Nevertheless, it is possible that these traditions preserve precious information
no longer available in older sources. Their validity should not be completely
rejected before they are analyzed in light of the newly discovered texts from
the Judaean wilderness.

M. Abot 1:3, which forms part of a section devoted to the chain of the tradition from Moses through the sages, reads as follows:

אנטיגנוס איש סוכו קבל משמעון הצדיק: הוא היה אומר אל תהיו כעבדים המשמשים את הרב
על מנת לקבל פרס אלא היו כעבדים המשמשים את הרב שלא על מנת לקבל פרס ויהי מורא
שמים עליכם.

Antigonus of Soko received (the Oral Torah) from Simon the Just. He used
to say: "Be not like the servants who serve the master in order to receive
wages, but be like the servants who serve the master without the expectation of receiving wages, and let the fear of heaven be upon you."[10]

After reproducing this passage, ARNA appends the following:

... כדי שיהיה שכרכם כפול לעתיד לבא. אנטיגנוס איש סוכו היו לו שני תלמידים שהיו שונין
בדבריו והיו שונין לתלמידים ותלמידים לתלמידים. עמדו ודקדקו אחריהן ואמרו מה ראו
אבותינו לומר דבר זה אפשר שיעשה פועל מלאכה כל היום ולא יטול שכרו ערבית. אלא אלו היו
יודעין אבותינו שיש עולם אחר ויש תחיית המתים לא היו אומרים כך. עמדו ופירשו מן התורה
ונפרצו מהן שתי פרצות צדוקים וביתוסים. צדוקים על שום צדוק ביתוסי על שום ביתוס. והיו
משתמשין בכלי כסף וכלי זהב כל ימיהם. שלא היתה דעתן גסה עליהם אלא צדוקים אומרים
מסורת הוא ביד פרושים שהן מצערין עצמן בעולם הזה ובעולם הבא אין להם כלום.

... So that your reward may be doubled in the age to come. Antigonus of
Soko had two disciples who used to study his words. They taught them to

their disciples, and their disciples to their disciples. These proceeded to examine the words closely and said: "Why did our ancestors see fit to say this thing? Is it possible that a laborer would do his work all day and not receive his reward in the evening? If our ancestors had known that there is another world and that there will be a resurrection of the dead, they would not have spoken in this manner." So they arose and separated themselves from the Torah and split into two sects, the Zadokites and the Baethusians: Zadokites named after Zadok, Baethusians after Baethus. They used silver vessels and gold vessels all their lives, not because they were ostentatious,[11] but the Zadokites said, "It is a tradition amongst the Pharisees to afflict themselves in this world, yet in the world to come they will have nothing."[12]

It seems that ARNA 5 attempts to solve two problems. The first concerns the identity of Antigonus and the second relates to his puzzling saying. The question of Antigonus of Soko's identity is particularly acute since unlike all the other sages who form part of the chain of tradition and are known from other mishnaic and talmudic sources, this sage is mentioned here and nowhere else. Yet he must have been an important partriarch, for he is the recipient of the *qabbalah* from Simon the Just and master of the first of the five pairs listed in Abot: Jose son of Joezer and Jose son of Johanan.[13] Antigonus, ARNA says, is to be identified by his infamous disciples, Zadok and Baethus, who propagated heresies that continued to plague the Jewish people for centuries. Antigonus, moreover, was not entirely innocent of this national tragedy since it was his ambiguous gnome that allegedly brought about the origin of these heresies. ARNA seems to be saying that were it not for their heretical doctrines, Zadok and Baethus would have been the first pair of the chain of tradition instead of Jose son of Joezer and Jose son of Johanan. In the context of the Mishnah and its sages, this is a serious charge against Antigonus. His shame was serious since his disciples initiated movements that spread vile heresies.

There are two ways to account for the presence of such a charge in ARNA 5. Either it represents an old tradition and may itself explain why Antignonus' teachings are not recorded elsewhere in the talmudic sources, or the author of ARNA or his source invented the anecdote to account for the mysterious identity of Antigonus. What appears evident, however, is that the puzzle of Antigonus' identity and his alleged teachings vis-à-vis the origin of sectarianism in Israel was not invented by ARNA but is intrinsic to the Mishnah and other sources which are absolutely silent concerning this otherwise unrecorded father. ARNA expresses its defense of Antigonus not only in the story of his disciples but also by apparently embellishing the saying in the Mishnah. ARNA adds: "so that your reward may be doubled in the world to come." Version B reads: "and you shall receive a reward as if you had observed them (the commandments?) in this world and the world to come."[14]

ARNA can be interpreted in two contradictory ways. At the outset it should be made clear that the purpose of the story in Abot de-Rabbi Nathan is distinct from that of the similar account in Karaite sources that will be discussed below. The latter's interest rests on the sectarianism of Zadok and Baethus, the former's on the relationship between Antigonus and his disciples. But it is this relationship that remains uncertain.

The ambiguity of Antigonus of Soko's saying, which was responsible for the schismatic movement, is documented by ARN. Unfortunately, ARN's account of the founders of Zadokite sectarianism is itself puzzling, lacking apparent clarity. In the first section of this citation, Zadok and Baethus question the propriety of servants laboring the whole day without receiving their due reward: "Why did our ancestors see fit to say this thing? Is it possible that a laborer would do his work all day and not receive his reward in the evening?" Misunderstanding their master, they think that he is saying that there is no reward and punishment. In other words, the doctrine of Zadok and Baethus did embrace reward and punishment. On the other hand, in the second part they say: "If our ancestors had known that there is another world and that there will be a resurrection of the dead, they would not have spoken in this manner." Again misunderstanding their master, the disciples attempt to follow what they imagine to be his teaching, concluding that he and the ancestors, i.e., the biblical tradition, do not recognize the ʿolam habba (the world to come) or the resurrection. The firt part of the account can be construed as meaning that Zadok and Baethus, in contrast to Antigonus, attempted to establish reward and punishment; the second, that they remained faithful to their master, who rejected the doctrine of resurrection.[15] Of course it is possible to interpret the second part in a still different way; i.e., Zadok and Baethus censured the ancestors as well as Antigonus for not being aware of the world to come and the resurrection. Thus the statement concerning the doctrine of the sectaries seems contradictory as to whether they did or did not accept the existence of the future world or resurrection. Both traditional and modern scholarship ignores the first part of this statement, in which Zadok and Baethus do seem to accept the doctrine of reward and punishment, but stresses the disciples' rejection of the Pharisaic doctrines of the world to come and the resurrection.[16] Furthermore, since the early Christian and rabbinic sources state that the Sadducees rejected resurrection, it follows, according to the generally accepted view, that ARN refers to this Judaean party.[17] Scholars go on to contest the historicity of ARNA 5, thereby denying that the appellation "Sadducees" is traceable to Antigonus' disciple Zadok.[18]

It is possible to account for the apparent inconsistency in the dissenting words of Antigonus' disciples by presuming a conflation. The first statement faults Antigonus for his failure to stress retribution, and usually the second phrase is interpreted in the light of the first, with אלא (but) inserted to hold the two views together. However, there seems to be no need for such a radical explanation. The supposition that Antigonus' disciple Zadok is the same person as the one to whom the Damascus Document attributes the discovery of 11Q Torah and whose monument seems to be recorded in the Copper Scroll may help make the statement in ARNA 5 coherent. Zadok's censure of Antigonus' Pharisaic doctrines seems to conform to the beliefs expressed in the works found in the Qumranic library. 11Q Torah and other writings all strongly emphasize reward and punishment.[19] Certainly, Antigonus' dictum to serve God even if God does not reward good deeds could not be reconciled with Qumran's central thesis—that God had chosen the members of the Commune and damned their enemies.[20]

On the other hand, the Qumranic doctrines contain nothing that would conflict with Zadok's other criticism of Pharisaic thought: the denial of the existence of the עולם הבא (the world to come) and resurrection. To be sure, the belief in the אחרית הימים (the end of days), the eschatological epoch, is fundamental for both Qumran and Pharisaism. But the disparity between Pharisaic and Qumranic eschatology is equally profound. Using the Mishnah as evidence, three basic elements may be attributed to early rabbinic eschatology: messianism, the world to come, and resurrection. Under messianism, the rabbis understood the restoration of the Davidic house as presaged by the prophets, especially Mal. 3:23. Messianism, according to the rabbis, assumed a renaissance of the ideal epoch when the son of Jesse would reign over a united Israel.[21] The restoration of the anointed from the loins of David was undoubtedly a prerequisite to the epoch when the souls and the bodies would be revived, the final stage of the coming end of days.[22] The exact meaning of the phrase "the world to come" is obscure.[23] It may allude to the messianic epoch or to the era of the resurrection of the dead. But it also seems to be a category of its own—perhaps a stage intermediate between the epochs of the Messiah and of resurrection. Although eschatology is one of the most important themes in the Dead Sea Scrolls, its true nature at Qumran seems to have eluded modern scholarship. Too often it has been taken for granted that Qumran's eschatological terminology is to be translated in a manner similar to its familiar meanings in early rabbinic and Christian writings. Take the term משיח (Messiah), for example, which the ancients rendered as *christos* (anointed). It came to mean the anointed scion of David who will at the end of days restore the ancient glory of Israel known from the days of David and Solomon. The Christians, to be sure, reinterpreted the term to refer primarily to salvation. But what does *mešyaḥ* mean in Qumranic texts? Clauses such as "until the establishment of the *mašuaḥ* of Aaron and Israel"[24] (sometimes *mašyaḥ* in either the singular or plural) have induced scholars to understand the Qumranic usage in light of the putative definition of messianism, i.e., Davidic kingship of God. What has divided the students of Qumran is whether the sectarians conceived of one or of two messiahs, one of Aaronide stock and the other descended from David.[25]

In fact, however, the term *mašuaḥ* and its cognates still seem to retain their scriptural connotation. The Mosaic books know only of the anointed priests, either the chief sacerdote or his assistants.[26] In no case does the canonical Torah ever refer to princes as anointed. The case is different in the historical and prophetic writings, where kings, especially the kings of Judah, are referred to as anointed.[27] The Qumranic Torah, in spite of its lengthy account of the royal charter, never alludes to the requirement of anointing the king. The term משיח אהרון וישראל (Messiah of Aaron and Israel) in CD and related texts makes sense only if understood as an epithet for or synonym to *kohen gadol* (high priest).[28] It follows that clauses such as "until the establishment of the anointed of Aaron and Israel" do not necessarily, perhaps not at all, refer to the messianic figure of the Jewish or Christian tradition but to the building of the eschatological sanctuary whose chief priest will bear the epithet of "the anointed of Aaron and Israel." In other words, whereas *mašyaḥ* in classical Judaism alludes to a divine kingship under a Davidic monarch, in the Qumranic writings the word designates the chief officer in the eschatological temple.

Not only is the classical content of messianism alien to the Qumranic sect, but so is the belief in the resurrection of the dead. Certainly the Dead Sea Scrolls contain no clear allusion to such a belief, and it is difficult to postulate the existence of such a doctrine at Qumran if it never found expression in the sect's vast writings. As to the *ʿolam habba,* this phrase is not attested in Qumranic literature either. It is difficult, however, to be dogmatic as to whether its equivalent was known to the sectaries, especially since the term remains largely undefined even in rabbinic writings. The upshot of this discussion is that the sect's eschatology diverged sharply from that of classical Judaism. Its exact nature remains an enigma.

The sectaries did have a belief in national immortality.[29] 11Q Torah conceives of this immortality in the eschatological sanctuary which, unlike its predecessors, will last forever. The Book of Jubilees likewise contrasts the ephemeral nature of the First and Second Temples with the eternal character of the structure it prescribes. The War Rule depicts the final victory of the children of light over those of darkness, resulting in the everlasting reign of God. Other Qumranic works, such as the pesherite writings, the Thanksgivings, and the Manual of Discipline, do speak of personal salvation, but only as part of a group. It seems noteworthy that this view, which finds the salvation of the individual in the group, was not an innovation of Qumran but rather a conservative doctrine that permeates Scripture, especially the Mosaic books.

Another obscure detail in Abot de-Rabbi Nathan may become understandable in light of the recovered sections from 11Q Torah: "For they used silver and gold vessels thoughout their lives not because they were ostentatious but because the Zadokites say, 'It is a tradition among the Pharisees to afflict themselves in this world, and in the world to come they shall have nothing.'" This sentence lacks clarity: first, because the manuscript tradition differs as to whether the enjoyment of precious metals applies to both disciples, as in the editio princeps, or only to one of them, apparently Zadok, as in some transmissions;[30] second, the word מסורת, generally meaning "tradition," hardly makes sense in the context where קללה (curse) or some such word would seem to be intended. That is to say, the Pharisees possess a curse in that they deprive themselves of the pleasures of this world and lack a belief in the world to come. The primary question, however, remains, What is the point of the use of silver and gold by Zadok and/or Baethus?

The recovered remnants of the Qumranic Torah seem to give a cogent answer to this question. One of the recurring formulas in the prescription for the future temple with respect to the walls of the various buildings or their furnishings is "all shall be overlaid with pure gold."[31] The requirement to have certain furnishings gilded goes back to the tabernacle,[32] but it is by and large missing from the biblical accounts of the Solomonic temple. It is entirely absent from the descriptions of the temple in Ezekiel 40–48 and in M. Middot. Only in the Qumran text of the future temple is it ordained that even ancillary structures such as the wash basin[33] and the staircases[34] must be absolutely covered with gold. To be sure, Eupolemus' account of the Solomonic temple does contain a fantastic amount of gold, but as was pointed out, this description seems to be indebted to the sectarian Torah.[35] This extraordinary emphasis on the precious metals in the future temple may explain the tradition in ARNA 5 of the ostentatious way of life ascribed to the disciples of Antigonus and the apology for such a behavior. Their use of silver and gold was intended, it is implied, to give a foretaste of the future temple, which would be fully gilded. There is also the fictive structure recorded in the Copper Scroll which contains stoas and exedras under which some of the sect's treasures were allegedly concealed.[36] As Abot de-Rabbi Nathan carefully explains, the apparent ostentation did not reflect an inclination to vanity, but an anti-Pharisaic polemic. The Pharisees, according to the Zadokites (if not according to Zadok and Baethus themselves), live a miserable life in this world and will have nothing in the hereafter—in contrast to the Zadokites, who are already regarded as possessing a foretaste of what extraordinary good there is in the future world.

The description of the gilding in ARNA 5 lends circumstantial evidence to the possibilities already outlined in the discussion of the sectarian eschatology. The statements which Abot de-Rabbi Nathan attributes to Zadok are not out of line with Qumranic theology. Certainly the concept of reward and punishment is central to Qumranic doctrine and Zadok's critique of Antigonus' presumed deemphasis, if not omission, of this teaching seems justified. On the other hand, the Dead Sea Scrolls fail to allude to a belief in the resurrection of the dead or in the *ʿolam habba,* doctrines apparently contested by Zadok according to ARN. Thus, nothing that the rabbinic tradition attributes to the schismatic disciples of Antigonus is inconsistent—and much in fact seems to be in harmony—with the sectarian literature of Qumran.

The main point, however, is that Abot de-Rabbi Nathan does contain a tradition that Zadok founded a sect in opposition to mainstream Judaism. Now that Qumranic writings attest that a certain Zadok was the first to discover the lost scroll given to Moses at Sinai, the question arises: Need we posit that Zadok, the disciple of Antigonus and the alleged founder of the Zadokites, is to be differentiated from his namesake, the apparent discoverer of the Qumranic Torah, or is it more reasonable, as we suggest, to consider that the Qumranic scrolls refer to the same person? We turn now to the Karaite evidence, which is more specific in the identification of Zadok and Baethus.

Al-Qirqisani on Zadok and Baethus

Thus far it has been shown that both Qumranic and rabbinic texts indicate that a certain Zadok who lived in post-exilic times played a significant role in the foundation of a sect that bore his name.[37] Interestingly, there exists a third source, the tenth-century Karaite author Abu Jusuf Ja'qub Al-Qirqisani, whose work on Jewish sectarians supplies sensational evidence that seems to link the disciples of Antigonus of Soko with the traditions found in the Damascus Document on the one hand, and with the Temple Scroll on the other. In 937 Qirqisani authored the *Book of Lights and Watch-Towers,* a large part of which was devoted to sects, the theme of a book written a century earlier by David ben-Marwan al-Muqammiz, from whom Qirqisani quotes extensively.[38] To enable the reader to evaluate the testimony of Muqammiz and Qirqisani, the relevant passages are included here in English translation:

1. Following the Rabbanites, the Zadokites appeared with their leaders, Zadok and Baethus. They (i.e., Zadok and Baethus) were, according to the Rabbanites, pupils of Antigonus of Soko, who succeeded Simon the Just and received instruction from him. Zadok was the first who exposed (the false views of) the Rabbanites by attacking them publicly, and he revealed some of the truth. He wrote a large book in which he attacked and criticized the Rabbanites. He did not adduce proofs for the things he said, but he wrote them as if from an oral tradition, except for one subject: the prohibition against (marrying) the daughter of the brother and the daughter of the sister. This he proved by the principle of *heqqeš* (analogy) with the (prohibition against marrying) the paternal or maternal aunt. As for Baethus, he used to say that the feast of Pentecost must fall on Sunday, which is the opinion of the Ananites and of the Karaite sect.[39]

2. Thereupon appeared the teaching of a sect called Magharians; they were

so called because their (sacred) books were found in a cave. One of them is the Alexandrian whose book is famous and (widely) known; it is the most important of the books of the Magharians. Next to it (in importance) is a small booklet entitled "The Book of Yaddua," also a fine work. As for the rest of the Magharian books, most of them are of no value and resemble mere tales.[40]

3. The account of the Zadokites, these are their doctrines: namely, they prohibit divorce, which is explicitly sanctioned in Scripture. Moreover, they make every month to be thirty days, and it is conceivable that in this matter they relied on the account of Noah. Also, they exclude the Sabbath from the total of the days of the feast of Passover, counting seven days in addition to the Sabbath, similarly with the feast of Sukkot. It is conceivable that it appeared to them that this obligation was from the passage in the book, "And on the eighth day he sent the people away" (1 Kgs. 8:66). Another verse says, "And on the twenty-third day of the seventh month, he sent the people away" (2 Chr. 7:10). The eighth day is the twenty-second, but if the Sabbath is excluded from the reckoning of the eight days, the eighth day is the twenty-third. David ben-Marwan al-Muqammiz has related some of their opinions. I shall make mention of him in the coming chapter.[41]

4. The Magharians fix the beginning of months by the appearance of the new moon. They adduce certain reasons in support of this (method); we shall mention them when we come to the discourse on the beginning of months and its indications. It is said that there are among them some who think that laughter is unlawful. Their interpretations of some passages in the Scriptures are altogether improbable and resemble foolish talk. David ben Marwan al-Muqammiz says in one of his books that the Sadducees ascribe corporeality to God and understand all the scriptural descriptions of Him which imply anthropomorphism in their literal sense. The Magharians are said to be opposed to this, i.e., they do not profess anthropomorphism; they also do not take these descriptions (of God) out of their literal meaning, but assert instead that these descriptions refer to one of the angels, namely, to the one who created the world. This (opinion) is similar to the view of Benjamin al-Nahawandi, which we shall explain later. But Baethus, who as we said was Zadok's companion, maintained, "The feast of Pentecost must fall on Sunday," which accords also with the views of our colleagues.[42]

Al-Qirqisani begins his account of the Zadokites by citing the rabbinic tradition that makes Zadok and Baethus disciples of Antigonus and goes on to explain their individual contributions to the development of sectarianism. In other words, at the very beginning, the Karaite historian makes it clear that he is using two sources here—one rabbinic and the other evidently Zadokite. The

Rabbanite source seems to be ARNA 5 or a similar tradition. It is difficult to establish what Qirqisani's Zadokite authorities were, but one would not go too far astray by conjecturing that he had before him works that went back to writings such as the Damascus Document, the Book of Jubilees, or even the Torah attributed to Zadok. The Cairo Genizah attests that some Qumran material still circulated in the tenth century and later.[43] Interestingly, Qirqisani, or rather his source here, David al-Muqammiz, explains the origin of the name of Magharians from the fact that their sacred writings were discovered in a cave. Does the Karaite author refer to caves in the Judaean wilderness? This may be the case, although the reports in Qirqisani on the various Jewish sects do suffer from obscurity and it is not always clear whether the Karaite author refers to sects still in existence in his own day or known to him only from their writings. What frustrates the reader is the author's terseness when referring to entire bodies of literature, of which hardly anything remains. It is only since the discovery of the Qumran library that some of Qirqisani's enigmatic statements can be unraveled.

Although Qirqisani frequently refers to the Rabbinates as a sect, he does grant that their doctrines had gained the ascendancy among the Jews in general prior to Zadok's exposition of their errors, since Rabbanite heresies had allegedly been introduced by Jeroboam I. In other words, Qirqisani presumes that the situation which existed in his own day had prevailed before Zadok arose to disagree with the doctrines of the Rabbanites. In so doing, Qirqisani is accepting the chain of tradition at face value. In contrast to Abot de-Rabbi Nathan, whose author is primarily interested in the teachings of Antigonus, Qirqisani's sole aim is to clarify the sectarian doctrines.

The question immediately arises as to whether this Zadok is to be identified with the one mentioned in CD 5:1–5. The differences are striking. The Damascus Document ascribes nothing to Zadok, only that the sealed book of the Torah was found in his day. According to Qirqisani, Zadok, the founder of the dissident movement, attacked the Rabbanites, disclosing the real nature of his dissatisfactions with Rabbinic Judaism. But Qirqisani added, "He did not adduce any proofs for the things he said, but he wrote them as if from an oral tradition, except for one subject, namely, the prohibition against (marrying) the daughter of the brother and the daughter of the sister. This he proved by the principle of *heqqeš* (analogy) with the paternal or maternal aunt."[44]

The discovery of the Damascus Document and 11Q Torah permits a glimpse into Qirqisani's sources, for both of these Qumranic texts prohibit marriage to one's niece. The Damascus Document says, concerning those who walk after *Ṣaw*,[45] "a man marries the daughter of his brother or the daughter of his sister. But Moses said, 'You shall not approach your mother's sister, she is your mother's kin.' The requirement concerning incest is written with regard to males but applies to women, so if the brother's daughter will uncover the nakedness of her father's brother, she is kin (as well))."[46] The argument here is polemical, for according to this passage, even the adversaries of the sect who can find no direct text for prohibition of the marriage ought to have derived it from the analogy of marriage with one's aunt. If the marriage to an aunt is incestuous, by extension, how can the marriage with a niece be sanctioned? But one need not question that the inspiration for this argument rests with the sectarian Torah, which the author could not cite since he was addressing people who had not accepted its sanctity. The prohibition is stated in 11Q Torah, "A man shall not marry his brother's daughter or his sister's daughter, it is an abomination."[47] Which of these two passages appears to be reflected in Qirqisani's account? The Karaite author makes three points concerning his source: (1) Zadok did not engage in polemics, limiting himself to general statements without bringing any proofs; (2) he prohibited marriage with the daughter of one's sister or brother; and (3) it is the only statement for which he did adduce proof, by citing the analogy from the biblical prohibition against marrying one's paternal or maternal aunt. In order to resolve the problem as to which work Qirqisani is relying on in these arguments, it is necessary to recall CD 5:7–11, which includes the quotation: "And Moses said: 'To the sister of your mother do not come near, she is the relative of your mother.' And the law of incest is written in the masculine but is equally applicable to females." To be sure, Qirqisani's third argument is found in the Damascus Document but not in 11Q Torah 66:16–17. The problem with assuming that he referred to the Damascus Document is that this is not the only statement for which it adduces proof, for it contains other polemical passages such as those dealing with polygamy and possibly divorce, for which Scripture is also cited.[48] A more basic problem with assuming that the reference here is to the Damascus Document is that Qirqisani seems to be referring to a book whose main subject is law,[49] whereas the Damascus Document is primarily theological and historical and only exceptionally becomes involved in legal polemics. It seems unlikely, therefore, that Qirqisani is referring to the Damascus Document.[50] Given the information now available, it appears that Qirqisani is reviewing 11Q Torah, which does prohibit the marriage of a niece, calling it an abomination.[51]

Qirqisani's other point, that the author of these prohibitions did not enter into polemics against his opponents, most certainly finds support in the extant fragments of the Qumranic Torah, whose author prescribes controversial ordinances, many of them intended to contrast with prevailing opinion, as well as with the canonical Torah, without introducing biblical support for his commandments.[52] The only problem with the presumption that Qirqisani here alludes to 11Q Torah 66:16–17 is that the present fragments do not contain the polemical statements attributed by Qirqisani to Zadok. But this last observation, that Qirqisani does not refer to 11Q Torah, remains uncertain since it happens that line 17 concludes col. 66, the top of col. 67 is missing, and the extant part of that parchment is blank. It may well be that the missing text on the top of col. 67 did contain the argumentative lines ascribed to it by Qirqisani. At any rate, the fact that a line in 11Q Torah brands the marriage of a niece as an abomination, analogous to the laws of incest duplicated from the canonical Torah, appears to reflect a polemical stance. Other evidence that ninth- and tenth-century Karaite writers possessed books by, or attributed to, Zadok which dealt with *qorbanot* (sacrifices)—presumably 11Q Torah—is discussed below.

Qirqisani also says that the Zadokites prohibited divorce even though Scripture explicitly sanctions it.[53] Prior to the discovery of the Qumranic Torah, scholars debated the question of whether CD 4:21, בחייהם (in their lifetime), prohibits only polygamy, as maintained by Ginzburg and Rabin,[54] or whether the use of this word implies that divorce is prohibited as well.[55] Even if Schechter is right regarding the meaning of this phrase in the Damascus Document, i.e., that it also includes divorce, it seems improbable that Qirqisani's source here is only CD 4:21, since this line is not clear and, at best, prohibits divorce only by implication.[56] Qirqisani, as far as is indicated, cited a source that prohibited it explicitly. Only 11Q Torah does so: "He (the king) shall not take in addition to her another wife, for she alone will be with him all the days of her life."[57] To be sure, the text of 11Q Torah only refers to the king, but by the time of Qirqisani, it was evidently taken to refer to all of Israel as well. Here again the evidence seems to suggest that Qirqisani had a source apart from the Damascus Document before him and that was 11Q Torah or a similar work.

On the other hand, there is some evidence that Qirqisani did have before him the text of CD 11:17–18: אל יעל איש למזבח בשבת כי אם עולת השבת כי כן כתוב מלבד שבתותיכם "Let no man offer on the Sabbath except the burnt offering of the Sabbath, for it is written, 'in addition to your Sabbath-offerings.'" The Karaite writer understood these lines, as do Rabin, Yadin, and Schiffman, as absolutely prohibiting the offering of sacrifices on the Sabbath.[58] Furthermore, Qirqisani seems to contradict many scriptural passages when he compares the differences in the two accounts of the festivities connected with the inauguration of the Solomonic temple as proof for the contention that the Sabbath was not reckoned as part of the seven days of Passover or the eight days of Sukkot.[59] But this prohibition, contrary to Yadin, is not found in the sectarian Torah and it certainly contradicts several ordinances in the Book of Jubilees, a work dependent on the scroll. The only source where Qirqisani, or al-Muqammiz, could find a basis for such an interpretation is CD 11:17–18, which lends itself to such a meaning, although, as pointed out above, it does not necessarily do so.[60] If this identification is correct, then the Karaite writers of the ninth and tenth centuries did utilize the Damascus Document in its present form, as it has come down to us in the Cairo Genizah. But this does not obviate the above-mentioned argument that Qirqisani or al-Muqammiz had before him the Qumranic Torah as well. In our view, then, it is presumed that Qirqisani's citation of a polemical reference to the marriage of a niece may be regarded as an allusion to the missing lines of col. 67 of 11Q Torah.

In addition to the probable availability of 11Q Torah and the Damascus Document, the Karaite writers of the ninth and tenth centuries must also have possessed a third Qumran work, perhaps resembling the Book of Jubilees. Qirqisani says that the Zadokites instituted a thirty-day month and twice states that the Feast of Pentecost was to fall always on a Sunday;[61] thus he indicates a Zadokite acquaintance with the Qumranic calendar, which is mentioned neither in the Damascus Document nor, evidently, in the Qumranic Torah, but is vehemently defended in Jub. 6:27-38. Does it follow, then, that the Karaite historian is alluding to the Book of Jubilees or to a work clearly dependent upon it? A possible hint that this is the case is Jubilees' embellishment of Genesis 7-8.[62] Jubilees not only mentions the solar calendar of thirty days, but does so in the account of Noah, evidently arguing that the solar calendar is imbedded in the 150 days of Gen. 7:11 and 8:3-4.[63]

The conclusion is inescapable. CD 5:5, when coupled with the Copper Scroll and the rabbinic and Karaite traditions, makes it virtually certain that Zadok is a real person.[64] The term *Ṣedoqym* in Qirqisani is equivalent to the *Beney Ṣadoq* in Qumran writings, not to the Sadducees of Josephus and the New Testament. Thus the treatment of Zadok and *Ṣedoqym* in Karaite literature attests to the existence of a continuous tradition that Zadok and his followers composed works such as the Qumranic Torah, the Book of Jubilees, and the Damascus Document, confirming what has been independently deduced from CD 5:5. The Karaite testimony also reaffirms the rabbinic tradition that identifies this Zadok as the disciple of Antigonus of Soko.

The Karaite testimony concerning Baethus is noteworthy as well. Both the rabbinic and the Karaite sources make Baethus a companion of Zadok and imply that he was his successor. The tradition in ARNA 5 and ARNB 10 regards Baethus as a contemporary of Zadok since both rebelled against the doctrine taught by Antigonus. The text clearly states, as does Qirqisani, that Zadok and Baethus were colleagues. But ARNA 5 and ARNB 10 say explicitly: "And two schisms arose from them, the Zadokites from the name Zadok; the Baethusians from Baethus." This statement suggests that from the beginning the two sects were clearly distinct. This is consistent with some statements in the talmudic tradition but departs from other references where the distinction is not clear. Since the sects were apparently closely related, it seems quite unlikely that they arose at the same time. What the rabbinic tradition is perhaps conveying, in its customary shorthand, is that Baethus was a disciple and successor to Zadok. Furthermore, Baethus introduced controversial elements that were not accepted by all the Zadokites. Thus the Zadokites and Baethusians were regarded by the rabbis sometimes as a single sect and sometimes as distinct movements.[65]

A similar ambiguity exists in the traditions transmitted by al-Qirqisani. Although he refers to Baethus as a companion of Zadok, Qirqisani also states that Zadok was the first to expose the Rabbanite errors, implying perhaps that Baethus' doctrines were enunciated thereafter.[66] Qirqisani attributes the view that the feast of the Pentecost must fall on Sunday to Baethus, although this opinion was shared by other sects, including the Karaites.[67] This seems to suggest that other calendrical reforms which Qirqisani ascribes to the Zadokites, such as the solar year in which each month has thirty days, also originated with Baethus.[68] In general, it may be inferred from the traditions preserved in Qirqisani that whereas Zadok was concerned with exposing the errors in the prevailing practices of Judaism in diverse areas, Baethus primarily advocated calendrical alterations.

One more point can be inferred from Qirqisani. Zadok, he says, differed from his successors in that he did not engage in debates but rather exposed the opposing views and stated his own opinions without adducing any proofs.[69] This seems to imply that the writers who followed Zadok, including Baethus, did just that. In other words, Baethus not only wrote books in which he presumably proposed his calendrical reforms, but unlike his predecessor, he did engage in polemics against the current practices of Judaism. Thus in spite of literary traditions which tend toward simplification in both Abot de-Rabbi Nathan and Qirqisani, the relationship between Zadok and Baethus resembles less that between co-founders of a sect and more that of a founder and reviser, such as the roles of Anan and Benjamin Nahawandi in the evolution of Karaism. Unlike Qirqisani, however, who takes no position on this subject, the talmudic tradition maintains that the Zadokites and the Baethusians long continued as two distinct groups.

What is the historical relationship between the two disciples of Antigonus of Soko? It would seem that the rabbinic and Karaite traditions make Baethus Zadok's younger contemporary. The Book of Jubilees may conceivably offer a clue to the identification of this Baethus. As has been shown above, the author of Jubilees is deeply indebted for his basic doctrines to 11Q Torah. To the information found in that source, the writer of Jubilees added a calendrical scheme. If so, Jubilees is to 11Q Torah what Baethus seems to be to Zadok. A logical consequence of this hypothesis is that just as Zadok may be regarded as the author of the Qumranic Torah, so Baethus would supposedly be the author of the Book of Jubilees. Intriguing as this possibility may be, it must be remembered that a personality by the name of Zadok is attested at Qumran, while what we know of Baethus remains obscure, coming exclusively from rabbinic and Karaite souces.

One point is clear: Ṣedoqym in Qirqisani does not necessarily or even primarily refer to the Sadducees, the patrician priests known from the writings of Josephus and the New Testament.[70] For Qirqisani, as well as for the author of Abot de-Rabbi Nathan, Ṣedoqym meant the followers of Zadok who, in the words of the rabbinic tradition, *pereś* (separated) himself from the Torah. Certainly neither the rabbis nor the Karaites would have admitted the alleged origin of Saducean nomenclature as going back to Solomon's priest and his descendants.[71] According to the Karaites, during the days of Solomon mainstream Judaism followed Karaite doctrine. It was Jeroboam who first introduced Rabbanite heresies into Judaism. For both Karaites and Rabbanites, the Sons of Zadok in Ezekiel 44 belonged to a line of legitimate priests, not to the heretics they labeled Ṣedoqym. There was never any doubt in rabbinic and Karaite historiography that the name Ṣedoqym goes back to Ṣadoq, the disciple of Antigonus. According to the Rabbanites, Zadok departed from the tradition by introducing heretical views. As the Karaites saw it, he restored the true meaning of the Torah that had been falsified since the days of Jeroboam. Both recognized the pivotal role of Zadok.

Zadok and Anan: The Qumranic Torah and the Karaites

Thus far the discussion has been restricted to al-Muqammiz and Qirqisani, since they alone among the Karaite writers record both Zadok and Baethus. We proceed now to deal with more Karaite and related sources that directly or indirectly seem to allude to Zadok or to his sectarian Torah.

Cogent as the arguments for the availability of Zadok's Torah to al-Qirqisani in 937 C.E. may seem to this writer, some readers may remain skeptical. What is the evidence that a copy of the Qumranic Torah was still available to the Karaite writers a dozen centuries after its composition? A critic may dismiss as unconvincing the evidence that Qirqisani attributed to Zadok the opposition to polygamy and divorce as well as to marriage to one's niece. Could it not be, one might ask, that Qirqisani's allusions refer not to the sectarian Torah but to the Damascus Document, which likewise alludes to these prohibitions, or to a work now lost? Fortunately, as this study underwent revision, additional testimony came to light that should, I think, prove convincing to even the most demanding reader. An unexpected dividend of this new evidence is the resolution of a puzzle that has split the historians of Karaism for more than a century. Did Anan ben David, the eighth-century founder of this sect, start something entirely new, as some historians have maintained;[72] or as others contend, did he build on the foundations of the ancient sectaries who flourished during the period of the Second Temple?[73]

The former argued that the Zadokites had disappeared soon after the destruction of the Second Temple in 70 C.E. and could not have influenced Anan and his Karaite followers. The latter, especially Abraham Geiger and Holdheim, countered that coincidence alone could not account for the similarities in the views of the ancient Sadducees and the Karaites, thus necessitating the presumption of Karaite indebtedness to the ancient sectarians.

Nearly a century ago, Abraham Harkavy, in his essay on the history of the ancient Jewish sects, cited the relevant Karaite evidence.[74] It is worth recalling that even prior to modern speculation on the possible linkage between the Zadokites mentioned in talmudic texts and the Ananites, savants such as Saadia Gaon (882–942), Abraham ibn Daud (1110–1180), and Maimonides (1135–1204)[75] routinely referred to the Karaite adversaries as *Ṣedoqym*. The evidence accumulated by Harkavy,[76] Hirschfeld,[77] Poznanski,[78] and Nemoy[79] sheds new light on the origin and development of the twelve hundred years of sectarian history.[80] What is crucial, however, is the fact of tenth-century citations from Zadok's writings for which there existed no source until the discovery of the sectarian scroll. All of these citations come from the disputations between Saadia Gaon and his opponents: the Palestinian coreligionists, on the one hand; and the Karaites, on the other. At issue with the Karaites was the antiquity of the Rabbanite reckoning of the calendar, which had abolished the ancient practice of attesting the beginning of the month by the visibility of each new moon. This revolutionary mode of reckoning, which laid down rules that barred any possibility of Passover ever falling on Monday, Wednesday, or Friday, was of relatively recent origin, from sometime between 600 and 800 C.E., probably nearer to the latter date. But Saadia, in response to the Karaite challenge to this mode of reckoning, blatantly asserted that the current mode of calendation went back to the days of Moses, and that reckoning by the visibility of the new moon was introduced by the Zadokites, whose founder was the disciple of Antigonus of Soko. Saadia, of course, knew better than that, but he was addressing himself to the lay population who were being drawn to the sectarians. The Karaite intellectuals easily refuted Saadia's false claims, and remnants of these retorts are preserved in various manuscripts which date from that time.

Indisputable proof that the text of the sectarian Torah was still known in the ninth century is the following citation from Saadia Gaon's polemics against the Karaites: "As for Judah of Alexandria, he says, 'Just as there is an interval of fifty days from the First Fruits of Barley and the First Fruits of Wheat, there are also fifty days from the First Fruits of Wheat and the First Fruits of Wine. (And the Feast of Wine) falls . . . at the end of the month of Tammuz. And between the First Fruits of Wine and the (season of the) First Fruits of Oil, fifty days, and the sacrifice of oil will be on the twentieth of Elul.'"[81] Citing this passage, Yadin attempts to create a chain of evidence for the existence of pentecontal feasts independent of the sectarian Torah.[82] In other words, this Judah of Alexandria, as well as the composer of the Temple Scroll, drew from other sources for the existence of these four Feasts of First Fruits. It seems more probable, however, that the Judah of Alexandria cited by Saadia is a Karaite author who had the sectarian Torah available to him.

This citation from Saadia Gaon, first published by Hirschfeld and reprinted by Poznanski,[83] has received much attention recently in connection with the pentecontal calendar found at Qumran. Jaubert and Yadin, however, have not recognized the significance of this fragment since they characterize it as a parallel source to the Qumranic material or, in the case of Yadin, to the so-called Temple Scroll.[84] In fact, however, this pentecontal calendar of the four Feasts of First Fruits—Barley, Wheat, Wine, and Oil—is a derivative of the Qumranic Torah, as no other text exists which ordains four Feasts of First Fruits. The name Judah of Alexandria also is of interest.[85] Although not further identified, we may presume that he is one of the Karaite opponents of Saadia from the Karaite community which flourished in Egypt. Since the fragment seems to be derived from Saadia's ספר הגלוי, composed in the first decades of the tenth century, it may be presumed that Judah lived either at that time or a generation or two earlier. Unfortunately, the context of the fragment is missing, though it is not unreasonable to postulate that it comes from a diatribe against the Rabbanites. On the other hand, this passage may be simply a remnant of a current calendar constructed by Judah for his Karaite coreligionists. In either case, this suggests that in the ninth or tenth century the Feast of First Fruits ordained in 11Q Torah continued to be observed among the Karaites of Egypt.

It seems not out of place, perhaps, to cite Philo's allusion to the Therapeutae of his own day, who likewise flourished in Alexandria.[86] Philo writes that "the people assemble after seven sets of seven days have passed, for they revere not only the simple seven but its square also, since they know its chastity and perpetual virginity. This is the eve of the chief feast which Fifty takes for its own, Fifty the most sacred of numbers and the most deeply rooted in nature, being formed from the square of the right-angled triangle which is the source from which the universe springs." The significance which Philo attributes to this feast as being the most distinct of the sect's observances suggests that these sectaries perhaps regarded 11Q Torah as a sacred text. Unlike the canonical Torah, in which Shavuot forms a routine feast, the sectarian Torah makes it the first of four successive seasons of First Fruits. Does this suggest the existence of a Qumranic diaspora in Alexandria in the first century C.E.?

Whether or not this is the case, there is no ambiguity in Saadia's citation of Judah of Alexandria. The passage quoted above forms part of a calendar which was typically Karaite.[87] It lists the First Fruits of Wine at the end (i.e., the twenty-ninth) of Tammuz and the Feast of First Fruits of Oil on Elul 20. These dates make it clear that the calendar is not the one found at Qumran, according to which these feasts would fall on the third day of the fifth month and on the twenty-second of the sixth month. On the other hand, the dates coincide perfectly with the Karaite calendar. The Karaites followed the Rabbanites in celebrating the fifteenth of Nisan according to a lunisolar reckoning. However, unlike the Rabbanites, who set the waving of the Omer on Nisan 16 (i.e., on the morrow of the Sabbath, which they interpreted as the first day of Passover), the Karaites understood morrow of the Sabbath literally, i.e., the Sunday after the beginning of Passover. Seven weeks later, also on a Sunday, the Karaites celebrated the feast of Shavuot. Now Judah of Alexandria's calendar diverges from the Rabbanite dating, according to which the Feast of New Wine would fall on the twenty-fifth of Tammuz and that of New Oil on the fifteenth of Elul.[88] But as the table on p. 158 shows, Judah of Alexandria's calendation corresponds perfectly with Karaite calendrical practice. The dates celebrated by Judah postulate that the fifteenth of Nisan and the first day of Nisan in that year fell on a Tuesday. According to the Karaites, the Omer was to be waved on the following Sunday, Nisan 20. Shavuot then fell on Sivan 10 in that year, the First Fruits of Wine on Tammuz 29, and the Feast of the First Fruits of Oil on Elul 20. All this provides indisputable evidence that some sectaries of Alexandria, apparently members of the faction-ridden Karaites, continued to observe precepts in the ninth and tenth centuries known to have been ordained only in 11Q Torah. We thus have a Qumranic-Karaitic diaspora a dozen centuries after the composition of the Qumranic Torah.

The Calendar of Judah of Alexandria

Nisan

S	M	T	W	T	F	S
		1	2	3	4	5
6	7	8	9	10	11	12
13	14	15	16	17	18	19
20*	21	22	23	24	25	26
27	28	29	30			

Tammuz

S	M	T	W	T	F	S
1	2	3	4	5	6	7
8	9	10	11	12	13	14
15	16	17	18	19	20	21
22	23	24	25	26	27	28
29*						

Iyar

S	M	T	W	T	F	S
				1	2	3
4	5	6	7	8	9	10
11	12	13	14	15	16	17
18	19	20	21	22	23	24
25	26	27	28	29		

Av

S	M	T	W	T	F	S
		1	2	3	4	5	6
7	8	9	10	11	12	13
14	15	16	17	18	19	20
21	22	23	24	25	26	27
28	29					

Sivan

S	M	T	W	T	F	S
					1	2
3	4	5	6	7	8	9
10*	11	12	13	14	15	16
17	18	19	20	21	22	23
24	25	26	27	28	29	30

Elul

S	M	T	W	T	F	S
			1	2	3	4	5
6	7	8	9	10	11	12
13	14	15	16	17	18	19
20*	21	22	23	24	25	26
27	28	29	30			

*This signifies the dates of the Pentecontal feasts.

Aside from al-Muqammiz, al-Qirqisani, and presumably Judah of Alexandria, there exists additional evidence for the continuity of the Qumran tradition in the tenth century. The following comes from a commentary on Exodus, attributed by Harkavy to Sahl Abu al-Sari,[89] whose apparent exegesis of Exod. 12:2 reads: "The ancients attempted to observe the new moon (for the setting of the new month). But Alfaiumi notes that the reason for this was Zadok and Baethus (who attempted to sabotage the traditional calendation). But the writings of the Zadokites are known and available to us and there is nothing whatsoever in them which that man (i.e. Alfaiumi) mentioned."[90] This passage contains the clearest proof of the continuity of the Qumranic tradition in the tenth century and provides further evidence that the founder of Qumran was believed to be a Zadok who had flourished during the Second Temple. Saadia Gaon, misusing the evidence of M. Rosh ha-Shanah 2:1, ascribed the origin of the talmudic practice of calendation by the visibility of the new moon to Zadok and Baethus. In other words, Zadok and Baethus, the disciples of Antigonus, like the Karaites of his own day, advocated the visibility of the new moon as a crucial element for setting the beginning of the month. According to Saadia, prior to Zadok and Baethus the lunisolar calendar had been determined by astronomical calculations alone. The author of this fragment retorted by calling Saadia a liar, saying that the writings of Zadok were extant and known to everyone but contained nothing of what Saadia ascribed to them.

Also of importance for our study is the continuation of this description: "For in the writings are found many things in which he opposed the Rabbanites of the Second Temple in matters concerning sacrifices and the like." What was the book which dealt with sacrifices and diverged from the traditional ritual? This reference could not be to the Damascus Document, for it contains only a few lines concerning sacrifices. Of course, it is possible that the Karaite writer is alluding to a work still lost, but at present such an assumption is superfluous. The contents of the book that Yadin calls the Temple Scroll and which I refer to as the Qumranic Torah correspond to a work which al-Sari identifies as "concerning sacrifices and the like." Certainly nearly half of the book, if not more, may be said to contain material relating to the rituals of the sanctuary. As Harkavy pointed out in 1893, there can be no question that this book ascribed to Zadok of the Second Temple was still extant, at least in Karaite circles, in the middle of the tenth century.

The positions of Qirqisani and Abu al-Sari were repeated in the twelfth century by Judah Hadassi, the author of אשכול הכופר, who reiterates the argument against Saadia by emphasizing the pivotal role of Zadok as the founder of the Zadokite movement.[91] It seems likely that the Zadokite writings attested to in the ninth and tenth centuries were still available to Judah Hadassi two centuries later.

The Karaite interest in Zadok was two-fold: first, the writings of Zadok still extant in their day seemed to be good ammunition for their arguments with the Rabbanites since both the Zadokite writings and the Ananites rejected the sanctity of the Oral Torah. For the Karaites, Zadok, the disciple of Antigonus, taught half the truth, Anan ben David the whole truth.[92] Second, it gave the Karaites proof that it was they, not the Rabbanites, who were the heirs of biblical Judaism. Zadok was not an innovator but the defender of the conservative views which were rejected by the radical Rabbanites. Incidentally, as was mentioned above, Karaite historiography traces the origin of the Rabbanites to Jeroboam, who had allegedly introduced it after the death of Solomon. In other words, Karaism represents the tribes of Judah and Benjamin while Rabbinism reflects the rebellious tribes of the northern kingdom. This argument parallels that of the Qumranic writers whose name for themselves is Judah and for their enemies is Manasseh and Ephraim. Is it not likely that the Qumranic writings inspired Karaite historians to identify the Rabbanites with Jeroboam and the Northern Kingdom?

The persistent tradition among the Karaite writers that the book dealing with the sacrifices, presumably the sectarian Torah, was authored by Zadok sheds new light on CD 5:1–5.[93] This passage claims that the scroll of the Torah which Moses received at Sinai had been sealed until the establishment of Zadok. There is here a direct conflict. The Karaite authors ascribed this book to Zadok himself, the Damascus Document ascribed it to Moses, who received it at Sinai. Which of these claims is correct? The following seems to have taken place. The author of the Damascus scroll and the Qumranites persisted in believing that Zadok was not the author of the sectarian Torah but merely its discoverer, thereby regarding it as at least equal if not superior to the canonical Law. Many of the Karaite factions, while aware of the Zadokite claims that this Torah was of Mosaic origin, rejected such an idea. Had they accepted the claim, they would have been required to accept the work's authority. They rationalized their stance by assuming that Zadok was not its finder but its author, and that Zadok, like Anan a millennium later, composed a Book of Commandments as a polemic against the Rabbanites. This made Zadok a forerunner of Anan, and thus the teachings of Zadok ought to be preserved and used against the Rabbanites, but it was unnecessary to follow them literally. On the other hand, a man like Judah of Alexandria must have given some credence to Zadok's own claims for the sanctity of his sectarian Torah.

Allusions to the Qumranic Sect in the Talmudic Literature

A puzzle, so far not solved, is the failure of the rabbinic tradition to allude directly to the Qumranic sect. Is it possible that the tannaitic sources do in fact make mention of the sectarians who flourished in the Judaean wilderness? There exists a universal assumption that *Ṣedoqym* and *Baytusym* in talmudic texts, when not inserted on account of censorship or by scribal alterations, refer to the Sadducean party which, according to Josephus and the New Testament, ruled in Jerusalem during the Second Temple. Now having shown that these terms may refer, at least in late rabbinic and Karaite literature, to the followers of Zadok, the question arises as to the identity of these terms in the Mishnah and Tosefta. Do they, as is generally taken for granted, always refer to the patrician Sadducees, or do the followers of Zadok and Baethus, known to us from the Qumran library, also receive mention? There is another possibility, that the rabbis of the Talmud no longer drew any distinction between the patrician Sadducees, recorded in Josephus, and the followers of Zadok, the disciple of Antigonus of Soko. Only a full analyis of the many texts which refer to the Zadokites and Baethusians can resolve these intriguing questions in the talmudic literature. For the sake of merely opening the issue, we cite several mishnaic and talmudic pasages which seem to fit the identification of the *Ṣedoqym* as the patrician Sadducees and point out other texts which, in spite of the prevailing view, may preferably be attributed to the Qumranite followers of Zadok. The resolution of still other pasages will require further investigation. In the following citations, the context makes it clear that the reference is to the patrician Sadducees:

(i) Megillat Taanit 10.

> *On the twenty-eighth of Tebet, the assembly was seated concerning matters of law.* As the *Ṣedoqym* were seated in the Sanhedrin (with) Jannaeus the king, and Salome the queen was seated next to him, there was not one Israelite sitting with them save Simeon son of Shetaḥ. (The people) raised questions and legal problems but they were not able to bring proof from the Torah. Simeon son of Shetaḥ said to them, "Anyone who knows how to adduce proof from the Torah ought to sit in the Sanhedrin." Once there was a controversial case and they could not adduce proof from the Torah except for one (Sadducean judge) who babbled against him saying, "Give me time and tomorrow I will answer." He (Simeon) gave him time. He went and sat by himself but was still unable to adduce proof from the Torah. The next day he was too ashamed to take his seat in the Sanhedrin, so Simeon son of Shetaḥ seated one of the disciples in his place. He said to them, "There are not to be less than seventy-one judges in the Sanhedrin." Thus he did every day until all of them (*Ṣedoqym*) were removed and the (legitimate) Sanhedrin of Israel was seated. The day that the Sanhedrin of the *Ṣedoqym* was removed and that of Israel was seated was proclaimed a festive day.

Whatever its historicity, this passage presumably refers to the patrician Sadducees, who, as attested by Josephus, were favored by Alexander Jannaeus over the Pharisees, here named simply Israel.[94]

(ii) Megillat Taanit 4.

> *On the fourteenth of Tammuz,*[95] *the book of decrees was abolished.* The book of decrees was before the *Ṣedoqym*: these deserve stoning, others are to be burned, still others to be slain by the sword, and others again are to be strangled. If during their deliberations someone would ask (for proof), they would show the inquirer the book. If he said (to them), "Whence do you adduce that this one is subject to stoning . . . ?" they did not know how to bring proof from the Torah. The sages said to them, "Is it not written, 'In accordance with the Torah which they shall teach you and according to the decisions which they shall tell you' (Deut. 17:11). It teaches that the laws are not to be written in a book."[96]

(iii) M. Sukkah 4:9

> Once a certain (priest) poured the (libation) water over his feet and all the people pelted him with their citrons.[97]

These and other passages conform to the popular disrepute of the Sadducees as boors and unlearned in the subtleties of the law. A telling example of this is found in the introductory paragraphs of M. Yoma, where the high priest is presumed to be illiterate and suspected of being sympathetic to the Sadducees. There is no need, then, to question that these passages allude to the patrician party of Jerusalem.

On the other hand, the passages cited below conflict with the stereotype of the boorishness of the Sadducees. Here the *Ṣedoqym* are as adept in midrashic dialectic as the sages. What is legitimate, however, is not proven by greater agility in scriptural analysis but on the basis of the legitimacy of their tradition and its authority. Theoretically, then, these texts may also refer to the patrician Sadducees, some of whom may have been learned. Nevertheless, given the Sadducean reputation for lack of learning and even lack of interest in the minutiae of the law—in contrast to the stringency found in Qumranic writings in matters of purity and defilement and in the literal interpretation of biblical texts—the presumption that the term *Ṣedoqym* refers to the Qumranic heretics seems cogent:

(i) Megillat Tannit 1 (M. Shekalim 3:1, 3; B. Menahot 65a)

> *These are the days upon which it is not permitted to fast. On some of them it is not permitted to mourn as well. From the first of the month of Nisan until the eighth, the Tamid was inaugurated; it is not permitted to mourn.* The Baethusians[98] used to say, "They accept the Tamid offering from individual donors. One person brings it one Sabbath, another brings it on the second Sabbath, while still another brings it on the third." How did they arrive at this? They said, "The one lamb thou shalt offer in the morning" (Num. 28:4), implying a

singular. The sages said to them, "You are not permitted to do this, for an offering must be brought by all of Israel, as it is said, 'Command the Israelites and say to them, "My sacrifice, My bread, for My offerings by fire, My pleasing odor, ye shall take heed to present to Me in its season"'' (Num. 28:2)."[99]

The dispute as to whether the daily sacrifice is to be taken from private offerings or from the temple treasury may be reflected in 11Q Torah 13:13–14, which takes its text from Lev. 7:8, making mention of the skin from the private sacrifice which the priest is permitted to keep for himself.[100]

(ii) Megillat Taanit 1 (M. Menahot 10:3; B. Menahot 65 a–b)

From the eighth of (Nisan) until the end of the season, a holiday is declared in which neither mourning nor fasting is permitted. Which holiday is this? It is the festival of Pentecost. Surely it was not necessary to record all the holidays mentioned in the scroll, but rather those over which they argued with the Baethusians, who used to say, "Pentecost always must fall on the day after the Sabbath, as it is written, 'You shall count from the day after the Sabbath' (Lev. 23:15)." The sages said to them, "The Sabbath of creation is called 'Sabbath' and days of the festivals are called 'Sabbath,' as it is written, 'On the first day (of Rosh ha-Shanah) is a Sabbath' (Lev. 23:24). The Day of Atonement is called 'Sabbath' as well, as it is written, 'You shall observe your Sabbath' (Lev. 23:32). All (special days) are called Sabbaths, as it is said, 'in addition to the Sabbaths of the Lord' (Lev. 23:38). It also says, 'Seven complete Sabbaths there shall be' (Lev. 23:15), and it is further written, 'Seven weeks you shall count' (Deut. 16:9). It says, 'The Feast of Weeks you shall keep, the First Fruits of the wheat harvest' (Exod. 34:22). 'On the Day of First Fruits when you present a cereal offering of new grain to the Lord during your (Feast of) Weeks' (Num. 28:26). It further says, 'You shall count from the day after the Sabbath, from the day you brought' (Lev. 23:15) and it says, 'You shall count fifty days' (Lev. 23:16). (In that case) your reckoning would not be fifty, but it could come to fifty-one, fifty-two up to fifty-six. Another line says, 'Seven days you should eat unleavened bread' (Exod. 12:15) and it is also written, 'Six days you shall eat unleavened bread' (Deut. 16:8). How can these two (disparate passages) be harmonized: seven days if reckoned from last year's grain and six days reckoned from the new grain? If you say, 'The day of the waving of the Omer is after the Sabbath' (i.e., Sunday), then it would not fall on the sixth day after the new grain."[101]

The stance taken by the Baethusians in the controversy with the Pharisees as to whether Pentecost should fall on a fixed day of the week is a distinctive feature of the Book of Jubilees, which became the basis for the Qumran calendar.[102] While this calendrical system is not necessarily evident in the Qumranic Torah, it is nevertheless clear that 11Q Torah sets the day of the raising of the Omer and the feast of Shavuot on the morrow of the weekly Sabbath, i.e., Sunday. Although this might have been the custom of other groups, as Qirqisani says,[103] the passionate differences between the groups are reflected in M. Menahot 11:3: "He used to call out three times for every matter, and they answered, 'Yea!' 'Yea!' 'Yea!' Wherefore was all this? Because of the Baethusians, who used to say: 'The Omer is not to be reaped on the morrow of the festival (Passover).'" Clearly their stance on this date makes the Zadokites (i.e., Qumranites) distinct from the rabbinic tradition.

(iii) Megillat Taanit 4

> Another opinion: From the book of decrees, the Baethusians used to say, "An eye for an eye, a tooth for a tooth."[104]

In the second section of the scholion, cited as "another opinion," the Baethusians are presented as supporters of a literal translation of the principle "an eye for an eye, a tooth for a tooth," also advocated in 11Q Torah 61:12. This is in contrast to the rabbis, who interpreted it as referring instead to monetary compensation.

(iv) M. Rosh ha-Shanah 2.1

> In a case when they (the Beth Din in Jerusalem) would not know him (the witness), they (the local Beth Din) sent with him another witness to attest to his reliability. Formerly, they received testimony concerning the new moon from anyone, but when the *mynym* (i.e. Baethusians) became disruptive, they decreed that they would only receive witnesses that they knew.

The visibility of the new moon played no role in the Jubilees calendar of thirty days per month plus four intercalary days throughout the year. The passionate resistance which the Baethusians maintained by allegedly hiring false witnesses to interfere with setting the calendar by the visibility of the new moon is understandable if the Baethusians supported the sectarian views recorded in Jubilees denouncing the lunisolar calendar.[105]

(v) M. Yadaim 4:6-7

> The Zadokites say, "We cry out against you, O ye Pharisees, for ye say, The Holy Scriptures render the hands unclean,' (and) 'The writings of Hamiram[106] do not render the hands unclean.'" Rabban Johanan b. Zakkai said, "Have we naught against the Pharisees save this!—for lo, they say, 'The bones of an ass are clean, and the bones of Johanan the high priest are unclean.'" They said to him, "As is our love for them, so is their uncleanness—that no man makes spoons of the bones of his father and mother."

He said to them, "Even so the Holy Scriptures: as is our love for them, so is their uncleanness; (whereas) the writings of Hamiram, which are held in no account, do not render the hands unclean." The Zadokites say, "We cry out against you, O ye Pharisees, for ye declare clean an unbroken stream of liquid." The Pharisees say, "We cry out against you, O ye Zadokites, for ye declare clean a channel of water that flows from a burial ground." The Zadokites say, "We cry out against you, O ye Pharisees, for ye say, 'If my ox or my ass have done any injury they are culpable, but if my bondman or my bondwoman have done an injury, they are not culpable'—if, in the case of my ox or my ass (about which no commandments are laid upon me) I am responsible for the injury that they do, how much more in the case of my bondman or my bondwoman (about whom certain commandments are laid upon me) must I be responsible for the injury that they do!" They said to them, "No!—as ye argue concerning my ox or my ass (which have no understanding) would ye likewise argue concerning my bondman or my bondwoman which have understanding?—for if I provoke him to anger he may go and set fire to another's stack of corn, and it is I that must make restitution!"

This passage from M. Yadaim lists four debates between the *Ṣedoqym* and the *Peruśym* which, in spite of general opinion, may not refer to the Patrician Sadducees:

1. Status of Scripture and other books with regard to cleanliness
2. Status of bones of dead with respect to purity
3. Status of *niṣṣoq* (uninterrupted flow of liquid) with regard to purity
4. Owner's responsibility for damage done by slaves or animals

In these passages, the Zadokites are not inferior to the rabbis in midrashic hermeneutics and are so regarded even by their rabbinic opponents—a far cry from the Sadducean high priest of M. Yoma 1:1–7 and from the illiterate and submissive *Ṣedoqym* in Megillat Taanit 4 and 10, who feel unsure of their own biblical antecedents. In the above mishnah we find learned men, on a par with the authors of CD 4–5, who can argue citation for citation. The presumption generally accepted that *Ṣedoqym* here means Sadducees cannot be defended once it is posited that some rabbinic citations refer to the Qumranites and their successors.

Recently discovered evidence substantiates this conjecture. Milik (*DJD* III, 225) quotes a fragment of a text which he labels 4Q Mishnah ("and concerning flowing liquids we say, 'they have no purity in them,' for the flowing liquids and their receptacle are to be regarded as one.") This passage provides the first external testimony for the historicity of M. Yadaim 4:7. The Qumranic writers agree that *niṣṣoq* (flowing liquids) do make the utensils unclean; moreover, they confirm that there existed an ancient controversy on that matter. "We say" in 4Q Mishnah corresponds to the polemical formula "The *Ṣedoqym* say . . . The Pharisees say . . . ." On the basis of this evidence, though fragmentary, it can now be asserted that M. Yadaim 4:7–8 reproduces a controversy between the sages and the Qumranic Zadokites.

A recent study by Joseph Baumgarten further substantiates the argument that what the Rabbis attributed to the *Ṣedoqym* frequently corresponds to the Qumranic tradition.[107] He discusses four controversies between the Pharisees and Sadducees (in our nomenclature, Zadokites) recorded in the Mishnah that are illumined by 11Q Torah. In three out of the four cases, including the question of *niṣṣoq*, Baumgarten argues, the Sadducean views harmonize with the stringency of the sectarian Torah in matters of ritual purity. The Pharisees permitted the contaminated priest who had immersed himself without waiting for the sunset of the seventh day (the *Ṭebul Yom*) to prepare the red heifer. The Zadokites, however, were strict in this matter, requiring the onset of evening prior to his engagement in the preparation of the ashes. The Zadokites as cited in the Mishnah (passage quoted above) make prescriptions with similar stringency for matters related to bones. Baumgarten cogently concludes, "We have found their complaints about Pharisaic laxities in the sphere of purity to be consistent with the laws found in the Temple Scroll and other Qumran writings."[108]

The chronological aspects of the *Ṣedoqym* mentioned in mishnaic and talmudic sources need to be discussed. The putative assumption that *Ṣedoqym* refers to the Sadducees, as it sometimes does, has given rise to the postulate that these discussions refer to the Pharisees and Sadducees of the period of the Second Temple and no longer had any relevance for the authors of the Mishnah in the second century C.E. But once it has been shown that some of the doctrinal elements and literary compositions of the Qumranic sect remained a living tradition at least as late as the tenth century, a new question presents itself. Must it be that all of the disputations with the Zadokites recorded in the Mishnah took place in the period of the Second Temple? Could it not be that some involved the sect's living adherents in the mishnaic era? The question does not refer only to possible stragglers who survived the *Ḥurban* and could still engage in disputes with Rabban Johanan ben Zakkai. It raises the issue whether a vibrant Qumranic sect continued which could have influenced Anan in 760 when he founded the movement eventually called Karaite. Harkavy attempted to explain the linkage between the sectaries of the Second Temple with the early Karaites by postulating that Anan searched for ancient writings that could serve as a basis for his opposition to the Rabbanites.[109] In other words, whatever Anan had rescued from the ancient Zadokites came only from books, not from a living tradition. This view sees unlikely. If one postulates a continuum from Zadok to Anan, it need not be accounted for on a literary basis alone. It seems more likely that the Ananites as well as the other movements that stood in opposition to the Rabbanites did not start completely *de novo,* but were inspired by what must have been remnants of older sects. It seems reasonable to presume that survivors of Qumran and their sympathizers elsewhere flourished during the centuries of the mishnaic and talmudic sages. It is they who account for the elements which bridge the Zadokites and the Ananites. It follows that *Ṣedoqym* in the Mishnah, Tosefta, and Talmuds need not be restricted to the heretics of the Second Temple, but could include groups who remained vibrant in spite of the growing predominance of Talmudic Judaism. The hypothesis that the *Ṣedoqym* were living opponents of the tannaim and amoraim, with a Torah and an exegesis of their own, makes sense in the light of the vehement anger directed toward them in the talmudic literature. A Qumranic diaspora, apparently presumed in Philo's account of the Therapeutae of Alexandria, links up with Judah of Alexandria cited by Saadia Gaon on the one hand and with the multiplicity of similar heresies in Mesopotamia and Persia on the other.

Greek Evidence

The credit or, as some scholars believe, the blame for identifying the Essene sect with the Zadokites of the Judaean wilderness belongs not to modern savants but to a Byzantine monk or monks who authored the versatile, if exasperating, lexicon of ancient Greek literature called the Suda. The Suda's entry under the heading of *Essaioi* (Essenes) reads as follows:

> Jews who are ascetics arising from those Pharisees and Scribes who were more extreme in their practice, offspring of Jonadab, the son of Rechab the righteous (or "the son of the Righteous"), are those who [possess] greater mutual love and piety than the other [groups]; they turn away from pleasure as evil, but they accept discipline, self-control, and not surrendering to the passions as a virtue. They disdain marriage for themselves, but they even take the young children of others, conduct their education like kinsmen, and mold them to their own practices. They reject every disgraceful act and practice every other virtue. They cultivate ethical discourse, enduring all things with contemplation. Thus Essenes are also called, the name reveals this, contemplatives, because the Essenes are more noble and thought to be considerably above the Pharisees, according to the populace.[110]

The author of this entry shows a familiarity with the accounts of the Essenes in Philo and Josephus and probably knew the frequent discussions about the sect in Christian literature, but was he also familiar with Zadokite writings?[111] The hint for such a possibility comes from the Suda's genealogy of the alleged founders of the Essenes: "Jonadab, son of Rechab *tou dikaiou*"—information which he did not get from either Josephus or Philo. Context alone permits two alternative translations of the epithet, either "the righteous" or, as a gentilic, "the son of the Righteous." Either way, the phrase seems to be a translation from the Hebrew *haṣṣadyq* or *Ṣadoq*. Whichever rendition one chooses, the interesting question is the source of the Suda's epithet linking the Rechabite's way of life with *ṣadyq* or Zadok. None of the Hebrew or Greek sources shows any recognition that Jonadab, the founder of the movement, was either called "the righteous" or that his grandfather or patriarch was named Zadok. Certainly there is no hint of it in Jeremiah 35. It seems likely that the Suda attribution of the honorific "righteous" or the gentilic "Zadok" to the alleged founder of the Essenes reflects a desire to link the ancient sectaries with the Christian monastic movement. Equally plausible, however, seems to be the postulate that the Suda's entry on the Essenes reflects an acquaintance by the eighth- or ninth-century Byzantine authors with a work such as the Zadokite fragments, whose main theme is devoted to the Commune, not referred to as much by the name *Yaḥad* as by the appellation "Men of Righteousness" or "Sons of Zadok." Another possibility is that the Suda's *tou dikaiou* assigns to Jonadab son of Rechab the title of Teacher of Righteousness.

One unexpected conclusion in this study has been the finding that the rabbinic traditions contain allusions to the Qumran sectaries. Certainly the rabbis and the Karaites conflated their views of the patrician Sadducees, known well from Josephus and the New Testament, with the followers of Zadok and Baethus, whose literature was in part still available in the tenth and eleventh centuries. Some of the references in rabbinic literature to *separym ḥiṣṣonym*[112] or *siprey Ṣedoqym* may in fact refer to sacred texts penned at Qumran. One may go even further. The putative assumption that the Qumranic sect ceased to exist after 70 is inaccurate. Many references in the Mishnah and Talmud to the *Ṣedoqym* seem to speak not of a sect of the past but of a continuous living tradition.[113] Abraham Geiger and Abraham Harkavy, on the basis of evidence available at that time, argued that Anan and his followers dipped deeply into the Sadducean writings, remnants of which were preserved in the Talmudic traditions.[114] Adolf Büchler and Solomon Zeitlin branded the Damascus Document a Karaite diatribe. These scholars were certainly partially correct. To be sure, Karaism cannot be linked with the patrician Sadducees. Nor did Karaism as a whole ever fully accept the Qumranic doctrines, but it borrowed enough from them to justify the traditional claim which identified Anan's Karaites with the disciples of Zadok and Baethus. Certainly Karaite historiography takes full cognizance of its Zadokite roots. The most dramatic evidence, however, of Karaite indebtedness to Zadok's sectarian Torah is, as we have seen, the calendar of the eighth and ninth centuries which notes the pentecontal feasts of First Fruits in an Ananite calendar. To a large extent, it may be said that the Karaite movement, or at least many of its factions, were part of the continuum of the Qumranic diaspora.

Chapter 5
Chronology

The Succession of the High Priests
and the Tobiads

When dealing with chronological questions, Qumranic scholarship usually starts with the proposition that only the Hasmonean and Roman periods have any relevance.[1] It will be shown in this chapter, however, that the roots of Qumran go back to the era of the Diadochi, especially to the time when Judaea was part of the Ptolemaic state. The rise of Zadok and his movement seems to have taken place at the end of the third and the beginning of the second century B.C.E.. Unfortunately, Josephus, so excellent for the Hasmonean and Herodian eras, is in this period terse and fragmented.[2] What he does supply has been the subject of heated debates. The chronology of the high priests after Jaddua, the last Aaronide chieftain mentioned in *AJ* 11:302 and 347, remains obscure. Jaddua appears at the end of the scriptural list of post-exilic high priests,[3] apparently the very last who served under Persian rule. What is known concerning his high-priestly successors in the post-biblical period comes from Josephus' list of high priests, supplemented by hints from other sources. The absence of a chronological framework is a serious impediment to the study of this era. The lacuna in Josephus' account is partly remedied by the Zeno papyri as well as the rabbinic tradition, which preserved facts not mentioned by the historian.[4] What follows is an attempt to create a chronological unit out of the information provided by these sources. The problem divides itself into two parts: (a) the chronology of the high priests from Onias I, who followed Jaddua, to Menelaus, sometimes referred to as Onias-Menelaus, and the chronology of the Tobiads, a clan of sheiks who controlled parts of Ammon from pre-exilic times, becoming influential and intermarrying with Jerusalem's aristocracy; (b) the chronology of the successors of the oral law listed in the Mishnah.

As to the high-priestly succession during the period of the Diadochi, Josephus names the following succession without recording anything significant about the terms of the first four:[5]

Onias I	Simon the Just, II
Simon the Just, I	Onias III
Eleazar	Jason
Manasseh	Menelaus (Onias-Menelaus)
Onias II	Alcimus

171

Nothing is known of the period of Onias I's priesthood except that Josephus names Jaddua as the high priest in the mythical account of the Jerusalem high priest's encounter with Alexander in 332 B.C.E.[6] Since he is listed as the successor of Jaddua,[7] Onias I presumably served in office after 332 B.C.E.. In rabbinic legends the figure who succeeded Onias I is Simon the Just.[8] If Josephus' chronology is accepted, the four successive high priests after Jaddua—Onias I, Simon I, Eleazar, and Manasseh—began their terms not earlier than circa 332 B.C.E. and continued until circa 240 B.C.E.; presumably throughout most of this period the office was held by Simon I. If some credence is to be given to the rabbinic tradition, Simon I ruled before 330.[9] Three high priests—Simon I, Eleazar, and Manasseh—then occupied this position between 332 and 240 B.C.E..

The crucial problem in this succession is to date the period of Onias II. *AJ* 12:157–179 names him as the high priest of a venerable age at the time when Joseph, son of Tobias, became the tax-farmer in Coele-Syria. The old man, Onias, had endangered the country by his failure to pay tribute to the Egyptian authorities. Here is the crux of the problem. Josephus states in two places that Joseph held the office of tax-farmer for twenty-two years.[10] The romanticized account of this Joseph contains information, however, that places Joseph's office after 193, when Ptolemy V Epiphanes was given Cleopatra by Antiochus III, with the taxes of Coele-Syria as her dowry.[11] This information being erroneous, the question has been whether credence can be given to the chronological elements of the account of Joseph's long service and, if so, when it took place. Tcherikover proposed that the visit of Joseph to Ptolemy took place during the reign of Ptolemy Euergetes (246–222 B.C.E.) in 242 B.C.E.; however, he argued that Joseph received the tax concession only during a later visit to the same ruler, between 230 and 220 B.C.E.[12] Many scholars have followed Tcherikover's lead; however, frequently Joseph's leasing of the right to tax Coele-Syria has been dated closer to 242 B.C.E.[13] If this is so, Onias, who is listed then as an old man, must have begun his priesthood some twenty years before that, around 260 B.C.E. Simon the Just II, successor to Onias II, would then have been assigned the implausibly long reign of circa 240–187, since we read of his death around 187 B.C.E. in *AJ* 12:224. The other problem with the conventional chronology is the time table of the Tobiads. Tobias, the sheik of Ammon, a correspondent of the Zeno papyri during the reign of Ptolemy II Philadelphus (282–246 B.C.E.), was the father of the aforementioned Joseph, the tax-collector whose death took place circa 187 B.C.E. according to *AJ* 12:224. Assuming Joseph became tax-collector at the age of thirty in 242, he would have been eighty-five at his death; if, however, he became tax-collector at forty, he then would have lived to the venerable age of ninety-five.

Although this chronology is not inconceivable, the proposal first made by Büchler seems more plausible, harmonizing more closely with what is known from Josephus and 2 Maccabees.[14] According to this reckoning, Joseph became tax-farmer in 219 B.C.E. under the rule of Ptolemy IV Philopator (222-205 B.C.E.), serving until the end of the Ptolemaic control of Coele-Syria in 198. Philopator, upon assuming office, wished to increase his revenue, which gave an opening to Joseph's ambitions. At that point, Onias was an old man; he died soon thereafter and was succeeded by Simon the Just II in 218-215 B.C.E.[15] If Joseph became tax-collector at the age of forty, he died at the age of seventy-seven years in 187. This coheres with Josephus, who apparently places the death of Simon II and Onias III's assumption of office after 187 B.C.E.[16] Simon the Just's rule, then, extended over thirty years, from circa 215 to 187-185, for he was still alive during the struggle among the heirs of Joseph over the paternal inheritance.[17]

As to Onias III, his office began sometime after 187, as attested in *AJ* 12:224, but he remained in office at the time of the accession of Antiochus IV Epiphanes in 175.[18] The question of when Onias III was replaced by his brother Jason does not have as clear a solution. Some scholars say that this occurred immediately after Antiochus IV's accession, others a year or two later.[19] After Onias had served three years, apparently in 172 or 170, the king replaced him with Menelaus, the Hellenizing high priest who was slain by Antiochus V Eupator circa 162 B.C.E.[20]

The virtue of this chronology is that it conforms to what is known from sources other than Josephus. 2 Macc. 3:11 reports that in 180 or 179 Seleucus IV ordered Heliodorus to sack the gold stored in Jerusalem's sanctuary. To dissuade Heliodorus from going through with this order, Onias noted that the temple's treasury contained the gold belonging to the powerful Tobiad sheik, Hyrcanus. In summary then, given the available evidence, the following chronology of the high priests seems plausible:

Jaddua—up to 330	Jason—175-173 to 172-170
Onias I—after 330	Menelaus—172-170 to 163-162
Simon I	Alcimus—163-162 to 159
Eleazar	Position unfilled—159 to 152
Manasseh	Jonathan—152 to 142
Onias II—240 to 218-215	Simon—142 to 134
Simon II—218-215 to 187-185	John Hyrcanus—134 to 104
Onias III—187-185 to 175-173	

The Chain of the Qabbalah

We have argued in this study that Zadok's unveiling of the new Torah marks the beginning of what eventually became the Qumran sect. It is this Zadok who may have been memorialized in a splendid monument, as attested in 3Q 15 (Copper Scroll) 11:2-7. The rabbinic and Karaite traditions name Zadok and a certain Baethus as the founders of two heretical movements. It was shown above that this tradition, though found only in texts edited during the ninth and tenth centuries, probably preserves valuable data for unraveling the roots of Qumran. But before evaluating this data, it is necessary to turn to the rabbinic chronology concerning Zadok.

Zadok in the rabbinic and Karaite traditions is the disciple of Antigonus of Soko, whose succession is found in M. Abot 1:1–4:

Prophets	Antigonus of Soko
Men of the Great Assembly	Jose son of Joezer
Simon the Righteous	and Jose son of Johanan

What is the time implied in this passage? Being a list that attempts to reveal the roots of the rabbinic tradition, i.e., the Pharisaic leadership, this part of the rabbinic chain has been the subject of many conjectures. For the subject under discussion, the dates of Simon the Just and Antigonus are of consequence. A subject of considerable controversy is the enigmatic institution known as the Great Assembly, considered to be of paramount importance by the rabbis. Opinion differs widely on the date and nature of the institution called in the Mishnah *Keneset Haggedolah* (Great Assembly).[21] In fact, however, the problem stems from modern scholarship, which refuses to recognize the rabbinic approach to ancient chronology. As Seder Olam and other talmudic sources make clear, the Great Assembly is a part-historical, part-fictive institution.[22] The historical reference to the assembly is recorded in Nehemiah 10, when Ezra led the people in affirming the covenant. Its fictive nature is shown in the abridgement of the period from the first year of the rebuilding of Jerusalem's temple by Zerubbabel until the time that the Macedonians conquered the Near East. Rabbinic chronography compressed a period of nearly two hundred years into fifty-two years, making Ezra and Nehemiah the contemporaries of Zerubbabel and the prophets Haggai, Zechariah, and Malachi on the one hand, and of Artaxerxes on the other.[23] Chronologically the "last" (literally, the remnant) of the men of the Great Assembly, by which Abot 1:2 dates Simon the Just, could only mean tht it was he who around 332 received Alexander the Great on his fictitious entry into Jerusalem.[24] It may additionally mean that Simon was the high priest at the time when prophecy formally ceased in Israel and the era of the *Ḥakamym* began. Traditionally it was considered that these events coincided with the beginning of the Seleucid era in 311/310 B.C.E. Strictly speaking, the rabbis compressed the period 522–312 B.C.E. into two generations, thus reducing the epoch of the Second Temple from 585 years to 420 years.

If taken literally, "Antigonus of Soko received (the Torah) from Simon the Just" means that he served as Simon's disciple. This, however, does not necessarily reflect the actual intention of the phrase. For Abot 1:4 tells us that Jose son of Joezer and Jose son of Johanan "received from Antigonus." It is generally taken for granted, perhaps correctly, that Jose son of Joezer and Jose son of Johanan, the first of the five pairs (*zugot*), died during the persecution by Antiochus IV (167–164 B.C.E.).[25] These two disciples are the first of the five pairs that end with Shammai and Hillel. Translated chronologically, the five *zugot* were intended to telescope some 236 years from the beginning of the Maccabean period in 167 B.C.E. to the destruction of the Second Temple in 70 C.E.[26] Here each of the pairs no doubt represents several generations; e.g., under the name of Hillel they actually embrace four generations (Hillel, Simon, Gamaliel, and Simon). Whatever the facts, Jose son of Joezer and his colleague are understood to have flourished during the time of the Syrian oppression and the Hasmonean liberation (170–164 B.C.E.).[27] The word קבל (received) therefore does not necessarily denote actual discipleship, but only that these sages were significant links in the chain. In the light of rabbinic chronology, Abot 1:3 dates Antigonus of Soko sometime between 311 and 170 B.C.E. In other words, during the period from the beginning of the Seleucid era in 311 B.C.E. until the time of the Hasmoneans he was the single personality whose name was worth preserving. The fact that Antigonus has no patronymic implies that he was a well-known personality who required no further identification. Since no teaching outside Abot is attested in the name of Antigonus—the tradition never mentions him elsewhere—why is he listed in the chain of the *qabbalah*? As recorded in Chap. 4, ARN suggests that the first pair, Zadok and Baethus, who in fact did study under Antigonus, were omitted on account of their sectarianism. Abot lists Antigonus in order to exculpate him from the misinterpretations ascribed to him by his disciples. In other words, the listing of Antigonus in Abot's chain of tradition was intended to allude to the rise of sectarianism under the leadership of Zadok and Baethus. Thus, the mention of Antigonus explains the terms "Zadokites" and "Baethusians," frequently mentioned in tannaitic texts.

In spite of his errant disciples, Antigonus himself was without blemish, a worthy representative, indeed the first recorded name, from the era of the sages, which had begun with the men of the Great Assembly. What Abot de-Rabbi Nathan really says is that the discipleship of Zadok made Antigonus significant enough to have been included as the intermediary between Simon the Just and Jose ben Joezer. In other words, according to Abot de-Rabbi Nathan, Abot 1:3 is intended to date the origins of the Zadokites and Baethusians, both frequently mentioned in the Mishnah and Talmud.

Since Abot de-Rabbi Nathan and presumably the Damascus Document claim that the Zadokite and Baethusian sects were founded by Antigonus' disciples, it is necessary to analyze further the range of the period that may be assigned to the first sage, who was neither a member of the Great Assembly nor one of the five *zugot*. As has been frequently noted, the name Antigonus is a Macedonian name, making him the first of the sages whose appellation

reflects Greek influence.[28] In fact, however, it shows more. The name was
probably given to a Jewish child as a tribute to Antigonus Monophthalmus,
who ruled Coele-Syria between 316 and 301 B.C.E.[29] It is doubtful that the
inhabitants of Soko would have dared to name their sons Antigonus after the
battle of Ipsus (301 B.C.E.), when the Ptolemies and the Seleucids successively
controlled the area. It was only during the Hasmonean period that this name
gained new popularity, as attested by the penultimate Hasmonean king,
Antigonus, son of Aristobulus (d. 37 B.C.E.). It follows that although Abot 1:3
suggests the period of Antigonus is between 311 and 170 B.C.E., the name
Antigonus itself makes it likely that the birth of this sage occurred before 301
B.C.E.

On the other hand, CD 1:1–10, it is argued below, dates Zadok's unveiling
of the new Torah in 196 B.C.E.[30] Presumably Zadok was not only the discoverer
of this new Torah but its author. He must have written this work sometime
before 196, say 200 B.C.E.[31] Can the chronology implied in the Qumranic writings be reconciled with what seems to be the rabbinic reckoning dating the
death of Antigonus around 240? If the two have validity, Antigonus was an
old man and Zadok must have been a young disciple of the venerable sage. In
the chronology assumed below, Zadok's death takes place about 170 B.C.E.[32] It
is not impossible, therefore, that Zadok, and perhaps Baethus, was in fact a
pupil of Antigonus of Soko, although the statement "disciples of disciples"[33]
may be construed as meaning that Zadok was not a disciple of Antigonus, but
that there was a master who was the student of Antigonus and the teacher of
Zadok. At any rate, since Qumran is absolutely silent concerning the antecedents of Zadok, even omitting the customary patronymic, attention must be
paid to the traditions imbedded in the rabbinic and Karaite literature. Thus it
may be presumed that Antigonus, the teacher of Zadok, taught during the
high-priesthood of Eleazar and Manasseh, and possibly that of Onias II.
Zadok, his disciple, presumably attained maturity during the period of Onias
II and Simon the Just II. Conjectural as this chronology is, it does support the
hypothesis that sectarianism began to take root in the third century B.C.E.

Chronography at Qumran

The recent trend in scholarship has been to date the beginning of the Qumran
sect in successively earlier time periods. The variety of propositions set forward to identify the wicked priest, i.e., one of the high priests in Jerusalem's
temple, will exemplify the point. It seemed to Cecil Roth and G. R. Driver that
the wicked high priest refers to one of the sacerdotes appointed by the Herodian rulers or by the Zealots who opposed them.[34] For Dupont-Sommer,
John Hyrcanus II (63–40 B.C.E.) was meant;[35] Carmignac and others, because
of the name of the Seleucid king recorded in Pesher Nahum, who was identi-

fied as Demetrius III (95–88 B.C.E.), believed that the wicked priest was Alexander Jannaeus (103–76 B.C.E.).[36] As a result of the paleographic study of the types of script, Cross and Vermes believe that either Simon the Hasmonean (142–134 B.C.E.)[37] or his brother Jonathan (152–142 B.C.E.) was meant.[38] Has the timetable of Qumran been set back far enough or will it continue to shift still further? The more important question concerns the methodology adopted to date the Qumran Commune. Is it valid to base the period of the sect's existence on a single conjecture, be it the identity of the wicked priest, the Kittim who invade the Holy Land, or some other historical figure? The answer is an emphatic negative. Diverse as the proposed chronological schemes are, at least four faulty premises undergird these studies: (1) that a movement of immense complexity, which possessed a literature of many genres, could have originated and reached full maturity within a single generation, say two or three decades; (2) that the roots of Qumran are to be sought during, or in the aftermath of, the Maccabean victory, never examining the possibility that they may antedate the persecution of Judaism during the reign of Antiochus IV; (3) that Josephus' *Jewish Antiquities* contains the key to resolve the puzzle of Qumranic chronology; and (4) that the chronological indices of the Dead Sea Scrolls are themselves worthless since their authors did not know or care about the past.

The chronology of Qumran proposed in this study rests on two elements, one seemingly simple, the other rather complex. Only when these two elements are mutually supportive is there a probability that one is on the right track. Internal and external consistency serve as controls against the tendency to confirm preconceived ideas. The simple element is that the chronology reported in the sect's own texts may in fact be historical. Although chronomessianic in form, these dates may be accurate. While chronography frequently tailors the timetable of events according to its own formulas, it does not follow that this is always the case. Why not start with the premise that CD 1:1–10, which dates the beginning of the sect in the three hundred and ninetieth year after the destruction of the Solomonic temple, records what the author thought actually occurred? It might be objected that since Ezra, the headings of the book of Daniel, Seder Olam, and the talmudic sages disregarded real chronology, the supposition that the Qumran sectaries accepted it is untenable. Daniel, for example, may be said to be interested strictly in chronomessianism. Certainly the rabbis tailor chronology to midrash, not vice versa. The answer to such a challenge is that the people of Qumran, like their Karaite successors, seem to have had an abiding interest in chronology. For the Damascus Document, chronology seems to be basic to its members rather than a result of its exegesis. The fact, therefore, that the other Jewish sects ignored precise historical sequence does not necessarily require the assumption that the author of the Damascus Document did likewise. Certainly the Karaites, who seem to have borrowed many Qumranic elements, tended to be stringent in their chronological statements, without question more so than their Rabbanite adversaries. Additional evidence that the dates given in CD 1:1–11 are roughly historical is found, as will be shown below, in Dan. 11:14. The timing of the events reported here brings independent evidence for the rough accuracy of the Damascus Document's chronology. Moreover, the fact that the complex data, i.e., the relative dating of the literature, coincides with this material is crucial evidence in support of the chronology proposed in this study. The evidence collected earlier in Chap. 2 suggests that the fragments of 11Q Torah are the first clearly identifiable documents of what eventually developed into a sectarian literature of many genres. The Book of Jubilees, a work seemingly devoted to the propagation of the sanctity of the Qumranic Torah, likewise belongs to the earliest stages of this heretical movement. On the other hand, the Thanksgivings (הודיות) and, especially, the Community Rule (סרך היחד) belong to the time when the Commune attained its maturity. The pesherite biblical commentaries were written in between these early and relatively late products of sectarian thought.

Aside from the complex literary history of the sect, the Qumranic writings may be made to tell the intricate story of the origin and early unfolding of the movement prior to its assuming the name of "men of the *Yaḥad* (Commune)." For historical purposes, 11Q Torah and Jubilees cannot be placed side by side with works such as the Community Rule and the Thanksgivings since the former still seem to be unaware of what we know as the Qumranic movement, while the latter takes it for granted. Only when the temporal implications of the diversity of Qumranic literature are taken into acount will the unfolding of its literary genres be discerned. Attention must also be paid to the sect's own timetable of its origin and early development. When the timetables of literary history and organizational development are synchronized to present a unified picture, the way will be opened toward resolving the problems surrounding the early chronology of Qumran.

The Sect's Own Timetable

However one treats the timetable given in CD 1:1–10, it ought not to be ignored—as has been the tendency of commentators on this treatise ever since its discovery. The opening lines of the Damascus Document read as follows:

> Therefore hear now, all you who know justice, and comprehend the words of God! For He tries all flesh and will judge all those who scorn Him. For because of the unfaithfulness of those who abandoned Him he hid his face from Israel and its sanctuary and delivered them up to the sword. But remembering the Covenant of the Patriarchs, He left a remnant to Israel and did not deliver them to destruction. And in the time of wrath, three

hundred and ninety years after He had delivered them into the hand of Nebuchadnezzar king of Babylon, He visited them, and caused a root of planting to spring from Israel and Aaron to possess His land and to grow fat on the good things of His earth. And they understood their iniquity, and recognized that they were guilty men. But they were like blind men, and like men who groping seek their way for twenty years. And God considered their works, for they had sought Him with a perfect heart; and He raised up for them a Teacher of Righteousness to lead them in the way of his heart.[39]

It is generally taken for granted that the two numbers in this passage are sheer literary devices not to be taken seriously since the cipher 390 years was intended to recall Ezek. 4:5, where the prophet tells how the Lord commanded him to lie on his side for 390 days to atone for Israel's sins. The number 390 and the twenty years, according to scholarly opinion, have no chronological value, having been intended as messianic numerology.[40] As first conjectured by Bruce, the 410 years form part of a larger number, the seventy sabbatical weeks of 490 years, which, according to Dan. 9:24, would elapse between the destruction of the temple and the eschaton.[41] Scholars find the deficit of eighty years in a forty-year period for the leadership of *Moreh Ṣedeq* and another forty years recorded in CD 20:15, which elapsed after his death, the symbolic equivalent of the duration of Israel's wandering in the wilderness. In other words, the 410 years have no intrinsic significance save as elements of the chronomessianic total of 490 years. Ezekiel's 390 days, translated here into years, serve as a convenient cipher for a chronomessianic numbering, but need not, according to the reigning view, concern the student of history.

There is no compelling reason to accept this hypothesis, which makes 390 years an element in the Danielic seventy sabbath years. None of the sect's texts found so far ever alludes to such a messianic chronology. In fact, if some of the conclusions mentioned below may be anticipated here, it seems probable that cols. 1–8 of the Damascus Document antedate Dan. 9:24–27. Daniel's seventy septads, based on Jer. 25:12,[42] which reckons from the destruction of the First Temple to the "end of days," is fundamental for the understanding of rabbinic chronology. But the writings of Qumran contain no trace of such messianic computation.[43] The addition of the two periods of forty years is used by modern scholars to discredit the sect's own timetable. In other words, whether or not the 410 years are historical, they ought not be disregarded as an adjunct of Danielic chronomessianism.

Messianic reckonings may be of little import to the modern reader, but they were of paramount significance to the author of the Damascus Document. Crucial as Dan. 9:24–27 may have been for later commentators, the remainder of that biblical book seems to ignore this section and alludes instead to other chronomessianic numbers. This is not the case in the Damascus

Document. The covenant of Damascus contains only two numbers, and both
are indispensable for determining the temporal boundaries of the treatise.
Not only the first preface, but the other two as well, are governed by the figure
of 390 years after the destruction of the temple by Nebuchadnezzar; and the
twenty-year era controls the body of the treatise.[44] In other words, the events
of cols. 1–8 of the Damascus Document, its author claims, occurred between
390 and 410 years after the Ḥurban. Ever since Adam and the patriarchs, the
author insists, the datum of redemption had been foretold. Now that the
eschaton presaged since creation is finally approaching, the writer makes these
numerals the cornerstone of the treatise. Again and again throughout the
work, the period 391–410 is referred to in phrases such as "the latter days,"[45]
"the latter generation,"[46] "their epochs,"[47] "the completion of the epoch of
those years,"[48] "in all these years,"[49] and "the epoch of evil."[50] The number
390 is a key datum for the understanding of the Damascus Document.

Can the words "And in the time of wrath, three hundred and ninety years
after He had delivered them into the hands of Nebuchadnezzar king of Babylon,"[51] be translated into a Julian date? Put simply, Nebuchadnezzar
destroyed the temple in 587 or 586 B.C.E. A subsequent 390 years would set the
end of this period in 197 or 196 B.C.E.. The era used here is not the one prevailing in Ezekiel and in other biblical texts that reckon from the time when
King Jehoiachin was transported to Babylon in 597 B.C.E., but eleven years
later, in the nineteenth regnal year of Nebuchadnezzar, i.e., 586 B.C.E., called
by the author of the Damascus Document and by Jewish chronography the
era of the (first) Ḥurban.[52] Presumably, as attested in Ezek. 40:1, both chronological systems, the era of exile and the era of the Ḥurban, were in use during
post-exilic times; thus there is a possibility that the author's reckoning of the
number of years which had elapsed since the destruction of the Solomonic
sanctuary approximated reality. What has apparently induced students of
Qumran to reject out of hand the translation of 390 after the Ḥurban as
197/196 B.C.E. is the extreme unlikelihood that the Qumranic Commune
could be dated that early. Rather than postulate such a chronology, it seemed
to them more reasonable to suppose that the Damascus Document's timetable
is not to be taken literally. It is worth recalling that archaeological evidence
gave impetus to a later date, tending to identify the wicked priest in this work
and in Pesher Habakkuk with John Hyrcanus II (63–40 B.C.E.) or Alexander
Jannaeus (103–76 B.C.E.).[53] To be sure, more recently this late chronology of
Qumran is being discredited, but scant attention has been paid to the sect's
own calculations.[54] The other argument, that no such era had been used at
that time and therefore none can be taken seriously, is contradicted not only
by the chronological prefixes used by Ezekiel, but also by the text itself, which
dates the origin of the sect according to this reckoning.

Although setting the date of the *Moreh Ṣedeq* in 197/196 B.C.E. differs from
the more recent scholarly consensus by some half a century, the primary evi-

dence permits no other chronology.[55] It is worth repeating that such luminaries as Eduard Meyer and Eugene Täubler, commenting on the Zadokite Fragments prior to the discovery of the Dead Sea Scrolls, dated their composition to the beginning of the second century B.C.E.[56] They viewed this document as reflecting the struggle between the priestly Oniads, who sided with Egypt, and the secularist Tobiads, who favored the Syrians. Certainly these savants were mistaken in postulating that the Zadokite movement had primarily political roots, but their chronology seems as cogent since the finding of the Qumranic library as it was heretofore. The eschaton began at the point that the Aaronide scion arose in the figure of the *Moreh Ṣedeq*. This figure, or as he is called in CD 5:5, Zadok, discovered the Book of the Law, which had been allegedly sealed for a millennium.

The First Twenty Years of the Sect: 196/195–177/176 B.C.E.

Taking the sect's own chronology at its face value, certain points of its history assume a new clarity. The author of the Damascus Document is not concerned with the setting up of a commune, an organization of which he seems to know nothing and which only appears in documents composed subsequently. Rather, he records the appearance of a new Aaronide planting, i.e., Zadok, who assumed the title of *Moreh Ṣedeq* in the three hundred and ninety-first year after the *Ḥurban*. Thereafter, he and his followers migrated to the region of Damascus. There Zadok and his followers proclaimed the new covenant, whose text and wording is recorded in CD 6:11–7:6. In essence, the new covenant called for an affirmation of the recently discovered Sinaitic Second Torah, which Zadok had found hidden in a sealed ark. The Damascene emigrés pledged to have no contact with the current sanctuary in Jerusalem, which they regarded as defiled since it did not conform to the divine prescriptions; thus the text of the "Mosaic" 11Q Torah was used to damn the existing sanctuary in Jerusalem.

At the time of the Damascene covenant, the emigrés believed that the beginning of the eschaton had arrived, but that a period of twenty years was necessary to bring it to fruition. The author refers to the bridging years as a time when the people act like the blind who grope in the darkness or, in the words of the prophet Hosea, "like a rebellious cow."[57] In other words, the new light of the new heavens, presaged by Isáiah, had appeared on the horizon, but the people, steeped in defilement, could not believe their own eyes. The purpose of the covenant of Damascus, as well as of the treatise that records it, was to make them realize that what they were seeing was not merely the appearance of truth but truth itself. Seemingly writing before the end of the twenty years of groping in the dark, i.e., 177/176 B.C.E., the writer fully expected that at the end of the twenty years the scoffer,[58] who acted as the chief priest in Jerusalem while the *Moreh Ṣedeq* was in exile, would be removed to make room for the

Aaronide planting that had been presaged since creation. A sacred city with an undefiled sanctuary, built and maintained in accordance with the Sinaitic ordinances, was what the Teacher of Righteousness and his adherents hoped for, not the Commune with a relatively small membership which eventually developed. At the time of the compostion of CD 1–8, the founding of the Commune was an event of the future.

Who presided over Jerusalem's sanctuary while the *Moreh Ṣedeq* was awaiting the call to return and thus can apparently be identified as the villain in the Damascus Document? As is generally recognized, Simon the Just II, son of Onias II and father of Onias III, was serving as high priest when in 198 or 197 B.C.E. Antiochus III's troops entered Jerusalem, ending the uninterrupted epoch of Ptolemaic occupation which had begun in 301. As stated above, it is likely that Simon II had assumed office circa 215 B.C.E.[59] He was succeeded by Onias III during the reign of Seleucus IV (187–175 B.C.E.), probably circa 185. In other words, during 195–175 B.C.E., the twenty years of the Damascene migration, two high priests held office, Simon the Just II and Onias III. But which of them is the איש הלצון, the religious leader branded "the scoffer" in CD 1:14?[60] The only likely answer is Simon the Just. He remained in office in 187 B.C.E., and perhaps even a year or two later, most of the twenty years that stretched from 196 to 176 B.C.E.

If the preceding reasoning is cogent, the vilification in CD 1:14–18 was directed against Simon the Just II. For the sake of balance let us place the Damascus Document's denunciations alongside Ben Sira's panegyric, evidently speaking of the same Simon:

CD 1:14–18	*Ben Sira 50:5–21*[61]
בעמוד איש הלצון אשר הטיף לישראל מימי כזב ויתעם בתהו לא דרך להשח גבהות עולם ולסור מנתיבות צדק ולסיע גבול אשר גבלו ראשנים בנחלתם למען הדבק בהם את אלות בריתו להסגירם לחרב נקמת נקם ברית	5. מה נהדר בהשגיחו מאהל ובצאתו מבית הפרכת. . . . 11. בעטותו בגדי כבוד והתלבשו בגדי תפארת: בעלותו על מזבח הוד ויהדר עזרת מקדש: 12. בקבלו נתחים מיד אחיו והוא נצב על מערכות: סביב לו עטרת בנים כשתילי ארזים בלבנון: ויקיפוהו כערבי נחל. . . . 20. אז ירד ונשא ידיו על כל קהל ישראל: וברכת ייי בשפתיו ובשם ייי התפאר: 21. וישנו לנפל שנית ...ל מפניו:
When the man of mockery arose who by his preaching let flow over Israel the waters of falsehood and led them astray in the roadless	5. How glorious he was when he appeared from the tent and came from behind the temple curtain! . . .

desert, bringing low the everlasting heights and departing from the paths of righteousness and removing the bound which their forefathers had established in their inheritance, that the curses of his covenant might cling to them, delivering them up to the avenging sword, the avenger of the covenant.

11. When he put on his gorgeous vestments and was robed in perfect splendour, and went up to the holy altar, he added lustre to the court of the sanctuary.
12. When he received the portions of the sacrifice from his brethren, as he stood by the altar hearth, his sons were like a garland, like cedar saplings of Lebanon, surrounding him like willows of the brook. . . .
20. Then Simon came down and raised his hands over the whole congregation of Israel with the blessing of the Lord on his lips, proud to pronounce the name of God.
21. and a second time they bowed in worship . . . before Him.

In spite of the polarity of the depictions, the striking feature of these accounts is their apparent agreement. This high priest, whether eulogized or damned, is portrayed as a most persuasive person, with a devoted following among the people. If only he had accepted Zadok's legitimate demands, the author of the Damascus Document seems to be saying, Israel's salvation would have arrived at the very beginning of the eschaton. But since he had not, the migrants pinned their expectations on his successor, who turned out to be Onias III.

If the איש הלצון (scoffer)[62] is to be identified with Simon the Just II, he is also the one addressed as Belial, whose person symbolizes Jerusalem's three sins: whoredom, wealth, and defilement of the sanctuary, all described at length in CD 4:14–5:11. Although Israel as a whole, save of course those who migrated to Damascus, seems to be guilty of the charges, it is Belial who is made responsible for the people's sinfulness. The ensuing polemics seem to be directed against him personally. In 5:18–19 he is compared to the evil spirit who, siding with the magicians of Pharaoh against Moses and Aaron, brought forth Jannes and Jambres, evidently to produce blood with black magic. Using humor, the author of the Damascus Document also says that Belial, in the person of the scoffer, presents the three evils mentioned above as *haṣṣedeq!*[63] If "the Just" (*haṣṣadyq*) was attached to Simon's name in his lifetime, it is conceivable that *haṣṣedeq* is a pun on the epithet; in the vocabulary of Satan, evil is good.

The postulate that the charges of whoredom, possessions, and defilement of the sanctuary are primarily directed against Belial's representative, i.e., the high priest now identified as Simon the Just, would explain puzzling aspects of the polemics in this passage. Into the diatribe on whoredom, CD 5:1 interjects, "And concerning the prince, it is written, 'He shall not multiply wives to himself.'" Could "the prince" be Simon the Just II or one of the Tobiad sheiks? A few lines further in the Damascus Document, another allusion appears. Among the charges leveled against the opponents of the sect is that "a man marries the daughter of his brother or the daughter of his sister."[64] As discussed ealier, this charge conforms to the sect's interpretation of Lev. 18:13,[65] a view not shared by traditional exegesis. It is worth recalling that according to the romance in *AJ* 12:160, Joseph the Tobiad's mother was a sister of Onias II, and Hyrcanus, Joseph's son, was prominent in Jerusalem in the early decades of the second century. Hyrcanus himself was the offspring of a marriage between Joseph and the daughter of his brother;[66] thus the marriage of a niece, according to contemporary documents, is attested in the high-priestly family.

The other two accusations, wealth and defilement of the sanctuary, may also have been directed to the person of the high priest. The author's detailing of the improper separation of the heave offerings under the category of *hon* may, as explained above, have referred to the disparity between the common mode of tithing at that time and the rules found in the *Seper Torah,* i.e., 11Q Torah.[67] There is no doubt that he also included under *hon* the unjust treatment of orphans and widows.[68] Eduard Meyer suspected that these words were directed against the Tobiad Joseph, who, with the support of Jerusalem's priesthood, sided with Antiochus III against Ptolemy V in the war over Coele-Syria.[69] Joseph had become the chief tax-farmer under the Ptolemies, and other members of the Tobiad clan gained control of the temple's treasury, which had become the equivalent of the people's bank where many placed their savings for safekeeping.[70] Was this also meant by *hon?* Rabin translates this phrase as "conveying uncleanness to the sanctuary,"[71] Vermes as "profanation of the Temple."[72]

Although the general meaning of the third charge is clear enough, the precise designation of the term טמא המקדש remains obscure. The avoidance of defiling the sacred is the main theme of the sectarian Torah.[73] But the epithet טמא המקדש seems problematic since it contains an adjective before a substantive with a definite article. Technically the phrase may be rendered "the most defiled of the temple," an epithet that would attain its full force only if hurled against Jerusalem's high priest. Thus it is not unlikely that all three charges—whoredom, possessions, and defilement—are primarily directed against the person of Simon the Just and his associates, an interpretation that makes the treatise's vilification quite pointed.

Pesher Habakkuk: Faith in the Moreh Ṣedeq
in Spite of Dashed Expectations

As we have seen, taking seriously the Damascene author's chronology results in a date for Zadok's discovery of the Book of the Law and his escape to the region of Damascus of 390 years after the *Ḥurban,* i.e., circa 196 B.C.E.. To the author of the Damascus Document, it seemed certain that before twenty years had elapsed, i.e., 196/195–177/176, the master would be welcomed as the truly anointed Aaronide priest[74] and would assume the office of the *kohen gadol* in Jerusalem. But when the promise was not fulfilled at the predicted time, the members of the sect must have been left in a quandry. How to deal with the disappointment of his followers now became the main task of the Teacher of Righteousness. He must have succeeded in part, for after his death we read of a prophecy in CD 20:14 presaging his return when forty years will have elasped. Thus we have three dates:

a. the date of the beginning of the eschaton, 390 years after the destruction (197/196 B.C.E.)
b. twenty years thereafter (i.e., 410 years—177/176), the presaged triumph of the *Moreh Ṣedeq*
c. some time before the end of forty years after his death, the expected return of the *Moreh Ṣedeq*

It is evident that this chronology contains a hiatus, for the relationship between the 410 years after the *Ḥurban* and the death of the *Morah Ṣedeq* is not recorded. It is therefore not known how much time, if any, elapsed from the end of the twenty years until his passing. What CD 20 does state, however, is that the fulfillment of the eschaton will take place before the end of forty years after his death.[75] In brief, the chronology can be stated as follows, using 586 as the first year of the era of the *Ḥurban:*

a. $586/585 + 390 + 20 + x$ (year 20 until date of death) $+ 40$
b. $586/585 + 390 = 197/196$
   $197/196 + 20 = 177/176$
   $177/176 + x + 40$

In other words, according to sectarian chronology, the eschaton began circa 197/196 B.C.E., followed by the period of groping in the darkness, which ended in 177/176 B.C.E. What remains unresolved is the time that apparently elapsed from the unexpected year of redemption until the death of the *Moreh Ṣedeq.* Let us review the case presented thus far. He announced himself as the anointed one in 196, pointing to his finding of the new version of the Mosaic Torah as a sign of the coming of the era predicted by the prophets. He gave himself twenty years in which to be accepted by the whole of Israel, when he would before 176 enter triumphantly into the holy city. But we do not know how many years elapsed from the time of the unfulfilled messianic dates until Zadok's death. It is possible, however, to read the chronology in a way that removes *x*, i.e., by placing his death at the end of the twenty years, i.e., 176/175. In this case, the forty years until his expected return would end in 136 B.C.E. What remains certain is that in spite of dashed hopes, faith in him remained undiminished among many of his followers.

Ample evidence exists that Zadok outlived the failure of his promise to be proclaimed the Messiah. This testimony comes from Pesher Habakkuk. It is important because this treatise is the only pesherite work whose beginning and end have survived. Also, it alludes to historical events, such as the wicked priest's persecution of the Teacher of Righteousness and the coming invasion of the holy land by the Kittim. Obviously, such persecution could not take place after the master's death, but did it occur during the twenty years of groping or thereafter? To answer this question, it is necessary to take a close look at Pesher Habakkuk, the only treatise aside from the Damascus Document that deals at length with the *Moreh Ṣedeq*'s lifetime. Much has been written on this commentary since Brownlee's editio princeps in 1948, yet its full import, its relation to the Damascus Document, and its sequential placement have escaped detection.[76] In order to present the structure of the treatise, it is necessary to look at its thrust and unity, as well as to examine its close link with the Book of Habakkuk.

This fascinating document consists of five segments[77] that form a single sermon which may be entitled, "Keep your trust in the *Moreh Ṣedeq*. God still assures his triumph!"

The five segments are:

1. 1:1–2:10 (Hab. 1:1–5): Those who have abandoned the master in adversity are people of little faith.
2. 2:10–6:12 (Hab. 1:6–13): The Kittim are a most-feared nation, but they, too, will ultimately submit to the authority of the *Moreh Ṣedeq*.
3. 6:12–8:3 (Hab. 1:14–2:4): Despite the *Moreh Ṣedeq*'s failure, the righteous shall live by faith in him.
4. 8:3–12:10 (Hab. 2:5–17): The evil priest persecutes the *Moreh Ṣedeq*.
5. 12:10–end (Hab. 2:18–20): The idolatrous nations will be destroyed in the day of judgment.

Of the known Qumran writings, with the exception of CD 1–8, Pesher Habakkuk is the only text that presumes a living *Moreh Ṣedeq*. CD 1–8 and Pesher Habakkuk ought, then, to be read side by side, keeping in mind, of course, that the former antedates the latter, since CD 1:11 speaks of his establishment and Pesher Habakkuk records his sufferings.[78] It follows that if CD 1–8 seemingly records events 390–410 years after the *Ḥurban*, the timetable of the incidents in Pesher Habakkuk presumably is subsequent to 410 years after the

Ḥurban. On the other hand, the death of the Teacher of Righteousness recorded in CD 20:14 took place after the events of this commentary; thus col. 20 of
the Damascus Document is to be considered part of a later work.[79] Translated
into the Julian calendar of Qumran postulated above, some time elapsed
between 175 B.C.E. and the master's death, an interval designated above as *x*.

What is the value of *x*? An internal analysis of Pesher Habakkuk may provide some hints. Although Pesher Habakkuk is less accommodating than the
Damascus Document in providing the exact dates of its subject-matter, it
does, or it did originally, give a temporal clue. After citing Hab. 1:1–2, the
commentator begins his exegesis with פשרו על תו[נ]חלת דור.[80] Habermann has
inserted the word "last" as the first word in 1:3, reading the phrase דור אחרון
(the last generation).[81] This interpolation is cogent since דור אחרון appears two
other times in the treatise. But what was the word which partially remains—
חלת [. . .]? Although a number of possibilities have been suggested, the likely
reading as proposed by Vermes is *teḥilat* (the beginning of), i.e., "the beginning of the last generation."[82] In other words, the exegete claims that Habakkuk's vision was intended to presage events whose significance can only be
understood in the light of the beginning of the last generation, that is to say,
the generation before the triumph of the *Moreh Ṣedeq*. The author of Pesher
Habakkuk is extending the period of waiting for the eschaton by *x*, which he
defines as the time of the last generation; or if the interpolation proposed
above be accepted, at the beginning of the last generation. This seems to be
the value of *x*. In Julian dates, then, *x* starts with 176/175 B.C.E. That is to say,
P. Habakkuk depicts events of that year or soon thereafter.

The Kittim, described by the author as a mighty nation, more powerful
than any other people,[83] are an indicator often used to date the Qumran commentary on Habakkuk. Although the majority opinion maintains that the
term refers here to the Romans,[84] as it does in the Septuagint text of Dan.
11:30, there exists no satisfactory explanation of the temporal aspects em-
bedded in the references to the Kittim. Some scholars, identifying the wicked
priest of this treatise as Alexander Jannaeus (103–76 B.C.E.), have said that
Pompey's invasion of the East in 64–63 B.C.E. was meant.[85] As the result of
recent studies tending to identify the wicked priest as one of the early Hasmoneans, Jonathan (152–142 B.C.E.) or Simon (142–134 B.C.E.), the passages that
mention the Kittim have once again become problematic.[86]

Significant as the allusions to the Kittim appear, they do not in fact provide
the key for placing this pesher in relationship to other Qumranic writings.[87]
The key does lie in the resolution of the treatise's main figures, the *Moreh Ṣedeq*
and the *kohen haraša*ᶜ. Most of the passages relating to the Kittim and other
idolatrous nations are merely supplementary, evidently inserted only because
the author of the commentary found it necessary to expound passages in
Habakkuk that deal with foreign nations as relating to the remarkable rise of
this western power. Although proportionately a third to a fourth of the

pesher, the description of the most feared nation in the world is subordinate to the main message. The *clef d'oeuvre* lies not so much in the commentary as in the prophetic book chosen for the pesher; and not only at the beginning of the biblical book, but in Hab. 2:2-3: "And the Lord answered me and said, 'Write the vision; make it plain upon tablets, so he who reads it may be fluent. For still the vision awaits its time; it hastens to the end—it will not lie. If it seems slow, wait for it; it will surely come, it will not delay.'" The meaning of these lines to the author of the pesher is self-evident.[88] The prophet forewarns against regarding the *Moreh Ṣedeq* as an impostor just because the predicted vision had not been realized.

The background for understanding this treatise is supplied by the work which preceded it. Both in terminology and content, CD 1-8 and Pesher Habakkuk appear to be intimately related, closer to each other in time of composition and possibly authorship than any other Qumranic writings. Terms such as מאס (despise), הון (possessions), דור אחרון (last generation), בוגדים (unfaithful), and כזב (lie) are all key words for understanding both documents. Central to the two works is the ברית חדשה (new covenant) and, above all, a living *Moreh Ṣedeq*.

Yet a sharp contrast separates the Damascus Document from Pesher Habakkuk. The former is permeated by a sublime optimism, as it relates a story of hope and expectation. The latter attempts to counter the air of despair and disappointment that seems to have enveloped the group. All the signs point, according to the Damascus Document, to the day of the eschaton, the time God had set at creation and promised to the patriarchs. The discovery of the new Torah and the appointment of an Aaronide leader, the finder of the awaited sealed scroll, marked the beginning of the end presaged to Moses and the prophets.

What seems to have separated the composition of this pesher from the Damascus Document is the relationship to the day of expectation. The latter precedes it, the former follows it. In this pesher we find a people who have believed almost beyond certainty that the redeemer would appear on top of the mountain on the morrow; that day has arrived, and there is no sign of his coming.[89] In the history of messianic movements, many such groups have left little or no trace. Others not only survived but found a new lease on life in the unfulfilled prediction. Pesher Habakkuk shows how the group that followed their master to Damascus managed not only to retain their faith in the *Moreh Ṣedeq*, but to use the failure as the beginning for what is now known as the Qumran Commune, which evidently developed into the Essene sect.

A master homilist, the author of the pesher uses the Book of Habakkuk to halt the distressing phenomenon of the people's loss of faith in the *Moreh Ṣedeq*. He does so in two ways. First, he invents a new hermeneutic. In the Damascus Document the term *pišro*, as pointed out above, still seems to have retained its original sense of an interpretation of a mysterious dream or the resolution of a puzzling passage.[90] As used in the new work, apparently written after the failure of the presaged eschaton, *pešer* assumes a new meaning: the clause-by-clause elucidation of the relevance of the prophetic words. It was one thing for the author of the Damascus Document to cite a variety of biblical lines as applicable to the current scene; it was more remarkable for this pesherite exegete to prove that every verse, even every word, of the ancient prophet was addressed directly to the current scene.

Introducing a new genre of biblical exegesis, the author appears to have been self-conscious in his hermeneutics. He uses Hab. 1:5 to show that the prophet himself foretold the *Moreh Ṣedeq*'s efficacy at interpreting Scripture for the current scene. In other words, the author of P. Habakkuk claims that this is not eisegesis; the prophet had actually intended his words to be interpreted as referring to the Teacher of Righteousness. This claim is made by introducing the second element. Instead of apologizing for the failure of the *Moreh Ṣedeq,* the interpreter, using the lines spoken by the prophet, attacks the sectarians who now doubt the truthfulness of the master's vision, calling them בוגדים (unfaithful):

> [The explanation of this concerns] those who have betrayed with the man of lies; for they [have] not [believed the words] of the Teacher of Righteousness (which he received) from the mouth of God. And (it concerns) those who betra[yed the] new [covenant]; for they did not believe in the covenant of God [and profaned] His [h]oly na[me]. And likewise, the explanation of this word [concerns those who will be]tray at the end of days: they are the violent . . . who will not believe when they hear all the things which will be[fall] the last generation from the mouth of the priest whom God placed in [the house of Jud]ah to explain all the words of his servants the prophets, by [whose hand] God has told all that will befall His people and [the nations].[91]

The introductory lines of 1QpHab claim that the prophetic books contain, in addition to their meaning for the time of the prophet, an eschatological meaning summarized under the term *pešer.*

Unlike the Damascus Document, which directs its arrows against the unfaithful of Jerusalem who were blind to the coming of the *Moreh Ṣedeq,* this treatise opens with an attack against those of the last generation during the eschaton who, because of a lack of faith, abandoned the master in the middle of his redemptive acts. Their lack of faith, the author says, is twofold. Like those whom Habakkuk himself witnessed, "the wicked surrounding the righteous,"[92] they do not trust God to overcome the lies with truth. Neither do many of the followers have faith in the *Moreh Ṣedeq* to provide the true interpretation of God's words, to לפשור (compose a pesher of) what the prophets had heard from God. Thus the pesher makes the prophet's vision real. What some see as the failure of the *Moreh Ṣedeq,* the author claims, was in fact a result of (a) the people's sinfulness in not following the Torah properly, and (b) a misunderstanding of what the *Moreh Ṣedeq* had really said.

After a hiatus in which the author diverts the reader with an exegesis of the remainder of Habakkuk 1 with reference to the Kittim, a mighty power which will conquer the world but which in turn will submit to the *Moreh Ṣedeq,* 1QpHab 6:12 resumes the main theme. In a segment remarkable for its literal rather than periphrastic exegesis, Hab. 2:1-3 is used to rekindle trust among the hesitant of the believers in the *Moreh Ṣedeq*:

> I desire to take my stand to watch and to station myself upon my stronghold; and I will spy out to see what He will say to me and what He will reply to my complaints. And the Lord answered and said to me: "Write down the vision and make it plain[93] upon the tablets so that he who reads it will be fluent." The explanation of this. . . . And God told Habakkuk to write down the things which will come to pass in the last generation, but the consummation of time he made not known to him. And as for that which he said, "he who reads it will be fluent," the explanation of this concerns the Teacher of Righteousness to whom God made known all the mysteries of the words of His servants the prophets. "For there is yet another vision relating to the appointed time; it speaks of the end and does not lie." The explanation of this is that the final time will last long and will exceed everything spoken of by the prophets; for the mysteries of God are marvelous. "If he tarries, wait for him; for he shall surely come and shall not delay." The explanation of this concerns the men of truth who observe the Law, whose hands do not slacken in the service of truth when the final time is delayed for them; for all the seasons of God come to pass at their appointed times according to His decree concerning them in the mysteries of His wisdom.[94]

The author claims that the *Moreh Ṣedeq* understood the prophetic words better than Habakkuk himself since God had given him the key words formerly only half-understood by those who first uttered them. The central slogan, taken from Hab. 2:2, was: "If he (i.e., the anointed) tarries, wait for him, for he shall surely come." Since there is no doubt that God had set the epochs of the world, He must have informed His chosen *Moreh Ṣedeq.* In contrast to the wicked, who have lost their trust in the master, "the righteous shall live by his faith."[95] The righteous, therefore, are the faithful who retain their trust in the Teacher of Righteousness. The pesherite writer, instead of apologizing for the unfulfillment of the prophecy of the *Moreh Ṣedeq,* takes the offensive by attacking the disbelievers.

The last third of the pesher resumes the theme found in the Damascus Document, the evil acts of the wicked priest in Jerusalem.[96] As the earlier portion of the treatise is devoted to the character of the Teacher of Righteousness, the commentary on Hab. 2:5-17 describes הכוהן הרשע (the wicked priest), who is called by the name of truth at the beginning of his establishment. The author here employs irony similar to that in CD 4:16–17, where the liar in Jerusalem, i.e., the high priest, was said to have practiced whoredom, possessiveness, and the defilement of the sanctuary under the banner of *ṣedeq* (righteousness).[97] The pesherite writer, however, expresses some sympathy for this man, recording the sect's expectations at the time of his assumption of office.[98] This compliment suggests that some of the new covenanters had hoped that the new high priest would welcome the *Moreh Ṣedeq* and his followers. But when the wicked priest started to rule, he became arrogant, he forsook God and despised the statutes on account of possessiveness, robbing, and amassing wealth with the men of violence who rebelled against God.

Using Hab. 2:7–8, 1QpHab 9:4–7 castigates the "latter priests of Jerusalem" who gather wealth from the booty of the nations, possessions which the author presages will fall into the hands of the Kittim, apparently the pagan victors, prior to the ultimate triumph of the *Moreh Ṣedeq*. At first glance these lines, as is generally supposed, appear to fit the Maccabean or Hasmonean rulers.[99] But a closer look makes the identification with any of the Hasmonean rulers questionable. To be sure, from Judah Maccabee to the days of Pompey's conquest of the Near East there was a rapid growth of Judaean territory. Is it this expansion to which the author of the pesher is objecting? This seems highly improbable in view of the writer's hostility to idolatry. The objection is not to the conquest of the lands, but to הון ובצע (wealth and robbery). The prediction that all of these possessions will ultimately fall into the hands of the Kittim makes little sense if the reference is to sections of the holy land.

Evil as the priests of Jerusalem were, their guilt consisted of following the wicked priest, who throughout the treatise remains the chief villain. The remainder of 1QpHab 8:3–12:10 focuses on the sufferings he had inflicted upon the Teacher of Righteousness. The specific accusations against the wicked priest are: (a) he seeks to oppress him;[100] (b) he is labeled "the preacher of lies" who builds Jerusalem with blood;[101] and (c) he pursues the *Moreh Ṣedeq* אבית גלותו (to [?] the house of his exile).[102] He appeared on the Day of Atonement to make the sectarians stumble in its observance, and the persecution continued thereafter. Although the details remain obscure, he planned to destroy the destitute, he defiled the sanctuary, and he committed abominations. Why did God permit such sufferings to be inflicted upon the Teacher of Righteousness?

In the only line that alludes to the imperfection of the *Moreh Ṣedeq*, Pesher Habakkuk ascribes his suffering to "his own sins as well as to those of his congregation."[103] This is a rather significant concession for a writer who has hitherto insisted on the infallibility of the master to whom God had revealed the hidden mysteries and who can discern the meaning of Habakkuk's words better than the prophet himself. It is not clear whether the tarrying of the predicted eschaton, mentioned above in 1QpHab 7:12, was also ascribed to the leader's sins. This granting of the master's failure is noteworthy only because it is unique in the early texts of the group. For the most part, the old answer remains unmodified—God sanctioned the persecution of the chosen to make the ignominy of the wicked even more visible to all. But the author does not conclude his work before revealing that the triumph of the *Moreh Ṣedeq* will rest not only on the demise of the wicked priest but also on the destruction of idolatry, to which the last segment of this work is devoted.

For both the date of the composition of Pesher Habakkuk and for the chronology presumed in the treatise, it is important to remember 1QpHab 11:4–8. These lines suggest that the author was writing while the Teacher of Righteousness was still alive. If the evidence accumulated in Chaps. 3–4 of this monograph is cogent, the death of Zadok provides the *terminus a quo* for this pesher. 1QpHab 7:7 can only be understood as having been written following the dashed expectations of the eschaton, but prior to the death of the Teacher of Righteousness. The phrase in 7:12: בהמשך עליהם הקץ האחרון (when the final time is delayed) takes cognizance of the crisis confronting the master. It argues, however, that the promised redemption will take place in spite of the delay. Since the redemption was to take place at the latest in 410 after the *Ḥurban,* the delay must refer to a period soon thereafter. This passage seems to date P. Habakkuk as having been composed during the period of dashed expectations when the eschaton, which was to take place before or during the year 410 after the *Ḥurban,* failed to materialize. Let us recall that CD 1–8 was written before this crisis. Only a short interval separates P. Habakkuk from the Damascus Document, but the mood is radically different. The latter is full of hope; the former attempts to console the despairing. In light of the chronology developed above, the period designated as x^{104} seems to be the time of P. Habakkuk.

To my knowledge, this study is the first to conclude that a significant portion of the works which constitute the Qumran corpus antedate the Maccabean rebellion. But this is not to say that such claims are unprecedented. As was remarked above, Eduard Meyer and Eugene Täubler had, before the discovery of the manuscripts in the Judaean wilderness, dated the sectaries of the Zadokite fragments at the turn of the second century B.C.E.[105] It is worth noting that Milik dates the composition of the Astronomical Enoch, fragments of which were found in Cave 4 at Qumran, as far back as the Persian period.[106] According to Milik, copy A of this Astronomical Enoch was written during the last quarter of the third century, or at the latest, toward the beginning of the second century B.C.E., at least a century after its composition. Whether or not one agrees with Milik's Persian date of 4Q Enastr, the library of Qumran attests to a literary tradition that goes back to the third century B.C.E. Only of late has the extent of the Graeco-Jewish literature that flourished at the end of the third and the beginning of the second century come to the attention of the public. Viewed from this perspective, the postulate that the Qumranic Torah, Jubilees, the Damascus Document, and now Pesher Habakkuk antedate the final composition of the Book of Daniel no longer seems so radical a revision.

As to the date of composition of Pesher Habakkuk, circa 170 B.C.E. seems likely. This date would correspond to about 416 after the *Ḥurban,* according to the reckoning used in the Damascus Document. This pesher could not have been written after the summer of 168 B.C.E. since the author, who describes the Kittim at length, seems to be completely unaware of Antiochus IV's breach of the sanctuary in that year. On the other hand, as already pointed out, the treatise could not have been written prior to 411 after the *Ḥurban,* i.e. 176/175 B.C.E. Presumably, the events described in Pesher Habakkuk, such as the wicked priest's assault on the Teacher of Righteousness on the Day of Atonement, according to sectarian chronology, took place between 175 and 170 B.C.E.

A number of problems would find resolution if this chronology is allowed. The passage relating to the Kittim in 1QpHab 2:10–6:12 is one instance. If, as a majority of scholars now maintain, Kittim refers to the Romans,[107] as in Dan. 11:30,[108] the pesher author's views seem to correspond to what is known of current public opinion as reflected in pagan sources: that Rome would continue its endeavor to liquidate the Seleucid Empire. Antiochus, who had been released as a hostage from Rome and been replaced in that capacity by the son of Seleucus IV, crowned himself Antiochus IV Epiphanes.[109] The Romans, who had humiliated the two preceding Seleucid rulers, Antiochus III and Seleucus IV, were not expected to treat Antiochus IV with any more kindness. The apparent prediction that the Romans would overthrow Antiochus IV and take over the Seleucid Empire in toto remained unfulfilled, however, at least for a century. This fact may serve as another indication for dating Pesher Habakkuk during the time of the expected invasion by Rome.

The Wicked Priest in the Habakkuk Commentary

Aside from the *Moreh Ṣedeq,* the central figure in the early Qumranic texts is the wicked priest. The title הכוהן הרשע appears only in the pesherite works and is not to be found in CD 1–8, written earlier, where the antagonist of the *Moreh Ṣedeq* is identified as Belial, or in CD 20, where he is named איש הכזב (the liar). The variation in vocabulary seems to suggest that these epithets do not necessarily refer to the same person, unlike the case of the Teacher of Righteousness, who is always to be identified as Zadok, whether the references are to current or future redemption.[110] Certainly the wicked priest in Pesher Habakkuk is not the same person who is identified as the opponent of the *Moreh Ṣedeq* in the Damascus Document or to whom Pesher Nahum attributes the hanging of people while alive.[111] The only constant in all those epithets is that they refer to the current high priest of Jerusalem's sanctuary.

It was argued above that the epithets hurled against the antagonist of the *Moreh Ṣedeq* in CD 1–8 refer to Simon the Just II, who held the office of high priest from 215 B.C.E. until circa 187 B.C.E. or shortly thereafter.[112] By 175, when Antiochus IV Epiphanes ascended to the Syrian kingship, as attested in Josephus, Simon's son Onias III had replaced his father as Jerusalem's high priest. The pesher on Hab. 2:5–6 makes it clear that a new high priest assumed office while the *Moreh Ṣedeq* was fighting for his life. This is the significance of 1QpHab 8:8–9: "Its interpretation concerns the wicked priest, who was called by the name of 'truth' at the beginning of his assumption of office." The best explanation of this phrase seems to be that the sectaries were expressing their disappointment with a priest in whom they had placed their hopes at the beginning of his rule. This could only be the case if he had assumed office after another high priest whom they did not find to their liking. In other words, the sect functioned during the tenure of both the wicked priest and his predecessor. Any chronology of the wicked priest in Pesher Habakkuk must take account of these two successive high priests. Postulating that the *Moreh Ṣedeq* first appeared in about 195 B.C.E. and that the year of the eschaton was either 196/195 or 195/194, 390 years after the *Ḥurban*, we must presume that Simon's death took place in the short period which occurred between 190 and 177 B.C.E., a time when the followers of Zadok were in a mood of exultation since the גלות (exile) was expected to end soon, with the master triumphantly entering the holy city. Some of the master's followers, if not he himself, expected the ecclesiastical leader to surrender his office to the newly anointed Aaronide scion. The fact that Onias did not do what the sectaries had expected of him sharpened their attack against him, resulting in charges not only of selling out to the enemy and of vanity, but of treachery as well: "And when he became ruler in Israel his heart became proud, and he forsook God, being unfaithful to the laws for the sake of possessions. He robbed and collected wealth (with) men of stealth who betrayed God."[113] The main accusation against the wicked priest, however, remains the acquistion of wealth (*hon*), a charge leveled with new fervor against the preceding high priest in CD 4–8. For not only was Onias III subject to the normal passion for acquiring possessions, but he exceeded his predecessors by taking from the neighboring peoples: "The wealth of nations he took, heaping sinful iniquity upon himself."[114]

What is significant is that the trait of acquiring wealth applies to the priests of Jerusalem as a whole, not only to the high priest. This fact, as well as the lack of any mention of the acquisition of territory, strengthens the evidence against the presumption that P. Habakkuk is referring to the Maccabean or Hasmonean priesthood. The only group whom the charges would seem to fit is the priesthood under the leadership of Onias III and, possibly after his removal, under his brother Jason. As is attested in Jerome's commentary on Daniel,[115] as well as in the charter of Antiochus III,[116] the sacerdotal authorities of Jerusalem had not only welcomed the Seleucid takeover of Coele-Syria in 198 B.C.E., but had rendered aid to the victor. The Tobiad clan, as is known from Ezra and Nehemiah, the Zeno papyri, and remaining monuments, exercised power over the Transjordan during the Persian and Ptolemaic reigns.[117] The Tobiad Joseph, the product of intermarriage with Jerusalem's priesthood, became the chief tax-farmer of Phoenicia as well as of Judaea. The wedding of the hereditary high-priestly rulers of the theocratic state with the Tobiad sheiks, evidently the wealthiest clan in a region stretching from Transjordan to Phoenicia, transformed the sanctuary from a sheer religious institution into a powerful house of finance, where the people entrusted their savings for safekeeping.[118] The Tobiads and the Oniads were deeply involved in the rivalry between the Seleucids and Ptolemies for supremacy in Coele-Syria, with Jerusalem accepting the promises of the Syrians in exchange for aid in wresting the area from Egyptian control. At the time of Onias III's accession to the high-priestly office after some two decades under Seleucid rule, some of the beneficial results of northern policy could be noticed in Jerusalem. Judaea seemed more prosperous than ever.[119]

Other consequences of, or perhaps coincidences with, Seleucid rule were less beneficial. A hitherto-unknown form of foreign influence, which gave rise to the term *hellenismos,* had penetrated some of Jerusalem's well-to-do families.[120] Travelers to Alexandria or Antioch as diplomats and tradesmen brought back to the holy city an ostentatious way of life. More slaves, as well as more silver and gold vessels, led to a loosening of family ties. Both the Syrian and Ptolemaic rulers had long favored Macedonian and Greek settlers, whose military colonies and urban settlements were given special privileges. Symbiosis between the Greek immigrants and the native landlords created the *polis,* a Hellenic enclave within an autochthonous population. Some of Jerusalem's wealthy, among them evidently members of the Tobiad clan, yearned for a royal charter that would bring Jerusalem within the growing circle of privileged *poleis*.[121] Others shuddered at the thought of introducing into the holy city a mode of living that would bring brothels and gymnasia, which to them smacked of the old, reputedly Canaanite practices. It goes without saying that little is known of how Jerusalem's population felt on these issues which some of the city's leading citizens were hotly debating. Most of our information comes from works that were written after Antioch IV's despoiling of the sanctuary in 169 B.C.E., his subsequent ban on the practice of Judaism two years later, and the revolt that ensued. Works such as 1–3 Maccabees as well as the writings of Josephus echo the Hasmonean hatred of Hellenism, at least the brand introduced by Antiochus IV. Daniel 7–12, written apparently around 165 B.C.E., mirrors the passions of the period when Judaism was banned.

Are there writings that may be said to reflect aspects of Jerusalem's mood in the first three decades of the second century, during the initial period of Seleucid rule? As is pointed out above, I believe that the Damascus Document was written circa 176 B.C.E., the commentary on Habakkuk some five years later. Together these two treatises reflect the attitude of Zadok's followers toward the Seleucid regime. In an interpretation of Deut. 32:33, the Damascus Document takes the clause "and the head of the serpents is cruel" to refer to "the head of the kings of Yavan," who were apparently to come to Jerusalem and take revenge.[122] The reference could only be to either a Ptolemaic or a Seleucid ruler, for only they controlled empires in which the phrase "head of kings" would make sense. The northern king appears more likely, especially since the author seems to have composed the treatise in Damascus. If so, and if the chronology outlined above is correct—i.e., that the Damascus Document was written circa 176 B.C.E.—the author alludes to Seleucus IV, who was assassinated in 175 B.C.E. As far as is known, the prophecy was never fulfilled because he was soon succeeded by his brother, Antiochus IV.[123] On the other hand, the commentary on Habakkuk, composed apparently during the reign of Antiochus IV, still seems to be unaware of the impending threat to Jerusalem from the new Seleucid king. Possibly this was because the new Syrian ruler was still not taken seriously since the Romans were expected to humiliate him as they had his father.[124] When the Kittim, i.e., the Romans, would bring an end to the Seleucid empire, the high-priestly state of Jerusalem would fall together with its powerful pagan master. This in fact happened, but it did not occur until more than half a century had elapsed. But the pesherite exegete must reflect the feelings of many native Judaeans who resented the Macedonian support of the Greek colonies and saw Rome as siding with the Orientals against the Greek kingdom. In predicting the Roman intervention against Antiochus IV, the writer of Pesher Habakkuk seems to be siding with anti-Seleucid elements in Jerusalem. The commentator's admonition against the "last priests of Jerusalem," who together with the wicked priest despoiled not only the native orphans and widows but also neighboring nations in order to accumulate wealth, seems particularly pointed if directed against the members of the pro-Seleucid party. At the time of Pesher Habakkuk's composition, Antiochus IV's march against Egypt in 170 and his breaching of the walls of the sanctuary a year later were still events of the future. As far as one can tell, Antiochus had sought the friendship of Judaea before his march southward. It was only after the humiliation in Egypt that he no longer needed native support for his military adventures and thus did not mind antagonizing the Jews.

An outline of the sequence of events postulated here presumes that the persecution of the Teacher of Righteousness described in Pesher Habakkuk took place after the affirmation of the covenant of Damascus, 410 years after the Babylonian exile. Instead of the expected redemption, a period of persecution had followed. The ecclesiastical authorities of Jerusalem had a free hand in punishing and even slaying their opposition coreligionists. The sectarian leader, who now proclaimed a newly established solar calendar, celebrated the seasons in accordance with the prescriptions of the Qumranic Torah. Onias evidently sent his agents to threaten the Teacher of Righteousness, who still remained in exile awaiting the anticipated invitation to enter the holy city as the anointed Aaronide priest.[125] The agents of the high priest delivered this threat, according to 1QpHab 11:7, on the Day of Atonement, which the sectaries observed at a time disparate from all of Israel. In other words, the high priest seems to have wished only to humiliate his opponent, not to slay him, for there is every indication that the *Moreh Ṣedeq* outlived the humiliation.[126]

At first sight, the pesherist's attacks on Jerusalem's high priesthood appear to be a response to the wicked priest's persecutions of the *Moreh Ṣedeq*. A closer reading of the Damascus Document and Pesher Habakkuk reveals, however, that the sectaries initiated the rivalry. As stated in CD 1:11 and throughout that treatise, the term *Moreh Ṣedeq* could only be understood as a contrast to the wicked priest, who by definition was Jerusalem's *kohen gadol* (high priest). The sectaries demanded nothing less than the unconditional surrender of the holy city to the *Moreh Ṣedeq*—a demand that must have been considered rebellion. That the Teacher of Righteousness was merely threatened and not slain may have been due to the fact that he himself had once been a member of Jerusalem's high priesthood; or that he was not taken too seriously by its leadership.

The significance of our discussion thus far lies in our new perception of Pesher Habakkuk. The exegetes of this treatise by and large treat it as a disconnected work held together solely by the prophetic book which it presumes to explicate. Most scholars believe "Kittim" refers to the Roman armies brought by Pompey in 63 B.C.E. Cross suggests that the pesherite manuscripts are autographs emanating from the Herodian period.[127] Accordingly, the Kittim may be taken to allude instead to the Roman armies who helped Herod expel the Hasmonean rulers from Jerusalem in 37 B.C.E. On the other hand, many of these same scholars identify the chief personalities alluded to in P. Habakkuk as figures found in the middle of the second century B.C.E.[128] This incoherence prompts the question raised by Carmignac as to whether the pesherite literature was penned by many writers or, as he assumed, was the product of a single author.[129] What all these scholars stress, however, is that Pesher Habakkuk, like the other pesherite fragments, is concerned with the atomistic understanding of phrases or words, paying little attention to the biblical book itself.

It is our view that the actual words of Habakkuk, and not only their pesher, play a crucial role in the message of 1QpHab. True, the Chaldeans become the Kittim and here and there the exegesis seems allegorical. But for the most part, the author considers a nearly literal interpretation of the prophetic text to be applicable to his own day. Even a paraphrase in English will suffice to demonstrate that the author thought Habakkuk was speaking of the group at Qumran:

> O Lord, how long shall I cry for help, and Thou wilt not hear? Or cry to Thee "Violence" and Thou wilt not save? Why dost Thou make me see wrongs and look upon trouble? Destruction and violence are before me; strife and contention arise. So the law is slacked and justice never goes forth. For the wicked surround the righteous, so justice goes forth perverted. Look among the nations and see; wonder and be astounded. For I am doing a work in Your days that You would not believe if told.[130]

> I will take my stand to watch and station myself on the tower, and look forth to see what He will say to me, and what I will answer concerning my complaint. And the Lord answered me: "Write the vision; make it plain upon tablets, so he may run who reads it. For still the vision awaits its time; it hastens to the end—it will not lie. If it seems slow, wait for it; it will surely come, it will not delay. Behold, he whose soul is not upright in him shall fail, but the righteous shall live by his faith. Moreover, wine is treacherous; the arrogant man shall not abide. His greed is as wide as Sheol; like death he has never enough. He gathers for himself all nations, and collects as his own all peoples." Shall not all these take up their taunt against him, in scoffing derision of him, and say, "Woe to him who heaps up what is not his own—for how long?—and loads himself with pledges!"[131]

Phrases such as the following seem to be literally translated into the current events of the sect: "O Lord, how long shall I cry for help, and Thou wilt not hear?" "For the wicked surround the righteous"; "For still the vision awaits its time; it hastens to the end—it will not lie. If it seems slow, wait for it; it will surely come, it will not delay"; "the righteous shall live by his faith." The fact that some other verses of Habakkuk did not apply quite as literally cannot negate the basic application of Habakkuk's prophecy to the author's own day. Moreover, these other verses seem difficult when applied to any age and their resolution by allegorical means appeared cogent to the pesherite writer. All in all, the Book of Habakkuk itself, quite apart from its commentary, had a contemporary application for the author of the pesher.

Carmignac and others have pointed to the author's careful distinction between the verbal perfect and imperfect to define time.[132] Perfects are employed when the author speaks of events of the past and imperfects for the future. This opinion appears to be cogent. Both past and future referred to what occurred durng the writer's lifetime. A close reading of the text confirms the impression that the book was composed not as an interpretation of the distant past, as many scholars maintain,[133] but as an elucidation of recent events. Thus the Teacher of Righteousness and the wicked priest were the author's contemporaries, or very nearly so. Suppositions such as that of

Cross, that the book was authored in Herodian times but the references are to Hasmonean and Maccabean princes, seem untenable.[134] On the other hand, Carmignac's view that all pesherite writings were penned by a single author is equally unacceptable.[135] Some fragments of this genre use the word *pešer* only once or twice while others reiterate the term almost constantly. There is also a difference between Pesher Habakkuk, which only occasionally uses allegory and attempts to use Habakkuk's words in a merely literal sense, and the other pesherite exegesis, which pays no attention to context or original meaning. It also seems unlikely that a single person would have had a monopoly on this genre of writing. It is not even necessary to assume that all pesherite writings—for example, Pesher Habakkuk and Pesher Nahum—were the product of a single generation. Moreover, in spite of the multitude of pesherite fragments, almost none outside the Habakkuk commentary mention the *Moreh Ṣedeq*. In a word, the dates of other pesherite fragments cannot determine precisely when Pesher Habakkuk was composed.

The mention of the Kittim does not refute this thesis. There seems to be no good reason to suppose that the Romans mentioned in 1QpHab are to be identified with Pompey's armies. Pompey's invasion was hostile, while the description of the Kittim in 1QpHab is not unfriendly. The author respects their martial valor at the same time that he despises their worship of idols. What 1QpHab reflects is an amazing sympathy for the Romans, whose deeds the writer knows only by hearsay. It is perhaps noteworthy that all the verbs alluding to the Kittim invariably employ the future sense.[136] Roman power played a vital role in the rivalry between the Seleucids and the Ptolemies long before the annexation of their kingdoms by the Roman Empire.

The assumption in this study that 1QpHab was composed during the *Moreh Ṣedeq*'s lifetime can find much support in the commentary's allusions to contemporary events. The account of the persecution of the *Moreh Ṣedeq* by the wicked priest, for example, contains a flair of immediacy, as do the allusions to the abuses of wealth and to the suffering of the poor. As has been pointed out above, an air of disappointment permeates the book. The basic chronology of this work presumes, therefore, that Pesher Habakkuk was composed before the death of the *Moreh Ṣedeq*.[137]

Pesher Nahum

A striking line in Pesher Habakkuk is the author's claim that the *Moreh Ṣedeq* had the authority (לפשור) to compose biblical commentaries which allegedly explained more than had been understood by the prophet himself.[138] Subsequent pesherite writers no longer required such justification. Furthermore, the hermeneutics in Pesher Habakkuk, contrary to what is generally assumed, rarely departs from the biblical text it interprets. These marks distinguish it from the other pesherite commentaries, a distinction which seems to have consequences for chronology as well. It was noted that the term *pišro* in CD 4:14 is still used in the restrictive sense of general interpretation rather than to designate a line-by-line commentary.[139] Pesher Habakkuk, then, seems to be the first example of this new genre of literature. One of the most interesting later examples is Pesher Nahum, which makes specific reference to Demetrius, Antiochus, the Kittim, and to the young lion who hangs the seekers of smooth things.[140] Such is the state of Qumran studies that, in spite of these many clues, no consensus exists as to the identity of the Seleucid monarchs mentioned here.[141] In light of the timetable proposed by our study, Demetrius may refer to Demetrius I (162–150 B.C.E.) or Demetrius II (145–139 and 129–125 B.C.E.).[142] CD 20:14–15, referring to forty years after the death of the *Moreh Ṣedeq*—therefore written before 130 B.C.E.—combined with Pesher Nahum, could refer to either Demetrius I or to the beginning of the reign of Demetrius II. Demetrius II became involved in Judaean matters when Jonathan successfully besieged the Acra (the citadel), which had been under Seleucid protection even after Judah's entry into Jerusalem in 164 B.C.E.[143] If the allusion is to this affair, the "hanging alive" in Pesher Nahum would then refer to the bloodbath of Jerusalem's Hellenizers. As to the other Seleucid monarch mentioned here, most scholars maintain that the reference is to Antiochus IV. But as the passage stands now, there is no reason to exclude Antiochus III (223–187 B.C.E.) from the list of possibilities. After all, it was during his reign that the sect made its appearance. Whatever the precise date of Pesher Nahum, it appears relatively late in the development of the genre, when the relation between the biblical text and its commentary was frequently oblique. Since Pesher Nahum was presumably composed when the Commune had become a mature institution, this work need not be brought into a discussion of the question concerning the roots of Qumran. Nevertheless, it is interesting that the vilification of the young lion who hangs the seekers of smooth things seems to use 11Q Torah, which denounces the desecration of those who had been crucified.[144] Pesher Habakkuk, however, was composed decades earlier while the Teacher of Righteousness was still presiding over the sectarians, probably 170 B.C.E.

Is Daniel's Reference to the Unfulfilled Vision an Allusion to Qumran?

The view that places the origin of Qumran at the beginning of the second century B.C.E. may have non-Qumranic support. Recent scholarship differs widely as to the nature and form of early sectarianism, but there seems to be a consensus that the distinctions between the Sadducean and Pharisaic parties on the one hand, and between these two and the Essenes on the other, originated during the Maccabean or post-Maccabean period.[145] 1 and 2 Maccabees, which cite the Hasideans who flocked to join in the revolt against Antiochus IV and who subsequently abandoned Judah Maccabee, at least for a while, seem to contain the first allusions to sectarianism, although opinion is divided as to whether these Hasideans are to be identified with the known Pharisees or with the Essenes.[146] Moreover, Josephus records that the split between the Pharisaic and Sadducean parties was in full swing during the reign of John Hyrcanus (134–104 B.C.E.).[147] This is taken to mean that the two parties could not be distinguished prior to the Maccabean period. Additional support for this thesis, according to some scholars, can be inferred from the fact that the Jewish historian inserts his first description of the sectarian ideologies into the midst of his account of Jonathan.[148]

Although this view has much to commend it, there is contrary evidence which modern scholarship has apparently ignored. Little can be concluded from the fact that Josephus does not allude to sectarianism prior to the Maccabean revolt. The possibility exists that his failure to mention any of these groups in an earlier age results not from the non-existence of sectarianism but from historiographic accident. By happenstance, 1 Maccabees is Josephus' source for the Jewish revolt and its aftermath. Like it, he begins his continuous account with Antiochus IV and devotes only a sentence or two to the time from the end of Alexander the Great's reign to the ascent of Antiochus IV. The story of the Tobiads is grafted onto *Jewish Antiquities* without background. Josephus' failure to mention the Pharisees, Sadducees, or Essenes in the pre-Maccabean epoch may then be due not to their non-existence but to the paucity of sources.

A more serious objection to the current consensus concerning the origin of Jewish sectarianism is the tendency to ignore such allusions as do exist. A case in point is Dan. 11:14, a passage first discussed by Porphyry and Jerome:

ובעתים ההם רבים יעמדו על־מלך הנגב ובני פריצי עמך ינשאו להעמיד חזון ונכשלו.

In those times, many will rise up against the king of the south. And breachers among your people will raise themselves to establish a vision, but they shall stumble.

Dividing the verse in the middle and relying on Porphyry, Jerome sees in v. 14a a reference to the alliance of Philip of Macedon and Antiochus the Great against Ptolemy and his allies.[149] Dan. 11:14b, on the other hand, calls attention to the division of Judaea into two factions, one favoring Antiochus and the other Ptolemy. An example of the latter is Onias, the high priest who fled to Egypt and built a temple there according to Jerome. Eduard Meyer identified the בני פריצי עמך (breachers among your people) with אשר פרצו גבול התורה (who breached the boundary of the law) of CD 20:25.[150] According to him, this was a Hellenizing, pro-Seleucid uprising against the faction which sided with the Ptolemies. For Meyer, the Tobiads were therefore the defenders of orthodoxy against the radical assimilationists. Accepting Meyer's interpretation of the verse as one unit, Eugene Täubler cited להעמיד חזון (to establish a vision) as evidence of a messianic uprising against the Ptolemies that was squelched by Scopas in 201/200 B.C.E. Thus Täubler removed the revolt from the realm of international politics, making it instead part of the religious fervor that swept Judaea at the time of the Seleucid conquest of Coele Syria.[151]

The Qumran library provides ample justification for rejecting the hypothesis that the Damascus Document's reference is to a political uprising against either the northern or the southern kingdom. But Meyer's other postulate, which links the rise of the breachers (Dan. 11:14b) with events recorded in the Damascus Document, deserves attention. His hypothesis fits well with the chronology proposed here dating the roots of Qumran between 195 and 170 B.C.E.[152] Linguistically, Daniel's wording echoes the vocabulary used in Pesher Habakkuk, which interprets חזון למועד (the vision is for the appointed time) as the *Moreh Ṣedeq*'s uprising against the authorities in Jerusalem.[153] By quoting the prophet, לוא יכזב (he did not lie), the pesherite author assures the members of the sect that the promised eschaton was not a false hope; the appointed time has merely been postponed.[154] In contrast to the promise, Daniel gives his comment on the success of the vision: ונכשלו (and they shall stumble).[155]

Daniel, defending the established authorities, and Pesher Habakkuk, which records the actions of the visionaries, employ similar vocabulary to describe this movement but render contrasting judgments on its efficacy. Daniel's attitude toward the sectaries is reflected in his choice of the word ינשאו (and they raised themselves up).[156] He considered them haughty and arrogant. If this interpretation is correct, Dan. 11:14a, "And in those times, many will rise against the king of the south," possibly refers to the Seleucid conquest of Coele-Syria in 198 B.C.E., whereas 14b alludes to the subsequent revolt of the visionaries (חזון) that was promulgated by Zadok and his adherents. Täubler's basic presumption that Dan. 11:14b records the rise of a messianic movement seems cogent. Thus Daniel, presumably written circa 165 B.C.E., provides the earliest and perhaps the only contemporary external attestation to the pre-Maccabean origin of the *Moreh Ṣedeq* and his followers.

The Date of Zadok and the Qumranic Torah

Drawing upon Qumranic, rabbinic, and Karaite testimony, the preceding pages put forth the hypothesis that the sectarian Torah is the precursor of all the writings that can be characterized as belonging to the sectarian Commune (*Yaḥad*). To validate this hypothesis, it was necessary to show as far as possible not only that all the Qumran sect's literature is dependent upon the Qumranic Torah, but also that its author explicitly or implicitly advanced a claim for its authoritativeness that is unequaled in post-biblical Jewish literature: God revealed to Moses not only the traditional Five Books of Moses, but also another Torah, to be hidden until the time of the eschaton.

Zadok's discovery of the *Seper Torah,* the copy given to Moses which had been sealed in an ark, marks the beginning of the eschaton. The fact that God revealed the secret location of the Torah, which had been hidden in an ark since the days of Joshua, indicated that Zadok was indeed a unique individual, the *Moreh Ṣedeq* or Teacher of Righteousness. Thus, as understood by the members of the sect, the term "Torah" did not refer exclusively to the Pentateuch, as it did for the rest of Israel, but also encompassed what is now available in the fragments of 11Q Torah. Qumranic literature shows a considerable evolution in the unfolding of the movement from a group of people trusting their master and following him into exile to the creation of a closely knit Commune (*Yaḥad*), and perhaps from it to the Essene heresy. But the sectaries never deviated from their basic trust in the *Moreh Ṣedeq* and the Torah he had recovered.

So far it has been argued that the external evidence, including works such as the Book of Jubilees, the War Rule, the Community Rule, and even perhaps the Book of Daniel, supports the postulate making the Qumranic Torah *the* first work, that is to say, the precursor of other Qumranic literature. The following pages analyze the text of 11Q Torah to determine whether or not its wording can be said to conform with the inferences from the external evidence. Fusing CD 1:1–10 with 4:13–5:6, it was shown that the sectarian Torah was composed prior to 196 B.C.E. when Zadok found the scroll in a sealed ark.[157]

Although CD 5:5 makes Zadok merely the discoverer of the lost *Seper Torah,* this study attributes to him its authorship as well. This is not to say that it was impossible for Zadok to have discovered an ancient scroll containing a copy of the Pentateuch which differed substantially from the current versions of the Mosaic writings. Indeed, it might be argued that the scroll reflects a collection of ancient sources rather than a novel composition. Theoretically at least, it is conceivable that the sectarian Torah was composed by someone prior to Zadok and that Zadok, as stated in CD 5:5, was merely its finder. Such a supposition would parallel the discovery of the book by Hilkiah, as recorded in 2 Kings 22. It seems apparent that what Hilkiah found was what we call the Book of Deuteronomy, directly ascribed to Moses. Few, however, would grant that Hilkiah in fact uncovered a work written by Moses. It is probable that the fifth Book of Moses was composed by Hilkiah and his circle in the second half of the seventh century. What applies to Deuteronomy is equally cogent for the *Seper Torah* discovered by Zadok. In theory the *Seper Torah* might itself be a composite of several authors; however, an analysis of the scroll, as is amply demonstrated in Chap. 1 of this monograph, gives the impression of a unified composition. This unity is reflected in the book's language, syntax, content, and theological underpinning. A supposition that elements of this work antedate the time of its alleged discovery would create complications leading nowhere. We must postulate that Zadok in fact composed this scroll which he presented as a copy of a Mosaic book that had been sealed in an ark for more than a millennium.

The external evidence accumulated thus far indicates that the work was composed not later than the first decade of the second century B.C.E. Is the internal data consistent with such an hypothesis? To begin with, it is perhaps useful to recall the contrasting conclusions of Yadin and Schiffman as to the nature and provenance of the Qumranic Torah.[158] Yadin sees nothing strange in placing the Qumranic Torah side by side with the other writings found at Qumran, such as the Community Rule, the War Rule, and the Damascus Document, all of which may be credited to the Essene sect that resided in the Judaean wilderness.[159] To be sure, a few problems exist. Why does much of the technical vocabulary of 11Q Torah diverge so sharply from that found in most other Qumranic texts? Yadin recognizes that 11Q Torah, for example, employs the term כוהן גדול (high priest, a title that is never used in the other Qumranic writings, where substitute epithets such as כוהן הראש (head priest) are used.[160] A comparison between the formulation of the law in 11Q Torah and the legal lore in CD 9–14 would reveal how disparate the two really are. For those who identify the Qumranites with the Essene sect, the polar attitudes to wine and oil are a problem. Not only are wine and oil not shunned as they were among the Essenes, according to Josephus, but they are made the center of the sacrificial rites.[161] The centrality of the sanctuary in the Qumranic Torah, and the profound interest in its dimensions and rites, seems antithetical to the many passages in the Community Rule where sacrificial offerings do not figure in the public meals.

Those characteristics which distinguish the sectarian Torah from Qumranic writings have led Schiffman and Levine to classify 11Q Torah as a text found in the sect's library but not composed by the sectaries.[162] In other words, according to Schiffman, the caves of the Judaean wilderness contained parchments that were regarded as sacred by Jews in general or by movements other than what is now understood as Qumran, as well as literary pieces that had no sanctity whatsoever. 11Q Torah, then, may be a case of incidental shelving.

Even if one grants the supposition that the Qumranic scribes copied manuscripts of writings formulated by opposing groups, a supposition that still needs validation, 11Q Torah cannot be said to have been one of them. The evidence for linking the scroll with the Qumranic literature, which Yadin has assembled in his introduction and commentary, cannot be dismissed just because there are some basic problems. It would be contrary to the known evidence to suggest that a stray copy of the sectarian Torah made its way into the caves of Qumran; fragments of four or five copies of the text have so far been identified and one may assume that more fragments will be found. The links between 11Q Torah and other Qumranic writings include features such as script, spelling, technical terminology, and characteristic phrasing that are peculiar to the Qumran sectaries. The evidence adduced in this study showing a common ideological infrastructure strengthens Yadin's hypothesis, if it needs strengthening, that 11Q Torah cannot be divorced from the Qumran tradition.

While any attempt to arrive at a date for the compostion of the sectarian Torah must begin with Yadin's extensive introduction to the text, his conclusions are doubtful. On the basis of the penmanship of scribes A and B in the remnants of the work acquired by Israeli authorities, Yadin believes that the two copyists wrote during the reign of Herod I (37–4 B.C.E.) or soon thereafter.[163] He identifies fragments of at least two more manuscripts among the scraps of the Qumran texts housed in the Rockefeller Museum in Jerusalem.[164] Relying on the paleographic studies of Avigad and Cross, he finds in one copy handwriting which was fashionable during the Hasmonean period.[165] By Hasmonean, Yadin means the second half of the rule of John Hyrcanus (143–104 B.C.E.) or during the reign of Alexander Jannaeus (103–76 B.C.E.). Not being a paleographer and knowing nothing that would contradict such dating of the fragments, I would like to accept Yadin's expertise, which sets the latest possible date of these fragments between 125 and 76 B.C.E.

It ought to be noted, however, that Yadin's chronology is contradicted by paleographic evidence, pointing to the existence of the Qumranic Torah at the beginning of the second century B.C.E.. Rockefeller 43.366, which includes remnants of the sectarian Torah as well as an unidentified fragment, is the point of departure.[166] Yadin describes this fragment as follows: "The date of this script is of special significance (for the dating of the scroll) for it is our oldest copy. There is no doubt this script is characteristic of the semi-ornate style of the middle Hasmonean period and that it resembles the script of Isa[a] and of 4Q Deut[a]. Hence this must be ascribed to approximately the last quarter of the second century B.C.E. (Prof. Avigad, who at my request kindly examined the script of Rockefeller 43.366, also concluded that it bears a distinct resemblance to Isa[a] and that it ought to be ascribed to the same time period) . . ."[167] Provisionally accepting Yadin's premise, the question arises as to why he chose the lower rather than the higher portion of the second half of the first century B.C.E. Yadin's date becomes even more problematic in light of the opinion of Cross, who places 4Q Deut[a] between the time of the Archaic and Hasmonean scripts, dating it to 175–150 B.C.E.[168] Moreover, according to John Strugnell there exists a hitherto-unpublished 4Q manuscript of the sectarian Torah unknown to Yadin. Professor Strugnell writes:

Both Yadin's MS, and the other fragmentary MS from 11Q of which he publishes parts in his volume of Supplementary plates (plates 35–37 and parts of 38–40), are of the 1st Century of our era. The 4Q fragments improperly labelled Rockefeller 43.366 are much earlier (roughly ca. 75 B.C.), but the work to which these fragments belong is not a copy of the "Temple Scroll," but a Pentateuch with frequent non-biblical additions; whether they are quotations from the Temple Scroll incorporated by that Pentateuch, or vice versa (i.e. bits of an earlier "wild" Pentateuch text used as a source by 11QT) remains to be seen. There is one group of 4Q fragments not yet published, which contains quotations from, or the text of, the Temple Scroll, or at least one of its sources: it is in a hand resembling that of the Qohelet fragment published by Muilenberg (BASOR #135 [1954] pp. 20 ff.) and would be difficult to date much later than 150 B.C.; without anticipating the forthcoming discussion of these fragments by their editor, one can say that this evidence, for at least one of the work's component parts, if not the work itself, compels a *pre*-Hasmonean date.[169]

Another problem with Yadin's dating is that he assumes that Rockefeller 43.366, allegedly written in 125 B.C.E., is an autograph. Since there is no reason for believing that this is the case, it follows that Rockefeller 43.366 is a copy of an archetype that antedates 125 B.C.E. According to Strugnell, however, as was stated above, Rockefeller 43.366 is made up not of fragments of the Qumranic Torah but fragments of additions to a standard Pentateuch, to be dated circa 75 B.C.E. In other words, Yadin's dating is problematic on three counts: first, Rockefeller 43.366 may be variously dated, from 125 B.C.E. to 75 B.C.E.; second, whatever their actual time of composition, the Rockefeller fragments appear to be citations from the sectarian Torah superimposed on the traditional Pentateuch and thus are necessarily antedated by their Qumranic archetype; and third, the availability of still other fragments going back to 150 B.C.E. or earlier necessitates an *a quo* date of the first half of the second century B.C.E. Thus paleographic testimony requires an assumption that the Qumranic Torah dates from some time before the middle of the second century B.C.E.

Common sense dictates that unless there is substantial evidence to the contrary, manuscripts are not considered autographs or near-autographs, and that some time must have elapsed between the time of the work's composition and the production of the copy that has survived. How much time one ought to assign to the interval between the presumed authorship and the earliest surviving remnants is an open question: a generation, half a century, a century? If paleography dates the oldest fragments of the Qumranic Torah to 100 B.C.E. and there is no indication that they are remnants of an autograph, everything else being equal, it can be presumed that there were antecedent originals around 150 B.C.E. Now, however, with the paleographic evidence cited by Cross and Strugnell, the date of the composition of the Qumranic Torah appears to be circa 200 B.C.E.[170] It will be argued below that there is nothing in the sectarian Torah that seems to contradict this paleographic argument.

Yadin maintains that there is subtantial internal evidence to synchronize the time of the work's authorship with the date of the surviving remnants in the Rockefeller Museum, set by him in the last quarter of the second century B.C.E. The evidence leading him to date the Qumranic Torah in 125–100 B.C.E., during the time of John Hyrcanus (134–104 B.C.E.), is of two sorts: linguistic and historical. Yadin sees a close kinship between the language of the fragments and that found in the Mishnah and cognate texts.[171] Words such as רובד (terrace), כיור (entablature), and ריס (measure of distance),[172] a phrase such as והיא רויה לו מן החוק (and she is fit for him by law), and the frequent use of the auxiliary היה (be) with ordinary verbs all show common links between the usage of Hebrew in the fragments and that of the talmudic sages. These and some other common features between the tongue of the *Ḥazal* (sages) and the lost work, Yadin argues, preclude the dating of the fragments before the Hasmonean period, when Hebrew must have been different.[173] Because of these similarities, Schiffman calls the Qumranic authorship of the scroll into question.[174] In my estimation, these scholars give too much weight to the half dozen or so words and phrases that seem to link the vocabulary and terminology of 11Q Torah with the tongue of the sages. To begin with, it is possible that some features of Mishnaic Hebrew go back to the third century B.C.E.[175] 11Q Torah contains few Aramaisms and no words of Greek origin, whereas the mishnaic treatises as well as the original Megillat Taanit contain loanwords from the Greek.[176] But the fragments of the Zadokite Torah do contain a number of foreign words, all evidently borrowed from the Persian.[177] In fact, the language of the Qumranic Torah, aside from quotations which, of course, are in the linguistic style of their own period, seems nearest to that of the Hebrew of the books of Ezra and Nehemiah. From the point of view of linguistic usage and technical vocabulary, there is nothing in 11Q Torah that excludes dating its composition during the late Persian or very early Hellenistic period, about 350–200 B.C.E.

What requires greater emphasis is Zadok's attempt, no matter how unsuccessful, to imitate slavishly the Hebrew of the traditional Torah. In his extensive work on the Hebrew grammar of the Dead Sea Scrolls, Qimron notes that some of the lengthened pronominal sufixes, such as *-kemah* and *-(h)emah,* as well as the afformative *-temah,* are characteristic of biblical texts in the Qumran scrolls.[178] Since this lengthening is also a striking feature of 11Q Torah, can it be that the scroll, even in this detail, is closer to its biblical archetype than scholars have presumed? The spelling of 11Q Torah reflects an attempt to mimic forms which its author considered archaic, thus strengthening the implicit claim for "Mosaic" authorship. In that case, it is not hard to understand how later Qumranic writers would have accepted Zadok's work as one of the two books of the Law given to Moses at Sinai.

Again and again, according to Yadin, the particulars in various ordinances seem to cohere with the Mishnah and with Josephus' report concerning the changes in the ritual instituted during the rule of John Hyrcanus.[179] The sectarian Torah devotes more than a column to the description of the chaining of the victims to the stands. From this evidence Yadin concludes that either the fragments' account echoes the current reforms of John Hyrcanus recorded in M. Maaser Sheni 5:15 and M. Sotah 9:10 or, as seems more likely to him, it inspired the innovations of the Hasmonean prince in this matter. In accordance with these changes, the newly found text fails to mention the requirement to recite the thanksgiving prayer over the tithes.[180] John Hyrcanus' reforms attempted to ameliorate the plight of the levites, and a concern for their welfare is reflected in the fragments. Yadin's major case for dating the work during the office of this high priest is based on the lengthy section that is devoted to the duties of the monarch.[181] The composition of this expansion of Deut. 17:14-20 seems appropriate during the time when Hasmonean power reached its peak. Yadin asserts that the rules of offensive and defensive warfare and the requirement that the army be entirely native, evidently banning mercenaries, seem inconceivable during the Persian period, when no Judaean army existed. He does not accept Dupont-Sommer's proposal to date the sectarian Torah during the Hellenistic period, a hypothesis based on the use of the word רכב in the sense of chariot instead of horse.[182] The polemics and the sectarian interests, which according to Yadin form the raison d'être of the newly found work, had no place in Judaean history prior to the Hasmonean period.[183] It was during the reign of John Hyrcanus, as reported by Josephus, that sectarianism became a major factor in the political and religious life of the Jews. In Yadin's view, the text of the Qumranic Torah was intended to refute many views of mainstream Judaism, which rabbinic literature otherwise preserved. It was precisely at the time of John Hyrcanus, then, or shortly thereafter, according to Yadin, that the unknown writer composed the sectarian scroll.

A close scrutiny of these arguments indicates that, even excluding the paleographic evidence which seems to contradict Yadin's conclusion, the case for dating this work during the rule of John Hyrcanus or soon thereafter is rather unconvincing. The parallels between the ordinances in the fragments and the Hasmonean reforms are too remote to serve as attestations of a similar date for the lost work. The problems of how to treat the sacrificial victims existed in any sanctuary where such offerings were a daily rite.[184] The lack of an ordinance to recite the thanksgiving prayer prescribed in Deut. 6:13-15 proves nothing: first, it is an argument *ex silentio* from a fragmentary work; second, the extant fragments cease at the beginning of Deuteronomy 23, and as far as anyone knows, the remaining sections may have contained a paraphrase of Deut. 26:13-15; third, the institutions of tithing and other priestly and levitical offerings in the fragments diverge so radically from the talmudic prescriptions as to preclude any parallels except at points where the two systems directly meet. Contrary to Yadin's argumentation, there seems to be nothing in cols. 56:12–60:12 that would appear to point to the days of John Hyrcanus or his successors. After all, John Hyrcanus never wore the crown and as high priest was ineligible for Israel's kingship.

The successors of John Hyrcanus did take it upon themselves to assume the royal diadem, but these claims were secular in nature and intended to impress the Oriental principalities.[185] The Pharisees and other religious groups never recognized these royalist claims, since kingship was in their view reserved exclusively for a scion of David.[186] The attitude to kingship in 11Q Torah seems to clash with the political thought of the Hasmonean period. According to Josephus, the Hasmoneans served as high priests of the temple as well as rulers of Judea, but were still subordinate, nominally at least, to the Seleucid king of the time. A new stage was attained, according to Josephus, only when Aristobulus (104–103 B.C.E.) assumed the title of *Basileus*.[187] Kingship then, in terms of secular power, represented a higher level of prestige and influence. In contrast to this, in the Qumranic Torah the high priest remains the sole authority, both as chief of state and as the interpreter of Torah. But since he could not leave the precinct of the sanctuary, as stated in Lev. 21:12, an office of kingship was established with a circumscribed role. What cols. 56–60 relate is that the duties and prerogatives of the king were limited to defense; in other words, he was a subordinate officer in the theocratic state headed by the *kohen gadol*. Yadin sees in 57:5–11, which describes an exclusively Jewish royal guard, a criticism of John Hyrcanus, who was the first of the Hasmonean rulers to employ pagan mercenaries. But the absence of permission to use mercenaries in the Qumranic Torah cannot be said to be directed against the Hasmonean prince. It is rather an indication of a sectarian lawgiver who probably could not even conceive of the thought that it might be necessary to retain idolaters to defend the holy city since the sanctuary was under divine protection. Thus the attitude toward kingship in 11Q Torah hardly coheres with the political situation during the Hasmonean period. On the whole, I cannot understand why the royal rules found in this work should be regarded as more relevant in the time of the Hasmoneans than during any other period of the Second Temple.[188]

The section of 11Q Torah on the constitution of the king is extraordinary in any period of Jewish history. It only makes sense if its author was composing prescriptions for the *aḥaryt hayyamym,* the messianic age. According to Yadin's view, the ordinances prescribed in the Qumranic Torah were rules to be applied to the current scene. All the author wanted was alterations in certain halakic practices for a restructured sanctuary. However, according to my understanding of the texts, the author wishes to have no share in the contemporary temple, which he regarded as utterly polluted. Under the guise of a consolidation of the Mosaic books, the author claims to present a theocratic system in a temple prescribed by God Himself. This does not mean that the author of this work does not reflect contemporary thought, only that his allusions to his own time were made unwittingly.

How then can the disparity between much of the terminology of the sectarian Torah and Qumranic literature, as pointed out by Schiffman, be accounted for? The answer is chronology. When Zadok wrote his Torah, he evidently did so to account for the lowly position of the Jews, an oppressed people who had been a buffer state between the northern and southern empires. Like his younger contemporary who is known to us by the pen name Daniel, Zadok was deeply impressed by the turns of fortune of the mightiest empires in the world during the Syrian wars. But where was the God of Israel? Why does God allow the idolaters' elephants to trample the holy land? Why the continuous suffering of Israel, not merely in recent years, but going back as far as the epochs of the judges and the monarchy? Why had the prophetic words of a new heaven and a new earth not come true? Both Daniel and Zadok were convinced that the fragility of the mighty powers was evidence of the impending new world presaged by the prophets Isaiah, Zechariah, Habakkuk, and Malachi, but they differed widely in their explanation of the causes of Israel's weakness and the power of the pagans. For Daniel, the introduction of the שקוץ משומם (detested abomination)[189] brought defilement to Jerusalem's sanctuary; for the author of the scroll, the sanctuary's impurity stemmed from its never having received divine sanction. As stated implicitly in 11Q Torah and explicitly in Jub. 1:10 and CD 6:12–14, all of the sanctuaries erected in the holy land were idolatrous, from the one built in Shiloh to the edifice rebuilt by Zerubbabel. Only the tabernacle of the wilderness, erected by Moses according to the Sinaitic blueprint, had been willed by God. It is no wonder that 11Q Torah considers the only worthy successor to the wilderness tabernacle to be the future edifice it prescribes. 11Q Torah's implicit condemnation of the current sanctuary as an abomination had far-reaching effects in the coming period of persecution. Dan. 11:33 and 1 and 2 Maccabees record the deep anguish felt by the people when Zeus Olympius was worshipped in the temple at Jerusalem by the slaughter of pigs. For the followers of Zadok, these abominations confirmed the intrinsic impurity of Jerusalem's shrine under the present leadership.

If this, as well as what was noted above in Chapter 1, represents the ideology of the author of 11Q Torah, it is difficult to presume such a vehement anti-hieronastic attitude developing in the aftermath of the Maccabean victory, the date assigned to 11Q Torah by Yadin and Ben Zion Luria. After all, with the expulsion of the idolaters from the sanctuary and its purification in 164 B.C.E., Jerusalem's temple reached its zenith with the universal acceptance of the celebration of Hanukkah.[190] This propelled the rebels into a position of leadership for the next hundred years and more. Many scholars have felt that the Qumranites repudiated Jerusalem's leadership because of the secular and Hellenistic tendencies of the Hasmonean rulers.[191] But this is not what the writings from the Qumranic library say. The Qumranic Torah vilifies not the new Greek way of life but the same idolatry that was berated by the Deuteronomist. Given the option of dating this treatise either before the Maccabean revolt or thereafter, an unprejudiced perusal of the fragments of 11Q Torah will, I think, persuade the reader of the former date.

Several sections of this study have demonstrated that the basic Qumran works not only are dependent on the Qumranic Torah but grant its superiority to the traditional Mosaic Torah.[192] The Book of Jubilees can only be understood as an attempt to propagate the sanctity of the newly discovered Law. Although the date of Jubilees is controversial, a pre-Maccabean date seems plausible.[193] Eupolemus, who presumably served as Judah Maccabee's envoy in 161 B.C.E., was apparently indebted to 11Q Torah,[194] but the dependence on the sectarian Torah becomes most evident in the Damascus Document and the pesherite texts cited above. The Damascus Document contains a chronology using the 390 and 410 years of the era of the destruction of the First Temple. Taken at face value, these dates seem to be 196/195 and 177/176 B.C.E., the former being the *ad quem* date for the Qumranic Torah. In other words, Zadok's supposed discovery of the text, which evidently took place in 196/195 B.C.E., assures us that 11Q Torah was composed in that year or earlier. The likely date, then, for the composition of the scroll, taking into account the internal and external evidence, is circa 200 B.C.E.. Since the discovery is ascribed to Zadok, the presumption that he was not only its discoverer but its author is plausible, unless we postulate that he was using the work of an unnamed writer, in which case the composition of the scroll took place some decades earlier.

As to the time of Zadok, he still seems to be living at the end of the twenty years, 170 B.C.E., at the time of the composition of Pesher Habakkuk, a treatise written to account for the non-fulfillment of the predictions outlined in the preceding treatise, the Damascus Document. Assuming that he was at the age of forty when he composed the Qumranic Torah, Zadok was born in 240 B.C.E. and lived at least sixty-five years. If one has to conjecture as to the date of Zadok's death, circa 170 B.C.E. seems a plausible guess, which assigns to him a seventy-year life-span. The allusion to forty years after his death in CD 20:14-15, referring to the date of the return of the Teacher of Righteousness, then alludes to 130 B.C.E. A very tentative chronological scheme follows:

Beginning of Antigonus' prominence	250 B.C.E.
Birth of Zadok	240 B.C.E.

Composition of 11Q Torah	200 B.C.E.
Three hundred and ninety-first year after the *Ḥurban*	196/195 B.C.E.
End of the groping in the darkness	177/176 B.C.E.
Nonfulfillment of the vision (P. Habakkuk)	176–170 B.C.E.
Death of Zadok	170 B.C.E.
His expected return after forty years	130 B.C.E.

Persian Culture during the Hellenistic Period

A major question which needs to be explored in order to explain events in second-century Judaea is, What was Jerusalem's dominant culture at the end of the third and the beginning of the second century B.C.E.? It is known that the Persian language and legal procedure penetrated deeply into Judaea during the two centuries of Achaemenid rule.[195] Can it be said that the Macedonian hegemony, which began in the days of Alexander and the Diadochi, transformed Jerusalem into a Greek *polis*? Current scholarly opinion would probably answer in the affirmative. A long string of scholars, including Bickerman, Tcherikover, and more recently Martin Hengel, have stressed the far-reaching results of Alexander's conquest of Judaea in 332 B.C.E. Hengel cites the romantic accounts of Joseph the Tobiad's adventures in Egypt and his alleged unconcern for the observance of Jewish law in contrast to the Book of Daniel, which does reflect such concern.[196] Following the work of Eduard Meyer, Bickerman and Tcherikover have postulated that the attempted Hellenization of Judaea by and large reflected the zeal of certain Jewish circles to exchange their houses of worship for gymnasia and that Antiochus IV's persecution of Judaism reflected the aims of Jewish reformers.[197] Three successive high priests, Onias III, Jason, and Menelaus, mirrored in their hostility to, sympathy with, and zeal for Hellenism the respective divisions of Jerusalem's population. Thus it is assumed that Hellenistic culture began to penetrate deeply into Jewish life at the end of the fourth century B.C.E.

Attractive as it may seem to students living in the modern period of Jewish history, this hypothesis ought to be rejected. There is nothing to indicate the deep penetration of Hellenization prior to the advent of Antiochus IV.[198] I fail to see Josephus' story of how Joseph came to think that he had slept with an Alexandrian prostitute as evidence of Tobiad zeal for the Greek way of life. The romances of Joseph and his son Hyrcanus do not relate, as is generally taken for granted, a flirtation with a Hellenized mode of living, but the problem of a provincial visiting the metropolis.[199] Tax-farming on behalf of the sovereign did not imply sympathy for the Macedonian civilization any more than Nehemiah's service as Artaxerxes' cupbearer reflected an alienation from Judaism. Even Daniel and his three companions were said to have served the

Babylonian and Persian rulers while remaining punctilious Jews. The point in the story of Joseph is that, in spite of the temptations, he ends up marrying his brother's daughter.[200] The common denominator of the Tobiad romance, of Daniel, and even of the Book of Esther, is that the protagonists remain faithful Jews while prospering in the service of a pagan monarch. On the other hand, there is no denying that the Macedonian rulers founded Greek colonies in the Near East, including Judaea, and that some Jews were attracted to the practices found in these military colonies or *poleis*. But it is clear from the lack of emphasis given to these topics in Jubilees that its author did not regard them as deserving serious concern, certainly not as compared to the issue of consumption of blood or the observance of the seasons in their proper calendrical settings.

The vilification of idolatry ought not to be interpreted as an allusion to Hellenism. Idolatry forms a major concern of the author of 11Q Torah, but as pointed out by Yadin,[201] it is the type of idolatry with which the writers of Deuteronomy, Deutero-Isaiah, and Ezekiel were preoccupied,[202] not the variety first appearing in the Book of Daniel, then in Maccabees and rabbinic literature. The biblical texts refer to the Canaanite cults, which were characterized by public and private deities. The new idolatry of Hellenism pertained primarily to political institutions such as the temples of Apollo and the gymnasia which served as symbols of the state. The idolatry alluded to in the Qumranic Torah is of the Canaanite type. Although a conclusive opinion is not possible since the treatise has not survived in its entirety, it is worth noting that the sectarian scroll does not seem to have touched on or alluded to the topic of circumcision and "uncircumcision," much treated in works written during and after the issue of Hellenization became prominent. Interestingly, Hellenization, which endangered the continuity of Judaism in the second century B.C.E., never receives its due emphasis in the Dead Sea Scrolls. In fact, it is hardly ever alluded to. The "uncircumcision" that is deplored in the Damascus Document and Pesher Habakkuk refers to stubbornness of the heart, a symbolism that ceases to be used in the Maccabean literature.[203] Yadin, in his late dating of 11Q Torah, has wondered why the author denounces a type of idolatry that seems inappropriate for the Hasmonean period. The presumption that the book was written at the end of the third century, before Hellenism penetrated the infrastructure of Judaea, may explain the absence of allusions to Hellenism. It is cogent to postulate that the apparent unconcern with the Hellenizing breaches into Judaean society may be ascribed to the fact that the roots of the sect were formed prior to the time when Greek influence became acute. For the sectaries of Qumran, it was the representatives of mainstream Judaism who were the enemies, not the Seleucid or Roman authorities.

The survival of Persian culture in Judaea long after the extinction of Achaemenid rule requires emphasis. One need only recall the influence of Arabic among Jews of Christian Spain, Spanish among the descendants of the

Jews who were expelled from the Iberian Peninsula, and German among Central European Jews who settled in Slavic lands to find analogies of how Persian culture and language could have remained a strong element until the advent of Antiochus IV, long after the Persian rule had ceased. Much of Daniel depicts the struggle between the Seleucids and the Ptolemies, but the superscriptions of the chapters dealing with this subject are ascribed to the reign of Neo-Babylonian and Achaemenid sovereigns.[204] The Book of Esther, which some scholars date circa 200 B.C.E. or later, reflects this influence by mocking Persian institutions.[205] Judging from books such as Esther, Tobit, and Daniel, the reign of the Persian rulers continued to capture the attention of Jewish writers long after the satraps had left Coele-Syria. Only the author of 1 Maccabees, a book evidently written at the end of the second century B.C.E., begins his story with Alexander the Great. Even a sophisticated writer such as Daniel refused to believe that the rule of the Diadochi was not ephemeral. Ironically, in spite of the Jewish resistance to Hellenism, it was Antiochus IV who effectively erased the remnants of Persian influence from Judaea.

The term "Persian" as used here is not necessarily limited to the culture emanating from Persepolis or Susa, but also embraces the Chaldean civilization, evident in a composition such as the Prayer of Nabonidus and to a lesser extent in Daniel 1–5. The proposition of the continued presence of Persian culture in Jerusalem's intellectual circles at the end of the third century B.C.E. may account not only for the setting of treatises such as Judith, Tobit, Esther, and much of Daniel, but also for certain aspects of some of the early works preserved among the Dead Sea Scrolls. The Qumran Targum of Job, the War Rule, and the Qumranic Torah all employ technical terms derived or borrowed directly from the Persian but are devoid of any Greek vocabulary.[206] The cosmology implicit in the Enochite astronomy and the Jubilees calendar seems to presume Oriental astronomical lore without any influence of Greek thought. The dimensions of the sanctuary formulated by the author of the Qumranic Torah, as was argued above, necessarily reflect an architecture whose elements were borrowed from an Oriental cosmogony and cosmography.[207]

Letters written circa 200 B.C.E. by Antiochus III provide more specific testimony of Persian influence. The epistles in *AJ* 12:138–146 were once suspected of being pseudepigraphs, but recent scholarship accepts them as genuine.[208] What characterizes these letters, in contrast to the usual correspondence emanating from the Seleucid chancellery, is their resemblance to the Achaemenid letters recorded in the books of Ezra and Nehemiah. Since Hellenistic epistolary style is known to have been distinctive, this resemblance to the Persian letters in the Bible may be accounted for by the supposition that the Jewish delegation to Antioch presented its requests in the form of drafts reflective of the scriptural style. Jack Love and Jacob Milgrom have called attention to an interesting clause in Antiochus III's letter to Ptolemy, his governor in Coele-Syria: "Nor is it lawful to bring in their skins (i.e., of unclean animals)."[209] This statement bears some resemblance to 11Q Torah 47:7–8: "Every skin of a clean beast which they may sacrifice in their cities they shall not bring into it (i.e., the holy city)." This ordinance is more stringent than the halakah, which sanctions the use of the skins of unclean animals for sacred purposes. It is also noteworthy that Antiochus III, or at least the Judaean drafter of the letter, was concerned about providing wood for the sanctuary: "The timber, moreover, shall be brought from Judaea itself and from other nations."[210] 11Q Torah 23–25 prescribes a feast of six days for the offering of new wood, a season first mentioned in a more modest form in Neh. 10:35 and 13:31. This is not to say that the similarities of Antiochus III's charter of 198 B.C.E. to some passages in the Qumranic Torah definitely date its compositon; only that the matter of the skins of unclean animals defiling the sanctuary is reflected in these letters composed at the beginning of the second century B.C.E.

Perhaps another hint suggesting that the composition of the Qumranic Torah occurred about 198 B.C.E. or a few years earlier is 11Q Torah 56:16: "And he shall not return the people to Egypt to wage war." The word למלחמה (to wage war) constitutes the author's addition to the citation from Deut. 17:16 and 28:68.[211] This may be an indication (a) that the author wrote prior to the time of Antiochus III's conquest of Coele-Syria; and (b) that the author of 11Q Torah was not one of those characterized by Josephus as having plotted with the Syrians against the Ptolemaic hegemony. This rule limits the prohibition against returning to Egypt to the specific purpose of waging war, thus sanctioning other relations, such as commerce.

The apparent influence of the books of Ezekiel and Ezra-Nehemiah upon the composition of the sectarian scroll provides additional evidence for dating 11Q Torah before the Maccabean period. Admittedly, the degree of the scroll's dependence on Ezekiel 40–48 still remains an unsettled problem. What cannot be questioned, however, is that along with Exodus 25–30 and 35–40, Ezekiel 40–48 forms the closest scriptural model for cols. 3–13 and 30–42 of the Qumranic Torah. Regardless of the details, the spirit that animated the exilic prophet to record the dimensions not only of the sanctuary but also of its courtyards, gates, and lampstands, and to relate these measurements to current cosmology is certainly duplicated by no other writer more clearly than the author of the Qumranic Torah.[212] These two writers also shared a concern for priestly prerogatives and perquisites, which went hand in hand with their description, in astonishing detail, of the separation of the defiled from the sacred. What both Ezekiel and Zadok attempted to attain was the highest degree of holiness. Also common to both writers is the willingness to propose new measurements and forms without regard to traditional texts, and to do so by invoking God's divine authority. Some three centuries separate Zadok from Ezekiel, but much of Jerusalem's ambience seems to have hardly changed. Aside from the Book of Ezekiel, the other non-Pentateuchal book that seems closest to 11Q Torah is Ezra-Nehemiah. The covenant proclaimed in Damascus, as was noted above, echoes the pact proclaimed by the people in Nehemiah 10.[213] But what seems most to underlie works such as the Temple Scroll, Jubilees, and the Damascus Document is a characteristic post-exilic messianism, a messianism which drew its inspiration from the exilic and post-exilic passages in Deuteronomy, Isaiah, Jeremiah, Ezekiel, and Malachi. The three elements of this eschatology were a new heaven,[214] a new covenant,[215] and a new temple.[216]

Whereas the messianism evident in the Qumranic Torah and the Book of Jubilees harmonizes with that of the post-exilic period, it hardly coheres with the messianic ideal that emerged with the Maccabean triumph. The basic difference between pre-Maccabean and post-Maccabean messianism seems to be reflected in different attitudes toward Zerubbabel's sanctuary. The repute of the Solomonic sanctuary, whether historical or mythologized, was such that the post-exilic house of God seemed a rather meager caricature of the former. Its stark prosaism contrasted strongly with the fabulous gilding of the days of David and Solomon. Such was Solomon's standing that two treatises incorporated into the canon, certainly written in post-exilic times, were attributed to the "wisest of all men," enhancing further the sanctuary erected by David's son. What is true of the physical appearance of Zerubbabel's temple applies also to its sanctity. One need only turn to the talmudic tradition to exemplify the contrast between the high state of purity attributed to the First Temple and the defilement of the Second. Although the talmudic literature emanates from a later period, it does seem to reflect in this instance the predominant post-exilic attitude. An example is Nehemiah's account of his visits to Jerusalem[217] and the lament of Hag. 2:3 and 9: "Who is left among you that saw this house in its former glory? How do you see it now? Is it not in your sight as nothing? . . . The latter splendor of this house shall be greater than the former, says the Lord of hosts; and in this place I will give prosperity, says the Lord of hosts"(RSV).

The removal of Zeus Olympus from the sanctuary in 164 B.C.E. had a cathartic effect upon Jerusalem's priests no less than on the Maccabean faithful. The Maccabean victory seemed a miracle, evidently proving to many that Jerusalem's shrine was a worthy structure in spite of its physical modesty. The immense pride in this sanctuary is reflected in works such as the Letter of Aristeas and the accounts retelling the story of Hanukkah. In a letter written apparently in 163 B.C.E., Judah Maccabee records at length how Nehemiah found the heavenly naphtha salvaged by Jeremiah from the fire of the First Temple and used it to kindle the altar of Zerubbabel's temple.[218] The feast of Hanukkah celebrates a new appreciation of Zerubbabel's sanctuary as much as it does its cleansing from pagan pollution. Josephus' histories, bare when dealing with the late Achaemenid rulers and the Diadochi, become voluminous for the Maccabean and Hasmonean eras. The pages of his work attest to the people's devotion to the central shrine of Judaism, with which numerous miracles were associated. As suggested by a report of Hecataeus of Abdera, writing circa 300 B.C.E., in pre-Maccabean times this devotion was directed not so much to the temple as to the high priest, a view also reflected in Ben Sira. Aside perhaps from the person of Judah Maccabee himself, the legendary figures of the Second Temple were the pre-Maccabean high priests, such as Simon the Just I and Simon the Just II. If, then, the Qumranic Torah may be said to have contained a single message, it is the repudiation of the current sanctuary as one not willed by God. This message remained a dogma throughout the sect's existence, being repeated in the Community Rule. But the repudiation, it would seem, could have originated only at a time when the standing of Jerusalem's current temple was regarded as inferior, not in the Maccabean age, when its repute reached its zenith. To be sure, as late as the rabbinic era, the Mishnah and the Talmud seem to underrate the Second Temple, a sentiment that may go back to the view that prevailed among the Pharisees.[219] But this sentiment may have had its roots in the pre-Maccabean epoch, though it would have found little support immediately after 164 B.C.E. At any rate, even the rabbis did not repudiate the celebration of Hanukkah, embellishing the event with the miraculous purification of the sanctuary. The Qumranic sect from its very inception, and its precursor in 11Q Torah, not only refused to recognize the Second Temple but regarded it as a source of defilement. Is it not curious that the voluminous literature found in the Qumran library, which is putatively dated to the end of the second or during the first century B.C.E., does not contain a single allusion to the feast celebrated on the twenty-fifth of Kislev? It is in particular this total rejection of the current sanctuary that makes the reigning hypothesis, which finds the roots of the Qumranic sect in the Hasideans who split off from the Maccabean rebels, seem unlikely.[220] The pious sectaries, the theory goes, wished to live in a higher state of purity than that observed by the Maccabean and Hasmonean rulers. Hence the vehement vilification, it is argued, of the sanctuary and Jerusalem's priesthood in Qumranic texts.

The views implicit in the Qumranic Torah, it seems to me, cannot be ascribed to the Hasideans. Neither can they be attributed to some extreme element of the Pharisees. As I see it, the reason that 11Q Torah rejects the holiness of the current sanctuary is not only, as the Hasideans maintained, that the priests of the day were unworthy preservers of its necessary sanctity, but rather that from its very beginning, i.e., since its erection, it had never possessed the proper state of holiness. Even the temple erected by David and Solomon was, according to the author of the Qumranic Torah, an idolatrous structure. The square dimensions of the true temple are intended to contrast with the rectangular sanctuary erected by Solomon. What is implicit in 11Q Torah seems quite explicit in the Damascus Document, where the history of Israel, beginning with the entry into Canaan, is represented as a single idolatrous epoch, relieved only by a few faithful who were the remnant, kept for the future redemption. The Damascus Document's ambiguous attiude to David, and presumably Solomon, is revealing. Since the author seems to have regarded David as one of the "remnant," the question arises, Why did he violate the prescriptions against royal bigamy? The answer given excuses his action on the grounds that the Book of the Torah which prohibited it had remained sealed in his day. The writer does not address himself to the next question, Why did it remain unrevealed? The implicit response to this query would be that David and his generation were unworthy of its revelation, which was therefore assigned to the scion of Aaron, Zadok. Had David known of its prescriptions as the opponents of the sect do, the author of the Damascus Document argues, he would have observed its provisions against polygamy. Of course, it is conceivable that some of the Hasideans who had been disappointed by the standards of purity and observance among the followers of Judah Maccabee eventually joined with the new covenanters of Zadok, but this may well have taken place after the platform of Damascus had been announced, as well as after the death of the Teacher of Righteousness, when the basic doctrine of the sect had essentially been shaped. But it seems unwarranted to postulate that the Hasideans, who had joined in the war against the Hellenizing polluters of the sanctuary, would have propagated views found in the Qumranic Torah. In other words, it would not be wrong to classify the Hasideans as conservatives, while the author of the sectarian Torah, Zadok, and his followers may properly be labeled radicals, if not revolutionaries. The rejection of Israel's history since the conquest of Canaan forms a fundamental precept of the Qumranic sect from its very beginning, and as such it has no parallel among Judaea's parties, except perhaps among some Christian groupings.[221] The Hasideans, on the other hand, aimed at attaining a state of purity that they ascribed to the priests of the Davidic sanctuary.

Thus, the Qumranic Torah as well as treatises such as the Book of Jubilees, the Damascus Document, and Pesher Habakkuk mirror the tensions of Judaean life during the third and early second centuries B.C.E. These books contain no inkling of the bitter struggle that was to occur after the advent of Antiochus IV Epiphanes in 175 B.C.E.

Zadok in the Literary Context of His Times

A glance at the personalities who are known to have been active in Jerusalem circa 200 B.C.E. reveals that an outburst of new ideas was filling the holy city during Simon II's high-priesthood. Among the figures who must have flour-

ished at this time was the young man of unusual imagination and talent who
eventually assumed the name Daniel. Then there was Simon, son of Joshua
son of Eleazar son of Sirah, known also as Ben Sira, who may be said to
represent the tradition of the learned priesthood—the ideal of fusing piety
with wisdom. His Ecclesiasticus attests to the continuity of a culture that
cherished the wisdom found in works such as Proverbs and Ecclesiastes. During this era in Jerusalem also lived Joseph son of Tobiah, an old man whose
name must have aroused terror throughout Syria, Phoenicia, and Palestine,
even if only a fraction of what is related about him is true. Joseph, the nephew
of Onias II, was a sheik and a descendant of the sheiks who had controlled
Ammon for half a millennium; a correspondent of Zenon, as well as an Egyptian bureaucrat during the reign of Ptolemy Philadelphus (283–247), he was
the chief tax-farmer of Coele-Syria according to Josephus, who also reproduces a romanticized account of his life.[222] Other leading Jerusalemites of the
period circa 200 B.C.E. included John son of Accos, who negotiated with
Antiochus III the privileges Judaea would receive for siding with him against
Ptolemy V Epiphanes (203–181 B.C.E.),[223] and John's son Eupolemus, who, as
was mentioned above, served as Judah's envoy to Rome in 161 B.C.E. and
authored some histories written in a vulgar Greek.[224] Not far from Jerusalem,
in a village called Modein, lived a priest named Mattathias the son of John,
the Hasmonean.

To these, if the chronology adduced in this study is valid, must be added the
name of Zadok, according to a persistent tradition the disciple of Antigonus of
Soko, who presumably wrote the Qumranic Torah and proclaimed himself
the *Moreh Ṣedeq* of the group in Damascus that launched what eventually
became the Essene movement. Somewhat later, the author of the remarkable
Book of Jubilees fused the traditional Torah with Zadok's newly discovered
Book of Law while alluding to the first rumblings of Hellenism in Judaea by
attacking nakedness and uncircumcision. The author of Jubilees must be
counted among the earliest adherents of Zadok's newly discovered Torah.

What may we determine about Zadok himself and his relationship to the
personalities of his time? Let us begin by presuming that the role of Zadok
was crucial as the immediate cause of the sectarian movement. 3Q 15 (Copper
Scroll) 11:2–7 and CD 5:5 confirm the rabbinic and Karaite traditions that
Zadok founded the sect which eventually became the group that settled at
Qumran and in a later period developed into the party known as the
Essenes.[225] It would seem that Zadok was married and had sons, which
accounts for the prominent place of the *Beney Ṣadoq* at Qumran. His burial site
became an important shrine of the sect.

11Q Torah, CD 1–8, and 1QpHab do reveal glimpses of the precursor of
Qumran. A number of texts stress that Zadok was of Aaronide descent, perhaps even from the high-priestly line of his namesake, the chief priest in the
days of David and Solomon. The name Zadok appears in both the pre-exilic

and post-exilic genealogical tables of the high priesthood. Matthew's genealogy of Jesus lists a certain Zadok as fifth in the post-exilic lineage of Joseph,
Mary's husband. According to a report in *AJ* 18:4 and 10, Saddok, a Pharisee,
was the co-founder together with Judas of Gamala of the "Fourth Philosophy," that gave rise to the Zealots. Josephus is silent concerning Saddok's
pedigree, but the possibility that he was of priestly descent need not be
excluded. And indeed, the collective name of the Aaronide officials who were
in charge of the temple and of Judaea was "the sons of Zadok." Born apparently in the last third of the third century B.C.E., Zadok must have been closely
related to Onias II and Simon the Just II, the successive high priests, and
through them with the powerful Tobiad clan, whose base was in Ammon, but
who intermarried with Jerusalem's ruling circles.

When delving into a text to extract information concerning its author, one
must distinguish the educational baggage the writer had acquired by assimilation from the personality he projects in his work. There is no doubt that the
study of the Torah formed the core of the schooling provided by Jerusalem's
educational facilities. In addition to whatever teaching was imparted by the
father, aristocratic, i.e., priestly, families must have hired tutors to instruct
their sons in the Mosaic Torah. As the child grew older, he was introduced to
the other books of Scripture, but for youngsters belonging to the priestly clans
the Torah, especially the sections relating to the sanctuary and its ritual, never
ceased to be the core subject. The passages committed to memory during
childhood assumed new meaning during apprenticeship, when the young
priests mastered the ritual routine and learned to negotiate the pathways and
corners of the sanctuary. Along with the clauses that prescribed the details of
the sanctuary and its ritual, it would seem that the priests mastered a symbolism which, though not recorded and therefore free to be improvised, gave
meaning to the repeated words. Fragments of these figurations have been preserved in writings such as Isa. 6:1–5, where the prophet depicts the throne of
God surrounded by seraphim, or Ezek. 1:4–28, where God is riding on the
chariots. The priestly lore taught that the punctilious observance of the prescribed dimensions and rites was a matter of great importance. Breaches in the
ritual would result in defiling the sanctuary and personal extinction. The les-
son was apparent from what had happened to Nadab and Abihu, who deviated from the norm.[226] The student would also have become cognizant of the
views expressed in the Enochite writings, which contained the popular cosmological and cosmogenic pictures of the universe assimilated into the dimensions of the temple, so that the sanctuary and its architecture came to
symbolize the universe.[227] To be sure, there were books in circulation, such as
Ecclesiastes, which claimed that nothing mattered. But being of priestly
stature and training, one knew better. As portrayed in the Song of Songs, even
the love of a woman was analagous to the presence of the holy in the chamber

of the sanctuary. It is quite doubtful that we can reconstruct the precise symbolism that a youth of the third century learned; what seems probable is that along with the formal study of Torah went a hermeneutic that attempted to give meaning to every word.

What little can be grasped of Zadok's educational background and his assimilation of it is inadequate to account for the composition of the Qumranic Torah. Some light may be shed on the mystery of the pseudonymity of the scroll by taking a glance at Jerusalem's literary scene at the end of the third and during the second century B.C.E. Ecclesiasticus is an exception to the pseudepigraphic rule of the time in that the real author attaches a colophon indicating his identity. Otherwise psalms are ascribed to David or Solomon, the latter also being credited with having authored the Song of Songs and Ecclesiastes. Perhaps likewise in circulation were the books known to us as the Wisdom of Solomon, the Odes of Solomon, and the Psalms of Solomon, all now classified as apocryphal or pseudepigraphic. Some writers chose to attribute their works to Enoch, Noah, Baruch, or Daniel. The same practice of attributing authorship to a notable figure of the past applies to the works composed by the members of the Qumranic sect. The eschewing of authorship by posing as the "finder" of an ancient manuscript is thus not an exclusive characteristic of the sectarians; a multitude of reasons prompt writers to conceal their identity. What is remarkable about ancient post-biblical literature is that so many authors did so.

What gave rise to this passion for pseudonymity? After all, the prophets did not hesitate to announce their visions under their own names. But the scribes who gained their livelihood by reproducing the pseudepigraphic writings did everything in their power to envelop in mystery not only the real authors, attributing their works to ante- or post-diluvian patriarchs or to angelic beings, but the "finders" of the allegedly ancient manuscripts, who were also not revealed. It is doubtful that the authors of these pseudepigraphs did what Moses de Leon did, aging the paper in which he had inscribed the holy Zohar.

Only in the case of 11Q Torah is the finder's name revealed, and this revelation may have been unintentional, only incidental to explaining why a Torah given at Sinai had not been observed by David. The resolution of this puzzling aspect seems to go back to the nature of post-exilic Judaism. Hand in hand with the catastrophe of the exile and the destruction of the sanctuary came the hope of redemption, as proclaimed by the prophets. Redemption did come in the form of successive proclamations of the Persian kings, but it expressed itself only in a pale shadow of what had been predicted by the seers. The post-exilic visionaries consoled the people, whose toil and suffering was becoming unbearable, with the assurance that the redemption had merely begun and that the future presaged a new heaven and a new earth. As these expectations were dashed, prophecy ceased. Thus the modest rebuilding of the sanctuary, restored walls for the holy city that gave but meager protection, and the constant pressure of the neighboring tribes, all of which characterized post-exilic Judaea, could in no way be considered the fulfillment of the prophetic visions in Ezekiel, Zephaniah, Haggai, Zechariah, and Malachi. The collapse of the Persian Empire under the pressure of Macedonia and the subsequent shifting fortunes of successive empires recalled for some the predicted wars between Gog and Magog. The never-ending Syrian wars, as well as the rise of Rome from a city to a world power during the third and second centuries B.C.E., gave new grist to writers who announced the impending coming of the anointed. The Book of Daniel, whose single theme is the setting of the eschaton, need not be seen as a novel expression of messianic expectation but as the most important treatise of this type which has found its place within the Hebrew Scripture.

Challenging Mainstream Judaism

It would seem that the messianic hopes which stirred the writer who chose the name Daniel also captured Zadok, probably Daniel's senior by a decade or two. Like Daniel, Zadok can be classified in modern vocabulary as a philosophical historian. But whereas the father of apocalyptic foresaw the redemption at the end of the eras of the four empires, Zadok viewed the eschaton as a strictly internal affair. It is worth recalling here what was suggested above, that the Qumranic Torah may be read in two ways. As Yadin has masterfully done, it may be seen as a work of learning, as an attempt to create a more coherent Torah by eliminating duplicate or seemingly contradictory material through conflation and harmonization, and by adding some supplementary material.[228] This approach appears to impose upon the text modern concepts of editing that were probably unknown to the author of 11Q Torah, and also ignores the significant role of crucial additions and alterations made by the author of the scroll.

In contrast, the hypothesis presented in this monograph views the conflation and harmonization of the legal lore of the Pentateuch as incidental to the author's purpose in composing the Qumranic Torah. The elements that stand out in 11Q Torah and which were probably paramount in the author's mind are the alterations, innovations, and supplements. Without question it was exceedingly important for the author to have a square sanctuary, not the rectangular one erected by Solomon and Zerubbabel. Of equal consequence were the three seasons of new fruits, instead of the single season of grain prescribed in the traditional Books of Moses. That the sacrificial rites for the Sabbaths and feasts depart from the Mosaic prescriptions and that an entirely new charter, unrecorded in Deut. 17:14-20, be observed by the king were considered of paramount significance by the writer.

These two approaches raise disparate problems concerning the sectarian Torah's author. In the first instance, the issue revolves around the nature of the erudition and the author's sources, questions ably discussed in Yadin's voluminous commentary and introduction. In the second approach, the enigma of the scroll raises issues other than those discussed by Yadin: (a) the question of heresy when a writer largely disregards the current Torah in favor of one composed by himself; (b) the willingness to challenge the Mosaic Torah by writing an entirely new version, a Torah in which God, speaking in the first person, addresses Moses at Sinai, and then presenting it as having been discovered in a sealed ark; (c) the readiness to reject the period from the entry into Canaan until the present—perhaps a millennium—as nothing but a sinful epoch. The basic question thus becomes not Yadin's query, How does the Qumranic Torah relate to the Qumranic sect on the one hand and to the mainstream of Judaism on the other? The question becomes, what made the writer—Zadok, we presume—compose a revolutionary document challenging traditional Judaism and then launch a movement that eventually developed into the Essene Commune?

The paucity of information concerning the last decades of the third century and the beginning of the second century B.C.E. leaves no choice but to rely on the indirect evidence available in books such as Daniel, Jubilees, and apparently the sectarian Torah, works whose authors flourished during the period under consideration. The current view, which maintains that the revolutionary period in Judaea began with the reign of Antiochus IV, can no longer be supported. Let us recall that redemption was the main theme of exilic Judaism, a yearning which remained unsatiated by the rebuilding of the temple under Zerubbabel. The fall of Persia and the coming of Alexander, followed by the incessant wars of the Diadochi and then the recurrent Syrian wars, were interpreted in Jerusalem as testimony to the battle between Gog and Magog. The victory of the Seleucids in 198 B.C.E., followed by Antiochus III's humiliation, seemed to attest to the downfall of pagan empires in the face of the coming kingdom of the Lord presaged by Malachi. Both Zadok and Daniel testify to the presence of this messianic expectation. The Book of Daniel was acceptable to mainstream Judaism, Zadok's work was branded as heretical. Inadequate as the information is, the Qumranic Torah is evidence of the existence of a new radicalism at the beginning of the second century B.C.E., a radicalism which based its validity on a return to the model of the Israelite camp at Sinai. This extremism found expression in a rejection of urbanism together with an idealization of the wilderness.

During the Persian period, Jerusalem had become an important trading center for the Phoenicians, and this role was expanded during the third century with both the decline of Tyre after the fall of Carthage and the rise of Greek colonization. The growth of the diaspora in distant lands became a

source of wealth for the holy city. The temple's treasury not only provided for
the sanctuary's ritual needs but fulfilled the functions of a banking institution.[229] Hellenization, although not as extensive as generally presumed, did
begin to make an appearance in the holy city. On top of this, as was discussed
above, came the alliance between Jerusalem's high priesthood and an enter-
prising clan in Transjordan, the Tobiads. All these developments reflected
Jerusalem's growing urbanization.

Some ecclesiastical circles must have viewed this growing urbanism with
horror. For them Jerusalem was not a city containing a sacred precinct, but an
extension of the temple. In other words, it was the temple and the sacred areas
that made Jerusalem what it was, a city of God. The hustle and bustle of a
metropolis apparently seemed abominable to many priests. Certainly numerous allusions in the Psalms reflect the growing idealization of the holy city.[230]
The halakah likewise transforms Jerusalem into a city which is an extension of
Mount Zion, in which worldly affairs, such as agriculture and commerce,
except for the service of pilgrims, were banned.[231]

What the rabbis did to a minor extent the Qumranic Torah accentuates,
transforming Jerusalem from a city having within its limits the precincts of the
temple into עיר המקדש (the city of the sanctuary). It is possible that the "city of
the sanctuary" envisaged in the sectarian Torah is not a rebuilding of the
temple in Jerusalem but a "New Jerusalem" which would, in a different area,
replace the city of that name. Certainly the dimensions of the courts in the
sectarian Torah exceeded the actual area of Jerusalem's Temple Mount.

As is to be expected, the city was of a lower degree of sanctity than the
courtyards of the sanctuary, from which it was separated by a רובד (terrace)[232]
and a חיל (rampart).[233] Cohabitation was prohibited according to the sectarian
Torah, thus excluding priestly families from the city.[234] The use of the skins of
animals not slaughtered in the temple according to ritual requirements was
limited to areas outside of the city.[235] Furthermore, no sewers were allowed in
it, a prescription which, according to Yadin and Milgrom, even bans any
excrement from the city of the temple.[236] If the exclusiveness of the city is not
sufficiently clear, it should also be noted that it was separated from its surrounding settlements by a buffer of thirty *ris* (3,000 cubits).[237] Thus the role of
the city, the "New Jerusalem," was to be an adjunct to the temple, thereby
excluding its function as the metropolis of Judaea, a role which it had actually fulfilled since Davidic times. And since the surrounding areas, as the
Qumranic Torah describes them, have only an agricultural function, its
author reflects a strong bias against urbanization. The priests and levites who
are not connected with the sanctuary and the twelve tribes are to dwell outside
the holy city and its buffer in מושבות (settlements).[238] The legislation of the
Qumranic Torah refers to the tilling of the land and husbandry. By special
dispensation, the slaughter of non-sacrificial animals was sanctioned, and

even the use of unclean animals for non-consumptive purposes. But what seems to be almost totally absent from the fragments of the sectarian Torah are passages similar to Exod. 21–22:16 which deal with trade or the sale of land. The "New Jerusalem" would be utterly sacred; everyday activity would be excluded. The hustle and bustle of the urban metropolis was not welcome. When compared with the Pentateuch and the Mishnah, this pastoral element becomes even more evident.

The Qumranic Torah implies what is stated explicitly in the Damascus Document, that only during their sojourn in the wilderness had Israel faithfully observed the Torah. This tenet gave new impetus to the doctrine idealizing the desert, a view which receives considerable emphasis in the Community Rule and the *Hodayot*. The Byzantine Suda, as noted above, saw a link between the Essenes and the Rechabites, who in the days of Jeremiah abandoned Jerusalem with its seductive entrapments for life in the wilderness. The rejection of urbanism and the idealization of the wilderness find concrete expression in the founding of the Commune in the desert of Qumran.[239]

Ever since Jeremiah there seems to have existed a tension between those who argued that the Law could be observed within the walls of a prosperous city and those who maintained this could only be done within the pristine wilderness of the desert. 11Q Torah, perhaps more than any other Qumranic treatise, seems to express this apparent revolt against the urbanization of the holy city and to call for a return to the tabernacle of the Exodus. The setting of this treatise is at Sinai, partly no doubt to assert its authority vis-à-vis the traditional Torah. But there may be another equally valid reason why its author set it in the period immediately after the Exodus. In contrast to the traditional Torah, which provides for a movable tabernacle in the wilderness and remains silent concerning the type of sanctuary to be constructed in the settled land, 11Q Torah asserts the permanence of the tabernacle of the wilderness. It does not merely reproduce the Mosaic structure, but preserves what the author regarded as its essential features. While reproducing the materials and sacred furnishings recorded in the Book of Exodus, it fits them into a tabernacle whose dimensions leave no doubt as to their permanence. Moreover, as emphasized by Yadin, the Qumranic Torah is characterized by its use of square dimensions. The tabernacle of the wilderness was rectangular, but the permanent temple was to recall the square shape of the breastplate with the twelve precious stones corresponding to the number of Israel's tribes.[240] Moses had built an altar with twelve stones at the foot of Sinai for the twelve tribes of Israel.[241] The author of the Qumranic Torah no doubt viewed the Mosaic altar at the foot of Sinai as a square which was to characterize the eternal sanctuary in the "New Jerusalem." The gates of the new sanctuary were to recall the manner in which the twelve tribes surrounded Mount Sinai. Thus the settlements in the holy land related to the city of the temple as did the

tribal encampments to the tent of meeting. A similar relationship existed
between the courtyards and their gates and the area designated as the *sanctum
sanctorum* in the sectarian Torah. The temple and its encampments thus mirrored a square universe in the center of which God would dwell. Both
features, the reshaping of the Mosaic furnishings and the square dimensions
of the new sanctuary, seem intended as a contrast to the historical sanctuaries
of Solomon and Zerubbabel.

The author of the Qumranic Torah, Zadok we presume, saw the future
reconstruction of Israel in a return to the ideals of the Rechabites, who were
moved by Jeremiah's glorification of the wilderness. A recent article by S.
Safrai documents the rabbinic allusions to the Essenes as Rechabites.[242] It is
not certain, but the migration to the *land* of Damascus may also reflect the
pastoral ideal, as may the establishment of the Commune in the wilderness of
Judaea. Essenism, as depicted by the ancient writers, attempted to create an
egalitarian society by an outright rejection of city life. The Therapeutai,
described in Philo, may reflect the attempt to make an urban copy of what had
hitherto been a pastoral utopia. The roots of Qumran, then, are not the stir-
ring events of the Maccabean uprising but the invisible turbulence hidden
behind the seeming serenity of the third century B.C.E. Deutero-Isaiah's new
light, Ezekiel's revival of dry bones and the war between Gog and Magog,
Habakkuk's expectation of the end, Malachi's return of Elijah—to mention
only a few visions—made the coming of the eschaton a constant preoccupa-
tion of Israelites during the post-exilic epoch. Of the three figures whose
works germinated during the last decades of the third and the beginning of
the second century B.C.E., the writings of Ben Sira seem to have been the least
affected by these expectations. The priestly circle that is reflected in Ecclesiasticus may perhaps be regarded as the group in which the Sadducean sect found
sympathizers. On the other hand, although the Book of Daniel became an
important document at Qumran, its powerful influence can only be gauged in
the mainstream of Judaism. Its inclusion in the canon of the *Tanak,* although it
was not written before 165 B.C.E., attests to the grip this work had on its contemporaries. In contrast to the Danielic messianism of the mainstream,
Zadok's advocacy of an eschatological sanctuary unfolded into a movement in
which the bringing of redemption became the principal goal of the sect. The
Commune called *Yahad* out of which the Essene movement sprang was thus
not an end in itself, but served as a prelude to the end of days.

Zadok combines two roles frequently found in redemptive movements. As
the presumed author of a Torah that prescribed the dimensions of the eternal
sanctuary, he links up with the prophets who, ever since Jeremiah, Deutero-
Isaiah, Zechariah, and Malachi, presaged the coming of the eschaton. But in
contrast to these prophets, who merely predicted the coming of the redemption, Zadok also put forward the claim of himself being the messianic figure
foretold by the prophets. He was both the author of the Qumranic Torah and

its chief protagonist. Jewish history knows of many figures who acted as redeemers and of others who acted as their presagers. As the "finder" of the sealed Torah and as the Teacher of Righteousness, Zadok embodied both roles.

11Q Torah gives us a glimpse into the mind of its author, shedding new light on the earliest stages of what, with the passage of time, developed into the Qumranic Commune. It would perhaps be erroneous to postulate that the composer of 11Q Torah and the Teacher of Righteousness viewed himself as either Elijah, the precursor of the Messiah, or as the Messiah himself. Neither 11Q Torah nor the literature that developed in its wake seems to contain any echoes of the messianic beliefs found in writings such as Malachi 3, where the Lord's coming is announced by the prophet, or in Sir. 48:10 and 1 Mac. 2:58, where Elijah serves as the precursor of the Messiah. But one may gain a better understanding of the beginning of Qumran if it is supposed that the author of 11Q Torah viewed himself as in a special kind of relationship to Moses. Perhaps the term "reincarnation" overstates Zadok's feelings while composing the sectarian Torah, which he was going to represent as a divine document hidden in an ark for a millennium. What seems apparent, however, is Zadok's strong identification with the ancient lawgiver.

This self-perception on the part of its author may account for features of 11Q Torah that are otherwise enigmatic. In a work that is largely modeled after the Mosaic books, the space in 11Q Torah devoted to the construction of the sanctuary seems disproportionate. Whereas some twelve chapters, one quarter of the Book of Exodus, are devoted to the building of the wilderness sanctuary, the author of 11Q Torah gives some twenty-eight columns to the building of his temple, retaining only thirty-eight for the remainder of the Law. This disproportion, as well as the endless repetition of the measurements of the sanctuary which far exceeds the biblical archetype, appears less puzzling if Zadok regarded himself as Moses *redivivus,* the one to whom God had given the commandments to erect the eternal sanctuary. On the other hand, the commandments in which he, as the surrogate of Moses, served merely as an intermediary between God and Israel, could be dealt with more briefly. Yadin has noted that the columns which are written in the third person instead of in the first (which is standard in the remainder of the scroll) comprise the priestly ritual.[243] The reason seems to be that, unlike the designing and building of the sanctuary, the sacrificial offerings were the exclusive domain of Aaron and his descendants. God, as the rabbis pointed out, spoke only to Moses on a regular basis, and to Aaron solely in exceptional cases. It would not have been fitting for a person who plays the role of high priest to compose a book that was intended to rival and perhaps outdo the Mosaic Law.[244] As the alter ego of Moses, however, the author of 11Q Torah could serve as the guide of both Aaron and Israel.

In the Qumranic Torah, when God addresses Moses in the first person, He is really addressing the latter-day Moses—i.e., the author. It may be said, therefore, that in composing the Qumranic Torah, Zadok acted in a dual capacity. First, as transmitter, he reproduced the words of God as God must have delivered them on Mount Sinai. Second, as addressee, he himself was the "thou" whom God was addressing. God said, "thou (Zadok) shalt make"; "thou (Zadok) shalt count"; "thou (Zadok) shalt sanctify." This dual capacity of addressee and executor is applicable to Moses only in certain instances, such as in his role as the shepherd and guide of Israel from the wilderness to the banks of the Jordan. In most of the commandments in the canonical Torah, however, Moses serves merely as the medium through which God's words are transmitted to Israel. In 11Q Torah, Zadok, acting as Moses' surrogate, is also assigned the task of executing God's prescriptions.

Put more simply, Zadok, whether consciously or not, set out to rival Moses, hoping to succeed where his predecessor had failed. Moses had brought the Torah to Israel in the wilderness, with the promised land as a reward for its observance. But soon after his death the people, attracted by the idolatry of the natives, spurned the Law. Even Nebuchadnezzar's destruction of the holy city and its sanctuary did not suffice to bring Israel back to the Torah. However, the advent of the new Law, i.e., 11Q Torah, which its author claimed had lain sealed in an ark until 390 years after the destruction of Jerusalem, would bring redemption to Israel: (a) the end of time, as promised by God to the patriarchs, would finally arrive; (b) Israel would be cleansed from idolatry; (c) the level of purity and separation between the profane and the sacred would be punctiliously observed; (d) the sanctuary, though designed and put together by Zadok and his assistants, would in truth be built by God to be His dwelling place forever; (e) life in the city of the temple and its surrounding settlements would be unconcerned with worldly matters but would focus on the sanctuary; and (f) in the absence of the pollution resulting from sinfulness, God would dwell in Israel's midst forever. In other words, unlike the ephemeral nature of the canonical Torah, 11Q Torah would endure forever.

The supposition of Zadok's self-identification with Moses sheds considerable light on the dawn of the Qumran movement. The epithet *Moreh Ṣedeq*, which the sect's founder adopted, was borrowed, as has been frequently noted, from Hos. 10:12. As we have shown, however, there was a more profound reason for the second half of the phrase: *ṣedeq* was but a variant of *Ṣadoq*, the name of the discoverer of the second Torah and the founder of the sect. Needless to say, the intrinsic meaning of *ṣedeq*, justice in a narrow definition and righteousness in the eyes of God in a broader sense, was not lost on the followers of Zadok.

Did the first part of the epithet, *moreh*, likewise have a meaning other than the obvious one? It would seem so. Scripture refers to Moses as shepherd, wise, man of understanding, pious (*ḥasyd*), and prophet, but never as *moreh* (teacher). Nonetheless, the Jewish perception of Moses was almost exclusively as teacher. This is certainly true in the rabbinic tradition, where *Morenu* (our master) or its synonym *Rabbenu* is the epithet always applied to Moses. This view need not be merely Pharisaic, but no doubt goes back to Exod. 4:12, "And I shall teach you," with regard to Moses' commissioning, and to Exod. 24:12, "the law and the commandment which I have written to teach them," referring to Moses on Mount Sinai. By adopting the title *Moreh* (or *Yoreh*) *Ṣedeq*, Zadok seems to have set forth a claim for Moses' mantle. The authorship of 11Q Torah plus the founding of a group ready to live by its prescriptions may have permitted him to make the invidious comparison between his predecessor and himself that is possibly suggested by his choice of a title. Moses, it would seem, was truly considered a *moreh,* but Zadok himself was to be regarded as the eternal *moreh*—the *Moreh Ṣedeq* or Teacher of Righteousness.

The audacity of composing such a book as 11Q Torah at a time when Israel as a whole had accepted the canonical Torah gives a glimpse into Zadok's character. This claim to Moses' mantle could be expected of a personality who had the audacity to compose a book which was to rival the canonical Torah. But Zadok did not claim mere equality with Moses; he sought superiority. The Torah of Moses was ephemeral, Zadok's eternal.

Notes to Chapter I

1. *Documents of Jewish Sectaries: Vol. 1: Fragments of a Zadokite Work* (Cambridge, 1910); reprinted with prolegomenon and bibliography by J. A. Fitzmyer (New York, 1970). It is instructive to see that scholars did not realize the extent of this new sect's significance. Even though fragments of the text have been found at Qumran, its relationship to the Qumranic writings has not been resolved. Examples of problems that still call for resolution include: the chronology of the lines of the Damascus Document, the identity of the מורה צדק (Teacher of Righteousness) and the בני צדוק (Sons of Zadok), as well as the literary relationship between the historical sections in cols. 1–8, the legal lore in cols. 9–16 and the concluding section of Ms. B. The nature and purpose of the treatise remain enigmatic, as they were at the time of the editio princeps.

2. See Fitzmyer's introduction and bibliography cited in n. 1. The most influential study prior to the discoveries in the caves of Qumran was that of L. Ginzberg, *Eine unbekannte jüdische Sekte* (New York, 1922), which has been translated into English as *An Unknown Jewish Sect* (New York, 1976). A more recent text, with translation and notes, is that of Chaim Rabin, *The Zadokite Documents* (Oxford, 2d ed., 1958).

3. M. Burrows (ed.), *The Dead Sea Scrolls of St. Mark's Monastery,* (New Haven, 1950–51), vols. I and II; new photographs by John C. Trever, *Scrolls from Qumran Cave I* (Jerusalem, 1972); E. L. Sukenik, *The Dead Sea Scrolls of the Hebrew University* (Jerusalem, 1955), ed. posthumously by N. Avigad and Y. Yadin. Some of the numerous fragments which have been published appear in the *Discoveries in the Judaean Desert* series. Brief discussions of major texts and fragments are to be found in Geza Vermes, *The Dead Sea Scrolls: Qumran in Perspective* (London, 1977). Joseph A. Fitzmyer lists texts and bibliographies in *The Dead Sea Scrolls: Major Publications and Tools for Study* (Missoula, Mont., 1977). *Revue de Qumran* provides a bibliographical list of new publications relating to the study of the Dead Sea Scrolls.

4. Many of these fragments are discussed by J. T. Milik in *Ten Years of Discovery in the Wilderness of Judaea* (Naperville, Ill., 1959), J. Strugnell (trans.). See also J. A. Sanders, "Palestinian Manuscripts 1947–1972," *JJS* XXIV (1973) 74–83.

5. *BJ* 2:136, 142, 159.

6. *The Temple Scroll* (Jerusalem, 1977) I–III and Supplement (Hebrew). Prior to this publication, the author discussed various aspects of the scroll in a number of articles: "Un nouveau manuscrit de la Mer Morte: 'Le Rouleau du Temple,'" *Académie des Inscriptions & Belles-Lettres: Comptes Rendus* (1967), 607–19; "The Temple Scroll," *Jerusalem Through the Ages* (Jerusalem, 1968), J. Aviram (ed.), 72–82 and plate 12 (Hebrew); "The Temple Scroll," *New Directions in Biblical Archaeology* (Garden City, 1969), D. N. Freedman and J. C. Greenfield (eds.), 139–48; "Pesher Nahum (4Qp Nahum) Reconsidered," *IEJ* XXI (1971) 1–12; "L'attitude essénienne envers la polygamie et la divorce," *RB* LXXIX (1972) 98–99; "The Gate of the Essenes and the Temple Scroll," *Qadmoniot* V (1972) 129–30 (Hebrew); for the English translation of this article see: *Jerusalem Revealed: Archaeology in the Holy City 1968–1974* (New Haven and London, 1976), 90–91; "Le Rouleau du Temple," *Qumrân: Sa piété, sa théologie et son milieu* (Louvain, 1978), M. Delcor (ed.), 115–19.

A number of translations of this astounding find have appeared: F. García, "El rollo del temple," *Estudios Biblicos* XXXVI (1977) 247–92; J. Maier, *Die Tempelrolle vom Toten Meer* (Munich, 1978): A Caquot, "Le Rouleau du Temple de Qoumran, "*ETR* LIII (1978) 443–500.

7. This provocative work has already been the subject of much discussion. Among the studies which have made their way to press are the following: Andre Dupont-Sommer's comments on Yadin's initial announcement, *Comptes-Rendus* (1967) 616–19; Jacob Milgrom, "The Temple Scroll," *BA* XLI (1978) 105–20; Milgrom, "Studies in the Temple Scroll," *JBL* XCVII (1978) 501–23; Joseph M. Baumgarten, review of *TS: JBL* XCVII (1978) 584–89; Ben Zion Luria, "Comments on the 'Scroll of the Sanctuary,'" *Beth Mikra* XXIII (1978) 370–86 (Hebrew); Manfred R. Lehman, "The Temple Scroll as a Source of Sectarian Halakhah," *RQ* IX (1978) 579–87; P. E.

Lapide, "Die Nachbarn der Urgemeinde: Einsichten aus der Tempelrolle der Essener von Qumran," *LM* XVII (1978) 273–75; J. Milgrom, "Comments concerning the Temple Scroll," *Beth Mikra* XXIII (1978) 494–507, XXIV (1979) 205–11 (Hebrew); B. A. Levine, "The Temple Scroll: Aspects of Its Historical Provenance and Literary Character," *BASOR* 232 (1978) 5–23; J. Milgrom, "'Sabbath' and 'Temple City' in the Temple Scroll," ibid., 25–27; Moshe Weinfeld, "'Temple Scroll' or 'King's Law,'" *Shnaton* III (1978–79) 214–37 (Hebrew); M. Mendels, "'On Kingship' in the Temple Scroll and the *Vorlage* of the Symposia in the Letter of Aristeas to Philocrates," *Shnaton* III (1978–79) 245–52 (Hebrew); M. Mishor, "On the Version of the Temple Scroll," *Tarbiz* XLVIII (1979) 173 (Hebrew); D. Flusser, review of *TS*: *Numen* XXVI (1979) 271–74; "The Temple Scroll from Qumran," *Immanuel* IX (1979) 49–52; J. Milgrom, "Further Studies in the Temple Scroll," *JQR* LXXI (1980) 1–17, 89–106; P.-E. Dion, "Le 'Rouleau du Temple' et les Douze," *Science et Esprit* XXXI (1979) 81–83; B. E. Thiering, *Redating the Teacher of Righteousness* (Sydney, 1979); G. Garner, "The Temple Scroll," *Buried History* XV (1979) 1–16; H. A. Mink, "Praesentation af et nyt Qumrans Krift," *DTT* XLII (1979) 81–112; J. M. Baumgarten, "The Pharisaic-Sadducean Controversies about Purity and the Qumran Texts," *JJS* XXXI (1980) 157–70; L. H. Schiffman, "The *Temple Scroll* in Literary and Philological Perspective," *Approaches to Ancient Judaism: Volume II* (Chico, Calif., 1980), W. S. Green (ed.), 143–58; M. Weinfeld, "The Royal Guard According to the Temple Scroll," *RB* LXXXVII (1980) 394–96; B. E. Thiering, "*Mebaqqer* and *Episkopos* in the Light of the Temple Scroll," *JBL* C (1981) 59–74; E. M. Laperrousaz, "Note à propos de la datation du Rouleau du Temple et plus généralement, des manuscrits de la Mer Morte," *RQ* X (1981) 447–52; J. Kampen, "The Temple Scroll: The Torah of Qumran?" *Eastern Great Lakes Biblical Society Proceedings* I (1981). Other studies on this scroll can be found in the notes to the rest of this chapter.

Postscript: The following items came to our attention after the book had been set in print: F. G. Martínez, "4QpNah y la Crucifixión: Nueva hipótesis de reconstrucción de 4Q 169 3–4 i,4–8," *Estudios Biblicos* XXXVIII (1979–80) 221–35; A. Caquot, "Le Rouleau du Temple," *Le Monde de la Bible* XIII (1980) 34–35; J. Maier, "Die Hofanlagen im Tempel-Entwurf des Ezechiel im Licht der 'Tempelrolle' von Qumran," *Prophecy: Essays presented to George Fohrer* (Berlin and New York, 1980), J. Emerton (ed.), 55–68; D. J. Halperin, "Crucifixion, the Nahum Pesher, and the Rabbinic Penalty of Strangulation," *JJS* XXXII (1981) 32–46; J. Milgrom, "The Paradox of the Red Cow," *VT* XXXI (1981) 62–72; M. Delcor, "Le statut du roi d'après le Rouleau du Temple," *Henoch* III (1981) 47–68; B. Jongeling, "A propos de la Colonne XXIII du Rouleau du Temple," *RQ* X (1981) 593–95; Y. Thorion, "Zur Bedeutung von גבורי חיל למלחמה in 11Q T LVII, 9," *RQ* X (1981) 597–98; "Zur Bedeutung von חטא in 11Q T," *RQ* X (1981) 598–99. Not seen was an article by A. S. van der Woude, "De Tempelrol van Qumran," *Nederlands Theologisch Tijdschrift* XXXIV (1980) 281–93.

8. In addition to Yadin's transcriptions (see n. 6), the two articles by Elisha Qimron have also been taken into consideration: "From the Work on the Historical Dictionary: The Text of the Temple Scroll," *Leshonenu* XCII (1978) 136–45 (Hebrew); "New Readings in the Temple Scroll," *IEJ* XXVIII (1978) 161–72. Departures from Yadin's transcription in this work are noted.

9. Yadin, *TS* I, 8. The next-longest is the Isaiah Scroll with 7.3 meters.

10. The changes, which give the book an archaic appearance, include the alteration not only of terms but even of spelling. See below, pp 4–9, 207.

11. 11Q Torah 4:1–13:8, 30:3–35:15.

12. 11Q Torah 13:8–29:6.

13. 11Q Torah 56:12–60:15. Even though the upper portion of col. 60 is missing, the mention of spoils (60:5, 8) would indicate that this column is a continuation of the "Torah of the King," which only includes cols. 56–59 according to Yadin.

14. In 11Q Torah 48–66, the author seems to be following the outline of Deuteronomy 14–22, omitting many sections.

15. In vol. III are found the photographs of the original manuscript. A supplementary volume includes photographs of the fragments found in the Rockefeller Museum. Vol. II consists of a

transcribed text with some reconstructions and an extensive commentary. At the end of this volume are found a reconstructed text and indices. Vol. I, the introduction, provides a study of the text, attempting to assess its role in Judaean and Qumran history. For much-deserved commendation for this monumental achievement, see Milgrom, *BA* XLI (1978) 120: Lehmann, *RQ* IX (1978) 579–80; Luria, *Beth Mikra* XXIII (1978) 370–86.

16. Although frequently used, the term "sacred literature" in the ancient Jewish context needs clarification. It embraces works ascribed to God Himself and is also extended to include writings He inspired; the further removed from God Himself, the less holy. Thus the Decalogue, the prophetic works, and the Psalms represent a descending hierarchy of sanctity. The meaning of sacred writings outside Scripture divided the ancients. The Pharisees would say that all the works which are now called Apocrypha or Pseudepigrapha come under the category of false writings, in other words, not included in the canon. The Qumran sect regarded anything composed by its members as inspired, though the relation of such writings to the scriptural text remains obscure. A third group regarded the Scriptures as never closed, as long as the literature was derived from the traditional writings. Certainly the current classification of canonical, apocryphal, and pseudepigraphic books lacks intrinsic meaning, reflecting attitudes current in late antiquity or during the Middle Ages. For some views on these problems see the following: Menahem Haran, "Problems of the Canonization of Scripture," *Tarbiz* XXV (1956) 245–71 (Hebrew): L. I. Rabinowitz and W. Harvey, "Torah," *EJ* XV, 1235–46; K. von Fritz (ed.), *Pseudepigrapha I* (Geneva, 1971); J. A. Sanders, *Torah and Canon* (Philadelphia, 1972); S. Z. Leiman, *The Canonization of Scripture: The Talmudic and Midrashic Evidence* (Hamden, 1976); N. Brox (ed.), *Pseudepigraphie in der Heidnischen und Jüdisch-Christlichen Antike* (Darmstadt, 1977).

17. Yadin, *TS* I, 60–73. Note particularly 63–65.

18. Milgrom, *BA* XLI (1978) 110–11; Maier, *Tempelrolle,* 11–12. Essentially this is also the view of Weinfeld, *Shnaton* III (1978–79) 214–37.

19. Yadin, *TS* I, 65–73.

20. Ibid., 70. See 1 Chr. 28:19 and Midrash Samuel 15:3. Yadin thinks 1 Chr. 28:19 provided the incentive and the justification for the author to compose this scroll (*TS* I, 70, 308. See also Lapide, *LM* XVII [1978] 274).

21. On the royal charter and the Temple Scroll, see Weinfeld, *Shnaton* III (1978–79), 214–37; *RB* LXXXVII (1980) 394–96. See also Yadin's notes to 11Q Torah 56–59.

22. Neh. 10:35, 13:31; 11Q Torah 23:1–25:1. See also M. Taanith 4:4–5.

23. Milgrom, *BA* XLI (1978) 109–15 speaks of "The Main Characteristics of the Composition," which include conflation, emendations, and glosses (109–12) and "Some Innovations . . ." (112–15).

24. J. M. Baumgarten quotes E. E. Urbach to the effect that Qumran writers, in contrast to the rabbis, drew no distinction between sacred scripture and sectarian compositions (*JBL,* XCVII [1978] 586). This view overstates the distinction. In fact, as indicated in the pesherite genre and other texts, a line of demarcation, even if not as sharp, did exist among Qumranites as well. The context of Urbach's remarks shows that he was speaking only of the Temple Scroll in this quotation, rather than of all Qumranic writings or all sectarian compositions ("The Talmudic Sage—Character and Authority," *Jewish Society through the Ages* [London, 1971], H. H. Ben-Sasson and S. Ettinger [eds.], 116–47, quotation on 126). Baumgarten cites this statement in support of his interpretation of 11Q Torah and Jubilees as "apocalyptic halakah." If I understand him correctly, Baumgarten regards the Temple Scroll as contemporary sectarian halakah which is at variance with mainstream Judaism. However, he also seems to say that the sect envisages another temple, a spiritual one, which is in contrast to the sanctuary described in 11Q Torah.

25. See n. 17 above. Z. W. Falk ("The Temple Scroll and the Codification of Jewish Law," *JLA* II [1979] 33–44) rejects Yadin's contention that it is a pseudepigraph. According to him, it is an early form of halakic composition, using the methods of midrash and the Oral Law to expand upon the Mosaic Torah. In other words, in spite of the fact that it diverges from rabbinic halakah

and is of sectarian origin, Falk views the scroll as a prototype of Mishnah and Tosefta. However, the scroll throughout never alludes to any oral tradition or midrash, but on the contrary vehemently insists on being a literal reproduction of God's words on Sinai. Incidentally, the terminology employed throughout the document is that of *mispaṭ, ḥoq,* and Torah rather than halakah.

26. Further examples can be found in Yadin's source analysis (*TS* I, 39–60), where such examples are marked "I."

27. This passage is found in the first person in Deut. 28:68, but the context for this reference appears to be Deuteronomy 17.

28. Yadin found fragments of letters on the outside of "wad y" which would suggest that there was at least one more column before the one which he labeled as "column 2" (*TS* I, 4–5). On the other hand, from what can be reconstructed of col. 2 it seems reasonable to suppose that this column is still a preface to the scroll; thus, more than one column before the one we find preserved seems unlikely (*TS* II, 1). For a discussion of the content of these introductory columns, see Chap. 2, pp. 42–48.

29. One of the most characteristic features of the scroll is that its author reproduces verbatim sections from the Torah—at least as it was before him—except that he alters the text to the first person to remove all doubt that God is speaking. This cannot be considered a minor alteration and is actually an important characteristic of a number of pseudepigraphic works. Moreover, this mode is rather ancient and is found in many pericopes of the Torah.

"The general procedure of the author is to alter the word 'Lord' to 'I,' 'me' and so forth.

"Furthermore, many sections which are supplementary to the Torah are also put in the first person. Nevertheless, there are sections where the style of the Torah is preserved and the word 'Lord' is not altered" (Yadin, *TS* I, 61). See also Milgrom, *BA* XLI (1978) 109.

30. Yadin believes that sections which are introduced in the Torah as uttered by God, such as Exod. 29 and 30:12–13, were left in the third person by the author of 11Q Torah. However, passages without an introductory attribution to God, many of which were from Numbers and Deuteronomy, the author altered to the first person to leave no doubt that the entire Mosaic Pentateuch was of direct divine origin. The problem with this hypothesis is that no one was more guilty of altering divine texts than the author of the Temple Scroll (Yadin, *TS* I, 62).

31. To be sure, especially after col. 47, the author increasingly reproduces Mosaic passages mechanically without altering them (e.g., 48:6, 51:19–21). In other cases he utilized second-person singular texts in Deuteronomy where they have a collective meaning and made them fit his syntactical format (55:15–21, 61:12–15, 65:2–5).

32. This is important for editing the text of 11Q Torah and was overlooked by Yadin in some cases; e.g., 11Q Torah 17:6, 25:4, 29:2.

33. Yadin understands בתים ומקורים to refer to buildings with ceiling joists (*TS* II, 140).

34. Exod. 20:2–7; Deut. 11:1; 12:28–31; 13:4, 13–15; 14:3, 22–26.

35. Exod. 25:23–30:38. That God addressed this charge to build the tabernacle only to Moses has been indicated by commentators: M. Noth, *Exodus* (Philadelphia, 1962), J. S. Bowden (trans.), 200 ff.; J. P. Hyatt, *Exodus* (London, 1971), 258–59. Note especially U. Cassuto, *A Commentary on the Book of Exodus* (Jerusalem, 1967), I. Abrahams (trans.), 328–29. The LXX writers understood this section to be addressed to Moses alone, as those few second-person plural statements in the Masoretic text appear in the singular in the LXX (e.g., 25:8–10).

36. This cannot be read "brothers" in the plural, as does Maier, *Die Tempelrolle,* p. 47.

37. 11Q Torah 60:16, "When you enter the land."

38. Commentators have noted the relationship between these two sections: Noth, *Exodus,* 274; Hyatt, *Exodus,* 328; R. E. Clements, *Exodus* (Cambridge, 1972), 238; B. S. Childs, *The Book of Exodus* (Philadelphia, 1974), 529–37. Critical questions such as which account was primary are of no concern here, for certainly the text was in its final form by the time of the composition of the scroll. Cassuto, *Exodus,* 452–53, gives an excellent analysis of the relationship of these accounts.

39. 11Q Torah reproduces only the furnishings of the wilderness tabernacle, not the architecture.

40. Yadin discusses linguistic questions in *TS* I, 21–34. Milgrom, *BA* XLI (1978), 109–12, gives some general comments. See also: Gershon Brin, "Linguistic Comments on the Temple Scroll," *Leshonenu* XLIII (1978) 20–28 (Hebrew); E. Qimron, "The Language of the Temple Scroll," *Leshonenu* XLII (1978) 83–98.

41. Milgrom, *BA* XLI (1978) 119. This phenomenon has evoked considerable discussion among students of the scrolls. Most of the earlier literature is cited in Jonathan P. Siegel, "The Employment of Palaeo-Hebrew Characters for the Divine Names at Qumran in the Light of Tannaitic Sources," *HUCA* XLII (1971) 159–72.

42. 11Q Torah 19:11, 21:12.

43. Ibid. 17:12, 21:14.

44. Ibid. 27:9, 51:8.

45. Ibid. 19:11, 27:8, 51:16.

46. Ibid. 21:9. See also 17:4, 18:13, 27:9.

47. Ibid. 21:9, 22:14, 27:5. See also 24:9.

48. Ibid. 63:5.

49. Eduard Y. Kutscher, *The Language and Linguistic Background of the Isaiah Scroll (1Q Isaᵃ)* (Leiden, 1974), 433, 440–45, has noted the numerous cases in which the Isaiah Scroll has lengthened the verbal afformatives and pronominal suffixes with the addition of the *hey*. Elisha Qimron, "A Grammar of the Hebrew Language of the Dead Sea Scrolls," (Diss., Hebrew University, 1976 [Hebrew]), notes in a summary, "Surprisingly, some of the lengthened pronouns (-*kemah*, -[*he*]*mah* and also the afformative -*temah*) are characteristic of Biblical texts only, though they appear occasionally in some others" (p. xiii). See his discussion, pp. 132, 242–47, where he lists examples. With the evidence from 11Q Torah now available, it seems that the lengthening of the Isaiah Scroll and other texts, as well as the peculiar spelling, is an imitation of the Temple Scroll. Recent conjectures that the peculiar spellings reflect the current pronunciation of Hebrew are unconvincing (Kutscher, pp. 446–51).

50. Gen. 17:2, 30:28, 34:12; Exod. 24:12; Num. 8:19; etc.

51. Exod. 15:17.

52. In commenting on an earlier draft of this manuscript, John Strugnell argued that these lengthenings are not archaic and reflect first-century C.E. endings.

53. Compare Yadin, *TS* I, 60–73.

54. See n. 59 for a discussion of this term.

55. 11Q Torah 51:11–15.

56. 11Q Torah 35:10–15, 37:8–12.

57. 11Q Torah 31:4–5.

58. 11Q Torah 21:8, 22:15.

59. This term has occasioned considerable debate. Jacob A. Milgrom, "A Prolegomenon to Leviticus 17:11," *JBL* XC (1971) 149–56; Jacob A. Milgrom, "Kipper," *EJ* X, 1039–44; Jacob A. Milgrom, "Atonement in the Old Testament," *IDBS*, 78–82; Baruch A. Levine, *In the Presence of the Lord* (Leiden, 1974), 56–77 and 123–27; Herbert Chanan Brichto, "On Slaughter and Sacrifice, Blood and Atonement," *HUCA* XLVII (1976) 19–55; E. P. Sanders, *Paul and Palestinian Judaism* (Philadelphia, 1977), 298–305. For another view, see: George Buchanan Gray, *Sacrifice in the Old Testament: Its Theory and Practice* (New York, 1971), 67–81. In 11Q Torah, J. Milgrom has suggested, the best translation of this term is "ransom" (*JQR* LXXI [1980] 3, 11).

60. A possible explanation is that the author considered the highest reward to be the eschatological one; God's dwelling is the supreme good which cannot be extended. A promise such as the one that God would make them multiply and cover the face of the earth was, by comparison, insignificant in the mind of the composer of 11Q Torah.

61. 11Q Torah 17:2, 4; 21:8, 9; 22:16; 25:9; 52:16; 59:12.

62. This theme first appears in Lev. 23:40, relating to the *lulab* during the Feast of Booths, but Deuteronomy regularly prescribes festal rejoicing during the feasts. Cf. M. Sukkah 5:1.

63. See the discussion of Jubilees below, pp. 42–48. Yadin, *TS* I, 34–60, presents a detailed précis of the contents of 11Q Torah.

64. See Yadin, *TS* I, 70 and 140–52. Yadin assumes a close relationship to the temple of Kings and perhaps Ezekiel, reconstructing some texts on the basis of that supposition. However, the evidence does not justify Yadin's hypothesis, as in no instance do any of the features that typify the Solomonic structure appear in the Temple Scroll.

65. 11Q Torah 4:4, 5; 46:5.

66. Ibid. 46:9.

67. Ibid. 5:13; 35:9–10; 37:6, 9; 42:8–9. See n. 77 below.

68. Ibid. 36:1–38:10; 39:11–16; 40:11–42:6. See also diagrams in Yadin, *TS* I, 189 and 195.

69. 11Q Torah 16–17.

70. Ibid. 19–21.

71. Ibid. 22–23.

72. Ibid. 23–25:1.

73. On the status of the levites and their portion, see Jacob Milgrom "A Shoulder for the Levites," in Yadin, *TS* I, 131–36 (Hebrew), and "Studies in the Temple Scroll," *JBL* XCVII (1978) 501–6.

74. For a different analysis, see Yadin, *TS* I, 163–84 (diagram—159) and II, 93–107.

75. Contrary to Yadin, who envisages only two altars (*TS* I, 186), 11Q Torah seems to make mention of three: the altar for incense (8:11), the altar for burnt offering (ordained in 3:14–15 and the subject of col. 11), and the altar of stone (12:11). The second altar was apparently devoted exclusively to the daily burnt offerings, while the altar of stone was for other sacrifices, such as sin, guilt, and peace offerings. On the other hand, see Rockefeller 43.366 (*TS* II, 34), which uses the term מזבח העולה (altar of the burnt offering) for private offerings.

76. 11Q Torah 35:8–9. Thus the Temple Scroll uses the term קודש קודשים differently than it is generally understood. In rabbinic texts קודש קודשים designates an area separated from the *heykal* by a double curtain. Present indications are that the author of 11Q Torah makes no mention of such a sanctum sanctorum.

77. 11Q Torah 35:10–15. Yadin (*TS* I, 182–84) and Milgrom (*JBL* XCVII [1978] 506) understand the stoa to be part of the *parwar*, in contrast to the view expressed here that this is not the case. The underlying problem is the exact meaning of the phrase סביב פרור (35:10).

78. Yadin devotes considerable space to the subject of the courts (*TS* I, 154–63, 186–214).

79. 11Q Torah 52:18. The *ris*, a Persian unit of distance, is used in Jubilees and in the rabbinic tradition (M. Yoma 6:4; Baba Kamma 7:7). Jastrow defines it as two-fifteenths of a mile (1475).

80. 11Q Torah 46:16.

81. Ibid. 46–66.

82. Ibid. 46–48.

83. Ibid. 48.

84. Ibid. 53–55.

85. Ibid. 54–56.

86. Ibid. 56.

87. Ibid. 56–60.

88. Yadin perceives the progression of the scroll to be from the innermost sacred area to the most profane area outside of the temple precincts, with supplementary material added at the end (Yadin, *TS* I, 38–60).

89. Contrast Yadin: "These examples clearly prove that the author of the scroll sought to create a Torah transmitted directly from God. This purpose most clearly explains the changes which the writer made, especially in the Book of Deuteronomy, while he left the prescriptions in Exodus, Leviticus, and Numbers—especially the laws concerning festivals and sacrifices—in the third person, for in the latter it is clearly established that they are the words of God. . . .

"Using the terminology of biblical criticism, it might be said that the writer alters the words of Moses which appear in D, changing them to the words of God by shifting them from the third to the first person. On the other hand, the words attributed to God in P he leaves in the third person" (*TS* I, 62). In fact, it would seem that Yadin's hypothesis does not explain the organization of the Temple Scroll and its relation to the Pentateuch.

90. There has been debate on the question of whether the Temple Scroll refers to hanging, a suggestion originally offered by Yadin: Y. Yadin, "Pesher Nahum (4QpNahum) Reconsidered," *IEJ* XXI (1971) 1–12; A. Dupont-Sommer, "Observations nouvelles sur l'expression 'suspendu vivant sur le bois' dans le Commentaire de Nahum (4QpNah. II, 8) à la lumière du Rouleau du Temple (11Q Temple Scroll LXIV, 6–13)," *Comptes-Rendus* (1972) 709–20; J. M. Baumgarten, "Does *TLH* in the Temple Scroll Refer to Crucifixion?" *JBL* XCI (1972) 472–81 (also *Studies in Qumran Law* [Leiden, 1977], 172–82; J. Massyngberde Ford, "'Crucify Him, crucify Him' and the Temple Scroll," *ExpT* LXXXVII (1976) 275–78; J. A. Fitzmyer, "Crucifixion in Ancient Palestine, Qumran Literature and the New Testament," *CBQ* XL (1978) 493–513.

91. *TS* I, 60.

92. See above, p. 12.

93. See the discussion between Levine and Milgrom concerning holiness in the Temple Scroll in *BASOR* 232 (1978) 5–27.

94. Yadin never seriously entertains this notion, even though he does mention the possibility in occasional phrases, e.g., *TS* I, 69. John Strugnell in a lecture delivered before the Seventh World Congress of Jewish Studies did advocate a theory of multiple authorship. Citing linguistic divergencies, Strugnell argues that the calendrical section (cols. 13–29) and the royal charter (cols. 56–59) are separate compositions. But he overlooks the book's phraseology, the I-thou-they passages, the courtyards, and the septimal numerology—items that indicate a single authorship.

95. 11Q Torah 56:18, 57:17–19. Yadin, *TS* II, 178, 182.

96. 11Q Torah 64:04–1; Deut. 21:15–17. Yadin, II, 201–2.

97. 11Q Torah 45:10–12, 15–18; 48:11–15.

98. 11Q Torah 52:11–12, 53:5.

99. 11Q Torah 54:8–18, 61:2–5.

100. If we interpret לא ירבה לו נשים as referring "even to the king," i.e., including all of the Israelites, then there is a contradiction with *gerušah* (divorcee) in 11Q Torah 54:4. A similar ambiguity is to be found in CD 5:1–2, where it states, "Concerning the prince it is written, 'He shall not multipy wives.'" The implication is that this prohibition only applies to the king. However, the Damascus Document goes on to cite the account of creation and the flood as proof for monogamy, thereby indicating that the prohibition of bigamy is universal. This incoherence still awaits resolution. For recent discussions of this passage, see the following: G. Vermes, "Sectarian Matrimonial Halakah in the Damascus Rule," *JJS* XXV (1974) 197–202; J. A. Fitzmyer, "The Matthean Divorce Texts and Some New Palestinian Evidence," *ThS* XXXVII (1976) 197–226; "Divorce among First Century Palestinian Jews," *Eretz-Israel* XIV (1978) 103–10; James R. Mueller, "The Temple Scroll and the Gospel Divorce Texts," *RQ* X (1980) 247–56.

101. 11Q Torah 64:6–9.

102. Yadin, *TS* I, 63–65.

103. See S. R. Hirsch, *The Pentateuch* (New York, 2d ed., 1971), I. Levy (trans.), V, 341–42, and Leiman, *Canonization*, 16–26. See also Josh. 8:31–32 and 23:6.

104. W. J. Harrelson, "Torah," *IDB* IV, 673, and D. N. Freedman, "Canon of the OT," *IDBS*, 130–32.

105. Concerning the question of Torah in Deuteronomy, see the following: O. Eissfeldt, *The Old Testament: An Introduction* (New York, 1965), P. R. Ackroyd (trans.), 155–56; B. Lindars, "Torah in Deuteronomy," *Words and Meanings* (Cambridge, 1968), P. R. Ackroyd and B. Lindars (eds.), 117–36; M. Weinfeld, *Deuteronomy and the Deuteronomic School* (Oxford, 1972), 64–65, 146–71, 336–39; L. Monsengeo Pasinya, *La Notion de NOMOS dans le Pentateuque Grec* (Rome, 1973); Leiman, *Canonization*, 16–26; J. A. Sanders, "Torah," *IDBS*, 909–11.

106. This phrase is neither Pentateuchal nor scriptural, even though it abounds in the Qumranic writings. *Mišpaṭ* seems to be borrowed from *kemišpaṭ* and *kemišpaṭam* of Numbers 29, which refer to the rules concerning the sacrificial drink offerings. Whether or not *mišpaṭ* here bears the meaning of rabbinic "halakah" is an open question. Recently the latter term has been used with reference to Qumran. Yadin, like Schiffman and Baumgarten, utilized this word. This usage seems inappropriate, since in rabbinics "halakah" has the precise meaning of the transmission of a body of laws not explicitly mentioned in Scripture. In Qumranic lore, *mišpaṭ* and its cognates seem to refer to a written tradition. The recent trend of generalizing from rabbinics to Qumran tends to conflate two distinct, perhaps irreconcilable, systems of legal transmission.

107. This is noted by Jacob Milgrom in his comments on an earlier draft of the manuscript. See Lev. 6:2, 7, 18.

108. Num. 29:6, 18, 21, 24, 27, 30, 33, 37.

109. See the prologue to Ben Sira, where the "Torah" is a clearly defined body of literature.

110. Josh. 8:31–34, 23:6; I Kgs. 2:3; II Kgs. 14:6, 23:2, 21; Ezra 10:3.

111. 11Q Torah 51:6–8. Note that the phrase *behar hazzeh* is never used in the levitical accounts concerning leprosy, but is borrowed from the account of the tabernacle (Exod. 25:40; 26:30; 34:2–4, 29–32).

112. Yadin, *TS* I, 56 and II, 177.

113. For the most part, the relationship between the norms of 11Q Torah and the halakah seems to be oblique. That is to say, the author presents his point of view without alluding to other interpretations of similar texts. After all, it would be beneath God to enter into polemics with an inauthentic hermeneutic. What the Temple Scroll reveals, then, is a tradition independent of and distinct from that of the halakah. Polemics generally suggests a recognition of the opposing view, which our author does not seem to grant.

114. 11Q Torah 56:1–11. Some readers suggest that only *Seper Torah* in 56:4 refers to the book, and that *Torah* (56:3, 7) refers to legal decisions. Such a modernistic division of concepts would probably have seemed strange circa 200 B.C.E.

115. 11Q Torah 56:12–60:15. For 60:1–15, see n. 13 above.

116. For the "torah of the king," see Yadin, *TS* I, 264–77, and II, 177–93.

117. For the use of this term in Deuteronomy, see the following: M. Tsevat, "Alalakhiana," *HUCA* XXIX (1958) 125–26; Hirsch, *Pentateuch* V, 341; Weinfeld, *Deuteronomy, 72*; A. Philips, *Deuteronomy* (Cambridge, 1973), 121–22; Thompson, *Deuteronomy, 12–14*, 206–7.

118. See *TS* I, 264–65.

119. Ibid. 268–70; II, 181 (11Q Torah 57:13–14). The conjunction may explain the meaning of *mišpaṭ hattorah*, where *mišpaṭ* refers to the particular and *torah* to the general.

120. 11Q Torah 59:7–13.

121. For a more detailed discussion on this subject, see below pp. 24–27.

122. That this text was used as Torah in the Qumran literature is demonstrated in Chaps. 2 and 3.

123. The name תורה חיצונית (unauthorized Torah) would portray in rabbinic terminology their view of this work.

124. 11Q Torah 29:3, 7, 8; 45:12, 13, 14; 46:4; 47:4, 11, 18; 51:7; 53:9; 56:5; 60:13.

125. According to Qimron, *Leshonenu* XLII (1978), 142, this should read נדריהמה instead of נסכיהמה as in Yadin's text.

126. For an explanation of this translation, see below, p. 23.

127. The reading here follows Yadin, but the scholar should be cognizant of Qimron's objection, *Leshonenu* XLII (1978) 142. Qimron reads הבריה (creation), which appears to be the reading in the normal photographs, but the mirror writing on the back of col. 31 may be read הברכה, if the photograph is a true representation of the original (*TS* III, plate 45:2).

128. The attitude of Qumran toward the temple has been the subject of considerable debate. A few discussions of this subject are: M. Baillet, "Fragments Araméens de Qumran 2. Description

de la Jérusalem Nouvelle," *RB* LXII (1955) 222–45 (see also *DJD* III, 84–89); M. Burrows, *More Light on the Dead Sea Scrolls* (New York, 1958), 363–78; J. Strugnell, "The Angelic Liturgy at Qumran—4Q Serek Shirot 'Olat Hashshabbat,'" *VTSup* VII (1960) 318–45; F. M. Cross, Jr., *The Ancient Library of Qumran and Modern Biblical Studies* (Garden City, N.Y., 1961), 101–6; B. Gärtner, *The Temple and the Community in Qumran and the New Testament* (Cambridge, 1965), 1–46; R. J. McKelvey, *The New Temple: The Church in the New Testament* (Oxford, 1969), 36–38; S. Fujita, "The Temple Theology of the Qumran Sect and the Book of Ezekiel" (Diss., Princeton, 1970); J.M. Baumgarten, *Studies in Qumran Law* (Leiden, 1977), 39–87.

129. Yadin, *TS* II, 89. See also I, 140–44.

130. Yadin's understanding of 29:7–10 and a similar viewpoint expressed by J. M. Baumgarten at the SBL meeting in Dallas (November 1980) give rise to what may be termed a periodic or staged eschatology. The sanctuary in this scroll is to be followed by a more sacred house of the Lord. Yadin believes that the author thought of the temple of Ezekiel 40–48 for the second eschatological period. Baumgarten tends toward viewing the second period as a time of a spiritualized presence of God, not a physical sanctuary (cf., *JBL* XCVII [1978] 588–89).

131. Maier, *Tempelrolle*, 89–90.

132. Ibid., 68.

133. See also J. M. Baumgarten, *JBL* XCVII (1978) 588.

134. See the following list of examples: עולם—9:14; 18:8; 21:9; 22:14; 25:8; 27:4; 29:7, 8; 35:9; 39:8; 45:14; 47:3; 50:19; 53:7; 55:10; 59:15; דורות—8:13; 19:8; 21:9; 22:14; 24:9; 27:5; כול הימים—29:10; 45:13; 46:4; 51:16; 59:15; 60:11.

135. Note the distribution of these terms throughout the scroll, including the sections on the festivals and the dimensions of the temple and its courts.

136. This view was expressed at the SBL meeting in Dallas (November 1980).

137. All the lexica consulted included a definition for this term with the sense of duration: *BDB,* 724–25: Koehler-Baumgartner, II, 680; Jastrow, II, 1042; Levey, III, 619. For biblical examples see: Judg. 3:26, Jonah 4:2. This may be an Aramaism: *BDB,* 1105. See Dan. 6:8, 13: 7:12, 25. It should also be noted that 11Q Torah 59:9 may be rendered as "while" and that 11Q Torah 42:16 most certainly requires this meaning.

138. In his commentary on the Book of Jubilees, Charles makes mention of this problem (*The Book of Jubilees* [London, 1902], 9). However, he changed what he thought would have been *hōs* (when) in the Greek text to *heōs* (until), which he considered closer to the meaning of the original text. In so doing, he did not notice that this second *ʿad* could not represent a break in the time sequence.

139. See above, pp. 9–12.

140. 11Q Torah 29:4. See above, pp. 17–21.

141. See Exod. 24:12 and 34:1. Cf. Exod. 31:18. Such an interpretation is also found in Jubilees, see below p. 47.

142. See below, pp. 91–94.

143. Yadin, *TS* II, 186, explains this column as a conflation of biblical texts which contain the blessings and curses.

144. Lev. 26:45.

145. Note that in the view of the Qumranic Torah, God is speaking at Sinai to Moses in the second Torah. By the time this Torah is discovered, Israel will already have backslid.

146. "This Torah" means 11Q Torah, of course.

147. This may be the explanation for the apparent absence of a Davidic Messiah from many Qumranic texts. Clearly the author rejects the view that Jehoiachin and his successors continue to be the anointed seed of David.

148. See below, p. 47. Cf. Jubilees 1 and CD 5:2–5.

149. 11Q Torah 59:9.

150. 11Q Torah 59:11–13.

151. See above, pp. 22–23.

152. Maier, *Tempelrolle,* 90, cites Lev. 26:42, where the covenant with Jacob is mentioned. But the reference to Bethel here implies that the author is not referring to the content of the covenant, but rather to the technical term (cf. Genesis 17).

153. Yadin, *TS* II, 92; I, 141–42.

154. See below, pp. 41–62.

155. Genesis 35.

156. Genesis 28.

157. Although it is possible that Bethel refers to God's promises in both Genesis 28 and Genesis 35, it is the latter that is emphasized here. Abraham and Isaac are not mentioned, as in Genesis 28, and the covenant in 11Q Torah refers to a time after the birth of the sons of Jacob. The top of col. 29 appears to discuss Sukkot, a festival also considered to have a relationship with Jacob in Genesis 35 (see Gen. 33:17, where Jacob journeyed to Sukkoth). It is clear that Jubilees understood it as referring to Genesis 35. See below p. 61.

158. 11Q Torah 51:7.

159. Unfortunately col. 67, which would have been based on the prohibitions forbidding the Ammonites and Moabites from entering the assembly of the Lord (Deut. 23:4–7), is lost. The last citation of a biblical text in the preserved remnants of the scroll is Deut. 23:1 (11Q Torah 66:12), i.e., the last reference which follows from the author's dependence on that biblical book for the structure of this portion of the scroll.

160. Exod. 12:42. For some studies on Moses, see H. M. Teeple, *The Mosaic Eschatological Prophet* (Philadelphia, 1957); W. A. Meeks, *The Prophet-King* (Leiden, 1967); H. Cazelles et al., *Moses in Schrift and Überlieferung* (Düsseldorf, 1963).

161. This phrase occurs three times in the Pentateuch: Gen. 49:1, Num. 24:14, Deut. 31:29. These references would appear to be intended to refer to the period after the conquest or during the monarchy.

162. See Jubilees 1, where this association is clear. This will be discussed below, 42–48.

163. See the discussion on "Purpose" above and n. 134.

164. This interpretation departs significantly from Yadin, who sees the sanctuary depicted here as nothing but an extension of the historical sanctuary, admittedly somewhat modified (*TS* I, 140–52). This should be remembered when restoring lacunae. With a writer such as the one who composed 11Q Torah, one can never be certain where copying will cease and innovation begin.

165. The relationship of the scroll to various textual traditions is discussed by Emmanuel Tov in an article to be published in *Eretz-Israel* in the Orlinsky festschrift.

166. B. Shabbat 116b.

Notes to Chapter 2

1. M. A. Knibb has published a new edition and translation of this important work: *The Ethiopic Book of Enoch* (Oxford, 1978). The second volume includes an introduction, translation, and commentary (see pp. 1–6 for a discussion of former editions of the text). R. H. Charles published a critical edition of this text, *The Ethiopic Version of the Book of Enoch* (Oxford, 1906) as well as a translation and commentary, *The Book of Enoch* (Oxford, 1893; revised, 1912).

2. This passage in Genesis seems to presume the existence of an Enochite literature. The enigmatic formulation of this passage, departing in form from the rest of Genesis 5, testifies to an extant Enochite tradition. These verses refute the argument that the Enochite literature was inspired by Gen. 5:21–24. As to the time of this passage, it would seem that it was an insertion into the body of Genesis 5, which originally treated Enoch no differently than the other patriarchs. The lore concerning Enoch was probably inspired by the fact that he was the seventh

after Adam. This in turn gave rise to an Enochite literature. Contrary to Milik, the link between the Genesis passage and the Aramaic Enoch is not a straight line, as Gen. 5:21–24 presumes a year of 365 days and the Aramaic Enoch one of 364 days. See J. T. Milik, *The Books of Enoch: Aramaic Fragments of Qumran Cave 4* (Oxford, 1976), 8–13, 273. Charles (*Enoch* [1893], 24–26) had already noted the antecedence of certain portions of Enoch to Jubilees.

On the Enochite tradition and Gen. 5:21–24 see these commentators: G. von Rad, *Genesis: A Commentary* (Philadelphia, 1961), J. H. Marks (trans.), 69–70; U. Cassuto, *A Commentary on the Book of Genesis* (Jerusalem, 1961), I. Abrahams (trans.), I, pt. 1, 282–85; E. A. Speiser, *Genesis* (Garden City, N.Y., 1964), 43.

3. Milik, *Enoch*, 8.

4. B. Z. Wacholder, *Eupolemus: A Study of Judaeo-Greek Literature* (Cincinnati, 1974), 75–76, 104, 288–93; Milik, *Enoch*, 8.

5. Jub. 4:17. On the date of Jubilees, see below, pp. 41–42.

6. Milik, *Enoch*, 8–13. J. C. Greenfield and M. E. Stone ("The Books of Enoch and the Traditions of Enoch," *Numen* XXVI [1979] 89–103) have questioned the assumption that the Astronomical Enoch was composed during the Persian period. They argue (a) that Gen. 5:23 does not necessarily imply the existence of Enochite astronomical writings, and (b) that if this passage does imply such a literature, it suggests a solar year of 365 days whereas the Astronomical Enoch has a year of 364 days. The weakness of their argument is that it does not note the peculiarities of this Enoch passage within the narrative of Genesis 5. It is the distinctive character of Gen. 5:22–24, which includes Enoch's walking with God as well as the 365 days, that necessitates the postulate of the existence of an Enochite source available to the author of this narrative. Unless 365 can be ascribed to sheer coincidence, the implication that Enoch was responsible for setting the year of 365 days cannot be denied. Thus an Astronomical Enoch, possibly oral but more probably written, antedates Gen. 5:22–24. Greenfield and Stone rightly point out the disparity between Gen. 5:23, a 365-day year, and the Astronomical Enoch, which they say has a year of 364 days. In fact, the Astronomical Enoch knows only of a lunisolar calendar consisting of 354 days, the normal Jewish lunar reckoning with the addition of an embolistic month. In this respect, Enoch could not be regarded as identical to the Qumran calendar which, as Jubilees 6 points out, totally ignored the lunar year. In brief, Gen. 5:22–24 implies an Enochite calendar of 365 days, the Astronomical Enoch has a lunisolar year with an intercalary month every three or five years, and Jubilees knows of a 364-day solar year. What is found here is an attempt to move from a strictly solar year to a solar year which would be divisible by the Jewish sabbath (week). The evolution from a year of 365 days to 364 was theologically inspired. Strictly speaking, the Qumran calendar is original with Jubilees and may not be ascribed to the Book of the Heavenly Luminaries, as stated by Greenfield and Stone. See below, pp. 53–60.

7. First published by E. Sachau, *Aramäische Papyrus and Ostraka* (Berlin, 1911), 40–55. See also A. E. Cowley, *Aramaic Papyri of the Fifth Century B.C.* (Oxford, 1923), 204–48.

8. Milik, *Enoch*, 8–13.

9. Jubilees Prologue, *APOT* II, 11.

10. Enoch 72:1. Knibb, *Enoch* II, 167.

11. 4Q Enastr[b] 7:ii:1–8. Milik, *Enoch*, 289–81.

12. The importance of the gates in this cosmological scheme may be reflected in the elaborate descriptions of the gates and courtyards in 11Q Torah 36–44.

13. 4Q Enastr[c] 1:ii:1–10, 13–20, and 4Q Enastr[b] 23. Milik, *Enoch*, 285–90.

14. Enoch 76:3–77:4. Knibb, *Enoch* II, 176–81.

15. Milik, *Enoch*, 273–75.

16. Enoch 72:8–14. Knibb, *Enoch* II, 168.

17. See p. 34 above. The following quotation is from 4Q Enastr[b] 7:iii:1–5 (Milik, *Enoch*, 281).

18. Enoch 73:3–74:9. Knibb, *Enoch* II, 171–73.

19. Jub. 6:23–28 (note especially 36–37).

20. Repeated recently in the articles by J. A. VanderKam, "The Origin, Character, and Early History of the 364-day Calendar: A Reassessment of Jaubert's Hypotheses," *CBQ* XLI (1979) 390–411; R.T. Beckwith, "The earliest Enoch Literature and its Calendar: Marks of their Origin, Date and Motivation," *RQ* X (1981) 365–403. See the discussion of the calendar in the Book of Jubilees.

21. 11Q Torah 30:7.

22. Ibid. 31:13.

23. Ibid. 33:9.

24. Ibid. 36:5.

25. Ibid. 40:9.

26. Ibid. 41:12.

27. Ibid. 36:8.

28. Ibid. 36:10.

29. Ibid. 41:14.

30. Ibid. 46:6.

31. Ibid. 31:10.

32. Ibid. 5:5 and 6:3.

33. Ibid. 36:9.

34. Ibid. 38:15.

35. Ibid. 39:15–16.

36. Ibid. 41:15.

37. Ibid. 40:12.

38. Two exceptions are Exod. 26:2 and 36:9, where the length of the curtain is twenty-eight cubits. This septimal number does seem to be significant, especially when compared with the curtain's width of four cubits, i.e., $4 \times 7 = 28$.

39. A major feature of the cosmological order is that the light of the moon, when full, is one-seventh of that of the sun (Enoch 73:3 and 78:4). Furthermore, the description of the waxing and waning of the moon is based on a division of its light into seven parts (Enoch 73:5, 78:6–9). This movement is depicted in greater detail, also from a septimal foundation, in the Aramaic fragments (Milik, *Enoch*, 278–84, 292). Even though a lunisolar calendar is not determinative in Enoch, the septimal year of 364 days finds frequent mention (Enoch 74:10, 12; 82:6). Finally, the vision of a quadrilateral earth includes seven high mountains (77:4), seven rivers (77:5), and seven large islands (77:8).

40. Knibb, *Enoch* II, 176–77. The Aramaic fragments of this chapter are found in Milik, *Enoch*, 284–91. Enoch 76:14 is found on p. 288.

41. 11Q Torah 31:10 and 38:14. The presumption that the gates, whether in Ezekiel 40–48, Enoch, or the Qumranic Torah, were intended to be linked with the movements of the celestial bodies rests on an ancient passage, Gen. 28:17: "How awesome is this place? This is none other than the house of God and this is the gate of heaven" (RSV). The midrash (Gen. Rabbah 69:7) points out that the foot of the ladder rested on the ground at Bethel and its slope reached the Jerusalem temple. Thus we find the conjunction of the house of God and the gate of heaven. The daily evening prayers likewise link the gates with the celestial bodies, and the synagogue liturgy contains many references to the gates of heaven, no doubt implying a relationship between the gates of the temple and the celestial movements (cf. Ps. 24:7, 9; 118:19). It is this tradition which Ezekiel, Enoch, and the Qumranic Torah express in their description of the temple gates.

42. 11Q Torah 39:11–13.

43. Ibid. 40:11–12.

44. See the ordinances for the festivals of the first fruits (11Q Torah 18:14–6; 19:3, 14–16; 21:1–3, 14–16; 22:12–13) and for the Offering of Woods (11Q Torah 23:7, 24:10–16), sections which are without Pentateuchal precedent. It is fair to presume, therefore, that the number twelve was of primary concern to the author of the Qumranic Torah.

45. The second story is found in 11Q Torah 31:6–7. Smaller dimensions are reflected in the description in 36:8–10.

46. 11Q Torah 5:8 (6:6), 30:3–31:9. Note especially 31:6–7. Yadin, *TS* I, 166, does not emphasize the unique aspects of this innovation.

The buildings specifically listed as being gilded are the בית־מסבה (house of the staircase), בית־כיור (house of the laver), and the gates. Though not mentioned specifically, the other buildings that formed part of the קדש קודשים (holy of holies) also presumably necessitated gilding. Note that the בית־הכלים (house of vessels) had to be modeled after the laver. Note also that the משקוף and the אדשכים had to be gilded.

47. Milik, *Enoch*, 8–13, 273–74. Ultimately, the Enochite literature is to be dated prior to the composition of Gen. 5:22–24, a passage which presumes its existence. The peculiar form of this passage, departing from the archetype of Gen. 4:17 and differing from the material surrounding it in Genesis 5, is a compelling reason to consider the availability of an Enochite source to the author. See above, p. 34.

48. Jub. 1:27, 29; 2:1.

49. Enoch 72:1, 11Q Torah 29:9–10, cf. Isa. 30:26.

50. This text was published by M. Baillet, "Un recueil liturgique de Qumrân, Grotte 4: 'Les Paroles des Luminaires,'" *RB* LXVIII (1961) 195–250.

51. *DSSE*, 202.

52. "The fourth day" appears in an unpublished fragment (*DSSE*, 202) and "Sabbath" is specified at 7:4.

53. M. Tamid 7:4.

54. I am grateful to Professor Strugnell for pointing out the so-called 4Q Mess Ar 1:5, which refers to תלחת ספריא (three books) by which the two-year-old child prodigy acquired his wisdom. These three books are not to be connected with any of the known biblical books but apparently belong to the Enochite lore. J. A. Fitzmyer ("The Aramaic 'Elect of God' Texts from Qumran Cave IV," *CBQ* XXVII [1965] 348–72) rightly rejected Starcky's assumption ("Un texte messianique Araméen de la Grotte 4 de Qumrân," *École des langues orientales anciennes de l'Institut Catholique de Paris: Mémorial du cinquantenaire 1914–1964* [Paris, 1964], 51–66) that these columns are messianic in character, but Fitzmyer's conjecture that they refer to Noah seems implausible, as Noah was considered a prodigy from birth (cf. 1QapGen 2 and Enoch 106–8), not at the age of two. It is conceivable that these Aramaic fragments describe the infancy of Enoch himself, how he acquired the beginnings of his wisdom when he discovered the three books which allegedly contained accounts of creation. The frequent reference to the *ʿyryn* (watchers) point in that direction. The three books available to this prodigy do not relate to the law which came at Sinai.

55. The Ethiopic text was first edited by A. Dillman in 1859 and reedited by R. H. Charles, *The Ethiopic Version of the Hebrew Book of Jubilees* (Oxford, 1895). Charles also published an English translation with a commentary under the title *The Book of Jubilees; or, the Little Genesis* (London, 1902), which was reprinted with short notes in his *APOT* II, 1–82. For the Greek fragments, see A. M. Denis, *Fragmenta Pseudepigraphorum Graeca* (Leiden, 1970), 70–102. He also discusses the fragments in his *Introduction aux Pseudépigraphes Grecs d'Ancien Testament* (Leiden, 1970), 150–62. J. C. VanderKam (*Textual and Historical Studies in the Book of Jubilees* [Missoula, Mont., 1977] 18–101) discusses the Hebrew fragments. See also A. Epstein, מקדמוניות היהודים (Vienna, 1887; new edition by A. Habermann, Jerusalem, 1956).

56. The Hebrew fragments mentioned in the previous note were found at Qumran. For the Hebrew title of Jubilees, see CD 16:3–4.

57. Charles, *Jubilees*, lviii–lxvi (also *APOT* II, 6–7).

58. *Textual*, 214–85.

59. Jub. 34:2–9; *Textual*, 218–29. The major argument is that the names of the cities in Jub. 34:4 are reflected in Judah Maccabee's northern battles, particularly the battle with Nicanor. See also Charles, *Jubilees*, lxii–lxiii, 200–204 (cf. 176–77 on Jub. 29:10).

60. Jub. 37–38:4; *Textual,* 230–38. See also Charles, *Jubilees,* 214–21.

61. *Textual,* 242–43. See also Charles, *Jubilees,* LX.

62. *Textual,* 245–46. See also Charles, *Jubilees,* LX.

63. *Textual,* 246–85. He sets the *terminus ad quem* at 140 B.C.E., on the supposition that the Qumran sectaries knew of Jubilees but that its author was not a member of the communal sect.

64. Aresa, Seragan, and Ma'anisakir (Jub. 34:4). Selo (Shiloh) and Ga'as (Yashar), if correct identifications, do not find mention in the Maccabean books, as VanderKam admits.

65. Taphu and Bethoron (Jub. 34:4).

66. Gen. 14:1–11.

67. Jub. 3:30–31.

68. Zeitlin dates Jubilees in the early post-exilic period, characterizing it as a book "written by a man, or a school of men, who opposed many of the pentateuchal laws and traditions" ("The Book of Jubilees: Its Character and Its Significance," *JQR* XXX [1940] 30). See also *The Rise and Fall of the Judaean State* (Philadelphia, 1968), I, 293–95. The position of this study departs from that championed by the eminent scholar.

69. Jub. 4:20. Jub. 23:16–31 has sometimes been regarded as post-Danielic, primarily because of the apocalyptic content of this section. There is nothing in this passage, however, that would seem to reflect a dependence on Daniel. On the other hand, it has been suggested that the internecine wars mirror Antiochus' persecution of Judaism and the divisions between the Hasideans and the Hellenizers (See the preceding discussion of VanderKam. Note also G. W. E. Nickelsburg, *Resurrection, Immortality, and Eternal Life in Intertestamental Judaism* [Cambridge, Mass., 1972] 46–47.) This would necessitate a post-Maccabean dating of our passage. Here again there is nothing to require such an interpretation. In fact, Jub. 23:16–31 contains little that is not found in the prophetic writings and has no allusion to events of the second century B.C.E.

70. Ezek. 14:14.

71. For the Enochite lore, see above, p. 34.

72. See Yadin's index *TS* II, 315, s.v. Jubilees.

73. See *TS* I:5, 39; II:1–2.

74. The contents of cols. 1 and 2 are described by Yadin as follows (*TS* II, 1): "The surviving lines reproduce the essence of Exod. 34:10–16, i.e., God's covenant with Israel—rewritten in the first person. This wording is most appropriate to the beginning of the scroll, which in its first section deals exclusively with the building of the temple, its furnishings, and with the designation of the feasts and their offerings. It is clear, therefore, that the author, while writing about the building of the temple, used the Mosaic ordinances for the tabernacle. Also Exod. 23:20 ff. and 34:10–16 are passages which deal with the covenant, preliminary to the ordinances of the tabernacle and its furnishings: Exodus 25 ff.—the design; Exodus 35 ff.—the execution. . . . As it is customary for this writer to conflate all the passages in the Torah on a given subject into a single unit, either by harmonization or exposition, he also inserts into this column portions from Deut. 7:1 ff., which reproduce the covenant found in the Book of Exodus. Very important to his work are the portions which appear only in Deuteronomy, i.e., the commandment to burn the idols (Deut. 7:5, 25) and the definition of idolatry as an 'abomination' (Deut. 7:25–26)." For a similar view, see Maier, *Tempelrolle,* 67. Milgrom, *BA* XLI (1978) 109, makes mention of its similarity to Jubilees.

75. As noted by Yadin, 11Q Torah 3:2, תכלת וארגמן (blue and purple), is found in Exod. 25:4 (*TS* II, 4). Since the Qumranic Torah is primarily dependent on Pentateuchal sources, this line seems to reflect Exod. 25:4a, rather than any of the passages in Chronicles also noted by Yadin. The word אשר in line 2 also appears in Exod. 25:3b. Yadin reads line 5, in the light of line 6, as dependent upon Deut. 7:25. It is more plausible to postulate that this line comes from Exod. 25:3, which also lists the metals to be collected for the adornment of the future tabernacle, the model for the sanctuary promised in 11Q Torah 3:4. Line 6 then would express the concern of the author that the תרומה (offering—Exod. 25:2–3) for the building of the sanctuary of the Lord not

be defiled. He could have in mind the skins of Exod. 25:6 since he elsewhere prohibits the defilement of skins coming into the holy city (11Q Torah 47:3–18).

76. The translation utilized in this text is that of the Revised Standard Version, with some modifications.

77. In addition to the items listed in n. 55 above, other studies on Jubilees include the following: H. Rönsch, *Das Buch der Jubiläen oder Die Kleine Genesis* (Leipzig, 1874); L. Finkelstein, "The Book of Jubilees and the Rabbinic Halaka," *HTR* XVI (1923) 39–61; "Some Examples of the Maccabean Halaka," *JBL* XLIX (1930) 20–42; C. Albeck, "Das Buch der Jubiläen und die Halacha," *Bericht der Hochschule für die Wissenschaft des Judentums* (Berlin, 1930), 3–60. More recent studies include: M. Testuz, *Les idées religieuses du livre des Jubliés* (Geneva, 1960); S. Tedesche, "Jubilees, Book of," *IDB* II, 1002–3; P. von der Osten-Sacken, *Gott und Belial* (Göttingen, 1969), 197–200; G. L. Davenport, *The Eschatology of the Book of Jubilees* (Leiden, 1971); G. W. E. Nickelsburg, Jr., *Resurrection, Immortality and Eternal Life in Intertestamental Judaism* (Cambridge, Mass., 1972); D. Patte, *Early Jewish Hermeneutic in Palestine* (Missoula, Mont., 1975), 131–236. For some of the numerous studies of the calendar in Jubilees, see below nn. 145, 148, 160, and 162.

78. Charles, *Jubilees*, 1–10. Only a few brief references to Exodus 34 appear in Charles's commentary, in the midst of numerous biblical citations. Scholars have had difficulty integrating the prologue and its content with the rest of Jubilees. See, e.g., Davenport, *Eschatology*, 10–18.

79. Exod. 34:5–7.

80. Jub. 1:5–18.

81. Exod. 34:8–9.

82. Jub. 1:19–21.

83. Jub. 1:22–26.

84. This perception of Israel's past history of idolatry is shared by the writer of the Damascus Document, who says this continued for 390 years (CD 1:5–6). See Chap. 3 below.

85. Jub. 1:26–29. This translation is from Charles, *Jubilees*, 7–9. This passage is newly translated by Davenport, *Eschatology*, 90–91.

86. Charles, *Jubilees*, 7–8, suggests that Jub. 1:26 refers to the Book of Jubilees itself, while 1:27 refers to the Pentateuch, i.e., the angel writes out the Torah and Moses writes down Jubilees. Charles himself expresses dissatisfaction with this explanation, since the angel is to write "till My sanctuary has been built among them for all eternity."

87. See the discussion in Chap. 1 above, pp. 21–30.

88. Jacob Milgrom, in commenting on an early draft of this book at the Centennial Meeting of the SBL (November 1980), proposed a novel interpretation of this phrase. As Milgrom understands it, "the first and the last" really means "from the first to the last," as expressed in 1 Chr. 29:29, 2 Chr. 9:29, 12:15, 16:11, etc.

89. E.g., 1QS 9:10, CD 20:8–9, 31. See also the discussion of the Second Torah below, pp. 91–94.

90. See p. 60 below.

91. Exod. 34:1.

92. Yadin deals extensively with these parallels: *TS* I: 75, 79–81, 84, 93, 100, 103–4, 108, 116, 127–28, 141–44, 271, 293, 304; II: 44, 54–55, 60, 91–92.

93. Cf. CD 9–14 and 1QS.

94. Jub. 2:19.

95. Jub. 2:22. Cf. Jub. 4:25, 6:3, 7:36, 16:23, etc. See also 11Q Torah 14:7, 16:13, 17:10, 20:8, 28:6, 34:14. These two treatises are unique in their constant reiteration of this theme.

96. In its generalized prohibition of any kind of labor, Jub. 2:25 uses the word טמא (defile), while in the biblical and rabbinic traditions, חלל (profane) would be expected. But טמא as a generalized prohibition of any labor on a sabbath or feast-day does fit 11Q Torah. See above, p. 12.

97. Jub. 50:10–11.

98. Yadin discusses this point and constructs his calendar from this perspective: *TS* I, 81,

95–96, 105. This view is based on CD 11:17–18 in the sectarian literature. See S. Schechter, *Documents of Jewish Sectaries* (Cambridge, 1910), L; C. Rabin *The Zadokite Document* (Oxford, 2d ed., 1958), 56–58; L. H. Schiffman, *The Halakhah at Qumran* (Leiden, 1975), 128–31; L. Ginzberg, *An Unknown Jewish Sect* (New York, 1976), 69–70.

99. Yadin, *TS* I, 96.

100. The conjectural reading of מלבד refutes arguments such as that proposed by Schiffman (*Halakhah,* p. 128), who says that in sectarian texts מלבד meant "instead of."

101. Sid Leiman, reading an early draft of this manuscript, suggested that *milbad* here means "only," i.e., only the sacrifices of the Sabbath. The Damascus Document reference could stand such an unsupported exegesis, but it seems inconceivable in Lev. 23:38. It is of course possible that the citation here is not from the canonical Pentateuch, where it is synonymous with *ʿal* in Numbers 28, but from a lost passage of 11Q Torah. *Milbad* is used in 11Q Torah 14 in the same manner and with the same meaning as in Numbers 28.

102. For this use of מלבד, see Lev. 9:17, Num. 28:32; 29:16, 22, 25, 28, 31, 34, 38.

103. Cf. A. M. Habermann, *The Scrolls from the Judean Desert* (Tel-Aviv, 1959), 195 (Hebrew).

104. 11Q Torah 60:6–8.

105. Jub. 49:16–18, 20–21.

106. Exod. 12:6. See also Charles, *Jubilees,* 255; Albeck, "Jubiläen," 13; Yadin, *TS* I, 79–81.

107. Apparently the Qumranic Torah and Jubilees use other passages from the Pentateuch, possibly Exod. 30:14, where all Israelites twenty years old and over are required to give a half-shekel as an offering to the Lord.

108. See M. Berakot 1:1, B. Berakot 9a, T. Pesaḥim 5:13.

109. 11Q Torah 48:16. See Finkelstein, *HTR* XVI (1923) 58.

110. Jub. 7:20–21.

111. Jub. 15:25.

112. Jub. 28:6. The author may have gotten this by taking the words of Laban literally.

113. 11Q Torah 35:6–7. See Exod. 28:41.

114. 11Q Torah 51:16–18. Deut. 16:18–20 does not prescribe death for the erring judge.

115. 11Q Torah 55:15–21. See Deut. 17:2–7.

116. 11Q Torah 64:7–9. Compare Exod. 19:16.

117. 11Q Torah 64:9–13. Compare Deut. 21:22–23.

118. 11Q Torah 66:1–3. See Deut. 22:23–24.

119. Jub. 15:26.

120. Jub. 16:9.

121. Jub. 20:4–5.

122. Jub. 30:7–10.

123. Jub. 33:10–17.

124. 11Q Torah 66:11–12.

125. Albeck, "Jubiläen," 24–25; Finkelstein, *HTR* XVI (1923) 54. These authors point out that Jubilees requires the covering of all blood, not just the blood of wild beasts and fowl, as in the rabbinic prescriptions.

126. Jub. 6:4–14.

127. Lev. 3:17, 7:26.

128. Deut. 12:15–28, 15:23.

129. 11Q Torah 52:11–12 and 53:5–6. Cf. Deut. 12:23–24. 11Q Torah 53:5–6, "thou shalt cover it with dust," appends Lev. 17:13 to Deut. 12:24. This conflation suggests that the author of the sectarian Torah would require the covering of the blood of all animals, in contrast to the halakah, which limits the requirement to the blood of wild beasts and fowl. See n. 125.

130. 11Q Torah 32:13–15.

131. Yadin, *TS* I, 127. See also Finkelstein, *HTR* XVI (1923) 52–53, and Albeck, "Jubiläen," 30–35. Note M. Maaser Sheni 5:1–2, 4.

132. Yadin, *TS* I, 81–99.

133. 11Q Torah 38:4, 43:5–12, 60:6–7.

134. 11Q Torah 60:2–4.

135. 11Q Torah 60:6–7. To be sure, Deut. 14:23 does designate the bringing of *ma'aser* (tithe) and *bikkurym* (first fruits) annually, but it does so without prescribing the festival.

136. Jub. 32:12.

137. Jub. 44:4.

138. Jub. 6:21.

139. 11Q Torah 19:9.

140. Jub. 1:1.

141. Jub. 6:1–18.

142. Jub. 14:20–15:34.

143. The origin of this festival seems to be alluded to in Neh. 10:35 and 13:31. See also M. Taanith 4:4–5 and M. Megillah 1:3.

144. Yadin, *TS* I, 81, 95, 105.

145. An explanation of this calendar can be found in A. Jaubert, *The Date of the Last Supper* (Staten Island, N.Y., 1965), 13–30. It is presented in tabular form by J. A. Fitzmyer, *The Dead Sea Scrolls: Major Publications and Tools for Study* (Missoula, Mont., 1977), 133. Pp. 131–32 provide an ample bibliography of major works on the Jubilees and Qumran calendar.

146. Yadin, *TS* I, 96.

147. Yadin, *TS* I, 81, would extend the festival seasons, which require additional festal offerings, by one day to make allowance for the prohibition against making sacrifices on the Sabbath. See above, p. 47.

148. Jaubert, *Date,* 31–52, claims that this calendar is the ancient, biblical calendar (cf. J. C. VanderKam, "The Origin, Character, and Early History of the 364-day Calendar: A Reassessment of Jaubert's Hypothesis," *CBQ* XLI [1979] 390–411). For a necessary refutation of this view, see J. M. Baumgarten, "The Calendar of the Book of Jubilees and the Bible," *Studies in Qumran Law* (Leiden, 1977), 101–14.

149. Yadin, *TS* I, 96.

150. Yadin, *TS* II, 44. However, Yadin's reading seems improbable in the light of what precedes and follows this defective line in the text.

151. Having assumed the sectarian calendar, Yadin (*TS* I, 95–96) proceeds to outline the year from that base. B. A. Levine ("The Temple Scroll: Aspects of its Historical Provenance and Literary Character," *BASOR* 232 [1978] 6–11) rightly takes issue with this assumption; however, I cannot agree that Leviticus need not refer to the Sabbath. J. Milgrom ("'Sabbath' and 'Temple City' in the Temple Scroll," *BASOR* 232 [1978] 25–26) disagrees with Levine, arguing that the Qumranic Torah is basing its calendar of festivals on the Sabbath day, even though this need not indicate the Qumran or Jubilees calendar.

152. See also 11Q Torah 11:11 of Yadin's restored text.

153. 11Q Torah 43.

154. 11Q Torah 14:10–15:1 and 25:1–10.

155. Even if Milik's dating is too high, the Astronomical Enoch cannot be later than the third century B.C.E. See the article by Greenfield and Stone in n. 6 above.

156. See pp. 35–40 above.

157. Ethiopic Enoch 72:1 (Knibb, *Ethiopic* II, 167).

158. Knibb, *Ethiopic* II, 173–75.

159. A misleading note by Charles on Enoch 74:12 is responsible for much confusion as to the relationship between the calendars in Enoch and Jubilees. While Charles in his 1893 edition translated "the moon brings in all the years exactly," and noted that this was in direct opposition to the statements in Jubilees 6 (p. 201), in his 1912 revision he read, "the sun and the stars bring in all the years exactly," and attached the note: "Our author advocates a sidereal year as does the

author of Jubilees" (p. 160). Knibb correctly translates this phrase, "And the moon conducts the years exactly." Thus Enoch cannot be reconciled with the Jubilees solar calendar. The calendar of Enoch is lunisolar throughout.

160. The putative view assumes that both Enoch and Jubilees present a solar calendar: Jaubert, *Date*, 17; S. Talmon, "The Calendar Reckoning of the Sect from the Judaean Desert," *Scripta Hierosolymitana* IV (Jerusalem, 1958), 177–79; F. M. Cross, Jr., *The Ancient Library of Qumran and Modern Biblical Studies* (Garden City, N.Y., 2d ed., 1962), 46; J. T. Milik, *Enoch*, 274; G. Vermes, *The Dead Sea Scrolls: Qumran in Perspective* (London, 1977), 176;

161. See p. 57 above.

162. A number of studies confirm that the Jubilees calendar and that of the Qumran sect are the same: D. Bartholemy, "Notes en marge de publications récentes sur les manuscrits de Qumran," *RB* LXIX (1959) 187–218, espec. 200–202; J. T. Milik, "Le travail d'édition des manuscrits de désert de Juda," *VTSup* IV (1957) 17–26, espec. 24–25; S. Talmon, *Scripta Hierosolymitana* IV (1958) 162–99; A. Jaubert, *Date*, 15–30; J. M. Baumgarten, "The Beginning of the Day in the Calendar of Jubilees," *Studies*, 124–30.

163. A. Jaubert, "Le calendrier des Jubilés et les jours liturgiques de la semaine," *VT* VII (1957) 35–61.

164. See above, pp. 38–40.

165. Jub. 6:35.

166. Charles, *Jubilees*, 24–25. A more extensive discussion of the heavenly tablets appears in his *Enoch*, 131–33. Other references to the heavenly tablets include Enoch 81:1, 2; 93:3; 103:2; 106:19; T. Levi 5:5; T. Asher 2:10, 7:5. Charles also lists references such as Enoch 47:3, which speaks of the "books of the living."

167. Most scholars have followed Charles (see previous note), who defines the term very broadly and understands it to be virtually synonymous with other phrases such as the "book of life (or the living)," "books of remembrance of good and evil deeds," "books of the saints," or "books of the angels." Cf. P. Volz, *Die Eschatologie der jüdischen Gemeinde im neutestamentlichen Zeitalter* (Tübingen, 1934), 290–92; R. Eppel, "Les tables de la Loi et les tables célestes," *RHPR* XVII (1937) 401–12; S. M. Paul, "Heavenly Tablets and the Book of Life," *JANES* V (1973) 345–53.

168. Charles, *Jubilees*, 24–25.

169. Jub. 6:29, 35; 16:28–29; 18:19; 21:10; 32:10, 15, 27–28; 34:18; 49:8, 17; 50:13.

170. Jub. 6:7–8 (cf. 4:5, 32).

171. Jub. 6:17, 21–22 (cf. 15:1–2, 16:13); 22:1.

172. See pp. 42–48 above.

173. Jub. 6:15–21. Scholars find in this description of the covenant with Noah the origin of the rabbinic notion that the Torah was given to Moses on this date: Charles, *Jubilees*, 52; Albeck, *Jubiläen*, 15–17; E. Lohse, "πεντηκοστη," *TDNT* VI, 48–49.

174. Jub. 1:1.

175. This phrase is not found in Enoch 72–82, which has been shown by Milik to antedate Jubilees (see above, p. 40), with the exception of 81:1–2, usually considered a later interpolation (Charles, *Enoch*, 188–89). It does appear in later literature, and the references have been listed in n. 166 above.

176. Gen. 28:10–22, 35:1–15.

177. Jub. 31:1–32:39. See the discussion of 11Q Torah 29 in Chap. 1, p. 21 ff.

178. Jub. 31:1–2 (cf. Exod. 19:10–15).

179. Jub. 32:21.

180. Literature which discusses this Jewish historian includes the following: J. Freudenthal, *Alexander Polyhistor* (Breslau, 1875), 104–30; P. Dalbert, *Die Theologie der Hellenistisch-Jüdischen Missionsliteratur unter Ausschluss von Philo und Josephus* (Hamburg, 1954), 35–42; A. M. Denis, *Introduction aux Pseudépigraphes Grecs d'Ancien Testament* (Leiden, 1970), 252–55; M. Hengel, *Judaism and Hellenism* (Philadelphia, 1974), 92–95; B. Z. Wacholder, *Eupolemus* (Cincinnati, 1974); N. Walter, *JSHRZ* I:2, 93–108.

181. *FGrH* 723. See Wacholder, *Eupolemus*, 44–52.

182. 1 Mac. 8:17; Hengel, *Judaism* I, 92; Wacholder, *Eupolemus*, 1–21; Walter, *JSHRZ* I:2, 95–97.

183. Clement of Alexandria, *Stromata* 1, 141, 1 (*FGrH* 723:4).

184. *PE* 9, 34, 4–16 (*FGrH* 723:2b). For the Greek text of Eusebius' work, see K. Mras, *Die Praeparatio Evangelica* (Berlin, 1954), 541–44. The translation used in the present work is from Wacholder, *Eupolemus*, 310–11.

185. Freudenthal, *Polyhistor*, 119.

186. Wacholder, *Eupolemus*, 174–75.

187. See below for the completion of this line.

188. Wacholder, *Eupolemus*, 175–78; Walter, *JSHRZ* I:2, 103.

189. Wacholder, *Eupolemus*, 177.

190. Yadin, *TS* II, 10.

191. LXX, 3 Kgs. 6:2: 40 × 20 × 25.

192. Yadin, *TS* II, 10.

193. Yadin, ibid., mentions this possibility, but rejects it as improbable.

194. Yadin, ibid., claims that the text as it is found in the scroll may be a scribal error and suggests that בניתה may represent the intent of the original author. Maier, *Tempelrolle*, 73, proposes, in addition, that the text may represent an archaic from of בנה borrowed from Ugaritic. In commenting on this manuscript, John Strugnell suggests reading וביאתה את האולם (and its entry, together with the porch).

195. 11Q Torah 5:13, 8:6, 12:15, 30:7, 31:10, 32:12, 34:15, 35:10, 38:12, 40:5, etc.

196. Yadin, *TS* II, 10–12.

197. See above, p. 39.

198. 11Q Torah 40:5–45:1.

199. Wacholder, *Eupolemus*, 177.

200. Ezek. 40:6–48; 43:1–4; 44:1–4; 45:19; 46:1–12, 19; 47:2; 48:30–34. Yadin, *TS* I, 146–48. See also Wacholder, *Eupolemus*, 186–87, and T. A. Busink, *Der Tempel von Jerusalem von Salomo bis Herodes* I (Leiden, 1970), 186–93.

201. 11Q Torah 36, 39:11–16, 40:11–42:6, 44:1–45:2.

202. *DJD* III 2Q 24:8, 3(p. 84). As in 11Q Torah (see p. 38 above), the septimal numbers also appear to play a major role in the description of the New Jerusalem. The dimensions of the buildings are constantly given in both cubits and קנין (reeds), the latter being seven cubits in length (*DJD* III, 5Q 15, pp. 189–193). In Ezekiel, the reed is only six cubits (40:5).

203. *CA* 1:198. See Yadin, *TS* I:184–86 and II:37.

204. If Eupolemus' text is emended to "twenty," the similarity of the two descriptions is even more apparent. See Wacholder, *Eupolemus*, 194–95; Walter, *JSHRZ* I:2, 104.

205. 11Q Torah 13:2.

206. 11Q Torah 13:5.

207. Yadin, *TS* II, 39. On the slaughterhouse see pp. 72–73.

208. 1 Kgs. 7:21 (2 Chr. 3:17) locates the two pillars one on the right and the other on the left, as does 11Q Torah 13:5.

209. 2 Kgs. 25:17 and Jer. 52:21–23.

210. 1 Kgs. 7:30 (2 Chr. 4:6).

211. 1 Kgs. 7:23 (2 Chr. 4:2).

212. Yadin, *TS* I, 168–73; II, 96–100. He considers 11Q Torah 31:10–33:7 to be a description of the בית כיור (house of the laver). Our text cites the *kyyor* in 5:10 (6:5) and then the *beyt kyyor*, which presumably contained the *kyyor* and was square rather than circular. The absence of any sculptured figures in the entire text implies a repudiation of the Solomonic structure, in which the sea stood on molten oxen.

213. Exod. 30:17–21. See Wacholder, *Eupolemus*, 193.

214. 11Q Torah 31:10.

215. 1 Kgs. 7:23.

216. Yadin cites a number of passages from King and Chronicles which allegedly served as a major source for the sectarian Torah. This seems not to be the case. To be sure, some terminology may have been borrowed from Kings and Chronicles (e.g., *parwar*); however, the absence of any substantial numerical similarities necessitates the conclusion that their influence on the Qumranic Torah was negative.

217. For the significance of septimal numbers in 11Q Torah, see above pp. 38–39.

218. Wacholder, *Eupolemus*, 190–93.

219. On the king's platform, see Wacholder, *Eupolemus*, 193–94. See also 2 Chr. 6:13.

220. 1 Kgs. 7:23 (2 Chr. 4:2).

221. Wacholder, *Eupolemus*, 187–90.

222. Note here that the Septuagint text of 1 Kgs. 7:31 (Hebrew, 7:45) inserts the words, "and the forty-eight pillars of the house of the king and of the house of the Lord."

223. Yadin, *TS* I, 178–82; II, 102–4.

224. Yadin, *TS* I, 182–84; II, 106–7.

225. Yadin, *TS* II, 106.

226. *BJ* 5:224.

227. Wacholder, *Eupolemus*, 196–201.

228. Yadin, *TS* I, 211–12; II, 138.

229. Wacholder, *Eupolemus*, 199.

230. Freudenthal, *Polyhistor*, 119–20.

231. *PE*, 30:8.

232. 11Q Torah 19:16, 21:5, 22:2 (cf. 21:2, 22:12, 23:10), 42:14, 57:12.

233. See above, p. 63.

234. S. Z. Leiman, *The Canonization of Hebrew Scripture: The Talmudic and Midrashic Evidence,* (Hamden, 1976), 28–30; B. Z. Wacholder, "The Letter from Judah Maccabee to Aristobulus: Is 2 Maccabees 1:10b–2:18 Authentic?" *HUCA* XLIX (1978) 125–26.

235. F. F. Bruce, "The Book of Daniel and the Qumran Community," *Neotestamentica et Semitica: Studies in Honor of Matthew Black* (Edinburgh, 1969), E. E. Ellis and M. Wilcox (eds.), 221–35.

236. Note that Yadin (*TS* II, 312) lists seven references to Daniel, none of which show 11Q Torah's dependence on that book.

237. See pp. 63–77 above.

238. See pp. 41–42.

239. The Hebrew text and commentary of this work was published by Y. Yadin, *The Scroll of the War of the Sons of Light Against the Sons of Darkness* (Jerusalem, 1955), (Hebrew) translated into English by B. and C. Rabin (same title, Oxford, 1962). For a brief analysis of the major commentaries on this scroll, see P. R. Davies, *1QM, the War Scroll from Qumran: Its Structure and History* (Rome, 1977), 11–20, even though he evaluates them only from the perspective of literary criticism.

While virtually all commentators note or assume the influence of Daniel on the War Rule, scholars differ as to the relationship of the War Rule to other Qumranic writings: A. Dupont-Sommer, *The Essene Writings from Qumran* (Cleveland, 1961), G. Vermes (trans.), 167; J. Carmignac, "La Règle de la Guerre," *Les Textes de Qumran* I (Paris, 1961), 85–86.

240. The influence of Ezekiel upon the War Rule is quite pervasive. J. van der Ploeg (*Le Rouleau de la Guerre* [Leiden, 1959],20) finds in the Rule original and secondary sections, with the former having been composed under the influence of Ezekiel 38–39.

241. See above, pp. 4–21.

242. 1QM 2:1 and 11Q Torah 31:4.

243. 1QM 3:15–18, 4:1–5 and 11Q Torah 22:2, 42:15, 57:4–5, 58:4.

244. 1QM 1:2 and 11Q Torah 44:14.

245. 11Q Torah 58:11.

246. 1QM 7:1–2 and 11Q Torah 57:2–3.

247. All translations of the War Rule are from Yadin's English edition, which is listed above (n. 239). Note Yadin's comments concerning this similarity (*TS* II, 91).

248. See above, pp. 9–12.

249. 1QM 7:10; 11Q Torah 3:2.

250. 1QM 2:3; 3:1, 7; 7:9, 16, etc.; 11Q Torah 36:7, 39:10–16, 40:12–41:17.

251. 1QM 2:5–6, 11Q Torah 13–29.

252. 1QM 3:13–14, 5:1–2; cf. 2:3, 7; 4:9–10; 6:10.

253. 11Q Torah 23:9–24:16.

254. Ibid. 39:11–13.

255. 1QM 7:3.

256. 11Q Torah 39:7, 40:6.

257. 1QM 7:4.

258. 11Q Torah 45:12–13.

259. Lev. 21:17–24. See *TS* I, 225; II, 136.

260. 1QM 7:6.

261. 11Q Torah 45:7–12.

262. Ibid. 58:17.

263. 1QM 2:1; 11Q Torah 31:4.

264. 1QM 2:3; 3:1, 7; 7:9, 16, etc.; 11Q Torah 36:7, 39:10–16, 40:12–41:17.

265. 1QM 2:5–6; 11Q Torah 13–29.

266. 11Q Torah 59:15.

267. Exod. 19:2, 24:4; Numbers 2.

268. This view differs from the commonly held opinion that the War Scroll represents a midrashic embellishment of Dan. 11:40–12:13 (Bruce, *Neotestamentica et Semitica*, 233).

269. 1QM 10:11; Dan. 2:22.

270. 1QM 10:11; Dan. 8:10.

271. 1QM 14:4.

272. Dan. 9:4.

273. 1QM 10:10.

274. Dan. 9:22 and 11:33.

275. 1QM 11:8 and Dan. 9:26.

276. Dan. 10:13 and 1QM 17:5–7. On Michael, See Yadin, *Scroll of the War*, 235–36.

277. 1QM 10:10.

278. 1QM 12:7.

279. Dan. 8:24.

280. Dan. 11:28, 30.

281. 1QM 2:2.

282. 1 Chr. 24:1–18, 25:9–31.

283. 1QM 2:1.

284. See above, pp. 53–59.

285. Note the many citations from Jubilees in his index, *Scroll of the War*, 364.

286. 1QM 2:6–14.

287. The heightened dualism of the War Scroll has been frequently noted, perhaps most notably by J. J. Collins ("The Mythology of Holy War in Daniel and the Qumran War Scroll: A Point of Transition in Jewish Apocalyptic," *VT* XXV [1975] 596–612), who seems to over-emphasize the Persian influence. Note the response of P. R. Davies, "Dualism and Eschatology in the Qumran War Scroll," *VT* XXVIII (1978) 28–36. A monograph on the subject of dualism at Qumran, which posits its introduction into the community through the War Rule, is that of P. von der Osten-Sacken, *Gott und Belial* (Göttingen, 1969).

288. Osten-Sacken (ibid.) notes the absence of a strict dualism in Jubilees; however, he then goes on to discuss the relationship between the angelology and dualism in that work.

289. CD 5:18.

290. *BJ* 2:137, 142.

291. The Hebrew texts of these works have been edited and vocalized in the following collections: A. M. Habermann, *The Scrolls from the Judaean Desert* (Tel Aviv, 1959), (Hebrew); E. Lohse, *Die Texte aus Qumran: Hebräisch und Deutsch* (Munich, 1964). Translations of the scrolls in collections include the following: J. Maier, *Die Texte vom Toten Meer,* (Munich and Basel, 1960), I and II; A. Dupont-Sommer, *The Essene Writings from Qumran* (Cleveland and New York, 1961), G. Vermes (trans.); J. Carmignac et al., *Les Textes de Qumran* (Paris, 1961), I and II; G. Vermes, *The Dead Sea Scrolls in English* (Middlesex, 2d ed., 1975).

292. See previous note.

293. *The Dead Sea Scrolls of St. Mark's Monastery* II (New Haven, Conn., 1951). Note that new photographs were published by F. M. Cross et al. (eds.), *Scrolls from Qumran Cave I* (Jerusalem, 1972), 125–47. In both editions, the photographs are by John C. Trever.

294. 1QS 1:11–12; 3:2; 5:2–3; 6:2, 17, 22, 25; 8:23; 9:7–9.

295. Major commentaries on this document include the following: P. Wernberg-Møller, *The Manual of Discipline* (Leiden, 1957); P. Guilbert, "La Règle de la Communauté" in *Les Textes de Qumran* I, 11–80; J. Licht, *The Rule Scroll; A Scroll from the Wilderness of Judaea: 1QS, 1QSa, 1QSb* (Jerusalem, 1965), (Hebrew); A. R. C. Leaney, *The Rule of Qumran and its Meaning* (London, 1966); J. Pouilly, *La Règle de la Communauté de Qumran* (Paris, 1976).

296. This reading is adopted by Lohse, *Texte,* 4.

297. 1QS 5:1.

298. 1QS 6:8.

299. 1QS 6:24.

300. 1QS 8:20.

301. 1QS 9:12.

302. 1QS 9:21.

303. 1QSa 1:1. Note that this formula continues in "The Messianic Rule."

304. 1QSa 1:6.

305. This may be a better explanation of many of those indicators which some scholars have taken to be evidence of a composite work: Guilbert, *Textes,* I, 12–15; Leaney, *Rule,* 113–116; Pouilly, *Règle,* 9–13, 85–103.

306. This viewpoint prompted E. F. Sutcliffe to write his work: *The Monks of Qumran* (Westminster, Md., 1960). See also more recently G. Vermes, *The Dead Sea Scrolls: Qumran in Perspective* (London, 1977), 87–90.

307. 1QS 6:4–6; 1QSa 2:17–20.

308. Cf. 11Q Torah 43:6–9.

309. 1QSa 1:8–10.

310. 11Q Torah 17:8, 39:11, 57:3.

311. 1QS 8:5–6, 8; 9:6; 10:4. Note especially 1QS 8:8, where it is preceded by *me'on*, a reference to the sanctuary.

312. 1QS 5:20.

313. 1QS 4:10.

314. 1QS 5:14.

315. 1QS 3:5–6.

316. 1QS 4:5; 5:13; 6:16, 22, 25; 7:3, 16, 25; 8:17, 24.

317. See above, pp. 10–12.

318. 1QS 2:21–22; cf. Exod. 18:21, 25; 11Q Torah 42:15, 57:4–5, 58:4.

319. Dupont-Sommer, *Essene Writings,* 97.

320. 1QS 10:1, 2, 3, 6.

321. See Levey, IV, 662.

322. 1QS 10:7–8.

323. 1QS 6:4–6; 1QSa 2:17–20.

324. The question of animal sacrifice at Qumran has been the subject of considerable debate. A few of the major studies follow: J. Strugnell, "Flavius Josephus and the Essenes: *Antiquities* XVIII.18–22," *JBL* LXXVII (1958) 106–15; F. M. Cross, Jr., *The Ancient Library of Qumran,* 100–103; L. Feldman (ed.), *Josephus* IX, p. 16, n. a; G. Klinzing, *Die Umdeutung des Kultus in der Qumrangemeinde und im Neuen Testament* (Göttingen, 1971), 20–49; E. P. Sanders, *Paul and Palestinian Judaism* (Philadelphia, 1977), 299–303; J. M. Baumgarten, *Studies,* 39–74.

325. 1QS 2:8; 3:6, 8; 5:6.

326. 1QS 8:6, 10; 9:4; 11:14.

327. 1QS 9:3–5.

328. 1QS 9:5–7.

329. Guilbert, *Textes* I, 57, uses 1QS 8:5 as evidence that the sect had not yet separated from the temple at the time of the composition of the Rule. Leaney, *Rule of Qumran,* 216, understands this phrase to mean that the community, i.e., the Commune, is to replace the temple.

330. Y. Yadin, "A Midrash on 2 Sam. vii and Ps. i–ii (4Q Florilegium)," *IEJ* IX (1959) 95–98; D. Flusser, "Two Notes on the Midrash of 2 Sam. vii," *IEJ* IX (1959) 99–109; J. M. Baumgarten, "The Exclusion of 'Netinim' and Proselytes in 4Q Florilegium," *Studies,* 75–87.

331. E. L. Sukenik, *The Dead Sea Scrolls of the Hebrew University* (Jerusalem, 1955), plates 35–58. Major commentaries include: J. Licht, *The Thanksgiving Scroll* (Jerusalem, 1957), (Hebrew); M. Mansoor, *The Thanksgiving Hymns* (Leiden, 1961); J. Carmignac, "Les Hymnes," *Textes* I, 129–280; S. Holm-Nielsen, *Hodayot: Psalms from Qumran* (Aarhus, 1961); M. Delcor, *Les Hymnes de Qumran (Hodayot)* (Paris, 1962).

332. Wernberg-Møller, *Manual,* 140.

333. John Strugnell and Joseph Baumgarten in private notes objected to this statement, arguing that some of the *Hodayot* reflect public prayer. Holm-Nielsen cites cols. 14, 16, and 17 (*EJ* XV, 1047) as evidence of public prayer in which the petitioner addresses the *Yaḥad.* All these passages show is that there are occasional allusions to the rules of the Commune in the midst of personal petitions (1QH 14:18). These passages do prove that the prayers were composed when the *Yaḥad* was fully developed.

334. The identity of the first-person singular in this work has been the subject of considerable debate. Beginning with Sukenik, some scholars have ascribed the hymns to the Teacher of Righteousness. More recently two monographs on the Teacher of Righteousness have been based on that assumption: G. Jeremias, *Der Lehrer der Gerechtigkeit* (Göttingen, 1963) and P. Schultz, *Der Autoritätsanspruch des Lehrers der Gerechtigkeit in Qumran* (Meisenheim am Glan, 1974). B. P. Kittel, (*The Hymns of Qumran: Translation and Commentary* [Chico, Cal., 1981], 9–10) does not agree. The term needs clarification. If *Moreh Ṣedeq* refers to the leading master of the Commune, such an assumption seems plausible (1QH 14:18–21). This study, however, presumes that *Moreh Ṣedeq* refers only to the founder of the sect, whose return is expected at the time of the eschaton. Since the *Yaḥad* and its organization are taken for granted in the hymns, their author could not have been the Teacher of Righteousness.

335. 1QH 2:31–32 (see also 6:19).

336. 1QH 4:38 (see also 14:12).

337. 1QH 5:9–12. For additional examples, see 1QH 6:4–5, 15:14–17.

338. 1QH 6:17–18.

339. 1QH 9:17–18.

340. 1QH 8:4–20.

341. 1QH 14:12.

342. 1QH 2:31–32, 4:7–16, 6:25–30, 7:10–12, 9:35, 10:27.

343. 1QH 4:38, 6:19–22, 13:5–6, 14:25–26, 15:15–21.

344. See n. 334 above.

345. See Chap. 3.

346. 1QS 6:7.
347. 1QS 8:1–4.
348. Cf. L. H. Schiffman, *The Halakhah at Qumran* (Leiden, 1975), 36–42 and 54–60.
349. For a discussion of these terms at Qumran, see below.
350. On this use of the term, see Schiffman, *Halakhah*, 22–32. For a different view, see N. Wieder, *The Dead Sea Scrolls and Karaism* (Oxford, 1962), 53–62. Note that both writers deal with the appearance of the term throughout the Dead Sea literature.
351. This characteristic has been noted by D. Patte, *Early Jewish Hermeneutic in Palestine* (Missoula, Mont., 1975), 300–302. I Rabinowitz ("*Pēsher/Pittārōn*: Its Biblical Meaning and its Significance in the Qumran Literature," *RQ* VIII [1972–75] 219–32) rightly emphasizes the difference between pesher and midrash, a point with which W. H. Brownlee (*The Midrash Pesher of Habakkuk* [Missoula, Mont., 1979], 23–28) takes issue. Other studies on this term include the following: O. Betz, *Offenbarung und Schriftforschung in der Qumransekte* (Tübingen, 1960), 77–80; L. H. Silberman, "Unriddling the Riddle: A Study in the Structure and Language of the Habakkuk Pesher (1Qp Hab.)," *RQ* III (1961–62) 323–64; A. Finkel, "The Pesher of Dreams and Scriptures," *RQ* IV (1963–64) 357–70. Recently M. P. Horgan (*Pesharim: Qumran Interpretations of Biblical Books* [Washington, 1979] 250–52) has shown the inadvisability of using "midrash" to describe the mode of interpretation at Qumran.
352. 1QpHab 1:13, 9:9–10, 11:2–12:10.
353. 1QpHab 2:12; 3:4, 9; 4:5, 10.
354. 1QpHab 11:2–8.
355. See below, pp. 185–99.
356. Jer. 25:11–12.
357. Dan. 9:24–27.
358. Targum Onkelos on Gen. 40:8.
359. See below, pp. 185–99.
360. See Chap. 5 below.
361. 4QpNah 1:2. While only the last half of the name is present in the fragments, there is no reason to seriously question the identification.
362. 4QpNah 1:3.
363. 4QpNah 3:3. The translation is that of G. Vermes, *DSSE* 233.
364. *DJD* V, 45. This text has incorporated the emendations of J. Strugnell, "Notes en Marge du Volume V des 'Discoveries in the Judaean Desert of Jordan,'" *RQ* VII (1970) 216.
365. 4Q 171, 4:9–15.
366. The importance of the forty years and the wilderness theme is discussed elsewhere; see pp. 78, 222–25.
367. *DJD* V, 67–68. Note Strugnell's different readings, *RQ* VII (1970) 238–41, particularly with regard to line 16. The translation is that of *DJD*.
368. Yadin may be correct in claiming that the prophetic reading should have been ספר התורה השנית (*TS* I, 303).
369. See above, pp. 42–48.
370. Yadin, *TS* I, 302–3.
371. See above, pp. 61–62.
372. This fragment was originally published by J. M. Allegro, "Further Messianic References in Qumran Literature," *JBL* LXXV (1956) 174–76.
373. See lines 5–6.
374. *DJD* V, 53.
375. Note that Strugnell (*RQ* VII [1970] 220) suggests that "Torah" may be the reading at the beginning of line 3. Our text also incorporates other alternate readings of Strugnell.
376. Note that ויאמר (and he said) may refer to a quotation from 11Q Torah, from the first columns in which God will have prescribed the construction of a sanctuary.

377. D. Flusser, *IEJ* IX (1959) 99–104. On the future sanctuary in 4Q Florilegium, see n. 330 above and the following studies: E. Fiorenza, "Cultic Language in Qumran and the New Testament," *CBQ* XXXVIII (1976) 159–77; A. J. McNicol, "The Eschatological Temple in the Qumran Pesher: 4Q Florilegium," *Ohio Journal of Religious Studies* V (1977) 133–41; D. R. Schwarz, "The Three Temples of 4Q Florilegium," *RQ* X (1979) 83–91.

378. For text and commentary see: J. M. Allegro, *The Treasure of the Copper Scroll* (Garden City, N.Y., 1960); J. T. Milik, *DJD* III, 201–302. This study uses Milik's text.

379. *DJD* III, 284. The translation of all quotations from the Copper Scroll is mine.

380. See below, pp. 119–21.

381. 11Q Torah 3:5.

382. Ibid. 3:8.

383. Ibid. 31:8.

384. Ibid. 36:10–11.

385. M. R. Lehmann, *RQ* IX (1978) 581.

386. The giving of the half-shekel for the temple is mentioned in 4Q 159 (*DJD* V, 6–7), which says it is given only once in each person's lifetime. Note the debate over this issue in *Tarbiẓ* XXXI (1961–62), which includes articles by J. Liver, D. Flusser, and M. Beer.

387. 11Q Torah 3:2.

388. 1Q 32 (*DJD* I, 134–35); 2Q 24 (*DJD* III, 84–89); 5Q 15 (*DJD* III 184–93, this also includes some Cave 4 fragments); 11Q JN ar (B. Jongeling, "Publication provisoire d'un fragment provenant de la grotte 11 de Qumrân [11Q Jér Nouv ar]," *JSJ* I [1970] 58–64 and "note additionelle," ibid., 185–86).

389. 1Q 32, Fl.

390. Ibid., F5. Note 11Q Torah 13:1–7 and the discussion above, p. 69.

391. 1Q 32, F14. Note that *galgillym* (wheels) also appear in 11Q Torah 34:4, 5, 9. Yadin, *TS* I, 181, suggests that 1Q 32, Fl, F5, and F14 belong together.

392. 2Q 24, F8.

393. Yadin, *TS* I, 174–75, 181, 186.

394. John Strugnell in a private communication.

395. The dimensions of the altar in the "New Jerusalem" include "twenty," the same measurement as given for the altar in 11Q Torah 12:9, according to Yadin, *TS* I, 186 and II, 37.

396. Jub. 6:21, 32:12, 44:4. See p. 53 above.

397. 1QS 6:4–6; 1QSa 2:17–20, See p. 85 above.

398. 1QH 10:24.

399. See Chap. 3, pp. 119–29.

Notes to Chapter 3

1. Without compelling reasons, in an act that reflects a disregard for common courtesy as well as a misunderstanding of the book's contents, this work has been rechristened the "Damascus Document." The alteration of the treatise's name from "Zadokite fragments" has helped to minimize a basic question in the comprehension of the Qumran library.

2. See above, p. 94.

3. A. Dupont-Sommer, *The Essene Writings from Qumran* (Cleveland and New York, 1962), G. Vermes (trans.), 383.

4. K. G. Kuhn, "Les Rouleaux de Cuivre de Qumrân," *RB* LXI (1954) 193–205; J. M. Allegro, *The Treasure of the Copper Scroll* (Garden City, N. Y., 1960), 56–62.

5. 5:6, 8.

6. *DSSE,* 272.

7. *DJD* III, 275–84.

8. The text used here is that of J. T. Milik, *DJD* III, 296. The English translation is mine.

9. 3Q 15, 11:9. *DJD* III, 259, 271, 274, has a discussion of this enigmatic name.

10. For a complete bibliography, see J. A. Fitzmyer's "Prolegomena" to the reprint of S. Schechter's *Fragments of a Zadokite Work* (New York, 1970), 25–34. The text utilized in this study is that of C. Rabin, *The Zadokite Documents* (Oxford, 2d ed., 1958). Photographs of the medieval text were published by S. Zeitlin, *The Zadokite Fragments* (Philadelphia, 1952). See further J. Murphy-O'Connor, "An Essene Missionary Document? CD II, 14–VI, 1," *RB* LXXVII (1970) 201–29; idem, "A Literary Analysis of Damascus Document VI, 2–VIII, 3," *RB* LXXVIII (1971) 210–32; idem, "The Critique of the Princes of Judah (CD VIII, 3–19)," *RB* LXXIX (1972) 200–16; idem, "A Literary Analysis of Damascus Document XIX, 33–XX, 34," *RB* LXXIX (1972) 544–64. He then presented the historical implications of these studies in "The Essenes and Their History," *RB* LXXXI (1974) 215–44. The other major historical study is that of H. Stegemann, "Die Entstehung der Qumrangemeinde" (Diss., Bonn, 1971). In addition to these, the translation and supplement of L. Ginzberg's work has appeared: *An Unknown Jewish Sect* (New York, 1976).

11. We are here following the order proposed by J. T. Milik (*Ten Years of Discovery in the Wilderness of Judaea* [Naperville, Ill., 1959], J. Strugnell [trans.], 151–52) with one exception. Along with other scholars, he assumes that the apparent duplication between pages 8 and 19 means that page 20 is a continuation of the same unit. See the following discussion for a different interpretation.

12. J. Murphy-O'Connor (*RB* LXXIX [1972] 544–64) regards this page as part of the unit, except for CD 20:1c–8a and 13c–17a, which he considers interpolations. These cannot be exceptions, since CD 20:25–27 seems to allude to the lines which Murphy-O'Connor regards as interpolations, especially 20:27, "days of its purgings," which refers to the removal of the wicked. See also J. Carmignac, "Comparaison entre les manuscrits 'A' et 'B' du Document des Damas," *RQ* II (1959–60) 53–67.

13. A basic difference between pages 1–8 and 20 is the presence or absence of the hope for a united Israel. Pages 1–8 speak of an eventual uniting of the two Israels, which is a view not contemplated on page 20. CD 4:11–12 is frequently understood as being indicative of the sect's irreconcilable differences with the rest of Israel (e.g., J. Maier, *Die Texte vom Toten Meer* [Munich and Basil, 1960], II, 47–48; E. Cothenet, "Le Document de Damas," *Les Textes de Qumran* [Paris, 1963], II, 161), but the context of this passage's quotation from Mic. 7:11 requires that it be understood as a forecast of the eventual reunification of Israel. J. Murphy-O'Connor (*RB* LXXVII [1970] 218) recognizes the inadequacy of the current interpretation, but sees the passage as an example of his "missionary document" hypothesis. CD 7:11–12 requires a similar interpretation, an expression of a hope for repentance and the eventual reunification of Israel.

14. This study distinguishes between "sect" and "commune." Sect (שבי ישראל, יודעי צדק, מחזיקים etc.) refers to the group as a whole, from its formation circa 200 B.C.E. to its extinction at Qumran. Commune (*Yaḥad* and its synonyms) denotes the second stage, when the group isolated itself from Israel, and is reflected only in the Qumranic stage, in literature such as the Community Rule and the Thanksgivings.

15. According to K. G. Kuhn (*Konkoranz zu den Qumrantexten* [Göttingen, 1960] and "Nachträge zur 'Konkordanz zu den Qumrantexten,'" *RQ* IV [1963–64] 163–234), this term is used fifty-three times in the Community Rule, the record of the regulations which were established to govern their common life.

16. CD 1:12, 2:1, 3:9, 7:20, 8:13.

17. In addition to its appearance in various Qumranic fragments, it appears fourteen times in the Community Rule, eighteen in the War Rule, seven in the Thanksgivings, and three times in the Messianic Rule.

18. CD 7:2, which quotes Lev. 19:17.

19. Cf. CD 7:15–16. See the discussion below, pp. 130–33.

20. See above, p. 46.

21. See above, p. 84 (cf. 1QS 9:10).

22. For the latter, see CD 2:17.

23. 1QM 2:14, 3:16, 4:10, 10:14; 1QSa 1:9, 15, 21.

24. For a fuller discussion, see below, pp. 108–9.

25. See Gen. 10:25.

26. For a fuller discussion of the three time periods, see below pp. 129–40.

27. See below, pp. 105–9.

28. בעצת הקדש (in the council of the holy) is also found in 1QS 2:25, 8:21; 1QM 3:4; 1QH 7:10; 1QSa 2:9. עצת appears even more frequently with יחד, thus "the council of the Commune," particularly in the Community Rule. Other modifiers include אל (God), תורה (law), and אנשי היחד (men of the Commune).

29. See below, pp. 185–93.

30. These words appear in combination in 1QS 1:5, 26; 5:4; 8:2; 9:17; 1QH 1:30. In addition, "justice" and "truth" are to be found in 1QS 4:2 and 24 as well as in 1QH 4:40, 11:30–31, and 14:15. "Truth," a word almost absent from CD 1–8, occurs at least forty-three times in the Community Rule and fifty-three times in Hodayot.

31. 1QS 1:26.

32. CD 1:4, 16; 3:10; 4:8, 9; 6:2; 7:21; 8:17.

33. CD 20:1, 15.

34. This outline of the material in CD 1–8 is in general agreement with that proposed by E. Cothenet (*Les Textes de Qumran* II, 133). For a different interpretation of the presentation of the material in CD 1:1–4:12, see the next section (p. 108). CD 6:1–11 seems to be a bridge passage with some similarities to the previous section, namely, references to the previous history of both Israel and the sect. J. Murphy-O'Connor (*RB* LXXVII [1970] 202–4) sees fit to omit this section from his hypothetical "missionary document." He perceives its uniqueness and on that basis postulates that it is a later composition than both what precedes and what follows, composed for the purpose of uniting the "missionary document" and the "memorandum" (*RB* LXXVIII [1971] 228–32). A. M. Denis (*Les thèmes de connaissance dans le Document de Damas* [Louvain, 1967], 124–30) understands this unit to be the conclusion to a section beginning at CD 4:6.

These scholars, as well as O. J. R. Schwarz (*Der Erste Teil der Damaskusschrift und das alte Testament* [Diest, 1965]) and H. Stegemann ("Die Entstehung der Qumrangemeinde"), consider the Damascus Document to be a compilation of materials from various times along with interpolations. But there seems to be no justification for such a bisection of texts. The integral harmonization of CD 6:1–11 with both what precedes and what follows would seem to be an argument for the literary unity of the document.

35. While Cothenet (see previous note) agrees with the divisions proposed here, he makes them three independent units rather than three parts of one literary unit, as proposed in this work. Due to this difference, he overlooks the parallelism of the three passages and finds only two, rather than three, historical admonitions. J. Murphy O'Connor (*RB* LXXVII [1970] 225–29) explains (a) and (b) as attachments to the "missionary document" for the purpose of countering apostasy within the group. Denis (*Connaissance,* 5–82) deals with CD 1–4:6a as a literary unit and divides it into three admonitions; however, he also overlooks to a great extent the parallel structure of (b) to (a) and (c).

36. CD 1:10.

37. This is the chronology proposed by F. F. Bruce, *The Teacher of Righteousness in the Qumran Texts* (London, 1957), 16–18. This hypothesis has been accepted by many of the scholars of Qumran as an explanation of the numbers proposed in the first chapter of the Damascus Document, even though they debate their value as historical indicators: M. Burrows, *More Light on the Dead Sea Scrolls* (New York, 1958), 193; Dupont-Sommer, *Essene Writings,* 121–22; G. Vermes, *The Dead Sea Scrolls: Qumran in Perspective* (London, 1977), 147–48. That the 390 years is not to be taken literally is also the stance of E. Wiesenberg, "Chronological Data in the Zadokite Fragments," *VT* V (1955) 284–308.

38. See previous note. It is worthy of mention that in this study by Bruce, as well as in his much

later work ("The Book of Daniel and the Qumran Community," *Neotestamentica et Semitica* [Edinburgh, 1969], E. E. Ellis and M. Wilcox [eds.], 221–35, note especially 230–33), the proposal to explain the dates of the Damascus Document in the light of Dan. 9:24 is advanced as a mere hypothetical proposal. It becomes "canon" only when other commentators bring it into their work as apparent fact.

39. While there are some similar vocabulary terms, these antedate the final edition of Daniel. Very little of the evidence cited by F. F. Bruce (*Neotestamentica et Semitica*, 221–35) concerns the Damascus Document directly; he rather shows the appearance of Danielic modes in Qumranic literature which this study considers to be later than both Daniel and the Damascus Document. J. Murphy-O'Connor (*RB* LXXVII [1970] 224) considers CD II:14–VI:1 to be devoid of Danielic influence.

40. The 390 years appears to have been adopted from Ezek. 4:5. While twenty does not have a biblical precedent, it would seem that the writer of the Damascus Document considered the period of forty years from Ezek. 4:6 too long a time for the period of groping, thus he divided that segment in half. The author was using Scripture rather than copying it. L. Ginzberg (*An Unknown Jewish Sect*, 258–60) interprets the phrase "to give them over to Nebuchadnezzar" (CD 1:6) as a late gloss. In his analysis, the 390 years refer to a period preceding the fall of the Temple and the twenty years refer to the twenty kings of the First Temple.

41. A. M. Denis (*Connaissance*, 102) says that because of a lacuna in CD 4:6, שלים הקץ (completion of the epoch) in CD 4:8 lacks the precision of a definite time. In fact, it refers to the end of the twenty years, קץ (epoch) being the period of twenty years. CD 4:8, then, refers to the end of that epoch, i.e., the end of the twenty years.

In a study of the terms for time, Jacob Licht ("Time and Eschatology in Apocalyptic Literature and in Qumran," *JJS* XVI [1965] 177–82) notes that periodization is one of the characteristic modes by which the apocalyptic writer makes sense of history. While he rightly finds less speculation about the detailed events of the future at Qumran, his study points to the specific content and meaning which each of these temporal phrases must have possessed.

42. CD 4:10–2. On this verse, see above, n. 13.

43. CD 1:7. The eschatological dimensions of the imagery of "plant" are examined by S. Fujita, "The Metaphor of Plant in Jewish Literature of the Intertestamental Period," *JSJ* VII (1976) 30–45. On this passage he follows the interpolation of the Qumran community as a spiritualized temple, and understands the origin of the group as the plant.

44. CD 1:11.

45. In CD 2:12 we find the title משיח (anointed one) and in CD 7:21 משיח אהרן וישראל (the anointed one of Aaron and Israel). Contrary to putative understanding, this term, whether in the singular or the plural, does not denote the same figure that is signified by "messiah" in rabbinic and Christian literature. As explained in Chap. 5 (n. 74), משיח אהרן at Qumran seems to be a synonym for the high priest. If so, the absence of the term כוהן גדול (high priest) in literature other than the Qumranic Torah need not be a serious problem. See Yadin, *TS* II, 49.

46. CD 1:14–15.

47. CD 4:13.

48. CD 4:14.

49. CD 4:19.

50. This identification was first proposed by Schechter (*Fragments*, xxxv), and while it is noted that we do not have the text, the proposal has not been seriously called into question: C. Rabin *Zadokite Documents*, 16; J. Maier, *Texte* II, 48; A. Dupont-Sommer, *Essene Writings*, 128; E. Cothenet, *Textes* II, 162; H. Kosmala, "The Three Nets of Belial (A Study in the Terminology of Qumran and the New Testament)," *ASTI* IV (1965) 91–113, see p. 91.

51. If this is so, it would be evidence of the influence of Jubilees on the Damascus Document. See above, p. 61.

52. CD 6:11a. Compare above, pp. 108–10.

53. See the discussions of this subject (pp. 90–92 and 188–90).

54. CD 6:11–7:9.

55. K. G. Kuhn (*Konkordanz,* 36–37, and RQ IV [1963–64] 183–84) lists 149 references to ברית, 18 in CD 1–8. ברית חדשה (new covenant) is found only at CD 6:19, 8:21 (19:34), 20:12. The last reference is a discussion of what happened to some of the people who later despised the covenant. As discussed above (p. 108), the ברית ראשונים (covenant with the former) in CD 1:4, 3:10, 6:2 refers to the history of Israel prior to the foundation of the sect. In the literature of the *Yahad,* subsequent to CD 1–8, the term seems to be so self-evident to the writers that it most frequently appears without any modifiers, occasionally as ברית יחד (covenant of the Commune) (1QS 3:11, 8:16) or ברית אל (covenant of God) (1QS 5:8, 11, 18, 19; 10:10, etc.).

56. CD 7:9–8:21.

57. On this order for the arrangement of pages 9–16, see J. T. Milik, *Ten Years,* 151–52.

58. J. Murphy-O'Connor (*RB* LXXIX [1974] 544–64) has recognized that page 20, beginning with 19:34, is a separate literary unit. However, he also argues for page 20 as a composite work, a step which seems unnecessary. The perception of page 20 as a continuation of page 8 (i.e., page 19) goes back to Schechter's editio princeps (xxxix–xlvi), in which he placed page 20 between pages 8 and 9 on the basis of the similarity of pages 8 and 19. This relationship has never been seriously challenged, and even Murphy-O'Connor's work does not raise this question because he is trying to isolate the smaller, individual units which the "compiler" had in his hand while writing, rather than to identify the larger units of material which make up the final product, the objective of this discussion.

59. See above, p. 100.

60. Schechter, *Fragments,* xxi.

61. A. Dupont-Sommer, *Essene Writings,* 129; J. Maier, *Texte* II, 48; E. Cothenet, *Textes* II, 164.

62. 1 Chr. 5:38–39. The finding of the book by Hilkiah is recorded in 2 Kings 22 and 2 Chronicles 34. Ginzberg, *Unknown,* 21; Rabin, *Zadokite,* 18.

63. This opinion is shared by P. Wernberg-Møller, "צדק, צדיק and צדוק in the Zadokite Fragments (CDC), the Manual of Discipline (DSD) and the Habakkuk-Commentary (DSH)," *VT* III (1953) 314–15.

64. This usage of the word appears quite frequently in Qumran texts, referring to persons who were viewed either positively or negatively by the writers: 4Q 174 (Florilegium), 1:11, 13; 4Q 175 (Testimonia), 24; 1QpHab 8:9; CD 1:14; 4:4; 5:17, 20; 6:10; 7:20; 12:23; 20:1, 5. Furthermore, the use of ויקם (and he shall establish) in the hiphil in CD 1:11 appears to be a synonym for עמוד, as does ויצמח (and he will cause to sprout) in CD 1:7. Note the use of these three terms in conjunction in 4Q 174 (Florilegium) 1:11–13.

65. See n. 62.

66. See 1 Kgs. 21:10–18.

67. See n. 61 above.

68. See discussion above.

69. Solomon sends Abiathar into exile (1 Kgs. 2:26–27) and then appoints Zadok in his place (1 Kgs. 2:35).

70. CD 4:4.

71. CD 6:10.

72. CD 7:20–21.

73. See also Wernberg-Møller (*VT* III [1953] 315), who claims this points to the Teacher of Righteousness but takes Ṣadoq as an adjectival reference. In a reference that has received no subsequent attention, H. J. Schoeps (*Urgemeinde; Judentum; Gnosis* [Tübingen, 1956], 74) identifies the Zadok of CD 5:5 with the Teacher of Righteousness and foresees the possibility that he is the father of the "sons of Zadok."

Rabin also claims to have received an oral communication from Yadin to this effect (see n. 96 below), but in a letter to the *Jerusalem Post* (Dec. 3, 1980) Yadin remains skeptical.

74. CD 1:9–10.

75. CD 1:11.

76. CD 1:14–18.

77. See parallel columns above, pp. 106–8.

78. CD 2:7–14. Note that פרוש קציהם (the determination of their epochs) in 2:9 is the same phrase used to describe the Book of Jubilees in CD 16:2–4.

79. CD 2:13. This line has been a very troublesome one for commentators, with Schechter admitting that he did not know what it meant (*Fragments*, xxxiii). Ginzberg (*Unknown*, 10, n. 13) reads this phrase as *ubperuš šamu šemoteyhem*, which he translates literally as "with distinctness they set their names," in the sense of behaving in such a manner that they are remembered. M. Burrows (*The Dead Sea Scrolls* [New York, 1955], 350) chooses a different interpretation: "And in the explanation of his name are their names." It would appear that Rabin (*Zadokite*, 9) has understood the intent of this line when he refers to Jub. 16:3, where the name of Isaac "is ordained and written in the heavenly tablets" before his birth.

80. CD 2:14–4:12.

81. See Jub. 6:7–14, 18–19; 7:23–26; 11Q Torah 52:11–12. This prohibition is discussed above on p. 52.

82. CD 3:21–4:4.

83. *Fragments*, xxi, xxxv.

84. Cothenet, *Textes* II, 159–60. Cf. Ginzberg, *Unknown*, 15, 194; Dupont-Sommer, *Essene Writings*, 127; Maier, *Texte* II, 47. O. Betz (*Offenbarung und Schriftforschung in der Qumransekte* [Tübingen, 1960], 181) interprets this as a reference to the three ecclesiastical groupings, the priests, the levites, and the laity.

85. "The 'Sons of Zadok the Priests' in the Dead Sea Sect," *RQ* VI (1967–69) 3–30, or *Eretz-Israel* VIII (1967) 71–81 (Hebrew). After the above was recorded in an early draft of this work, Joseph Baumgarten kindly forwarded to me his enlightening treatment of *ṣedeq* in Qumranic writings ("The Heavenly Tribunal and the Personification of *Ṣedeq* in Jewish Apocalyptic," in *Aufstieg und Niedergang der Römischen Welt* [Berlin and New York, 1979], W. Haase [ed.], II, 219–39). He, even more than Liver, shows the unique position of *ṣedeq*, *Ṣadoq*, and *Beney Ṣadoq*, in the Dead Sea Scrolls, a relationship not found in other Jewish sources.

86. See Ginzberg, *Unknown*, 15.

87. Matt. 1:23 and Isa. 7:14.

88. CD 4:9–12.

89. J. A. Fitzmyer ("Divorce among First-Century Palestinian Jews," *Eretz-Israel* XIV [1978] 107–8) notes the Damascus Document's possible indebtedness at this point to Jub. 7:20–21: "Noah began to enjoin upon his sons' sons . . . to . . . guard their souls from fornication and uncleanness and all iniquity. For owing to these three things came the flood upon the earth, namely, owing to the fornication wherein the Watchers against the law of their ordinances went a-whoring after the daughters of men, and took themselves wives of all which they chose: and they made the beginning of uncleanness." See the next section (p. 119) for a more complete discussion of the three sins.

90. CD 4:21.

91. Deut. 17:17.

92. Schechter, *Fragments*, xxxvi; Rabin, *Zadokite*, 18; Maier, *Texte* I, 52; Dupont-Sommer, *Essene Writings*, 129; Cothenet, *Textes* II, 162.

93. L. H. Schiffman (*The Halakhah at Qumran* [Leiden, 1975], 30) dispenses with the need to insert the negative by defining נגלה as a term designating a revealed text, i.e., revealed to the sectaries. For the similarity of this definition to the use of the term by the Karaites, see N. Wieder, *The Judean Scrolls and Karaism* (London, 1962), 53–62. Ginzberg (*Unknown*, 21), on the other hand, emends the *yod* of ויטמן to a *hey*, and understands this latter term to refer to the Torah.

94. See above, p. 112.

95. See p. 114 above for the arguments that this reference must be understood in a messianic time-period. It has been suggested that this identification of Zadok would be exceptional in a work that employs cryptic sobriquets for contemporary figures. It should be recalled that references to contemporary names, though rare, are not unheard-of at Qumran, e.g., Antiochus and Demetrius in 4QpNahum.

96. In the corrigenda to the second edition of *The Zadokite Documents*, Rabin refers to an oral communication from Y. Yadin in which it is suggested that Zadok in CD 5:5 is the Teacher of Righteousness. This suggestion is based on the statement in As. Mos. 1:17.

97. See above, p. 109. Jacob Weingreen has argued that the title of *Moreh Ṣedeq* is a claim for authoritativeness: "The Title *Mōṛēh Ẓedek* (Teacher of Righteousness?)," *From Bible to Mishnah: The Continuity of Tradition* (Manchester, 1976), 100–14. The messianic associations of the title are explored by Roy A. Rosenberg, "Who Is the *Moreh haṣṢedeq?*" *JAAR* XXXVI (1968) 118–22.

98. CD 1:9. This is basic to many reconstructions of the history of the sect: Cross, *Ancient Library*, 132–34; Vermes, *Dead Sea*, 147–48. See the discussion above, pp. 108–9.

99. CD 1:7. In this analysis the new planting is the Teacher of Righteousness.

100. 3Q 15, 11:2–7. See the previous discussion of this reference, pp. 99–100.

101. Yadin discusses the possibility that the "sealed *Seper Torah*" of CD 5:2 may be the Qumranic Torah (*TS* I, 302), but also suggests that this work may have been inspired by 1 Chr. 28:19 (*TS* I, 70, 308). P. E. Lapide ("Die Nachbarn der Urgemeinde," *LM* XVII [1978] 273–75) thinks both passages refer to this scroll.

102. See above, pp. 115–16.

103. Those who attempt to explain this choice of the three evils do so by attributing them either to opponents of the sect or to current practices: Schechter, *Fragments*, xvii–xviii; Ginzberg, *Unknown*, 127–30; C. Rabin, *Qumran Studies* (Oxford, 1957), 55–59; Dupont-Sommer, *Essene Writings*, 128–30; G. Jeremias, *Der Lehrer der Gerechtigkeit* (Göttingen, 1963), 95–106; H. Kosmala, *ASTI* IV (1965) 99–109; J. Murphy-O'Connor, *RB* LXXVII (1970) 220–22; Fitzmyer, *Eretz-Israel* XIV (1978) 105.

104. See above, p. 112.

105. See above, p. 115.

106. Ginzberg, *Unknown*, 19–20, 127–31; Rabin, *Zadokite*, 17. Other scholars maintained that this phrase referred to both: Schechter, *Fragments*, xxxvi; P. Winter, "Ṣadoqite Fragments IV 20, 21 and the Exegesis of Genesis 1:27 in Late Judaism," *ZAW* LXVIII (1956) 71–84; Dupont-Sommer, *Essene Writings*, 129; Cothenet, *Textes* II, 163; G. Jeremias, *Lehrer*, 100. J. Murphy-O'Connor (*RB* LXXVII [1970] 220) thinks this forbids two marriages in a lifetime.

107. 11Q Torah 57:17–18. See Yadin, *TS* I, 270–74. G. Vermes finds confirmation in the Qumranic Torah for the position which he had adopted, i.e., only polygamy is prohibited ("Sectarian Matrimonial Halakhah in the Damascus Rule," *JJS* XXV [1974] 197–202). Yadin is supported by J. A. Fitzmyer (*Eretz-Israel* XIV [1978] 103–10). J. R. Mueller also argues that both divorce and polygamy are prohibited for the commoner as well as the King ("The Temple Scroll and the Gospel Divorce Texts," *RQ* X [1978] 247–56).

108. 11Q Torah 56:18.

109. CD 5:6–7.

110. CD 5:7–8.

111. CD 5:8–9. Biblical support is summoned from Lev. 18:13.

112. On this passage see Yadin *TS* I, 284–85, and II, 211.

113. Yadin, *TS* I, 272–74; J. A. Fitzmyer, *Eretz-Israel* XIV (1978) 105. Neither of them accepts that this prohibition in 11Q Torah was intended only for the king.

114. See the discussion of this literature in Chap. 4.

115. See the discussion of the chronology in Chap. 5, pp. 181–99.

116. CD 5:12.

117. CD 5:20–21.

118. CD 2:6.

119. On the place of this unit in the structure of the work, see n. 34.

120. The two most common interpretations which שבי has received were already mentioned by Schechter in his discussion of CD 4:2 (*Fragments*, xxxv). He said it could mean either *šeby* (captivity) or *šabey* (repentants) and chose the former as the most likely alternative, based on his understanding of the use of the term in CD 6:5. Ginzberg (*Unknown*, 15) chose the other alternative and translated it as "penitent." I. Rabinowitz ("A Reconsideration of 'Damascus' and '390 Years' in the 'Damascus' ['Zadokite'] Fragments," *JBL* LXXIII [1954] 16–17) follows Schechter and assumes that these references are to the past history of Israel. Many others have accepted the definition of *šabey* as "penitents" or "converts": Habermann, *Megillot*, 80; Maier, *Texte* II, 43–44 (on CD 2:5); Dupont-Sommer, *Essene Writings*, 127, 131; Cothenet, *Textes* II, 160; E. Lohse, *Die Texte aus Qumran: Hebräisch und Deutsch* (Munich, 1964), 77; Vermes, *DSSE*, 100, 102. Rabin (*Zadokite*, 13) thinks this is a shorthand for שבי פשע ישראל (turned from the impiety of Israel), based on the use of the term שבי in CD 2:5. S. Iwry ("Was There a Migration to Damascus? The Problem of שבי ישראל," *Eretz-Israel* IX [1969] 86) interprets this phrase geographically as referring to those who returned from exile. J. Murphy-O'Connor (*RB* LXXVII [1970] 211–12) understands CD 4:2 in a similar manner.

121. CD 6:1–2.

122. CD 5:2–3 alleges that Zadok found the sealed Sefer Torah in an ark (ארון). Rabin (*Zadokite*, 18) thoughtfully interpolates הברית (of the covenant), but this interpolation is objectionable. If the hidden Torah was in the ark all the time, why was it not opened earlier? Was the ark not destroyed in 586 B.C.E.? It is preferable to understand ארון as a box in which the scroll was found. One can then presume that ארון refers not to the ark of the covenant, but to a container in which, according to Zadok, the ancient text had been hidden since Joshua. If this reasoning is cogent, the quotation of Num. 21:18 in CD 6:3–4 assumes a new meaning. The Damascus Document seems to be saying that Zadok claims to have found the sealed Torah in a box, a באר (well or pit) in the nomenclature of the Numbers passage. This may explain the Qumranic tradition of wrapping parchments and placing them in containers in caves, thus contributing to the preservation of the sect's library.

123. CD 6:1–8.

124. CD 6:10–11.

125. CD 1:1.

126. CD 4:16–17.

127. The role of this text in studies of this manuscript has not been fully appreciated. Schechter (*Fragments*, xxxviii) thought that this phrase meant there were special rules for those who entered the sanctuary of the sect. Ginzberg (*Unknown*, 30–31) took issue with this interpretation and stated that it was a reference to the Jerusalem temple. The purpose of the covenant was to avoid the temple because those in control had defiled it. J. M. Baumgarten (*Studies in Qumran Law* [Leiden, 1977], 41–42) accepted this viewpoint as well in an early article (it originally appeared in 1953), but then modified his stance, stating that this was one of the duties of the covenant (*Studies*, 70–71). The latter viewpoint is quite common: Maier, *Texte* II, 51; Dupont-Sommer, *Essene Writings*, 132; Cothenet, *Textes* II, 166–167; L. H. Schiffman, *Halakhah*, 129. J. Murphy-O'Connor (*RB* LXXVIII [1971] 216–18) suggests that it is an introduction to the "memorandum" which follows the well midrash.

128. In addition to L. Feldman's note on this passage in the Loeb edition of Josephus and the bibliography cited there (IX, 16–17), see also: R. de Vaux, *Archaeology and the Dead Sea Scrolls* (Oxford, 1973), 12–16; J. M. Baumgarten, "The Essenes and the Temple—A Reappraisal," *Studies*, 57–74; J. Nolland, "A Misleading Statement of the Essene Attitude to the Temple," *RQ* IX (1978) 555–62.

129. See above, pp. 22–24.

130. See above, pp. 46–47.

131. 11Q Torah 35:13–14.

132. 11Q Torah 51:8–9. See also p. 11 above. Other references include 11Q Torah 16:12; 35:11; 46:10, 17; 48:13.

133. 11Q Torah 57:20–21.

134. 11Q Torah 53:9–54:7, 29:6 (cf. Elisha Qimron, "From the Work on the Historical Dictionary: The Text of the Temple Scroll," *Leshonenu* XCII [1978] 142 [Hebrew]).

135. 11Q Torah 60:5 (cf. 2:10–11, 55:6–11, 62:13–15).

136. Cf. Ezek. 22:26.

137. 11Q Torah 27:8–9.

138. 11Q Torah 47:3–4. See also p. 10 above.

139. CD 6:18–19.

140. 11Q Torah 8:8–11.

141. A reconstruction of the lines from 11Q Torah 13:17 to 14:1 suggests a somewhat fuller text than that contained in Yadin's interpolation, which simply reproduces the Masoretic text of Num. 28:9–10, consisting of twenty-one words.

142. CD 6:18.

143. These festivals occupy 11Q Torah 18–25 and 43, an extraordinary amount of space to devote to a subject that has but little Pentateuchal warrant. See Chap. 1 and the discussion of Jubilees in Chap. 2.

144. The provisions in 11Q Torah document the deviation of that work from the biblical provisions in Leviticus 16 and Num. 29:7–11: (a) 11Q Torah 25:14 includes the goat for the sin offering in its list of sacrifices to be accompanied by cereal and drink offerings, but Num. 29:11 lists it after the latter. (b) For the sin offering of purgation, 11Q Torah 25:16 lists two rams, making a total of three rams required for the rite, a prescription without precedent in the Mosaic ordinances. The priest offers one of these rams on behalf of himself and the house of his father, but in Lev. 16:6 and 11, the bullock is sacrificed for this purpose. (c) 11Q Torah omits any mention of the laying on of hands while the chief priest confesses all the iniquities of the people.

145. See p. 53 ff. above for a discussion of the Jubilees calendar and the related bibliography.

146. Certainly the *terminus ad quem* for the calendar is the event recorded in 1QpHab 11:4–8, where the wicked priest persecuted the Teacher of Righteousness while in exile, apparently in Damascus, on the Day of Atonement.

147. This change in the calendar is anticipated in CD 3:14.

148. CD 6:20.

149. Deuteronomy 26.

150. 11Q Torah 43:3–5.

151. 11Q Torah 52:7–9. *Terumah* may also be connected to the preceding phrase of the Damascus Document, that the offering be brought in accordance with the sect's calendar.

152. As understood by the rabbis, גר apparently means "proselyte" and does not refer to "stranger" as in the Bible. See the following occurrences: 4Q 174 (Florilegium) 1:4; 4QpNah 2:9; CD 14:4, 6. However, 11Q Torah 40:6 appears to be an imitation of the biblical usage.

153. CD 6:20–7:1.

154. CD 6:20–21.

155. Pp. 124–27.

156. CD 7:2.

157. Schechter, *Fragments*, xxxix; Cothenet, *Textes* II, 169.

158. CD 7:3–6, 19:1–2.

159. This has been discussed in Chap. 1, p. 10.

160. 11Q Torah 16:12.

161. 11Q Torah 35:8–9.

162. 11Q Torah 35:11–13.

163. 11Q Torah 51:8–10.

164. CD 7:6–6a.

165. The reading of Ms. B. (19:3), where אשר היה מקדם (which was from of old) is also found in the text, does not refer to the sectarian groupings, as Dupont-Sommer says (*Essene Writings*, 133), but to when they led a normal life in Jerusalem prior to their flight to Damascus.

166. CD 7:6a–9, 19:2–5. The text here followed is Rabin's conflation of the two manuscripts.

167. See Deut. 23:15, where "camp" is also a synonym for private life; if they live in camps, then they may marry.

168. Ginzberg, *Unknown*, 32–33; Milik, *Ten Years*, 91–92; Cross, *Ancient Library*, 80–81; Vermes, *Dead Sea*, 97. While these scholars agree that "camps" refer to something other than a central commune, there is no such unanimity on the location of the place of exile.

169. Neh. 10:30; CD 3:12, 20; 7:13.

170. Neh. 10:32–40; CD 3:14–15, 6:12–20.

171. Neh. 10:30, 33, 35–37; CD 6:12–7:3.

172. Neh. 10:38–40; 11Q Torah 18:10–22:16, 38:4, 43:2–17, 60:6.

173. 11Q Torah 23:1–25:1.

174. According to Dupont-Sommer (*Essene Writings*, 132), this is a reference to the promise of eternal life.

175. If מחנות (camps) was an indication of the intention to form separate groups, this would be the exception. The context in which this term appears in the Damascus Document makes this meaning unlikely.

176. J. Liver, *RQ* VI (1967) 3–30. For a discussion of this line in the Damascus Document, see above, p. 115.

177. See Chap. 4, 161, for a discussion of these terms.

178. Schechter, *Fragments*, xviii–xxii.

179. In addition to the articles by Liver and Baumgarten mentioned in n. 85 above, see also the following works on the *Beney Ṣadoq*: P. Wernberg-Møller, *VT* III (1953) 310–15; R. North, "The Qumran 'Sadducees,'" *CBQ* XVII (1955) 164–88; D. Hill, "Δικαιοι as a Quasi-Technical Term," *NTS* XI (1964–65) 296–302; J. Le Moyne, *Les Sadducéens* (Paris, 1972), 75–93.

180. *DJD* I: 78.

181. *DJD* V: 44. See also J. Strugnell, "Notes en marge du volume V des 'Discoveries in the Judaean Desert of Jordan," *RQ* VII (1970) 214–15.

182. Lohse, *Qumran Texte*, 246–47; originally published by J. M. Allegro, "Further Messianic References in Qumran Literature," *JBL* LXXV (1956) 174–75.

183. An extensive discussion of Pesher Habakkuk is to be found in Chap. 5.

184. 1QpHab 9:8–12. Commentators usually ascribe the iniquity in this passage to the wicked priest: Dupont-Sommer, *Essene Writings*, 265; Carmignac, *Textes* I, 108–9; W. H. Brownlee, *The Midrash Pesher of Habakkuk* (Missoula, Mont., 1979), 153–54. For a further discussion of this passage, see Chap. 5, 191.

185. See texts XII–XIV above. In this study I argue that Pesher Habakkuk is antecedent to the other pesherite works (p. 188) and to CD 20.

186. *DJD* V: 53. I have adopted the reading of Strugnell, *RQ* VII (1970) 222.

187. J. Liver, *RQ* VI (1967) 3–30.

188. Of some importance for this discussion are the cases which Baumgarten has noted in which Ṣadoq and ṣedeq appear to be interchangeable; e.g. in 1QS 9:14, which reads *Beney Ṣadoq*, but the Cave 4 fragment of the same text reads *Beney ṣedeq* (*Aufstieg und Niedergang*, II, 235).

Notes on Chapter 4

1. M. Abot 1:3; ARNA 5; ARNB 10.

2. The latter spelling is based on the Greek name Βοηϑος (*AJ* 15:320).

3. The traditional texts of ARNA 5 and ARNB 10 are found in Solomon Schechter, אבות דרבי נתן

(Vienna, 1877), 13a–b. This passage was re-edited by L. Finkelstein, *The Pharisees and the Men of the Great Synagogue* (New York, 1950), 43 (Hebrew). A translation of ARNA 5 can be found in Judah Goldin, *The Fathers According to Rabbi Nathan* (New Haven, 1955), 39. ARNB 10 is translated by A. J. Saldarini, *The Fathers According to Rabbi Nathan, Version B* (Leiden, 1975), 85–89.

4. A. Geiger, *Urschrift und Uebersetzungen der Bibel* (Breslau, 1857), 101–6. Note also his article, "Sadducäer und Pharisäer," *JZWL* II (1863) 11–54. See also the following summaries of research on this question: L. Finkelstein, *The Pharisees: The Sociological Background of Their Faith* (Philadelphia, 1938) II, 663, n. 20; J. Le Moyne, *Les Sadducéens* (Paris, 1972), 155–63; *Schürer* II, 405. This view is now standard. See for example Kaufmann Kohler, *JE* X, s.v. "Sadducees," 630–34; A. C. Sundberg, *IDB* IV, s.v. "Sadducees," 160–63; S. Zeitlin, *The Rise and Fall of the Judaean State* (Philadelphia, 1968), I, 183.

5. The latter reference, found only in the Hebrew text of Ben Sira, was of course unavailable to Geiger.

6. Geiger's viewpoint (see n. 4 above) was taken up by Wellhausen (*Die Pharisäer und Sadducäer* [Reisswald, 1874]), who rejected the testimony of ARNA 5 (p. 46). Most scholars have followed in this tradition, making minor variations in the hypothesis. In addition to the works listed in n. 4, see also the following: H. Grätz, *Geschichte der Juden* (Leipzig, 4th ed., 1888), III, 88; G. F. Moore, *Judaism in the First Centuries of the Common Era* (New York, 1971—1st ed., 1927), 69–70; R. Meyer, *TDNT* VII, 35–43; G. Vermes, *The Dead Sea Scrolls: Qumran in Perspective* (London, 1977), 118–19. Geiger's hypothesis was disputed by J. Derenbourg (*Essai sur l'histoire et la geographie de la Palestine* [Paris, 1867], 452–56), who said that the names arose from insulting sobriquets hurled by the Pharisees and Sadducees at one another. T. W. Manson ("Sadducee and Pharisee—The Origin and Significance of the Names," *BJRL* XXII [1938] 144–59) challenged both the identification of the name with the high priest of David and the validity of the account in ARNA 5; however, his alternative was deemed unacceptable. The Abot de-Rabbi Nathan account is taken more seriously by E. Meyer (*Ursprung und Anfänge des Christentums* [Stuttgart and Berlin, 1921] II, 290–91), who thinks it provides a more satisfactory solution to the question than the accepted explanation. E. Baneth (*Ursprung der Ṣadoḳäer und Boëthosäer* [Dessau, 1882]), argues that Zadok and Baethus, under the influence of Epicurean thought, founded the Sadducean sect during the reign of John Hyrcanus. See also H. D. Mantel, "The Sadducees and the Pharisees," *WHJP* VIII, 99–123; E. Bammel, "Sadducäer und Sadokiden," *ETL* LV (1979) 107–15; M. Stern, "Aspects of Jewish Society: The Priesthood and the Other Classes," *CRINT* I: 2, 561–630.

7. See the comments of Schechter to this passage, *Abot de-Rabbi Nathan* 13b.

8. A. Guttmann, "Tractate Abot—Its Place in Rabbinic Literature," *Studies in Rabbinic Judaism* (New York, 1976), 102–14. This article originally appeared in *JQR* XLI (1950) 181–93.

9. L. Finkelstein has advanced the argument for the priority of large sections of Abot de-Rabbi Nathan to M. Abot: "Introductory Study to 'Pirke Avot,'" *JBL* LVII (1938) 13–50; *Introduction to the Treatises Abot and Abot of Rabbi Nathan* (New York, 1950), 4–59 (Hebrew). In this hypothesis, he has been followed by Saldarini, *Version B*, 8–16. J. Goldin (*The Fathers*, xxi) says that ARNA was composed not much later than the third century.

10. This text is a translation from C. Albeck, *Six Orders of Mishnah* (Jerusalem, 1968) IV, 353 (Hebrew).

11. Finkelstein (*Pharisees and Men of the Great Synagogue*, 43) adopted a singular reading for this phrase, so that it would have to be interpreted as referring only to Zadok or only to Baethus.

12. ARNA 5. The text is that of Schechter, 13b. The corresponding text in ARNB as found in Schechter's edition reads as follows:

. . . תקבלו עליהם שכר כאלו עשיתם בעולם הזה ובעולם הבא. ב' תלמידים היו לו צדוק וביתוס וכיון ששמעו את הדבר הזה שנו לתלמידיהם. ותלמידיהן אמרו דבר מפי רבן ולא אמרו פירושו. אמרו להן אילו הייתם יודעים שתחיית המתים מתן שכרן של צדיקים לעתיד לבוא היו אומרים כן. הלכו ופירשו להן ויצאו מהם שתי משפחות צדוקים וביתוסים צדוקים לשם צדוק וביתוסים לשם ביתוס

and you shall surely receive a reward for observing them, as if you had performed them in this world and in the world-to-come. He (Antigonus) had two disciples, Zadok and Baethus.

When they heard this saying, they taught it to their disciples. Their disciples quoted the statement, but not its elaboration. They said to them, "If you had known that the resurrection of the dead is the reward of the just in the age to come, would they (perhaps "you") have spoken thusly?" They went and withdrew. Two clans came out of them, the Zadokites and the Baethusians, the Zadokites named after Zadok and the Baethusians named after Baethus.

13. Abot 1:4.

14. Schechter 13a–b.

15. That Zadok and Baethus rejected resurrection is the putative understanding of this passage. See sources cited in n. 3 and n. 4.

16. Moore, *Judaism* I, 69–70; Finkelstein, *Pharisees: Sociological Background* I, 153; Idem, *Pharisees and the Men of the Great Synagogue,* 42–44; Le Moyne, *Sadducéens,* 117; Saldarini, *Version B,* 85; *Schürer* II, 406–7.

17. M. Sandhedrin 10:1; B. Sanhedrin 90b; Matt. 22:23; Mark 12:18; Luke 20:27, etc.

18. See above, n. 4 and n. 6. Note, however, Moore (*Judaism* I, 70), who grants the possibility that the rabbinic tradition preserves the name of a historical personage who played a leading role in the Sadducean movement.

19. For example, see CD 20:3–13, 25–27; 1QS 4:7–14; 11Q Torah 59:1–21.

20. 1QS 2:5–18.

21. For a discussion of messianism in rabbinic literature, see, among others, the following: S. Schechter, *Aspects of Rabbinic Theology* (New York, 1961—original, 1909), 97–115; J. Klausner, *The Messianic Idea in Israel* (New York, 1955), W. F. Stinespring (trans.), 391–517; E. E. Urbach, *The Sages: Their Concepts and Beliefs* (Jerusalem, 1975), I. Abrahams (trans.), 308–14, 653–92; B. Z. Wacholder, *Messianism and Mishnah: Time and Place in the Early Halakhah* (Cincinnati, 1979).

22. Klausner, *Messianic Idea,* 413–19; Urbach, *Sages,* 652.

23. Klausner, *Messianic Idea,* 408–19; Urbach, *Sages,* 651–52.

24. CD 12:23–13:1, 20:1.

25. Most scholars accept the theory of two Messiahs at Qumran: K. G. Kuhn, "The Two Messiahs of Aaron and Israel," *The Scrolls and the New Testament* (New York, 1957), K. Stendahl (ed.), 54–64; M. Burrows, *More Light on the Dead Sea Scrolls* (New York, 1958), 297–311; F. M. Cross, Jr., *The Ancient Library of Qumran and Modern Biblical Studies* (Garden City, N.Y., 1961), 219–21; R. E. Brown, "The Teacher of Righteousness and the Messiah(s)," *The Scrolls and Christianity* (London, 1969), M. Black (ed.), 37–44, 109–12; G. Vermes, *The Dead Sea Scrolls,* 184–86; *Schürer* II, 550–54. Other scholars have disputed this hypothesis: W. S. LaSor, *The Dead Sea Scrolls and the New Testament* (Grand Rapids, Mich., 1972), 100–103. A select bibliography on this subject is to be found in J. A. Fitzmyer, *The Dead Sea Scrolls: Major Publications and Tools for Study* (Missoula, Mont., 1977), 114–18.

26. Exod. 28:41, 30:30, 40:15; Lev. 4:3, 5, 16; 6:15; 7:35–36; 10:7; 21:10–12; Num. 3:3; 6:13.

27. 1 Sam. 24:7, 11; 26:9, 11, 16, 23; 2 Sam. 1:14, 16; 19:22, etc.

28. 1QS 9:11; CD 12:23, 19:10, 20:1.

29. G. W. E. Nickelsburg, Jr. (*Resurrection, Immortality and Eternal Life in Intertestamental Judaism* [Cambridge, Mass., 1972], 144–67) recognizes the absence of these terms at Qumran and opts for a national view of immortality; however, he finds individual immortality portrayed in the predestinarian views of 1QS 3–4 and the Hymns.

30. See n. 11 above.

31. 11Q Torah 3:5, 8, 9, 12; 7:13; 26:6; 31:8; 32:10; 36:11; 39:3; 41:16.

32. Note particularly the utensils and furnishings prescribed in Exodus 25 and 28, which are then made in Exodus 37 and 39.

33. 11Q Torah 32:10.

34. Ibid. 31:8.

35. See above, pp. 62–77.

36. See above, p. 95.

37. CD 5:1–5 and ARNA 5.

38. The Arabic text of Qirqisani's *The Book of Lights and Watchtowers* was published by L. Nemoy, *Kitāb al-Anwār wal-Marāqib: Code of Karaite Law* (New York, 1939). An English translation of the section dealing with the sects (vol. I of the work just mentioned) had already been executed by the same scholar, "Al-Qirqisani's Account of the Jewish Sects and Christianity," *HUCA* VII (1930) 317–97. See also W. Bacher, "Qirqisani, the Karaite and His Work on Jewish Sects," *JQR* VII (1895) 687–710. I wish to thank Prof. Moshe Assis, who read through the relevant portions of the Arabic text and provided the basis for the translation here.

39. Nemoy, *Kitāb* I, 11 (I.2.7); *HUCA* VII, 326 (2.4).

40. Nemoy, *Kitāb* I, 11–12 (I.2.8); *HUCA* VII, 326–27 (2.5).

41. Nemoy, *Kitāb* I, 41 (I.6); *HUCA* VII, 363 (6). It should be noted that the quotation from 2 Chr. 7:10 seems to have been missing from the Arabic text from which Nemoy made his translation.

42. Nemoy, *Kitāb* I, 41–42 (1.7); *HUCA* VII, 363–64 (7).

43. P. Kahle, *The Cairo Geniza* (Oxford, 2d ed., 1959), 17.

44. Lev. 18:12–14.

45. Cf. Hos. 5:11; CD 4:19.

46. CD 5:8–11.

47. 11Q Torah 66:15–17. On the relationship of these two statements, see the discussion in Chap. 3, 126.

48. See also "on the eighth day" (Qirqisani, chap. 6, #3 above), where Qirqisani mentions a law also found in CD 11:18, that "no one may bring a burnt offering on the Sabbath." According to Qirqisani, Zadok ruled that the Sabbath day is not to be counted as part of the seven-day festive offerings.

49. "He (Zadok) wrote a large book in which he attacked and criticized the Rabbanites" (Qirqisani 2:4, #1 above).

50. Note that CD 11:18 does adduce biblical proof: "for thus it is written, 'apart from your Sabbath-offerings' (Lev. 23:38)."

51. 11Q Torah 66:17.

52. Al-Muqammiz and Qirqisani draw a strong distinction between the ancient Zadokite and Baethusian doctrines and those of the Karaites, thus testifying to the distinction between Qumran and Karaite sectarianism. This distinction was rejected most emphatically by Solomon Zeitlin in his many articles in *JQR*: XXXIX (1948–49) 337–63; XL (1949–50) 57–78; XLI (1950–51) 1–58, 251–75; XLIV (1953–54) 85–115; LIV (1963–64) 89–98; LVII (1966–67) 28–45; and a number more. He has been supported in his stand by S. B. Hoenig in *JQR*: XLVIII (1957–58) 371–75; XLIX (1958–59) 209–14; LIII (1962–63) 274–76; LIV (1963–64) 334–39; LIX (1968–69) 24–70. In addition to the arguments advanced by most scholars dating the scrolls to a much earlier time-period, the identification of Qumran with Karaism is disputed by N. Wieder, *The Judean Scrolls and Karaism* (London, 1962), 253–57.

53. See Qirqisani, chap. 6 (#3 above).

54. L. Ginzberg, *An Unknown Jewish Sect* (New York, 1976), 19–20, 127–31; C. Rabin, *The Zadokite Documents* (Oxford, 2d ed., 1958), 17. More recently this position has been adopted by G. Vermes, "Sectarian Matrimonial Halakhah in the Damascus Rule," *JJS* XXV (1974) 197–202.

55. See Chap. 3, n. 106 and 107.

56. Schechter, *Fragments of a Zadokite Work* (Cambridge, 1910), xxxvii. It should be noted that the Qumranic Torah does permit divorce, as the גרושה (divorcee) is mentioned at 5:4 (see p. 125 above for a more detailed discussion).

57. 11Q Torah 58:17–18.

58. See above, pp. 48–50.

59. Lev. 23:33–36, Num. 29:12–38, Deut. 16:13–15.

60. See above, pp. 48–50.

61. See Qirqisani, chap. 6 (#3 above) on the thirty-day month. Pentecost is mentioned in chap. 2.7 (#1 above) and in chap. 7 (#4 above).

62. Jub. 5:23–6:38.

63. Jub. 5:27. In addition to the polemic against any form of lunar reckoning (Jub. 6:32–38), note the repetition of the non-Pentateuchal additions which the author of Jubilees made to the dates recorded in Genesis 7–8. I am referring to the feast that was to be observed on the new moon of the first month of each of the four three-month cycles, which the writer of Jubilees had woven into the Noah story in order to buttress his account of the calendar (Jub. 5:22–30, 6:25–31). On the other hand, Jubilees never mentions that the Feast of Pentecost was to fall on a Sunday. In fact, it never discusses the weekly calendar.

64. See the previous chapter for a discussion of Zadok.

65. Cf. ARNB 10, which implies that the heresies arose in the days of the disciples of Zadok and Baethus. For the distinction between the Zadokites and Baethusians in rabbinic texts, see below pp. 160–67.

66. Qirqisani, chap. 2:4 (2:7 in Arabic text) (#1 above).

67. Ibid.

68. Qirqisani, chap. 6 (#3 above).

69. Qirqisani, chap. 2:4 (2:7 in Arabic text) (#1 above).

70. *Schürer* II, 381–82, 404–14. See also the discussion in the previous chapter, pp. 135–40.

71. The reference to Zadok in CD 5:5 is discussed in Chap. 3, p. 113.

72. E.g., Leon Nemoy and Joseph Heller in *EJ* X, 762–63.

73. S. Holdheim, מאמר האישות (Berlin, 1861), 117–73; A. Geiger, "Sadducäer und Pharisäer," *JZWL* II (1863) 33–34; idem, *Das Judenthum und seine Geschichte* (Breslau, 1865) II, 55–62.

74. "לקורות הכתות בישראל," a supplement to H. Graetz, דברי ימי ישראל (Warsaw, 1907), S. P. Rabinowitz (trans.), III, 493–511.

75. Maimonides considered the Zadokites, the Baethusians, and the Karaites to be one sect. Judah Halevi in his work *Kuzari* distinguished between the Zadokites, who repudiated Antigonus, and the Karaites, who he said originated in the days of Salome. Azariah de Rossi, on the other hand, claimed that the name "Essene" mentioned in Philo and Josephus referred to the Baethusians. For the full discussion, see Azariah de Rossi, מאור עינים (Wilna, 1866), 90–97.

76. Harkavy, p. 495 (see n. 74 above).

77. H. Hirschfeld, "The Arabic Portion of the Cairo Genizah at Cambridge," *JQR* XVI (1904) 98–112.

78. S. Poznanski, "Anan et ses écrits," *REJ* XLIV (1902) 161–87.

79. L. Nemoy, *Karaite Anthology: Excerpts from the Early Literature* (New Haven, 1952). See pp. 4, 50, 201, etc.

80. A number of recent scholars have also made the claim that the Qumran sect was one of the sources of Karaism: P. Kahle, "The Karaites and the Manuscripts from the Cave," *VT* III (1953) 82–84; C. Rabin, *Qumran Studies* (Oxford, 1957), 87; Wieder, *Judean Scrolls*, 254–57.

81. Hirschfeld, *JQR* XVI (1904) 103; slightly reedited by Poznanski, "Philon dans l'ancienne littérature judéo-arabe," *REJ* L (1905) 26; *TS* I, 97.

82. *TS* I, 97–99.

83. See n. 81 above.

84. *TS* I, 97–99; A. Jaubert, *The Date of the Last Supper* (Staten Island, N.Y., 1965), Isaac Rafferty (trans.), 40, n. 19.

85. Isidore Levy (*Recherches esséniennes et pythagoriciennes* [Geneva and Paris, 1965], 12–14) thinks he is the same person as the anonymous Alexandrian whom Qirqisani considered to be a member of the Magharians (Nemoy, *HUCA* VII [1930] 326–27 [2.5], passage #2 above). As proposed earlier by Poznanski (*REJ* L [1905] 27), J. Baumgarten identifies Judah of Alexandria with Philo, who is sometimes referred to as Judas in the Church fathers ("4Q Halakah[a] 5, the Law of *Hadash,* and

the Pentacontad Calendar," *JJS* XXVII [1976] 41; also in *Studies,* 136). But our fragment comes from Saadia, who as far as we know never cites Philonic writings. At any rate, this passage is part of Saadia's polemics against the Karaite reckoning. Alexandria, and Egypt in general, contained an important Karaite community in the ninth and tenth centuries. The descendants of Anan are known to have lived there.

86. *De Vita Contemplativa,* 64. Incidentally, Philo only records a single Feast of First Fruits celebrated by the Therapeutae.

87. The Karaite calendar underwent many changes without ever being fully settled. The principle adopted by all groups was that the waving of the Omer and Shavuot must fall on a Sunday. Nahawandi's proposal to imitate the reckoning now found at Qumran was not accepted. The Karaite calendar does find mention in the medieval work on calendation by Albiruni, which was translated by C.E. Sachau, *The Chronology of Ancient Nations* (Pall Mall, England, 1879), 68–69, 278. He had published the Arabic text a year earlier. For a discussion of the Karaite calendar and its history, see the works of S. Poznanski in the *Encyclopaedia of Religion and Ethics* (New York, 1922), J. Hastings (ed.), III, 118–20; VII, 662–63; Z. Ankori, *Karaites in Byzantium* (New York, 1959), 292–353 (the sources for the Karaite calendar are listed on p. 292, n. 1).

88. According to these dates, the calendar departs from the rabbinic in another respect. The month of Ab, which in rabbinic calendation always has thirty days, here has twenty-nine.

89. A. Harkavy, זכרון לראשונים (St. Petersburg, 1891) V, 225.

90. Harkavy, p. 495 (see n. 74 above).

91. S. Pinsker, *Lickute Kadmoniot; zur Geschichte des Karaismus und der karäischen Literatur* (Vienna, 1860); Poznanski, *REJ* XLIV (1902) 177.

92. Harkavy, p. 495 (see n. 74 above).

93. The fact that the Karaites regarded themselves as followers of Zadok and copied the Qumranic writings may account for the preservation of the Qumranic Psalter in Arabic; cf. J. Strugnell, "Notes on the Text and Transmission of the Apocryphal Psalms 151, 154 (=Syr. II) and 155 (=Syr. III)," *HTR* LIX (1966) 278–81.

94. For the text of Megillat Taanit, see H. Lichtenstein, "Die Fastenrolle: Eine Untersuchung zur jüdisch-hellenistischen Geschichte," *HUCA* VIII/IX (1931–32) 342–43; S. Zeitlin, *Megillat Taanit as a Source for Jewish Chronology and History in the Hellenistic and Roman Periods* (Philadelphia, 1922), 67; B. Z. Luria, *Megillath Ta'anith (with Introductions and Notes)* (Jerusalem, 1964), 181 (Hebrew). The translation in this work is based on Lichtenstein's text.

95. This is the reading according to Zeitlin, *Megillat Taanit,* 66 (n. 165), and Luria, *Megillath Ta'anith,* 130.

96. Lichtenstein, 331: Zeitlin, 66; Luria, 130 (full references in n. 94 above). The question of whether the debates recorded in the scholion to Megillat Taanit are historical is still problematic. But even assuming that these incidents did not occur on the recorded date, they do seem to have an independent value. They apparently preserve accounts which would have been lost if they had not become attached to the Scroll of Fasts; thus the debate between the Pharisees and Sadducees may have been historical even though it was not related to the fourteenth of Tammuz. In fact, it should be noted that the issue of the identity of Ṣedoqym in the Mishnah and Tosefta, as well as in the scholions, is independent of the problem of the historicity of the recorded incidents.

97. In B. Sukkah 48b, this is attributed to one of the Ṣedoqym, in T. Sukkah 3:6 to a *Baytusy* (see Lieberman, תוספתא כפשוטה, II:2, 881). In *AJ* 13, 372, Alexander Jannaeus is the object of derision.

98. An alternate reading is Ṣedoqym (Luria, *Megillath Ta'anith,* 87). Note that in this and the next passage, the Baethusians are listed instead of Zadokites. It seems that the Baethusians are mentioned particularly in calendrical controversies. Compare Qiraisani as cited above, who also appears to connect Baethus with calendrical innovations. M. Rosh ha-Shanah 2:1 lists the *Mynym,* but the same account in T. Rosh ha-Shanah 1:15 and in B. Rosh ha-Shanah 22b names the Baethusians as participants in intercalatory controversies.

99. Lichtenstein, 323; Zeitlin, 228; Luria, 87 (see n. 94 for full references).

100. The insertion of Lev. 7:8 into a citation from 11Q Torah 13:13-14 seems peculiar. A possible explanation is that it was inserted for polemical reasons to make a point about the privacy of the offering. Compare Yadin's notes, *TS* II, 41-42, for a different point of view.

101. Lichtenstein, 331: Zeitlin, 65; Luria, 95 (see n. 94 for full references). In spite of the many citations, the crucial scriptural passage is missing: "And on the morrow after the passover, on that very day, they ate of the produce of the land, unleavened cakes and parched grain" (Josh. 5:11). Certainly, 11Q Torah 18:10-13 confirms the view which the rabbis attribute to the Baethusians. Compare Qirqisani above, p. 153.

102. This calendar is discussed in Chap. 2.

103. Chap. 2.4 (2.7 in Nemoy's Arabic text) (passage #1 above). See the discussion of the calendar above, pp. 156-58.

104. Lichtenstein, 331; Zeitlin, 66; Luria, 130 (see n. 94 for full references).

105. See n. 98 for the reading *Baytusym* in this text. The only time that the Mishnah uses *Baytusym* is in discussions of calendrical subject-matter, which seems to corroborate the calendrical reforms which Qirqisani attributed to Baethus (chap. 2:4 [2:7 in Nemoy's Arabic text—passage #1 above]). See the discussion of the Jubilees calendar in Chapter 2.

106. Homer?

107. "The Pharisaic-Sadducean Controversies about Purity and the Qumran Texts," *JJS* XXXI (1980) 157-70. That there are two kinds of *Ṣedoqym* in talmudic literature had already been noted by G. R. Driver in *The Judaean Scrolls: The Problem and a Solution* (Oxford, 1965), 259-66. Of course, I cannot accept the thesis that the non-Sadducean references refer to a group which takes its name from the Saddok who together with Judas founded the fourth philosophy.

108. *JJS* XXXI (1980) 168-69.

109. "Anan ben David," *JE* I, 554.

110. A. Adam, *Antike Berichte über die Essener* (Berlin, 2d ed., 1972), 59.

111. A recent work on the offspring of Jonadab of Rechab, as they appear in rabbinic literature, and the great similarity of this portrait to descriptions of the Essenes, has been published by S. Safrai, "The Sons of Yehonadav ben Rekhav and the Essenes," *Bar Ilan Annual* XVI–XVII (1979) 37-58 (Hebrew).

112. M. Sanhedrin 10:1.

113. B. Shabbat 108a.

114. See above, p. 156.

Notes to Chapter 5

1. In the earlier discussions of the history of Qumran, there was, of course, considerable difference of opinion concerning the historical provenance of the Commune. There were those who argued for a first-century c.e. date, centering around the year 70 c.e.: C. Roth, *The Historical Background of the Dead Sea Scrolls* (New York, 1959); G. R. Driver, *The Judaean Scrolls: The Problem and a Solution* (Oxford, 1965). The most outspoken advocates of a medieval date for the scrolls were S. Zeitlin and S. B. Hoenig in their articles in the *Jewish Quarterly Review* (see Chap. 4, n. 52 above).

2. *AJ* 11:347-12:246. On this period of Jewish history, see the following discussions and accompanying bibliographies: J. Derenbourg, *Essai sur l'histoire et la geographie de la Palestine* (Paris, 1867), 41-56; H. Gräetz, *Geschichte der Juden* (Leipzig, 2d ed., 1902), II:2, 206-91; V. Tcherikover, *Hellenistic Civilization and the Jews* (Philadelphia, 1959), S. Applebaum (trans.), 1-89; M. Hengel, *Judaism and Hellenism* (Philadelphia, 1974), J. Bowden (trans.), I, 6-57; *Schürer* I, 137-63.

3. Neh. 12:11.

4. See p. 172 ff. below.

5. *AJ* 11:347-12:246, particularly 12:156-59. See also V. Tcherikover, *WHJP*, VI, 105-14.

6. *AJ* 11:326–39. See R. Marcus's discussion of the high-priestly succession in Appendix B of the Loeb edition of Josephus (Cambridge, Mass., 1933), VII, 732–36.

7. *AJ* 11:347.

8. Abot 1:2.

9. There is a rabbinic tradition that it was Simon the Just who encountered Alexander the Great: B. Yoma 69a; scholion to Megillat Taanit on Kislev 21.

10. *AJ* 12:186, 224.

11. *AJ* 12:154.

12. *Hellenistic Civilization*, 128–30.

13. M. Stern ("Notes on the Story of Joseph the Tobiad [Josephus, *Antiquities*, XII, 154 ff.]," *Tarbiz* XXXII [1962] 35–47 [Hebrew]) and M. Hengel (*Judaism*, I, 267) place the beginning of Joseph's tax collection in 240 or 239 B.C.E. Others are closer to Tcherikover's suggestion: E. Meyer, *Ursprung und Anfänge des Christentums* (Stuttgart and Berlin, 1921), II, 129–31; B. Mazar, "The Tobiads," *IEJ* VII (1957) 235; S. Zeitlin, *The Rise and Fall of the Judaean State* (Philadelphia, 1968) I, 64; *Schürer* I, 140.

14. A. Büchler, *Die Tobiaden und die Oniaden* (Vienna, 1899), 60–62, 69–70. R. Marcus, in his notes to the Loeb edition of Josephus (VII, 82–83), seems to accept Büchler's argumentation, but suggests that the twenty-two-year period began during the reign of Ptolemy Euergetes.

15. G. F. Moore, "Simon the Righteous," *Jewish Studies in Memory of Israel Abrahams* (New York, 1927), G. A. Kohut (ed.), 348–64; R. Marcus, *Josephus* (London 1933), VII, 732–36.

16. *AJ* 12:224.

17. *AJ* 12:229.

18. *AJ* 12:237.

19. Tcherikover, *Hellenistic Civilization*, 158–61, 187; E. Bickermann, *Der Gott der Makkabäer* (Berlin, 1937), 12–16; Hengel, *Judaism* I, 275–80; *Schürer* I, 149.

20. 2 Mac. 4:23.

21. L. M. Barth, "Synagogue, The Great," *IDBS*, 844–45. See also S. Zeitlin, "The Origin of the Synagogue," *PAAJR* II (1930–31) 79–81, and Hugo Mantel, "The Era of the Men of the Great Assembly," in *Chapters in the History of Jerusalem during the Period of the Second Temple* (Jerusalem, 1981), Izhak Ben-Zvi (ed.), 22–46 (Hebrew). The view that this refers to the great assembly of 1 Mac. 14:27–45 in which Simon is appointed high priest cannot be substantiated; E. Rivkin, *A Hidden Revolution* (Nashville, 1978), 215–20, 236.

22. Seder Olam 30. A discussion and listing of the talmudic evidence is to be found in L. Finkelstein, *The Pharisees and the Men of the Great Synagogue* (New York, 1950), 45–50 (Hebrew). The following chapters of his work deal with the origins of this institution.

23. Seder Olam 30.

24. B. Yoma 69a; scholion to Megillat Taanit on Kislev 21.

25. 1 Mac. 7:16–17; Gen. Rabbah 65:22. Many scholars connect these two passages: C. Albeck, *Introduction to the Mishna* (Jerusalem, 1959), 25 (Hebrew); A. Guttmann, *Rabbinic Judaism in the Making* (Detroit, 1970), 34; A. J. Saldarini, *The Fathers According to Rabbi Nathan, Version B* (Leiden, 1975), 89. For an argument against this identification, see S. B. Hoenig, *The Great Sanhedrin* (Philadelphia, 1953), 29–30.

26. In addition to the following references, see the bibliography on the Pharisees and Sadducees in *Schürer* II, 381–82; L. Zunz, *Die Gottesdienstlichen Vorträge der Juden historisch entwickelt* (Frankfurt a.M., 1892), 38–39; Finkelstein, *The Pharisees and the Men of the Great Synagogue*, 40–45; C. Albeck, *Introduction*, 216–18; Guttmann, *Rabbinic Judaism*, 33–39; S. Zeitlin, *Rise and Fall* I, 207–8, 412–34; Rivkin, *Hidden Revolution*, 235–36. The rabbinic traditions concerning the *zugot* are collected by J. Neusner in *The Rabbinic Traditions about the Pharisees before 70* (Leiden, 1971), I, 60–159, 184–340.

27. I. Broydé in *JE* VII, 242; M. D. Herr in *EJ* XVI, 853–54.

28. *EJ* III, 67; Zeitlin, *Rise and Fall* I, 309; M. Hengel, *Judaism and Hellenism*, I, 64, 128, 143.

29. E. Will, *Histoire Politique du Monde Hellénistique (323–30 av. J. C.)* (Nancy, 1966), I, 47–70; E. J. Bickerman, *Chronology of the Ancient World* (London, 1968), 210–11.

30. See p. 180.

31. Of course, 196 B.C.E. is not intended to be a literal date. It is just as possible, in fact, that Zadok "discovered" the scroll a decade or two earlier.

32. See pp. 185–93.

33. ARNB 10.

34. They both opted for Eleazar ben Hananiah, captain of the temple: C. Roth, *The Historical Background of the Dead Sea Scrolls* (New York, 1959), 11–14; G. R. Driver, *The Judaean Scrolls: The Problem and a Solution* (Oxford, 1965), 267–84.

35. A. Dupont-Sommer, *The Essene Writings from Qumran* (Cleveland, 1967), G. Vermes (trans.), 351–57; K. Elliger, *Studien zum Habakkuk-Kommentar vom Toten Meer* (Tübingen, 1953), 270–74.

36. M. H. Segal, "The Habakkuk 'Commentary' and the Damascus Fragments," *JBL* LXX (1951) 136–40; M. Delcor, *Essai sur le Midrash d'Habacuc* (Paris, 1951), 61–68; J. Carmignac et al., *Les Textes de Qumran* (Paris, 1963), II, 53–54.

37. F. M. Cross, Jr., *The Ancient Library of Qumran and Modern Biblical Studies* (Garden City, N.Y., rev. ed., 1961), 137–56; "The Early History of the Qumran Community," *New Directions in Biblical Archaeology* (Garden City, N.Y., 1969), D. N. Freedman and J. C. Greenfield (eds.), 76–79. Other scholars have made a similar proposal: W. F. Albright and C. S. Mann, "Qumran and the Essenes: Geography, Chronology, and Identification of the Sect," *New Directions* (see Cross reference), 19; R. de Vaux, *Archaeology and the Dead Sea Scrolls* (Oxford, 1973), 117; G. W. E. Nickelsburg, "Simon—A Priest with a Reputation for Faithfulness," *BASOR* 223 (1976) 67–68.

38. G. Vermes, *The Dead Sea Scrolls: Qumran in Perspective* (London, 1977), 150–51. An increasing number of students of Qumran have accepted this identification: J. T. Milik, *Ten Years of Discovery in the Wilderness of Judaea* (Naperville, Ill., 1959), J. Strugnell (trans.), 84–89; E. F. Sutcliffe, *The Monks of Qumran* (Westminster, 1960), 42–49; G. Jeremias, *Der Lehrer der Gerechtigkeit* (Göttingen, 1963), 69–78; H. Stegemann, "Die Entstehung der Qumrangemeinde" (Diss., Rheinische Friedrich-Wilhelms-Universität, Bonn, 1971), 202–9; J. Murphy-O'Connor, "The Essenes and Their History," *RB* LXXXI (1974) 229–33; M. Hengel, *Judaism* I, 224; M. A. Knibb, "The Dead Sea Scrolls: Reflections on some Recent Publications," *ExpT* XC (1979) 297.

39. CD 1:1–11, Dupont-Sommer's translation, *Essene Writings,* 121–22.

40. One of the few scholars to take the chronological proposals of the Damascus Document seriously is E. Meyer, whose work is discussed below, n. 56. The same can be said for H. H. Rowley, "The History of the Qumran Sect," *BJRL* XLIX (1966–67) 203–32. I. Rabinowitz ("A Reconsideration of 'Damascus' and '390 Years' in the 'Damascus' ['Zadokite'] Fragments," *JBL* LXXIII [1954] 33–35) takes the numbers literally, but applies them to the end of the First Temple. S. Hahn ("Zur Chronologie der Qumran-Schriften," *AcOr* XI [1960] 181–89) attempts to work out the chronology of the Damascus Document from the timetable of Seder Olam. M. Black, (*The Scrolls and Christian Origins* [New York, 1961], 19–20), who accepts Onias III as the Teacher of Righteousness, takes the chronology seriously; however, the rise of this personage is attributed to the end of the twenty years, thus around 175 B.C.E.

41. *The Teacher of Righteousness in the Qumran Texts* (London, 1957), 17–18; *Biblical Exegesis in the Qumran Texts* (Grand Rapids, Mich., 1959), 59–62. Bruce's conjecture has been accepted as fact by later scholarship: Vermes, *Dead Sea Scrolls,* 147–48.

42. This is apparent from the chronology of the destruction of the First and Second Temples—Seder Olam 28–30; cf. B. Z. Wacholder, "Chronomessianism: The Timing of Messianic Movements and the Calendar of Sabbatical Cycles," *HUCA* XLVI (1975) 201–18.

43. Bruce (see above n. 41), to his credit, was careful to state this conjecture in a circumscribed form. He still emphasized the hypothetical nature of this theory in the much later essay, "The Book of Daniel and the Qumran Community," *Neotestamentica et Semitica* (Edinburgh, 1969), E. E. Ellis and M. Wilcox (eds.), 232.

44. For a literary analysis of the Damascus Document which undergirds this hypothesis, see Chap. 3, pp. 105–10.

45. CD 4:4; 6:11.

46. CD 1:12.

47. CD 2:10. On the significance of these terms in Qumran literature, see J. Licht, "Time and Eschatology in Apocalyptic Literature and in Qumran," *JJS* XVI (1965) 177–82.

48. CD 4:8–9.

49. CD 4:12.

50. CD 6:10, 14.

51. CD 1:5–6.

52. 2 Kgs. 25:8–9. For the word חורבן (destruction), Ezek. 40:1 uses הכתה העיר (the city was smitten); however, the same prophet frequently uses חורבה (desolate): Ezek. 25:13; 29:9; 33:24, 27; 35:4; 36:33; 38:8, etc. See B. Z. Wacholder, *Essays on Jewish Chronology and Chronography* (New York, 1976), vii–viii.

53. See n. 35 and n. 36 above.

54. For example, see Vermes, *Dead Sea Scrolls,* 147–48.

55. John Strugnell raised the question of whether Zadok may have been one of the unrecorded high priests who served between 159 and 152 B.C.E. Others have suggested that Zadok refers to Simon *Ḥaṣṣadyq* (the Righteous). It seems unlikely that Simon the Just or any of the unknown high priests is intended in CD 5:5.

56. E. Meyer, "Die Gemeinde des neuen Bundes im Lande Damaskus: Eine jüdische Schrift aus der Seleukidenzeit," *Abhandlungen der preussischen Akademie der Wissenschaften* (Berlin), Phil.-hist. Kl., IX (1919) 1–65; E. Täubler, "Jerusalem 201 to 199 B.C.E.: On the History of a Messianic Movement," *JQR* XXXVII (1946–47) 1–30, 125–37, 249–63. See below for a further discussion of the views contained in these works.

57. Hos. 4:16. See CD 1:13.

58. CD 1:14.

59. See p. 173.

60. A number of scholars who argue that Jonathan is the wicked priest claim that this designation does not include the "scoffer" or the "liar": Stegemann, "Entstehung," 200–228; Murphy-O'Connor, *RB* LXXXI (1974) 229–38; Knibb, *ExpT* XC (1979) 298.

61. The Hebrew text is from *The Book of Ben Sira: Text, Concordance and an Analysis of the Vocabulary* (Jerusalem, 1973), pp. 62–63 (Hebrew). The identity of Simon II follows from the preface to the work, where the writer, describing himself as the grandson of the author, claims that he began translating it in the thirty-eighth year of the reign of Euergetes. This would have to be Euergetes II; thus he devoted himself to the translation in 132 B.C.E. This would make his grandfather a contemporary of Simon the Just II. The date of this high priest has been discussed above, p. 173.

62. CD 1:14.

63. CD 4:16. This has already been discussed in Chap. 3.

64. CD 5:8.

65. See above, p. 126.

66. *AJ* 12:186–89. Rabin (*Qumran Studies,* 91) notes a number of instances from the time of Herod.

67. See above, pp. 131–33.

68. CD 6:16–17.

69. Meyer, *Ursprung* II, 127–28.

70. 2 Mac. 3:6, 10–12.

71. *Zadokite Documents,* 16.

72. *DSSE,* 101.

73. See Chap. 1., p. 12.

74. It ought to be emphasized that the Qumranic literature does not know of the concept of

the משיח (anointed) in its Greek translation *Christos,* where it refers to the anointed eschatological figure of the Davidic seed. In Qumran writings, where the term is משיח or משוח, occasionally in the plural, it refers to the anointed priests, i.e., the high priest and his assistants. The high priest upon assuming office is, of course, anointed, but as for the king, his anointment is stated in the biblical tradition but is not recorded in the Qumranic Torah. This may reflect an omission, but it ought to be noted that the king in Qumran, as in the Testament of the Twelve Patriarchs, is subordinate to the high priest. The phrase משיח אהרון וישראל (anointed of Aaron and Israel) appears to be nothing but a synonym for the כוהן גדול (high priest). 11Q Torah devotes a section to the anointment of the high priest but ignores this with respect to the king. Thus there is no objection to the use of the word "Messiah" at Qumran as long as it is understood as an eschatological term, but certainly not in its rabbinic meaning. See Chapter 4, p. 145.

75. CD 20:15. Though the forty years refers, of course, to the wilderness and the proverbial reign of kings such as David and Solomon, for the author of the Damascus Document this also represents a positive date which appears in later literature of the Commune as well: 4QpPs 37, 2:7–8; 1Q 22 (Sayings of Moses), 2:5. The pesher on Psalm 37 seems to have been composed after the death of the *Moreh Ṣedeq* but prior to the completion of the forty years of evil: Jub. 50:4; CD 20:15. The War Rule is also based on a forty-year epoch (Dupont-Sommer, *Essene Writings,* 172–73; 1QM 2:6–14).

76. W. H. Brownlee, "The Jerusalem Habakkuk Scroll," *BASOR* 112 (1948) 8–18. Photographs of the scroll were published a few years later: M. Burrows et al., *The Dead Sea Scrolls of St. Mark's Monastery* (New Haven, 1950), I. Brownlee has an extensive bibliography in his new work, which includes an introduction, text, translation, and commentary: *The Midrash Pesher of Habakkuk* (Missoula, Mont., 1979), 5–15.

77. Students of this work do not usually divide it into literary units but rather assume that it is an ongoing commentary. This approach fails to take account of the genius of its author.

78. The similarity of the historical allusions in the two works is noted by M. H. Segal, even though he dates Pesher Habakkuk slightly earlier than the Damascus Document: "The Habakkuk 'Commentary' and the Damascus Fragments (A Historical Study)," *JBL* LXX (1951) 131–47.

79. See Chap. 3, above, pp. 101–5.

80. Brownlee, *Midrash Pesher,* 37.

81. A. M. Habermann, *The Scrolls from the Judaean Desert* (Tel-Aviv, 1959), 43 (Hebrew). He is followed in this reading by Carmignac, *Textes* II, 93, and Vermes, *DSSE,* 235.

82. Vermes, *DSSE,* 235. The prevailing reading seems implausible: Dupont-Sommer, *Essene Writings,* 258; E. Lohse, *Die Texte aus Qumran: Hebräisch und Deutsch* (Munich, 1964), 229. תוחלה (expectation) does appear in 1QH 9:14, but its position is syntactically unusual. Neither in Scripture nor in the Qumran scrolls is this word used in a temporal relationship, as would be the case here. What is true of תוחלת applies also to מחלת (sickness) (Habermann, *Scrolls,* 43) or to נחלת (inheritance) (one of the alternatives cited by Brownlee, *Midrash Pesher,* 38). In this text the author is interpreting the introductory lines of Habakkuk. The reading תחלת (beginning) commends itself because: (a) it seems proper for the hermeneutics of an introductory verse (cf. Hos. 1:1), (b) a word with a temporal meaning is required to fit the words that follow: "(last) generation," and (c) a very similar use is found in 1QpHab 8:9.

83. 1QpHab 2:12, 14; 3:4, 9; 4:5, 10; 6:1, 10; 9:7.

84. K. M. T. Atkinson, "The Historical Setting of the Habakkuk Commentary," *JSS* IV (1960) 238–63; F. F. Bruce, "The Dead Sea Habakkuk Scroll," *ALUOS* I (1958–9) 12–14; J. T. Milik, *Ten Years of Discovery in the Wilderness of Judaea* (Naperville, Ill., 1959), J. Strugnell (trans.), 64–65; Cross, *Ancient Library,* 123–24; Dupont-Sommer, *Essene Writings,* 341–51; Vermes, *Dead Sea Scrolls,* 149–50. H. H. Rowley identifies the Kittim as the Seleucids (*BJRL* XLIX [1966–67] 219).

85. Delcor, *Essai,* 61–68; Carmignac, *Textes* II, 53–54.

86. See p. 177 above.

87. In contrast to what is presented in this study, most commentators on Pesher Habakkuk

have ignored, with the exception of the passages dealing with the Kittim, the contents and structure of the prophetic book. Such a presentation presumes a unified formula for the pesher; that is
to say, the hermeneutics of 1QpHab is thought to be identical to that of the other peshers. This is
not the case, however, since Pesher Habakkuk as well as the pesherite elaboration of Isa. 24:17 in
CD 4:14 seems to diverge from the other pesherite fragments.

88. 1QpHab 6:12–7:14.

89. 1QpHab 7:9–14. Many commentators ascribe this to the "air" of the times rather than
relate it to the specific situation of the sect: K. Elliger, *Studien zum Habakkuk-Kommentar vom Toten
Meer* (Tübingen, 1953), 195; Dupont-Sommer *Essene Writings*, 263; J. Maier, *Die Texte vom Toten
Meer* (Munich and Basel, 1960), II, 146; Brownlee, *Midrash Pesher*, 120.

90. CD 4:14. See p. 111 above.

91. 1QpHab 2:1–10. Murphy-O'Connor, *RB* LXXXI (1974) 233–38, takes the passages dealing
with the "man of lies" as representative of a clearly defined split between two leaders in the Qumran movement. According to his hypothesis, the man of lies is not the wicked priest.

92. Hab. 1:4.

93. Brownlee, *Midrash Pesher*, 109–10, speculates that the pesherite text may have read בער (to
make empty), which makes no sense. באר (make plain) alludes to Deut. 1:5 and serves as a synonym for *pešer*. In the pesherite understanding of this verse, God addresses the commentator as
well as the prophet by revealing to the former the eschatological dimension of the tablets.

94. 1QpHab 6:12–7:14. Brownlee's definition of pesher (*Midrash Pesher*, 23–28) as a third category of midrash after midrash halakah (legal) and midrash aggadah (homiletical) creates more
problems than it solves. K. Stendahl, *The School of St. Matthew* (Lund, 1954), 184, accepted this definition, first advanced in 1953. This approach links a book such as Pesher Habakkuk with early
rabbinic hermeneutics reflected in the Mishnah and Talmud. This tends to obscure the relationship between the biblical text and the rabbinic commentator, making him appear to disregard
both the text and the content of the scriptural passage. No traditional midrash ever ignores
altogether the historical meaning of the scriptural text. The rabbis did claim that it contained
additional meanings. 1QpHab, and other peshers even more so, is absolutely oblivious to the historical meaning of Scripture. Thus Habakkuk is censured by the pesherite writer for perceiving
God's words as referring to the prophet himself rather than to the Teacher of Righteousness. Only
perhaps in the Song of Songs, where the literal meaning did not conform to current morality, was
the allegorical given a primary meaning. The contrast between midrash and pesher might be
stated as follows: in midrash the historical meaning still remains basic no matter how much it is
expanded by metaphorical hermeneutics, while Qumranic exegesis sees the allegorical or eschatological as basic and the historical as secondary. Calling a product of pesherite exegesis a midrash obfuscates the contrasting hermeneutics. Christian biblical hermeneutics includes both
pesher and midrash types, even though the search for Christ in the Hebrew Scriptures tends to
make it more of the former. There are those who have sought to explain the hermeneutics of the
pesher without resort to midrash: Elliger, *Studien*, 150–64; E. Osswald, "Zur Hermeneutick des
Habakuk-Kommentars," *ZAW* LXVIII (1956) 243–56; I. Rabinowitz, "*Pêsher/Pittârôn*. Its Biblical
Meaning and Its Significance in the Qumran Literature," *RQ* VIII (1973) 219–32; M. P. Horgan,
Pesharim: Qumran Interpretations of Biblical Books (Washington, 1979), 249–59. In an attempt to
resolve this impasse, L. H. Silberman was forced to rely too heavily on Danielic similarities:
"Unriddling the Riddle: A Study in the Structure and Language of the Habakkuk Pesher
(1QpHab)," *RQ* III (1961–62), 323–64.

95. Hab. 2:4.

96. 1QpHab 8:3–12:10.

97. See Chap. 3, p. 129.

98. 1QpHab 8:8–9.

99. With the exception of Carmignac (*Textes* II, 109), who thinks this is a reference to the sect
itself, when its hopes of being returned to Jerusalem would be fulfilled, scholars agree that later

Hasmonean rulers are here being discussed: Cross, *Ancient Library*, 124; Dupont-Sommer, *Essene Writings*, 264; Vermes, *Dead Sea Scrolls*, 151–52; Brownlee, *Midrash Pesher*, 152.

100. 1QpHab 9:10–12.

101. Ibid. 10:9–13.

102. Ibid. 11:4–8.

103. Ibid. 9:9–10; Dupont-Sommer (*Essene Writings*, 265) translates this as follows: "The explanation of this concerns the Wicked Priest whom, because of the iniquity committed against the Teacher of Righteousness and the men of his council, God delivered into the hands of his enemies." Such an understanding of this passage is shared by most students of this work: Elliger, *Studien*, 204; Silberman, *RQ* III (1961–62) 350–51: Carmignac, *Textes* II, 109; Lohse, *Texte*, 239; Vermes, *DSSE*, 240.

104. See above, p. 185.

105. See above, p. 181.

106. See Chap. 2, p. 34.

107. See p. 187 above.

108. See LXX, Dan. 11:30.

109. O. Morkholm, *Antiochus IV of Syria* (Copenhagen 1966), 34–38; E. Will, *Histoire Politique du Monde Hellénistique (323–30 av. J. C.)* (Nancy, 1967), II, 259–60.

110. Students of Qumran differ as to whether *Moreh Şedeq* is a title embracing two or more individuals, or whether it alludes, at least in Qumranic writings, to a single person. This study supports the latter position, in part because the term does not appear in the later Qumranic writings, such as the Thanksgivings or the Manuals. Admittedly, the term *Moreh Şedeq* does appear in rabbinic literature, but there it has a meaning completely disparate from that found at Qumran. A brief article on this other possibility was written by G. W. Buchanan, "The Office of Teacher of Righteousness," *RQ* IX (1977) 241–43.

111. B. Z. Wacholder, "A Qumran Attack on the Oral Exegesis? The phrase *'šr btlmwd šqrm* in 4Q Pesher Nahum," *RQ* V (1964–66) 575–78.

112. See p. 182 above.

113. 1QpHab 8:9–11.

114. Ibid. 8:12.

115. Jerome's Commentary on Dan. 11:14.

116. *AJ* 12:138–44.

117. The chronology of members of this clan has been discussed at the beginning of this chapter, p. 172 ff. Josephus' account of the history of this group is found in *AJ* 12:154–236. Many of the papyri and inscriptions relevant to the history of the Tobiads are discussed by B. Mazar, "The Tobiads," *IEJ* VII (1957) 137–45, 229–38, and Hengel, *Judaism* I, 27–29, 47–55, 267–77. In addition to the bibliography cited by R. Marcus in the Loeb edition of Josephus (VII, 767–68, 770–71), see the following treatments of Tobiad history: Tcherikover, *Hellenistic Civilization*, 127–42, 153–74; Zeitlin, *Rise and Fall* I, 60–66; M. Stern, "Notes on the Story of Joseph the Tobiad (Josephus, *Antiquities*, XII, 154 ff.)," *Tarbiz* XXXII (1962) 35–47 (Hebrew); V. Tcherikover, "Social Conditions," *WHJP* VI, 87–114.

118. 2 Mac. 3:6, 10–12.

119. From the account in 2 Maccabees, it would appear that the reputation of fabulous wealth probably exceeded the temple's actual holdings.

120. 2 Mac. 4:13. See also 1 Mac. 1:11–15.

121. Bickermann, *Gott der Makkabäer*, 53–65; Tcherikover, *Hellenistic Civilization*, 159–66; Hengel, *Judaism* I, 277–83.

122. CD 8:11–12.

123. O. Morkholm, *Antiochus IV*, 38–50; E. Will, *Histoire Politique*, II, 254–59.

124. Morkholm, *Antiochus IV*, 54–55; Will, *Histoire Politique*, 259–60.

125. This must have occurred on the tenth of Tishri, with Tishri a solar month of thirty days.

126. This is in contrast to those like Brownlee who maintain that this is a reference to an attempt to slaughter the Teacher of Righteousness. Brownlee (*Midrash Pesher*, 187) finds support for this interpretation in the references to the blood in 1QpHab 9:8 and 12:1.

127. *Ancient Library*, 114–15.

128. See n. 34–n. 38 above.

129. *Textes* II, 47–48.

130. Hab. 1:2–5 (RSV).

131. Hab. 2:1–6 (RSV).

132. Carmignac, *Textes* II, 49–50; Horgan, *Pesharim,* 248.

133. E.g., Cross, *Ancient Library*, 113–15.

134. Ibid.

135. Carmignac, *Textes* II, 47–48.

136. This congruency was pointed out to me by John Kampen.

137. On the other hand, 1QpHab allegorizes the term "Lebanon" as equivalent to the *ʿaṣat Ḥayyaḥad* (council of the Commune). One must suppose, therefore, that the *Yaḥad* came into existence prior to the death of the *Moreh Ṣedeq*. There is nothing intrinsically difficult about such an assumption except that, as far as we know, the early books, such as the Damascus Document do not contain any allusions to such an institution. I am inclined, therefore, to accept a suggestion by John Kampen, whose share in this study is considerable, that 1QpHab was composed not before but after the death of the *Moreh Ṣedeq,* and during the lifetime of the wicked priest. The virtue of such an assumption is that it would account for the echoes of contemporary events without necessarily being tied to the chronology of Zadok's lifetime. In other words, if we date Zadok's death to 170 B.C.E., Pesher Habakkuk was composed soon thereafter. About this time, also, the *ʿaṣat Ḥayyaḥad* came into being. A basic tenet of this Commune was the belief, attested in the supplement to the Damascus Document, that the *Moreh Ṣedeq* would reveal himself within forty years after his death.

138. 1QpHab 2:6–10. לפשור (to compose a pesher) seems to refer to a claim which alleges that the pesherite commentator relates to the prophet as does the interpreter of dreams to the dreamer.

139. See p. 111 above.

140. The fragments are published as 4Q 169 in *DJD* V, 37–42.

141. A bibliography of earlier studies on these fragments is provided by J. Fitzmyer, "A Bibliographic Aid to the Study of the Qumran Cave IV Texts 158–186," *CBQ* XXXI (1969) 63–65.

142. Most frequently these fragments have been thought to concern Demetrius III: J. M. Allegro, "Further Light on the History of the Qumran Sect," *JBL* LXXV (1956) 89–95; Milik, *Ten Years,* 72–73; Cross, *Ancient Library,* 124–26; Dupont-Sommer, *Essene Writings,* 268; Y. Yadin, "Pesher Nahum (4QpNahum) Reconsidered," *IEJ* XXI (1971) 1–12; *DSSE,* 65. Demetrius I was proposed by H. H. Rowley, "4QpNahum and the Teacher of Righteousness," *JBL* LXXV (1956) 188–93. He noted that *AJ* 12:156 mentions that Antiochus IV crucified people, thereby responding to the major argument for placing the activities described in the pesher in the time of Alexander Jannaeus.

143. *AJ* 13:121–23.

144. 11Q Torah 64:8–13.

145. Cross, "The Early History of the Qumran Community," *New Directions in Biblical Archaeology,* 67–68; *Schürer* II, 400–403, 412–14, 585–90.

146. In the literature cited in the previous note, we see that recent scholarship has tended to relate the Hasideans to the origins of both groups.

147. *AJ* 13:288–98.

148. 13:171. See *Schürer* II, 401.

149. Jerome's Commentary on Dan. 11:14. *FGrH* 260, F44–45 (IIB, 1223–24).

150. Meyer, *Ursprung* II, 127–28.

151. "Jerusalem 201 to 199 B.C.E. On the History of a Messianic Movement," *JQR* XXXVII (1946–47) 1–30, 125–37, 249–63; note especially 16–30.

152. See p. 185 above. A similar group seems to be referred to in Dan. 11:34.

153. 1QpHab 7:5–8 on Hab. 2:3.

154. Ibid.

155. Dan. 11:14. The author of the Damascus Document (2:17) uses the same word to describe the failings of the past.

156. Dan. 11:14.

157. See pp. 178–84.

158. See n. 162.

159. *TS* I, 295–98, 304–06. According to Ben Zion Luria, the Essene movement only began after Alexander Jannaeus' persecution of the Pharisees. See his article, "Comments on the Scroll of the Sanctuary," *Bet Mikra* III (1968) 370–86 (Hebrew). On the basis of the congruency of Qumran with the Essenes, this scholar then advances the thesis that the Qumranic Torah was composed toward the middle of the first century B.C.E.

160. *TS* I, 298.

161. *BJ* 2:123, 133.

162. L. H. Schiffman, "The *Temple Scroll* in Literary and Philological Perspective," *Approaches to Ancient Judaism: Volume II* (Chico, Calif., 1980), W. S. Green (ed.), 143–58; B. A. Levine, "The Temple Scroll: Aspects of its Historical Provenance and Literary Character," *BASOR* 232 (1978) 7.

163. *TS* I, 15–18.

164. Ibid.

165. N. Avigad, "The Palaeography of the Dead Sea Scrolls," *Scripta Hierosolymitana* IV (1958) 56–87; F. M. Cross, Jr., "The Development of the Jewish Scripts," *The Bible and the Ancient Near East: Essays in honor of William Foxwell Albright* (New York, 1961), G. E. Wright (ed.), 133–202.

166. *TS* III (Suppl.), plates 38 and 40, for photographs of these fragments.

167. *TS* I, 16–18.

168. Cross, "Development of the Jewish Scripts," 138, 166–73. See also Avigad, *Scripta* IV, 69.

169. A letter from Professor Strugnell, dated April 28, 1981, for which I am grateful. The letter continues: "I write now that I have just finished holding my own seminar on the Temple Scroll, with some interesting results. On the general question of date we tended to follow you into pre-Antiochus times, and to find that neither Yadin's precise dates under Hyrcanus or Jannaeus, nor his proposed close associations with the theology of the Qumran sect, had any evidence in its favor."

170. This would still not be the oldest non-biblical text found at Qumran. Milik dates the remnants of the Astronomical Enoch to the end of the third century or to the early second century B.C.E. (*Enoch,* 273).

171. *TS* I, 31–33.

172. 11Q Torah 52:18. This word is missing from Yadin's concordance to 11Q Torah.

173. *TS* I, 34.

174. Schiffman, "Philological and Literary Method," 9–13.

175. M. H. Segal, *A Grammar of Mishnaic Hebrew* (Oxford, 1927), 1–20; C. Albeck, *Introduction to the Mishnah* (Jerusalem, 1959), 130 (Hebrew); E. Y. Kutscher, *EJ* XVI, 1590–1607; *The Language and Linguistic Background of the Isaiah Scroll (1 Q Isaᵃ)* (Leiden, 1974), 8–15.

176. Kutscher, *EJ* XVI, 1604–5.

177. *TS* I, 34. The most obvious example is found at 11Q Torah 41:16 (אדשכים). See my review of *Le Targum de Job de la grotte XI de Qumran* (Leiden, 1971), J. P. M. van der Ploeg and O. P. and A. S. van der Woude (eds.), in *JBL* XCI (1972) 414–15. Kutscher (*EJ* XVI, 1589) does speculate that a few words in the Dead Sea Scrolls may have been influenced by Greek or Latin, but these instances are highly questionable.

178. E. Qimron, "A Grammar of the Hebrew Language of the Dead Sea Scrolls" (Diss., Hebrew University, Jerusalem, 1976), 133, 241–47 (Hebrew).

179. *TS* I, 178–80, 297.

180. Deut. 26:13–15.

181. 11Q Torah 56:12–60:12. *TS* I, 264–77, 297, and his commentary to the relevant section in vol. II.

182. A. Dupont-Sommer, in his response to Yadin's announcement of the discovery of the Temple Scroll, *CRAIBL* (1967), 618.

183. *TS* I, 296–306.

184. M. Sotah 9:10.

185. The numismatic evidence supports this view. The title "king" appears on Hasmonean coins, with one exception, in the Greek only; the Hebrew legend is *Kohen Gadol*. The exception, a coin of Alexander Jannaeus, does have the title "king" in Hebrew, but this was probably intended merely as a translation of the Greek, not the traditional meaning of *melek*. See Dov Genachowski, *EJ* V, 716; *Schürer* I, 602–6. Certainly John Hyrcanus never styled himself king, either in Greek or in Hebrew.

186. This is true in spite of B. Kiddushin 66a, which seems to concede the right of kingship to Alexander Jannaeus but objects to his holding the office of the high priesthood.

187. *BJ* 1:70; *AJ* 13:301.

188. M. Weinfeld ("'Temple Scroll' or 'King's Law,'" *Shnaton*, III [1978–79] 214–37 [Hebrew]) makes the royal constitution the central thesis of 11Q Torah, comparing it with Hellenistic and Roman constitutions. See also his more recent article, "The Royal Guard according to the Temple Scroll," *RB* LXXXVII (1980) 394–96. His argument lacks cogency, and there is nothing in Graeco-Roman literature that, except for remote parallels, compares to what is stated in 11Q Torah. For a comparison of 11Q Torah and the concept of kingship in the Letter of Aristeas, see D. Mendels, "'On Kingship' in the Temple Scroll and the *Vorlage* of the Symposia in the Letters of Aristeas to Philocrates," *Shnaton*, III (1978–79) 245–52 (Hebrew). If a dependence had been demonstrated, it might have been useful for the dating of both documents. But there is little here to necessitate a presumption that either of these writers used the other.

189. Dan. 9:27, 11:31, 12:11.

190. See B. Z. Wacholder, "The Letter from Judah Maccabee to Aristobulus: Is 2 Maccabees 1:10b–2:18 Authentic?" *HUCA* XLIV (1978) 89–133 and the literature cited therein for a discussion of the rededication of the temple.

191. Milik, *Ten Years*, 80–83; Cross, *Ancient Library*, 129–35; Vermes, *Dead Sea Scrolls*, 150–56; *Schürer* II, 586–87.

192. B. E. Thiering (*Redating the Teacher of Righteousness* [Sydney, 1979], 205–6) dates this work to the Herodian period, but she does regard it as the earliest text emanating from the Commune. This, of course, clashes with the paleographers discussed above. See also her article, *"Mebaqqer and Episkopos* in the Light of the Temple Scroll," *JBL* C(1981) 59–74.

193. See Chap. 2 above, pp. 40–41.

194. See Chap. 2 above, pp. 62–77.

195. See pp. 214 ff. below. The Persian resistance to Hellenism has been studied by S. E. Eddy, *The King Is Dead: Studies in the Near Eastern Resistance to Hellenism 334–31 B.C.* (Lincoln, 1961), 3–80.

196. Hengel, *Judaism*, I, 267–72.

197. E. Meyer, *Ursprung*, II, 121–66; Bickermann, *Der Gott der Makkabäer*; Tcherikover, *Hellenistic Civilization*, 90–174.

198. The only exception would seem to be the name Antigonus of Soko.

199. Hengel, *Judaism* I, 268–72.

200. *AJ* 13: 187–89.

201. *TS* I, 39; II, 1–3.

202. The culture reflected in the Book of Tobit could also be added to this list.

203. 1QpHab 8:10, 11:13; CD 2:18; 3:5, 12; 8:8, 19; 19:20, 33; 20:10.

204. Dan. 1:1, 2:1, 7:1, 8:1, 9:1, 10:1.

205. O. Eissfeldt, *The Old Testament: An Introduction* (New York, 1976), P. R. Ackroyd (trans.), 509–10; *IDB* III, 151; *IDBS* 280.

206. In addition to p. 207 above, see 1 QapGen 20:8 and Fitzmyer's commentary, *The Genesis Apocryphon of Qumran Cave I: A Commentary* (Rome, 1966), 111–12.

207. See Chap. 2, pp. 39–41.

208. On the history of this question, see R. Marcus's discussion in Appendix D of the Loeb edition of Josephus, VII, 743–66. See also Tcherikover, *Hellenistic Civilization,* 82–89.

209. *AJ* 12:146. J. Love, "The Ban on Animal Skins in Jerusalem: A Comparison between the Temple Scroll and the Second Decree of Antiochus III," unpublished, Berkeley, 1978; J. Milgrom, "Further Studies in the Temple Scroll," *JQR* LXXI (1980) 98; see also *TS* I:240.

210. *AJ* 12:141.

211. *TS* II, 178.

212. Yadin, *TS* I, 146–48.

213. See p. 134.

214. Isa. 30:26, 65:17, 66:22.

215. Isa. 61:8; Jer. 31:31–34, 32:36–41.

216. Isaiah 54, 60; Ezekiel 40–48.

217. Neh. 2:11–20.

218. On the authenticity of this letter, see B. Z. Wacholder, *HUCA* XLIX (1978) 89–133.

219. B. Z. Wacholder, *Messianism and Mishnah: Time and Place in the Early Halakhah* (Cincinnati, 1979); J. A. Goldstein, *I Maccabees: A New Translation with Introduction and Commentary* (Garden City, N.Y., 1976), 547, n. 1.

220. Milik, *Ten Years,* 80–83; Cross, *Ancient Library,* 129–35; Vermes, *Dead Sea Scrolls,* 150–56; *Schürer* II, 586–87.

221. This statement is not contradicted by the existence of pesherite commentaries on Samuel, or by the fact that Qumranic writings are heavily dependent on the Hebrew Scriptures. That the . pesherite texts could be given a "true" meaning made them acceptable to the authors of the Dead Sea Scrolls.

222. All of the above personalities have been discussed earlier in this chapter.

223. 2 Mac. 4:11.

224. See Chap. 2, pp. 62–77.

225. See Chap. 3 and 4 above.

226. Lev. 10:1–7; Num. 26:61.

227. Enoch 72–82. See Chap. 2 above, pp. 39–41.

228. See Chap. 1, p. 2–3.

229. 2 Mac. 3:6–7, 9–12.

230. See, e.g., Ps. 122.

231. See T. Negaim 6:2. For parallel passages see A. Guttmann, "Jerusalem in Tannaitic Law," *HUCA* XL-XLI (1969–70) 251–75=*Studies in Rabbinic Judaism* (New York, 1976), 236–60.

232. 11Q Torah 46:5.

233. Ibid. 46:9.

234. Ibid. 45:11–12.

235. Ibid. 47:7–8.

236. Ibid. 46:13–16. *TS* I, 229–35; J. Milgrom, "The Temple Scroll," *BA* XLI (1978) 114–15.

237. 11Q Torah 52:18.

238. Compare the use of this term in Yadin's concordance, *TS* II, 287.

239. Note the group seeking righteousness and justice who flee to the wilderness in 1 Mac. 2:29–38.

240. Exod. 28:16. In commenting on an earlier draft of this manuscript, Jacob Milgrom pointed out that the extant text does not actually say whether or not the settlements were square but conceded that its author may have intended to reflect that which is articulated in Ezekiel 48.

241. Exod. 24:4.

242. S. Safrai, "The Sons of Yehonadav ben Rekhav and the Essenes," *Bar Ilan Annual* XVI–XVII (1979) 37–58.

243. *TS* I, 61–62.

244. The author's identification with Moses may account for the rather favorable apportionment of the perquisites to the levites, as noticed by J. Milgrom (*TS* I, 131–36; *BA* XLI [1978] 117–19; *JBL* XCVII [1978] 501–6), compared to the premiums assigned to them in the Pentateuchal exemplar.

Citations

I. HEBREW SCRIPTURES

Genesis
1:14 – 38
1:14–19 – 59
1:16 – 38
2:1–3 – 48
4:17 – 242
5:21–24 – 34
5:22–24 – 241n, 243n
5:23 – 241n
7–8 – 268n
7:11 – 153
8:3–4 – 153
10:25 – 257n
14 – 139
14:1–11 – 244n
17 – 240n
17:2 – 235n
28 – 240n
28:10–22 – 248n
28:17 – 242n
30:28 – 235n
33:17 – 240n
34:12 – 235n
35 – 240n
35:1–15 – 248n
40:8 – 254n
44:3 – 40
49:1 – 240n
49:10 – 93

Exodus
4:12 – 229
12 – 51
12:2 – 54, 159
12:6 – 246n
12:15 – 163
12:42 – 240n
15:17 – 235n
15:17–18 – 94
18:21,25 – 252n
19:2 – 251n
19:3 – 61
19:10–15 – 248n
19:16 – 246n
20:2 – 9
20:2–7 – 234n

21–22:16 – 225
23:20ff – 244n
24 – 13, 47
24:4 – 251n, 281n
24:12 – 229, 235n, 239n
24:12–18 – 45
25 – 43, 244n, 266n
25–30 – 13, 215
31:18 – 239n
34 – 13, 43–47, 62
34:1 – 6, 60, 92, 239n, 245n
34:1–9 – 44
34:2–4 – 238n
34:5–7 – 245n
34:8–9 – 245n
34:10 – 6, 21
34:10–16 – 43–44, 244n
34:18–20 – 56
34:22 – 163
34:29–32 – 238n
35 – 43, 244n
35–40 – 8, 215
36:9 – 242n
37 – 266n
39 – 266n
40:15 – 266n

Leviticus
3:17 – 246n
4:3, 5, 16 – 266n
6:2, 7, 18 – 238n
6:15 – 266n
7:8 – 163, 270n
7:26 – 246n
7:35–36 – 266n
9:17 – 246n
10:1–7 – 280n
10:7 – 266n
16 – 263n
16:6,11 – 263n
17:13 – 246n
18:12–14 – 267n
18:13 – 126, 184, 261n
19:17 – 256n
19:17–18 – 133
19:23–24 – 52
21:10–12 – 266n
21:12 – 209

21:17–24 – 251n
23 – 13, 54
23:9–21 – 55
23:15 – 59, 163
23:15–16 – 55
23:15–21 – 55
23:16 – 163
23:24 – 163
23:32 – 163
23:33–36 – 267n
23:38 – 50, 163, 246n, 267n
23:40 – 236n
26 – 20, 25
26:14–15 – 25
26:42 – 25–26, 240n
26:44–45 – 29
26:45 – 239n

Numbers
1:32–35 – 79
2 – 81, 251n
3:3 – 266n
6:13 – 266n
8:19 – 235n
20:3–5 – 5
21:18 – 108, 262n
24:14 – 240n
26:61 – 280n
27:19 – 113
27:21 – 113
28 – 55, 246n
28–29 – 13, 50, 54
28:2 – 163
28:4 – 162
28:9 – 50
28:9–10 – 49, 263n
28:26 – 56, 163
28:32 – 246n
29:6ff – 238n
29:7–11 – 263n
29:12–38 – 267n
29:16ff – 246n
30 – 15
30:3–10 – 16

Deuteronomy
1:5 – 275n

4:44–45 – 18
5:24–25 – 8
6:13–15 – 208
7 – 43, 44
7:1ff – 244n
7:5,25 – 244n
7:25–26 – 244n
11:1 – 234n
12:15–28 – 246n
12:23–24 – 246n
12:28–31 – 234n
13:4 – 234n
13:13–15 – 234n
14–22 – 232n
14:3 – 234n
14:22–26 – 234n
14:23 – 247n
15:23 – 246n
16:8 – 163
16:9 – 163
16:9–10 – 56
16:13–15 – 267n
16:18–20 – 246n
17:2 – 5
17:2–7 – 246n
17:8–11 – 19
17:11 – 162
17:11–20 – 3
17:14–18 – 17
17:14–20 – 20, 25, 26, 208, 222
17:16 – 5, 215
17:17 – 117, 124, 125, 126
21:5 – 6
21:13 – 85
21:15–17 – 237n
21:22–23 – 246n
22:23–24 – 246n
23 – 208
23:1 – 240n
23:4–7 – 240n
23:15 – 264n
26 – 263n
26:13–15 – 208, 279n
27–28 – 20
28 – 25
28:36 – 25
28:68 – 25, 215, 234n

31:29 – 240n
32:28 – 104
32:33 – 196
33 – 40
33:4 – 19

Joshua
5:11 – 270n
8:31–32 – 237n
8:31–34 – 238n
23:6 – 237n, 238n

Judges
2:10 – 117
3:26 – 239n

1 Samuel
24:7,11 – 266n
26:9,11,16,23 – 266n

2 Samuel
1:14,16 – 266n
19:22 – 266n

1 Kings
2:3 – 238n
2:26–27 – 259n
2:35 – 259n
6:2 – 65
7:21 – 249n
7:23 – 71, 249n, 250n
7:30 – 249n
7:31 – 250n
8:66 – 149
21:10–18 – 259n

2 Kings
14:6 – 238n
22 – 113, 124, 203, 259n
23:2,21 – 238n
25:17 – 249n

Isaiah
6:1–5 – 218
7:14 – 260n
24:17 – 110, 117, 119, 275n
30:26 – 243n, 280n

54 – 280n
60 – 280n
61:8 – 280n
65:17 – 280n
66:22 – 280n

Jeremiah
25:11–12 – 254n
25:12 – 179
31:31–34 – 280n
32:36–41 – 280n
35 – 168
52:21–23 – 249n

Ezekiel
1:4–28 – 220
4:5 – 179, 258n
4:6 – 258n
14:14 – 244n
22:26 – 263n
25:13 – 273n
29:9 – 273n
33:24, 27 – 273n
35:4 – 273n
36:33 – 273n
38–39 – 250n
38:8 – 273n
40–47 – 22
40–48 – 147, 215, 239n, 242n, 280n
40:1 – 180, 273n
40:5 – 249n
40:6–48 – 249n
43–44 – 116
43:1–4 – 249n
44 – 141, 155
44:1–4 – 249n
44:15 – 115, 118, 119, 136
45:19 – 249n
46:1–12 – 249n
46:19 – 249n
47:2 – 249n
48 – 281n
48:30–34 – 249n

Hosea
1:1 – 274n
4:16 – 273n

5:11 – 267n
10:12 – 228

Jonah
4:2 – 239n

Micah
7:11 – 256n

Habakkuk
1 – 190
1:1-2 – 187
1:1-5 – 186
1:2-5 – 198
1:4 – 275n
1:5 – 189
1:6-13 – 186
1:14-2:4 – 186
2:1-3 – 190
2:1-6 – 198
2:2 – 190
2:2-3 – 188
2:3 – 278n
2:4 – 275n
2:5-6 – 194
2:5-17 – 186, 190
2:7-8 – 191
2:18-20 – 186

Haggai
2:3 – 216
2:9 – 216

Malachi
1:10 – 130
3 – 227
3:23 – 145

Psalms
24:7,9 – 242n
118:19 – 242n
122 – 280n

Daniel
1-5 – 214
1:1 – 280n
2:1 – 280n

2:22 – 251n
6:8,13 – 239n
7-12 – 195
7:1 – 280n
7:12,25 – 239n
8:1 – 280n
8:10 – 251n
8:16 – 81
8:24 – 251n
9 – 90
9:1 – 280n
9:4 – 251n
9:21 – 81
9:22 – 251n
9:24 – 179, 258n
9:24-27 – 179, 254n
9:26 – 251n
9:27 – 279n
10:1 – 280n
10:13 – 251n
10:21 – 81
11:4 – 113, 114
11:14 – 178, 201, 202, 276n, 278n
11:28 – 251n
11:30 – 187, 193, 251n
11:31 – 279n
11:33 – 210, 251n
11:34 – 278n
11:40-12:13 – 251n
12:11 – 279n

Ezra
2:63 – 113, 114
6:3 – 65
10:3 – 238n

Nehemiah
2:11-20 – 280n
7:65 – 113
8:1 – 18
10 – 134, 174, 216
10:1 – 103
10:30 – 264n
10:32-40 – 264n
10:35 – 134, 215, 233n, 247n
12:11 – 270n
13:31 – 134, 215, 233n, 247n

1 Chronicles
5:38 – 113
5:38–39 – 259n
24:1–18 – 251n
25:9–31 – 251n
28:19 – 233n, 261n
29:29 – 245n

2 Chronicles
3–5 – 64
3:3 – 65
3:15–17 – 69
3:17 – 249n
4:1 – 68
4:2 – 71, 249n
4:6 – 249n
6:13 – 250n
7:10 – 149, 267n
9:29 – 245n
12:15 – 245n
16:11 – 245n
34 – 259n

II. Apocrypha and Pseudepigrapha

Assumption of Moses
1:17 – 261n

Ben Sira
prologue – 18
48:10 – 227
50:5–21 – 182–183
51:12 – 116, 141

Enoch
47:3 – 248n
72–73 – 39
72–82 – 34, 35, 59, 60, 98, 248n, 280n
72:1 – 57, 241n, 243n
72:8–14 – 36
73 – 57
73:3 – 242n
73:3–74:9 – 37
73:5 – 242n
74:10 – 242n
74:10–75:2 – 57–58
74:12 – 242n, 247n

76 – 39
76:3–77:4 – 35–36
76:14 – 242n
77:4,5,8 – 242n
78:4 – 242n
78:6–9 – 242n
81:1,2 – 248n
82:6 – 242n
93:3 – 248n
103:2 – 248n
106–108 – 243n
106:19 – 248n

Jubilees
prologue – 34
1 – 44–48, 61, 92, 94, 239n, 240n
1:1 – 56, 60, 62, 247n, 248n
1:4 – 56
1:4–29 – 124
1:5–18 – 245n
1:10 – 210
1:19–21 – 245n
1:22–26 – 245n
1:26 – 13, 245n
1:26–29 – 24, 245n
1:27 – 243n, 245n
1:29 – 24, 47, 81, 243n
2:1 – 243n
2:17–33 – 48
2:19 – 245n
2:22 – 48
2:24 – 48
2:25 – 245n
3:10 – 51
3:30–31 – 244n
3:31 – 51
4:5 – 248n
4:17 – 241n
4:20 – 42, 244n
4:25 – 245n
4:31–32 – 51
4:32 – 248n
5:22–30 – 268n
5:23–6:38 – 268n
5:27 – 268n
6 – 55–56, 81, 241n, 247n
6:1–18 – 247n

6:3 – 245n, 260n
6:4–14 – 246n
6:7–8 – 248n
6:7–14 – 260n
6:15–21 – 248n
6:17 – 248n
6:18–19 – 260n
6:20–38 – 53
6:21 – 247n, 255n
6:21–22 – 248n
6:21ff – 98
6:22–38 – 58
6:23–38 – 38, 241n
6:25–31 – 268n
6:27–38 – 153
6:29 – 248n
6:32–38 – 268n
6:35 – 60, 248n
7:20–21 – 246n, 260n
7:23–26 – 52,260n
7:36 – 52, 245n
14:20–15:34 – 247n
15:1–2 – 248n
15:25 – 246n
15:26 – 246n
16:9 – 246n
16:13 – 248n
16:23 – 245n
16:28–29 – 248n
18:19 – 248n
20:4–5 – 246n
21:10 – 248n
21:12–14 – 53
22:1 – 248n
23:16–31 – 244n
28:6 – 246n
29:10 – 243n
30:7–10 – 246n
30:15–16 – 110
30:21–22 – 110
31–32 – 28
31:1–2 – 248n
31:1–32:29 – 248n
32 – 48
32:10 – 248n
32:12 – 247n, 255n
32:15 – 248n
32:21 – 248n
32:27–28 – 248n

33:10–17 – 246n
34:2–9 – 243n
34:4 – 244n
34:18 – 248n
35:5–8 – 81
44:4 – 247n, 255n
49 – 40
49:8 – 248n
49:10–12 – 51
49:16–18 – 246n
49:17 – 51, 248n
49:20–21 – 246n
50:1–4 – 81
50:4 – 81, 274n
50:10–11 – 49
50:13 – 248n

1 Maccabees
1:11–15 – 276n
1:14–15 – 42–43
2:29–38 – 280n
2:58 – 227
4:46 – 114
7:16–17 – 271n
8:17 – 249n
14:27–45 – 271n

2 Maccabees
3:6 – 273n, 276n
3:6–7 – 280n
3:9–12 – 280n
3:10–12 – 273n, 276n
3:11 – 173
4:9–15 – 42
4:11 – 63, 280n
4:13 – 276n
4:23 – 271n

Testament of Asher
2:10 – 248n
7:5 – 248n

Testament of Levi
5:5 – 248n

III. New Testament

Matthew
1:23 – 260n

5:17 – 32
22:23 – 266n

Mark
12:18 – 266n

Luke
20:27 – 266n

Revelation
21:22–23 – 22

IV. Qumran

Astronomical Enoch
4QEnastr[b] 7:ii:1–8 – 34–35
4QEnastr[b] 7:iii:1–5 – 37, 241n
4QEnastr[b] 23 – 35
4QEnastr[c] 1:ii:1–10, 13–20 – 35

Blessings (1QSb)
3:22–23 – 139

Community Rule (1QS)
1:5–257n
1:11–12 – 252n
1:24–26 – 104
1:26 – 257n
2:5–18 – 266n
2:8 – 253n
2:21–22 – 252n
2:25 – 257n
3–4 – 266n
3:2 – 252n
3:5–6 – 85
3:6,8 – 253n
3:11 – 259n
3:20 – 139
3:21–22 – 139
4:2 – 257n
4:5 – 252n
4:7–14 – 266n
4:10 – 252n
4:14 – 275n
4:24 – 257n
5:1 – 252n
5:1–2 – 139
5:2–3 – 252n
5:4 – 257n

5:6 – 253n
5:8 – 259n
5:8–9 – 139
5:11 – 259n
5:13 – 252n
5:14 – 85
5:18 – 259n
5:19 – 259n
5:20 – 252n
6:2,17,22,25 – 252n
6:4–6 – 252n, 253n, 255n
6:7 – 254n
6:8 – 252n
6:16,22,25 – 252n
6:24 – 252n
7:3,16,25 – 252n
8:1–4 – 254n
8:2 – 257n
8:4–10 – 87
8:5 – 253n
8:5–6 – 252n
8:6 – 253n
8:8 – 87, 252n
8:10 – 253n
8:15 – 103
8:16 – 259n
8:17 – 252n
8:20 – 102, 252n
8:21 – 257n
8:23 – 252n
8:24 – 252n
9:3–5 – 87
9:4 – 253n
9:5–7 – 253n
9:6 – 252n
9:6–7 – 95
9:7–9 – 252n
9:10 – 84, 245n
9:11 – 266n
9:12 – 252n
9:14 – 264n
9:17 – 257n
9:21 – 252n
10:1 – 252n
10:2 – 252n
10:3 – 252n
10:3–8 – 89
10:4 – 252n
10:6 – 252n

10:7–8 – 252n
10:8 – 86
10:10 – 259n
10:13 – 104
11:14 – 253n

Copper Scroll (3Q15)
1:1–4 – 94
5:6,8 – 99
11:2–7 – 100, 112, 173, 217
11:9 – 256n

Damascus Document (CD)
1–4:6a – 257n
1–8 – 101–105, 108, 109, 111, 112, 134, 135,
    137, 138, 139, 179, 180, 183, 186, 188, 192,
    193, 194, 219, 231n, 257n, 259n
1:1 – 262n
1:1–10 – 176, 177, 178–179
1:1–11 – 178
1:1–12 – 103, 108
1:1–2:1 – 105–108, 115
1:1–4:12 – 257n
1:1–7:19 – 135
1:3–6 – 104
1:4 – 257n, 259n
1:4–9 – 114
1:5 – 108
1:5–6 – 104, 119, 180, 245n
1:6 – 258n
1:7 – 108, 109, 119, 259n
1:9 – 118
1:9–10 – 260n
1:10 – 257n
1:11 – 108, 109, 186, 197, 258n, 259n, 260n
1:12 – 256n, 273n
1:13 – 273n
1:14 – 182, 259n, 273n
1:14–15 – 110
1:14–18 – 182–183, 260n
1:15 – 127
1:16 – 257n
2:1 – 115, 256n
2:2–13 – 105–107, 115
2:2–14 – 115
2:5 – 262n
2:6 – 128
2:7–14 – 260n

2:10 – 273n
2:12 – 109
2:13 – 109, 260n
2:14 – 115
2:14–3:12 – 115
2:14–4:12 – 105–107, 260n
2:14–6:1 – 258n
2:17 – 257n, 278n
2:18 – 280n
3:5 – 280n
3:9 – 256n
3:10 – 257n, 259n
3:12 – 264n, 280n
3:12–4:12 – 115
3:14 – 263n
3:14–15 – 264n
3:19 – 109
3:20 – 264n
3:21 – 136
3:21–4:4 – 260n
3:21–5:12 – 136
4–5 – 165
4–8 – 194
4:1 – 129
4:1–9 – 116
4:2 – 262n
4:2–12 – 116
4:4 – 114, 259n, 273n
4:6 – 257n, 258n
4:8 – 257n, 258n, 273n
4:9 – 109, 257n, 273n
4:9–12 – 260n
4:10–11 – 109
4:10–12 – 258n
4:11–12 – 256n
4:12 – 109, 110, 116, 273n
4:12–13 – 118
4:12–6:11 – 105
4:12–8:21 – 119
4:13 – 110
4:13–5:6 – 203
4:14 – 110, 200, 275n
4:14–5:11 – 183
4:16 – 273n
4:16–17 – 129, 191
4:17 – 103
4:19 – 110, 267n
4:19–5:11 – 97

4:20–21 – 120, 125
4:20–5:11 – 133
4:21 – 117, 152
4:21–5:2 – 117
4:21–5:5 – 125
5:1 – 184
5:1–2 – 237n
5:1–5 – 124, 150, 160, 267n
5:2 – 261n
5:2–3 – 126, 262n
5:2–4 – 117
5:2–5 – 127, 239n
5:2–7 – 112
5:4 – 99, 116
5:4–5 – 117
5:5 – 102, 112, 113, 114, 118, 119, 129, 139,
    153, 181, 203, 219, 259n, 261n, 273n
5:6–7 – 121
5:6–11 – 126
5:7 – 122
5:7–8 – 120, 126
5:7–11 – 151
5:8 – 184
5:8–9 – 126
5:8–11 – 150–151
5:12 – 127
5:15–21 – 127
5:17 – 104, 259n
5:18 – 252n
5:18–19 – 183
5:20 – 259n
5:20–21 – 127–128
6:1–2 – 262n
6:1–8 – 262n
6:1–11 – 105, 128, 257n
6:1–7:9 – 105
6:2 – 257n, 259n
6:3–4 – 262n
6:4 – 109
6:5 – 104, 262n
6:6 – 110
6:10 – 114, 259n, 273n
6:10–11 – 262n
6:11 – 108, 110, 258n, 273n
6:11–14 – 129–130
6:11–7:6 – 181
6:11 – 7:9 – 259n
6:12–14 – 210

6:12–20 – 264n
6:12–7:3 – 264n
6:14 – 273n
6:14–16 – 130
6:15–17 – 121
6:16–17 – 273n
6:17 – 122
6:17–18 – 123
6:18 – 124, 263n
6:18–19 – 131
6:19 – 104, 124, 132, 259n
6:20 – 124, 132
6:20–7:1 – 132
6:21 – 121
6:23 – 104
7:1 – 120, 133
7:1–2 – 120
7:2 – 133, 256n
7:3 – 122
7:3–6 – 133
7:4–6 – 135
7:6–6a – 263n
7:6a–9 – 134
7:9–8:21 – 259n
7:13 – 264n
7:15–16 – 256n
7:18 – 110
7:19 – 110
7:20 – 110, 256n, 259n
7:20–21 – 114
7:21 – 110, 257n, 258n
8 – 259n
8:5 – 120
8:6 – 120
8:8 – 280n
8:11–12 – 276n
8:13 – 256n
8:16 – 111
8:17 – 257n
8:19 – 280n
8:21 – 259n
9–14 – 102, 105, 111, 204, 245n
9–16 – 111, 231n
10:14 – 48
11:17–18 – 49, 50, 152, 246n
11:18 – 50, 267n
12:23 – 259n, 266n
12:23–13:1 – 266n

13:16 – 103
14:4,6 – 263n
15-16 – 105, 111
16:2-4 – 260n
16:3-4 – 243n
19 – 259n
19-20 – 111
19:1-2 – 133
19:2-5 – 134
19:10 – 266n
19:13 – 264n
19:20 – 280n
19:33 – 280n
19:34 – 111, 259n
19:35-20:1 – 103, 137, 138
20 – 110, 139, 193, 259n, 264n
20:1 – 257n, 259n, 266n
20:1-31 – 101-104
20:1c-8a – 256n
20:3-13 – 266n
20:5 – 259n
20:8-9 – 245n
20:10 – 280n
20:11 – 108
20:12 – 259n
20:13-15 – 137, 138
20:13c-17a – 256n
20:14 – 185, 187
20:14-15 – 138, 200, 211
20:15 – 108, 179, 257n, 274n
20:20-21 – 263n
20:25 – 201
20:25-27 – 256n, 266n

Florilegium (4QFlor). *See* Misc. Qumranic Texts:
    DJD V

Genesis Apocryphon (1QapGen)
2 – 243n
20:8 – 280n

Messianic Rule (1QSa)
1:1 – 252n
1:1-2 – 139
1:6 – 252n
1:8-10 – 252n
1:9,15,21 – 257n
1:24 – 139

2:2-3 – 139
2:9 – 257n
2:17-20 – 252n, 253n, 255n

"New Jerusalem" (*DJD* III)
Fragments cited on pp. 95-96, 249n

Patriarchal Blessings (4QPBless)
3 – 137
3-6 – 92-93

Pesher Habakkuk (1QpHab)
1:1-2:10 – 186
1:3 – 187
1:13 – 136, 254n
2:1-2 – 136
2:1-10 – 189
2:6-10 – 277n
2:10-6:12 – 186, 193
2:12,14 – 254n, 274n
3:4,9 – 254n, 274n
4:5,10 – 254n, 274n
5:9-11 – 136
6:1,10 – 274n
6:12-7:14 – 190, 275n
6:12-8:3 – 186
7:4-5 – 136
7:5-8 – 278n
7:7 – 192
7:9-14 – 275n
7:12 – 191, 192
8:1-3 – 136-137
8:3-12:10 – 186, 191, 275n
8:8-9 – 194, 275n
8:9 – 259n, 274n
8:9-11 – 194
8:10 – 280n
8:12 – 194
9:4-7 – 191
9:7 – 274n
9:8 – 277n
9:8-12 – 264n
9:9-10 – 137, 254n, 276n
9:10-12 – 276n
10:9-13 – 276n
11:2-8 – 254n
11:2-12:10 – 254n
11:4-6 – 137

11:4-8 – 192, 263n, 276n
11:7 – 197
11:13 – 280n
12:1 – 277n
12:10ff – 186

Pesher on Micah (1Q14)
8-10:6 – 138
10:5 – 137

Pesher Nahum (4QpNah)
1:2 – 254n
1:3 – 254n
1:4-8 – 232n
2:9 – 263n
3:3 – 91

Pesher on Psalm 37 (4Q171).
   See Misc. Qumranic Texts: *DJD* V

Qumranic Torah (11QTorah)
1-2 – 22, 60, 92
1-13 – 15
2 – 13, 21, 29
2-12 – 21
2-52 – 17
2:1 – 4, 6
2:1-15 – 42-44
2:10-11 – 263n
3 – 29, 48, 75
3-13 – 1, 13, 215
3-29 – 22
3:2 – 95, 244n, 251n
3:3 – 80
3:4 – 9, 27, 47, 244n
3:4-8 – 6
3:5 – 95, 266n
3:5-6 – 244n-245n
3:8 – 95, 266n
3:9,12 – 266n
3:15 – 68
4-6 – 14, 75
4:1-13:8 – 232n
4:4-5 – 236n
4:5-6 – 66
4:7-10 – 65-67
5:5 – 242n
5:8 – 243n

5:8-11 – 67-68, 75
5:13 – 236n, 249n
6:3 – 242n
6:6 – 243n
7:13 – 266n
8:6 – 249n
8:8-11 – 123, 263n
9 – 75
11:11 – 247n
12 – 76
12:7-16 – 69
12:8-13 – 68-69
12:9 – 255n
12:11 – 14
12:15 – 249n
13 – 18, 75
13-14 – 124
13-29 – 1, 13, 15, 21, 54, 237n, 251n
13:1-7 – 69-70, 255n
13:2,5 – 249n
13:8-29:6 – 232n
13:13-14 – 163, 270n
13:17 – 50
13:17ff – 131
13:17-14:1 – 263n
14 – 246n
14:1 – 131
14:7 – 245n
14:9 – 54
14:10-11 – 49
14:10-15:1 – 247n
14:13 – 49
16-17 – 236n
16:5 – 10, 123
16:10 – 49
16:10-12 – 121
16:12 – 133, 263n
16:13 – 245n
17:2 – 235n
17:2-4 – 9-10
17:4 – 235n
17:6 – 234n
17:6-29:2 – 124
17:7 – 50-51
17:8 – 51, 252n
17:8-9 – 50
17:10 – 245n
17:12 – 235n

18–23 – 52
18–25 – 85, 263n
18:10 – 55
18:10–13 – 270n
18:10–22:16 – 264n
18:13 – 235n
18:14–16 – 242n
19–21 – 236n
19:3 – 242n
19:9 – 56
19:11 – 55, 235n
19:13 – 55
19:14–16 – 242n
19:16 – 250n
20:8 – 245n
21:1–3 – 242n
21:2 – 250n
21:4–7 – 80
21:5 – 250n
21:8 – 235n
21:8–9 – 10
21:9 – 235n
21:12 – 55, 235n
21:14 – 235n
21:14–16 – 242n
22–23 – 236n
22:2 – 250n
22:12 – 250n
22:12–13 – 242n
22:14 – 235n
22:15 – 235n
22:16 – 235n
23–25:1 – 236n
23–35 – 215
23:1–25:1 – 53, 233n, 264n
23:7 – 242n
23:9–24:16 – 251n
23:10 – 250n
24:9 – 235n
24:10–16 – 242n
25:1–10 – 247n
25:4 – 234n
25:9 – 12, 235n
25:10–27:10 – 124
25:13–14 – 49
25:14,16 – 263n
26:6 – 266n

26:7 – 10
27:5 – 235n
27:5–6 – 49, 123
27:8 – 235n
27:8–9 – 10, 123, 131
27:9 – 235n
28:6 – 245n
29 – 13, 18, 48, 94, 240n
29:2 – 234n
29:2–10 – 27
29:3 – 238n
29:3–4 – 4
29:3–10 – 21–23
29:4 – 239n
29:6 – 4, 263n
29:7 – 238n
29:7–10 – 239n
29:8 – 238n
29:8–10 – 30, 47
29:9–10 – 79, 94, 243n
29:10 – 21, 28, 48, 61, 92
30–35 – 14
30–42 – 215
30–43 – 21
30–46 – 1, 15, 36
30:3–31:9 – 243n
30:3–35:15 – 232n
30:7 – 242n, 249n
31:4 – 250n, 251n
31:4–5 – 235n
31:6–7 – 243n
31:8 – 95, 266n
31:9 – 4, 8
31:10 – 242n, 249n
31:10–13 – 70–71
31:10–33:7 – 249n
31:13 – 242n
31:14 – 242n
31 – 76
32:6 – 10
32:10 – 266n
32:12 – 249n
32:12–15 – 7
32:13–15 – 52
32:14–15 – 11
33:9 – 242n
34 – 76

34:2-6 – 72–74
34:4 – 255n
34:5 – 255n
34:5-8 – 52
34:9 – 255n
34:14 – 245n
34:15 – 72–74, 249n
35 – 76, 87
35:6-7 – 246n
35:8-9 – 10, 14, 70, 72–74, 85, 133, 236n
35:9-10 – 236n
35:10 – 249n
35:10-14 – 121
35:10-15 – 73, 74, 235n, 236n
35:11 – 263n
35:11-13 – 10, 133
35:13-14 – 131
36 – 75, 249n
36-44 – 241n
36-45 – 14
36:1-38:10 – 236n
36:5 – 242n
36:7 – 251n
36:8 – 242n
36:8-10 – 243n
36:9 – 242n
36:10 – 242n
36:10-11 – 95
36:11 – 266n
37:6 – 236n
37:8-12 – 235n
37:9 – 236n
37:11-12 – 11
38:4 – 247n, 264n
38:12 – 249n
38:15 – 242n
39:3 – 266n
39:7 – 251n
39:8-9 – 95
39:10-11 – 5
39:10-16 – 251n
39:11 – 252n
39:11-13 – 39, 251n
39:11-16 – 236n, 249n
39:15-16 – 242n
40:5 – 249n
40:5-45:1 – 249n

40:6 – 251n, 263n
40:9 – 242n
40:11-12 – 39
40:11-42:6 – 236n, 249n
40:12 – 242n
40:12-41:17 – 251n
41:12 – 242n
41:14 – 242n
41:15 – 242n
41:16 – 266n, 278n
42:8-9 – 236n
42:14 – 250n
42:15 – 250n, 252n
42:16 – 239n
43 – 124, 132, 247n, 263n
43:2-17 – 121, 131, 264n
43:3-5 – 132
43:5-12 – 247n
43:6-9 – 252n
44:1-45:2 – 249n
44:5 – 8
44:14 – 250n
45:4 – 122
45:4-7 – 10
45:7-12 – 251n
45:10 – 5
45:10-12 – 237n
45:11-12 – 280n
45:11-14 – 122–123
45:12 – 5
45:12-13 – 251n
45:12-14 – 10, 238n
45:14 – 5
45:15-18 – 237n
46 – 76
46-48 – 236n
46-66 – 236n
46:1-3 – 74–75
46:3-4 – 5
46:4 – 238n
46:5 – 236n, 280n
46:6 – 242n
46:6-8 – 6
46:7-8 – 5
46:9 – 236n, 280n
46:9-10 – 11
46:9-12 – 7

46:10 – 263n
46:13–16 – 7, 280n
46:16 – 236n
46:16–18 – 122
46:17 – 263n
47–52 – 1
47–54 – 15
47:3–4 – 5, 131
47:3–7 – 11, 123
47:3–18 – 245n
47:4 – 238n
47:7–8 – 215, 280n
47:9 – 5
47:11 – 5, 238n
47:12–13 – 5
47:15–16 – 5
47:17–18 – 5
47:18 – 238n
48 – 236n
48–66 – 232n
48:6 – 234n
48:11–15 – 237n
48:13 – 263n
48:14–17 – 122
48:16 – 246n
50:5–7 – 18
50:17 – 19
50:17–19 – 11, 123
51:5–10 – 123
51:6–7 – 7, 8
51:6–8 – 10, 19, 123
51:7 – 238n, 240n
51:8 – 235n
51:8–9 – 131
51:8–10 – 11,133
51:11–15 – 235n
51:16 – 235n
51:16–18 – 246n
51:19–21 – 234n
52–66 – 1
52:7 – 15
52:7–9 – 124, 132
52:9 – 9
52:10 – 5
52:11–12 – 52, 237n, 260n
52:14–15 – 5
52:16 – 5, 9, 235n
52:18 – 236n, 279n, 280n

52:19–21 – 7
53–55 – 236n
53–66 – 17
53:5 – 237n
53:5–6 – 52
53:9 – 238n
53:9–54:7 – 121, 263n
53:14 – 16
53:14–21 – 5
54–56 – 236n
54–66 – 15
54:4 – 16, 237n, 267n
54:8–18 – 237n
55:6–11 – 121, 263n
55:15–17 – 5
55:15–21 – 234n, 246n
56 – 236n
56–59 – 232n
56–60 – 80, 209, 236n
56:1–9 – 19
56:1–11 – 238n
56:3–4 – 19
56:4–5 – 9
56:5 – 238n
56:12–21 – 17
56:12–60:12 – 209, 232n, 279n
56:12–60:15 – 238n
56:16 – 215
56:16–18 – 25
56:17–18 – 5
56:18 – 16, 120, 125, 126, 237n
56:18–57:18 – 125
56:20–21 – 20
57–58 – 17
57–60 – 31
57:1 – 20
57:2–3 – 250n
57:3 – 252n
57:4–5 – 250n, 252n
57:5–11 – 209
57:11–15 – 80
57:12 – 250n
57:13–14 – 238n
57:14 – 20
57:17–18 – 120, 125
57:17–19 – 237n
57:20–21 – 121, 131
58:4 – 250n, 252n

58:11 – 250n
58:17 – 251n
58:17–18 – 152
59 – 13, 20, 24–27, 48
59:1–21 – 266n
59:7–13 – 20
59:9 – 239n
59:11–13 – 239n
59:12 – 235n
59:12–13 – 12
59:13 – 94
59:15 – 251n
60 – 14, 17
60:2–4 – 247n
60:3–4 – 52
60:5 – 121, 232n, 263n
60:6 – 264n
60:6–7 – 247n
60:6–8 – 246n
60:6–9 – 124
60:8 – 232n
60:10–11 – 6
60:12–14 – 11–12
60:12–66 – 15
60:13 – 238
60:16 – 234n
61:1–15 – 238n
61:2–5 – 237n
61:11–12 – 51
61:12 – 164
61:12–15 – 234n
62:13–15 – 121, 263n
63:3 – 6
63:5 – 235n
63:10–15 – 15
63:14–15 – 85
64:04–1 – 237n
64:6–9 – 237n
64:6–13 – 15
64:7–9 – 246n
64:8–13 – 277n
64:9–13 – 246n
66:1–3 – 246n
66:11–12 – 246n
66:11–14 – 120
66:12 – 240n
66:15–17 – 120, 151
66:16–17 – 126

66:17 – 267n
67 – 152, 153

Sayings of Moses (1Q22)
2:5 – 274n

Testimonia (4Q175)
See Misc. Qumranic Texts: *DJD* V

Thanksgivings (1QH)
1:30 – 257n
2:31–32 – 88, 253n
4:7–16 – 253n
4:38 – 88, 253n
4:40 – 257n
5:9–12 – 88
6:4–5 – 253n
6:17–18 – 253n
6:19 – 253n
6:19–22 – 253n
6:25–30 – 253n
7:10 – 257n
7:10–12 – 253n
8:4–20 – 253n
9:14 – 274n
9:17–18 – 253n
9:35 – 253n
10:24 – 255n
10:27 – 253n
11:30–31 – 257n
13:5–6 – 253n
14 – 253n
14:12 – 253n
14:15 – 257n
14:18 – 253n
14:18–21 – 253n
14:25–26 – 253n
15:14–17 – 253n
15:15–21 – 253n
16 – 253n
17 – 253n

War Scroll (1QM)
1:2 – 250n
1:8–9 – 81
1:9 – 79
1:17–2:2 – 81
1:17–2:3 – 80

2:1 – 250n, 251n
2:2 – 251n
2:3 – 79, 251n
2:5–6 – 80, 251n
2:6–14 – 251n, 274n
2:7 – 251n
2:14 – 257n
3:1 – 79, 251n
3:4 – 257n
3:7 – 79, 251n
3:13 – 81
3:13–14 – 251n
3:15–18 – 250n
3:16 – 257n
4:1–5 – 250n
4:9–10 – 251n
4:10 – 257n
4:13 – 79
5:1–2 – 251n
6:10 – 251n
7:1–2 – 250n
7:3 – 251n
7:4 – 251n
7:6 – 79
7:9 – 79, 251n
7:10 – 79
7:16 – 79, 251n
9:15–16 – 81
10:10 – 251n
10:11 – 251n
10:14 – 257n
11:8 – 251n
12:7 – 251n
13:11–12 – 82
14:4 – 251n
17:5–7 – 251n
17:6–9 – 81
17:7–8 – 79

Miscellaneous Qumranic Texts

a) Biblical Manuscripts
    1QIsa[a] – 9, 205, 232n
    4QDeut[a] – 205
    11QtgJob – 214
b) *DJD* V
    4Q159 – 255n
    4Q169 – 277n
    4Q171 (*Pesher on Ps. 37*)
        2:2–3 – 91–92

2:7–8 – 274n
3:15–19 – 137, 138
4:7–9 – 91
4:9–15 – 254n
4Q174 (*Florilegium*) – 253n, 255n
    1:1–13 – 93–94
    1:4 – 264n
    1:11–13 – 259n
    1:17 – 139
4Q175 (*Testimonia*)
    24 – 259n
4Q177
    1:5 – 92
    1:10–11 – 92
    1:12–16 – 92
c) 4QMess ar (*Aramaic Messianic Text*)
    1:5 – 243n

V. RABBINIC LITERATURE

Mishnah

Berakot
1:1 – 246n

Maaser Sheni
5:1–2 – 246n
5:4 – 246n
5:15 – 208

Pesahim
5:1 – 50
10:9 – 51

Shekalim
3:1,3 – 162

Yoma
1:1–7 – 165
6:4 – 236n

Sukkah
4:9 – 162
5:1 – 236

Rosh ha-Shanah
2:1 – 159, 164

Taanith
4:4–5 – 233n, 247n

Megillah
1:3 – 247n

Sotah
9:10 – 208, 279n

Baba Kamma
7:7 – 236n

Sanhedrin
10:1 – 266n, 270n

Abot
1 – 142
1:1–4 – 174
1:2 – 174
1:3 – 142, 175, 176, 264n
1:4 – 174, 266n
5:5 – 75

Zebahim
5:8 – 50

Menahot
10:3 – 163
11:3 – 164

Tamid
7:4 – 243n

Middot
4:6 – 75

Yadaim
4:6–7 – 164–166

Tosefta

Pesahim
5:13 – 246n

Sukkah
3:6 – 269n

Rosh ha-Shanah
1:15 – 269n

Negaim
6:2 – 280n

Babylonian Talmud

Berakot
9a – 246n

Shabbat
108a – 270n
116b – 240n

Yoma
69a – 271n

Sukkah
48b – 269n

Rosh ha-Shanah
22b – 269n

Kiddushin
66a – 279n

Sanhedrin
90b – 266n

Menahot
65a – 162
65a-b – 163

Midrash

Genesis Rabbah
65:22 – 271n
69:7 – 242n

Midrash Samuel
15:3 – 233n

Targum

Targum Onkelos on Gen 40:8 – 254n

Miscellaneous Rabbinic Texts

Abot de-Rabbi Nathan, Version A
5 – 141–148, 150, 153, 264n, 265n, 267n

Abot de-Rabbi Nathan, Version B
10 – 142, 143, 153, 264n, 265n, 266n, 272n

Megillat Taanit
1 – 162–163
4 – 162, 164, 165
10 – 161, 165

Seder Olam
28–30 – 272n
30 – 271n

VI. Classical Authors

Eusebius

Preparatio Evangelica (PE)
9,30,1–9,34,18 – 75
9,30,8 – 250n
9,34,4–16 – 63–77, 249n

Josephus

Against Apion (CA)
1:198 – 249n

Jewish Antiquities (AJ)
11:302 – 171
11:326–39 – 271n
11:347 – 171, 271n
11:347–12:246 – 270n
12:138–144 – 276n
12:138–146 – 214
12:141 – 280n
12:154 – 271n
12:154–236 – 276n
12:156 – 277n
12:157–179 – 172

12:160 – 184
12:186 – 271n
12:186–189 – 273n
12:224 – 172, 173, 271n
12:229 – 271n
12:237 – 271n
13:121–23 – 277n
13:187–189 – 279n
13:288–98 – 277n
13:301 – 279n
13:372 – 269n
15:320 – 264n
18:4 – 220
18:10 – 220
18:19 – 130

Jewish War (BJ)
2:123, 133 – 279n
2:136 – 231n
2:137 – 252n
2:142 – 231n, 252n
2:159 – 231n
5:224 – 250n

VII. Miscellaneous Texts

al-Qirqisani

Kitāb al-Anwār wal-Marāqib
I,11 (I.2.7) – 148–154, 267n, 268n, 270n
I,11–12 (I.2.8) – 148–149
I,41 (I.6) – 149, 152–153, 267n, 268n
I,41–42 (I.7) – 149, 153–154, 268n

Suda
167–168

Modern Authors

Abrahams, I., 234n, 241n
Ackroyd, P. R., 237n
Albeck, C., 245n, 246n, 248n, 265n, 271n, 278n
Albright, W. F., 272n
Allegro, J. M., 254n, 255n, 264n, 277n
Ankori, Z., 269n
Assis, M., 267n
Atkinson, K. M. T., 274n
Avigad, N., 205, 231n
Aviram, J., 231n
Bacher, W., 267n
Baillet, M., 40, 101, 238n, 243n
Bammel, E., 265n
Baneth, E., 265n
Barth, L. M., 271n
Bartholemy, D., 248n
Baumgarten, J., 166, 231n, 232n, 233n, 237n, 238n, 239n, 247n, 248n, 253n, 260n, 262n, 264n
Beckwith, R. T., 242n
Beer, M., 255n
Ben-Sasson, H. H., 233n
Betz, O., 254n, 260n
Bickerman(n), E., 212, 271n, 272n, 276n, 279n
Black, M., 272n
Bowden, J., S., 234n
Brichto, H. C., 235n
Brin, G., 235n
Brown, R. E., 266n
Brownlee, W. H., 186, 254n, 264n, 274n, 275n, 276n, 277n
Brox, N., 233n
Broyde, I., 271n
Bruce, F. F., 108, 179, 250n, 251n, 257n, 258n, 272n, 274n
Büchler, A., 168, 172, 271n
Buchanan, G. W., 276n
Burrows, M., 84, 231n, 239n, 257n, 260n, 266n, 274n
Busink, T. A., 249n
Caquot, A., 231n, 232n
Carmignac, J., 176, 197, 198, 199, 250n, 252n, 253n, 256n, 264n, 272n, 274n, 275n, 276n, 277n
Cassuto, U., 234n, 241n
Cazelles, H., 240n

Charles, R. H., 24, 41, 42, 44, 60, 78, 239n, 240n, 241n, 243n, 244n, 245n, 246n, 247n, 248n
Childs, B. S., 234n
Clements, R. E., 234n
Collins, J. J., 251n
Cothenet, E., 115–116, 256n, 257n, 258n, 259n, 260n, 261n, 262n, 263n
Cowley, A. E., 241n
Cross, F. M., 177, 197, 199, 205, 206, 239n, 248n, 252n, 253n, 261n, 264n, 266n, 272n, 274n, 276n, 277n, 278n, 279n, 280n
Dalbert, P., 248n
Davenport, G. L., 245n
Davies, P. R., 250n, 251n
Delcor, M., 231n, 232n, 253n, 272n, 274n
Denis, A. M., 243n, 248n, 257n, 258n
Derenbourg, J., 265n, 270n
Dillman, A., 243n
Dion, P. E., 232n
Driver, G. R., 176, 270n, 271n
Dupont-Sommer, A., 86, 99, 112, 176, 208, 231n, 237n, 250n, 252n, 257n, 258n, 259n, 260n, 261n, 262n, 264n, 272n, 274n, 275n, 276n, 277n, 279n
Eddy, S. E., 279n
Eissfeldt, O., 237n, 280n
Elliger, K., 272n, 275n, 276n
Emerton, J., 232n
Eppel, R., 248n
Epstein, A., 243n
Ettinger, S., 233n
Falk, Z. W., 233n
Feldman, L., 253n, 262n
Finkel, A., 254n
Finkelstein, L., 245n, 246n, 265n, 266n, 271n
Fiorenza, E., 255n
Fitzmyer, J. A., 231n, 237n, 243n, 247n, 256n, 260n, 261n, 266n, 277n, 280n
Flusser, D., 93, 232n, 253n, 255n
Ford, J. Massyngberde, 237n
Freedman, D. N., 231n, 237n
Freudenthal, J., 64, 76, 248n, 249n, 250n
Fritz, K. von, 233n
Fujita, S., 239n, 258n
Garcia, F., 231n
Garner, G., 232n

Gärtner, B., 239n
Geiger, A., 141, 156, 168, 268n
Genachowski, D., 279n
Ginzberg, L., 112, 125, 152, 231n, 246n, 256n, 258n, 259n, 260n, 261n, 262n, 264n, 267n
Goldin, J., 265n
Goldstein, J. A., 280n
Grätz, H., 265n, 268n, 270n
Gray, G. B., 235n
Green, W. S., 232n
Greenfield, J. C., 231n, 241n
Guilbert, P., 252n, 253n
Guttman, A., 265n, 271n, 280n
Habermann, A. M., 187, 243n, 246n, 252n, 262n, 274n
Hahn, S., 272n
Halperin, D. J., 232n
Haran, M., 233n
Harkavy, A., 156, 159, 168, 268n, 269n
Harrelson, W. J., 237n
Harvey, W., 233n
Heller, J., 268n
Hengel, M., 212, 248n, 249n, 270n, 271n, 272n, 276n
Herr, M. D., 271n
Hill, D., 264n
Hirsch, S. R., 237n, 238n
Hirschfeld, H., 156, 157, 268n
Hoenig, S. B., 267n, 270n, 271n
Holdheim, S., 156, 268n
Holm-Nielsen, S., 253n
Horgan, M. P., 254n, 274n, 277n
Hyatt, J. P., 234n
Iwry, S., 262n
Jacoby, F., 249n
Jaubert, A., 157, 247n, 248n, 268n
Jeremias, G., 253n, 261n, 272n
Jongeling, B., 232n
Kahle, P., 267n, 268n
Kampen, J., 232n, 277n
Kittel, B. P., 253n
Klausner, J., 266n
Klinzing, G., 253n
Knibb, M. A., 240n, 248n, 272n, 273n
Kohler, K., 265n
Kosmala, H., 258n, 261n
Kuhn, K. G., 99, 255n, 256n, 259n, 266n

Kutscher, E. Y., 9, 235n, 278n
Lapide, P. E., 232n, 233n, 261n
Lapperrousaz, E. M., 232n
LaSor, W. S., 266n
Le Moyne, J., 264n, 265n, 266n
Leaney, A. R. C., 252n, 253n
Lehmann, M. R., 95, 231n, 233n, 255n
Leiman, S. Z., 233n, 237n, 246n, 250n
Levine, B. A., 204, 232n, 235n, 237n, 247n
Levy, I., 237n, 268n
Licht, J., 252n, 253n, 258n, 273n
Lichtenstein, H., 269n, 270n
Lieberman, S., 269n
Lindars, B., 237n
Liver, J., 116, 141–142, 255n, 264n
Lohse, E., 248n, 252n, 262n, 264n, 274n, 276n
Love, J., 214–215
Luria, B. Z., 210, 231n, 233n, 269n, 270n, 278n
McKelvey, R. J., 239n
McNicol, A. J., 255n
Maier, J., 22, 23, 30, 231n, 232n, 233n, 234n, 239n, 240n, 244n, 249n, 252n, 256n, 258n, 259n, 260n, 262n, 275n
Mann, C. S., 272n
Manson, T. W., 265n
Mansoor, M., 253n
Mantel, H. D., 265n, 271n
Marcus, R., 271n, 276n, 280n
Marks, J. H., 241n
Martinez, F. G., 232n
Mazar, B., 271n, 276n
Meeks, W. A., 240n
Mendels, D., 232n, 279n
Meyer, E., 181, 184, 192, 201–202, 212, 265n, 272n, 273n, 279n
Meyer, R., 265n, 271n
Milgrom, J., 9, 23, 30, 214, 224, 231n, 232n, 233n, 234n, 235n, 236n, 237n, 238n, 244n, 245n, 247n, 281n
Milik, J., 34, 35, 39–40, 56, 100, 101, 105, 165, 192, 231n, 243n, 247n, 248n, 255n, 256n, 259n, 264n, 272n, 274n, 277n, 278n, 279n, 280n
Mink, H. A., 232n
Mishar, M., 232n
Monsengwo Pasinya, L., 237n

Moore, G. F., 265n, 266n, 271n
Morkholm, O., 276n
Mras, K., 249n
Mueller, J. R., 237n, 261n
Muilenberg, J., 206
Murphy-O'Connor, J., 256n, 257n, 258n,
   259n, 261n, 262n, 272n, 273n, 275n
Nemoy, L., 156, 267n, 268n
Neusner, J., 271n
Nickelsburg, G. W. E.,244n, 245n, 266n, 272n
Nolland, J., 262n
North, R., 264n
Noth, M. 234n
Osswald, E., 275n
Osten-Sacken, P. von der, 245n, 251n
Patte, D., 245n, 254n
Paul, S. M., 248n
Philips, A., 238n
Pinsker, S., 269n
Ploeg, J. van der, 250n
Pouilly, J., 252n
Poznanski, S., 156, 157, 268n, 269n
Qimron, E., 9, 207, 232n, 235n, 238n, 263n
Rabin, C., 101, 125, 152, 184, 231n, 246n,
   256n, 258n, 259n, 260n, 261n, 262n,
   264n, 267n, 268n, 273n
Rabinowitz, I., 254n, 262n, 272n, 275n
Rabinowitz, L. I., 233n
Rivkin, E., 271n
Rönsch, H., 245n
Rosenberg, R. A., 261n
Rossi, A. de, 268n
Roth, C., 176, 271n, 272n
Rowley, H. H., 272n, 274n, 277n
Sachau, E., 241n, 269n
Safrai, S., 226, 270n, 281n
Saldarini, A. J., 265n, 271n
Sanders, E. P., 235n, 253n
Sanders, J. A., 231n, 233n, 237n
Schechter, S., 1, 99, 101, 112, 115, 152, 246n,
   258n, 259n, 260n, 261n, 262n, 263n,
   264n, 265n, 266n, 267n
Schiffman, L. H., 152, 204, 207, 210, 232n,
   238n, 246n, 254n, 260n, 262n, 278n
Schoeps, H. J., 259n
Schultz, P., 253n
Schürer, E., 265n, 266n, 268n, 270n, 271n,
   277n, 279n, 280n

Schwarz, D. R., 255n
Schwarz, O. J. R., 257n
Segal, M. H., 272n, 274n, 278n
Siegel, J. P., 235n
Silberman, L. H., 254n, 275n, 276n
Speiser, E. A., 241n
Starcky, J., 243n
Stegemann, H., 256n, 257n, 272n, 273n
Stendahl, K., 275n
Stern, M., 265n, 271n, 276n
Stone, M. E., 241n
Strugnell, J., 205–206, 231n, 235n, 237n,
   238n, 243n, 249n, 253n, 254n, 255n,
   256n, 264n, 269n, 273n
Sukenik, E. L., 88, 231n, 253n
Sundberg, A. C., 265n
Sutcliffe, E. F., 252n, 272n
Talmon, S., 248n
Täubler, E., 181, 192, 202, 273n
Tcherikover, V., 172, 212, 270n, 271n, 276n,
   279n, 280n
Tedesche, S., 245n
Teeple, H. M., 240n
Testuz, M., 245n
Thiering, B. E., 232n, 279n
Thompson, J. A., 238n
Thorion, Y., 232n
Tov, E., 240n
Trever, J. C., 231n, 253n
Tsevat, M., 238n
Urbach, E. E., 233n, 266n
VanderKam, J., 41, 42, 78, 242n, 243n, 244n,
   247n
Vaux, R. de, 262n, 272n
Vermes, G., 40, 100, 177, 184, 187, 231n,
   237n, 248n, 252n, 257n, 261n, 262n,
   264n, 265n, 266n, 267n, 272n, 273n,
   274n, 276n, 279n, 280n
Volz, P., 248n
Von Rad, G., 241n
Wacholder, B. Z., 241n, 248n, 249n, 250n,
   266n, 272n, 273n, 276n, 278n, 279n, 280n
Walter, N., 248n, 249n
Weinfeld, M., 232n, 233n, 237n, 238n, 279n
Weingreen, J., 261n
Wellhausen, J., 265n
Wernberg-Møller, P., 252n, 253n, 259n,
   264n

Wieder, N., 254n, 260n, 267n, 268n
Wiesenberg, E., 257n
Will, E., 272n, 276n
Winter, P., 261n
Woude, A. S. van der, 232n
Yadin, Y., 1, 2, 3, 4, 6, 13, 15, 17, 19, 20, 21, 23, 24, 30, 42–43, 47, 49, 52, 53, 54, 55, 65–66, 69, 71, 72, 73, 75, 77, 78, 79, 81, 92, 96, 124, 152, 156, 157, 159, 204–210

passim, 213, 222–225 *passim,* 227, 231n, 232n, 233n, 234n, 235n, 236n, 237n, 238n, 239n, 240n, 244n, 245n, 246n, 247n, 249n, 250n, 251n, 253n, 254n, 255n, 259n, 261n, 270n, 277n, 280n
Zeitlin, S., 101, 168, 244n, 256n, 265n, 267n, 269n, 270n, 271n, 276n
Zunz, L., 271n

Subjects

Aaron, 28, 82, 87, 127, 128, 129, 227
Aaronide planting, 108, 109
Abot de Rabbi Nathan, 150, 154, 175. *See also* Citation Index
Abraham, 53
Abraham Ibn Daud, 156
'aḥarit hayyamym, 29, 209
Acquisitiveness, 119, 121, 129, 134, 183, 184, 191, 194
'ad, 23–24, 239n
Adam and Eve, 125
Ahikar, 34
Albiruni, 269n
Alexander, 174, 271n
Alexander Jannaeus, 177, 187, 205, 269n, 277n, 278n, 279n
Alexander Polyhistor, 62–63
Alexandria, Egypt, 269n
Alfaiumi, 159
Altar, 236n
Anan ben David, 155–160, 166, 269n
Angels, 82, 245n, 251n; angel of presence, 45, 46; Gabriel, 78, 81, 90; Mastema, 78, 127; Michael, 78, 81; Raphael, 78; Sariel, 78; Uriel, 40
Animals, 52, 125, 224, 245n, 253n. *See also* Birds
Anointing, 146, 147, 274n
'anšey Ṣedeq, 112, 114
Antigonus, son of Aristobulus, 176
Antigonus Monophthalmus, 176
Antigonus of Soko, 141–148, 174, 175–176, 268n, 279n
Antiochus III, 63, 172, 184, 200, 214, 215
Antiochus IV, 41, 42, 78, 90, 97, 173, 175, 177, 193, 195, 200, 212, 214, 218, 223
Aristobulus, 209
Ark, 262n
Astronomy, 34–37
Astronomical Enoch, 34–40, 56, 98, 192n, 241n, 278n
Atonement, 86–87
Baethus, 141–144, 147, 148, 153–154, 175, 176, 269n
Baethusians, 162, 163, 164, 175, 267n, 268n, 269n, 270n
Belial, 111, 117, 118, 127, 129, 183, 184
Ben Sira, 217, 219, 226, 238n

Benjamin (tribe), 78
beryt, 21, 22. *See also* Covenant
Beney Ṣadoq, 99, 112, 115–116, 118, 119, 129, 135–140, 141, 153, 155, 168, 219, 220, 231n, 259n, 264n. *See also* 'anšey Ṣedeq
Bethel, 28, 61, 240n
Bigamy, 16–17, 117, 124–126, 133, 218, 237n. *See also* Fornication; Polygamy
Birds, 75
Blind, 123
Blood, 52, 55, 60, 61, 115–116, 213
Book of the Heavenly Luminaries, 241n
Cairo Genizah, 1, 150, 153;
Calendar: Baethusian, 154, 163–164, 269n; Enochite, 38, 57–59, 241n, 242n, 247n–248n; Jubilees, 53–60, 62, 132, 153, 163–164, 214; Karaite, 156–159, 269n; lunisolar, 38, 54–59, 62, 164, 241n, 242n; solar, 53, 55, 59, 81, 86, 97, 98, 153, 154, 196, 241n; Zadokite, 149
Camp at Sinai. *See* Temple, eschatological: Sinai encampment
Canaan, 28
Canon, 233n
Capital punishment, 51
Chaldeans, 197
Christianity, 146–147
Chronomessianism, 177, 179
Circumcision, 41, 51
Clement of Alexandria, 62, 63
Cohabitation, 85, 224
Coins, 279n
Communal life, 134. *See also* Property, renunciation of
Commune vs. sect, 256n
Community Rule (1QS), 33, 83–88, 98, 102, 103, 104, 110, 137, 146, 178, 203, 204, 217, 225, 245n, 256n
Copper Scroll (3Q15), 147, 153
Covenant, 20–21, 22, 28, 31, 43, 103, 104, 111, 115, 129–135, 216, 241n, 262n
Damascus Document (CD), 41, 101–140, 150, 160, 175, 185–189, 202, 204, 211, 216, 219, 225, 231n
Damascus, migration to, 103, 104, 110, 128, 129, 132, 134, 138, 181, 226
Daniel, Book of: and Community Rule, 87–88; and Hellenism, 212, 213; and

Jubilees, 42, 77; and messianism, 177, 222, 226; and Persian culture, 214; and Qumranic Torah, 33, 77–78, 203, 223, 226; and War Rule, 80–81; and Zadok, 210, 219

David, 94, 112–114, 115, 117, 125, 218

Day of Atonement, 54, 90, 123–124, 131, 191, 193, 197

Decalogue, 233n

Defilement, 12, 15, 18–19, 51, 85, 131; of sanctuary, 119, 121–124, 129, 134, 183, 184, 210, 217, 245n. *See also* Purity

Deification, 139

Demetrius I, 200

Demetrius II, 200

Demetrius III, 177

Deutero-Isaiah, 213

Deuteronomy, 3–4, 12–13, 15, 16–17, 124, 203, 213, 216, 234n, 236n, 237n, 244n

Diadochi, 171, 214, 217, 223

Diaspora, Qumranic, 166–167

Divorce, 16–17, 125–126, 127, 133, 151, 152, 237n, 267n, 261n

dorot, 239n

Dreams, 61, 90, 277n

Dualism, 81–83, 88–89, 97

Ecclesiastes, 220

Ecclesiasticus. *See* Ben Sira

Education of priests, 220–221

Egypt, 28

Eleazar ben Hananiah, 272n

Eleazar (biblical priest), 117, 125

Eleazar, high priest, 171, 172, 173, 176

Eli, high priest, 76

'emet, 257n

Enoch, 33–40, 99, 220, 241n, 248n. *See also* Astronomical Enoch

Epicureans, 265n

Eschaton; and Damascus Document, 114, 130, 135, 179, 180, 181, 185; and Daniel, 179, 222, 226; and Jubilees, 124; and Pesherite texts, 90, 91–92, 97, 187, 189, 194; and Pharisees, 145; and Qumranic Torah, 22–24, 29–30, 33, 40, 130, 135, 145, 181, 203, 209–210, 226, 228; and Thanksgivings, 88. *See also* Messiah; Messianism; New heaven; New Jerusalem; New planting; Temple, eschatological

Essenes, 83, 130, 167, 188, 200–201, 203, 204, 214, 219, 225, 226, 268n, 270n, 278n

Eternal life, 264n

Eupolemus, 62–77, 211, 219

Eusebius of Caesarea, 62–63

Eve, 51, 125

Exodus, Book of, 8–9, 227

Ezekiel, 68, 78, 213

Ezra, 134, 174, 207, 214, 215

Feast of Weeks. *See* Shavuot

Festivals, 54–56, 97. *See also* Calendar

First fruits, seasons of, 30, 50, 52–53, 54–56, 85, 86, 97, 132, 156–158, 222, 242n, 247n, 269n. *See also* Shavuot; Wine and oil; Wood offering

Fornication, 51, 117, 120, 124, 129, 133, 134, 184. *See also* Bigamy; Polygamy

Flood, 51, 52. *See also* Noah

Gates, 39, 80, 242n. *See also* Temple

Gog and Magog, 222, 223

Genesis, 28, 41, 53

ger, 263n

God, to dwell among Israelites, 12, 21, 24, 97, 228, 235n

Gold and gilding, 13, 39, 68, 95, 143, 147, 243n

Great Assembly, 174, 175

Hadassi, Judah. *See* Judah Hadassi

Halakah, 234n, 238n

Halevi, Judah. *See* Judah Halevi

Hanging, 237n

Hanukkah, 211, 216

Hasideans, 217–218, 277n

Hebrew orthography. *See* Orthography

Hecataeus of Abdera, 68, 217

Hellenism, 42, 195, 212–213, 219, 224

Herod I, 205

High priests, 13, 16, 80, 146, 165, 171–173, 184, 185, 194, 195, 197, 204, 209, 220, 258n, 263n, 273n, 274n, 279n. *See also* Priests and Priesthood

Hilkiah, 112–113, 116, 203

Hodayot. *See* Thanksgivings

Holy of Holies, 14, 73, 85, 87

Hurban, 110, 111, 118, 180

Hyrcanus, the Tobiad, 184

Idolatry, 12, 43, 46, 191, 192, 228, 244n

Immortality, 146. *See also* Eternal life

Impurity. *See* Defilement

Incest, 51, 52

Intermarriage, 44, 51–52

Isaac, 26on

Isaiah, 2d. *See* Deutero-Isaiah

Israel, 83, 97, 102, 218, 223, 256n

Jacob, 21, 28, 48, 61, 92

Jaddua, high priest, 171, 172, 173

Jason, 173, 212

Jehoiachin, 239n

Jeremiah, 226

Jeroboam, 150, 160

Jerome, 194, 201

Jerusalem, 96, 104, 212, 219, 220, 223–224. *See also* New Jerusalem; Temple

Job, 42

Johanan ben Zakkai, 166

John Hyrcanus, 41, 78, 201, 205, 207, 208–209, 279n

John, son of Accos, 219

Jonadab, 167–168, 270n

Jonathan, high priest, 41, 273n

Jonathan, the Hasmonean, 177, 187

Jose, son of Joezer, 143, 174–175

Jose, son of Johanan, 143, 174–175

Joseph, 79, 90

Joseph, the Tobiad, 172, 173, 184, 195, 212, 213, 219

Josephus, 1, 65, 83, 173, 177, 217. *See also* Citation Index under Classical authors

Joshua, 117

Josiah, 124

Jubilee year, 86

Jubilees, Book of, 41–62, 89; its date, 41–42, 98, 218; as apocalyptic, 233n; and Baethus, 154; and Baethusians, 163, 164; and Community Rule, 86, 87; and Damascus Document, 50, 115, 258n, 26on; and dualism, 82; and Enoch, 34; and eschatological temple, 146; and eschaton, 239n; and Exodus, 44–45; and Genesis, 240n; and Hellenism, 213; and Karaites, 153; and messianism, 216; and Persian culture, 214, 236n; and Qirqisani, 150; and Qumranic Torah, 33, 54, 61–62, 96–98, 135, 178, 203, 211, 219; and War Rule, 77–83 *passim*, 97, 98

Judah (tribe), 78, 160

Judah Hadassi, 159

Judah Halevi, 268n

Judah Ha-Nasi, 142

Judah Maccabee, 63, 77, 216

Judah of Alexandria, 156–158, 160, 268n

Judas of Gamala, 220

Judith, Book of, 214

kapparah, 12, 24

Karaites, 1, 148–160, 177–178, 26on, 267n, 268n, 269n

kedušah, 16

Kings and kingship, 16, 26, 125, 126, 146, 152, 209, 237n, 261n, 274n, 279n. *See also* Royal charter

Kittim, 78, 90, 94, 137, 186, 187, 191, 196, 197, 200, 274n, 275n

Kohen gadol. See High priests

Kol hayyamym, 239n

Laban, 246n

Letter of Aristeas, 216, 277n

Levi, 110, 119

Levites, 14, 85, 115–116, 208, 224, 236n, 281n

Light and darkness, 82–83, 88

Love, 132–133

Lying priest, 102, 103, 109, 110, 111, 127, 191, 273n. *See also* Scoffing priest; Wicked priest

Maccabees and Maccabean Period, 41, 175, 176, 177, 201, 202, 205–218 *passim. See also* Hasideans

Maccabees, Books of, 173, 201, 210, 213, 214

Magharians, 149–150, 268n

Maimonides, 268n

Malky-ṣedeq, 139

Manasseh, king of Judah, 113

Manasseh, high priest, 171, 172, 173, 176

Manual of Discipline. *See* Community Rule

Marriage, 44, 51–52; to niece, 17, 97, 126–127, 133, 150-151, 152, 153, 184

Mašyaḥ. See Messiah

Matthew, Gospel of, 220

Megillat Taanit, 207, 269n, 271n

Menelaus, 173, 212

Messiah, 29, 93, 145, 239n, 258n, 274n

Messianic Rule, 102, 256n

Messianism, 145–146, 216, 222, 223, 227, 261n

Midrash, 89, 234n, 254n, 275n

Mishnah, 207, 234n; Abot, 175, 265n; Middot, 30, 147; Yoma, 162

Mišneh Torah, 20

mišpat, 18–19, 20, 234n, 238n

Monasticism, 85

Moon, 36–38, 39, 40, 57–58

Moreh hayyaḥyd, 138

Moreh Ṣedeq: his anointing, 102; his
authoritativeness, 261n; as biblical commentator, 137, 189–191, 199; and chron-
olgy; 108–109, 179; and Daniel, 202; his
death, 104; and eschaton, 97, 128, 137,
140; his seeming failure, 91, 186–192; his
identity, 231n, 276n; and Jonadab, son
of Rechab, 168; as messianic figure,
138–139, 261n; and Onias III, 272n; as
persecuted, 135, 137–138, 186, 191,
196–197, 199, 263n; and Pesher Habakkuk, 90, 136–139, 186–199; as redeemer,
137; his resistance, 117; return after
death, 104, 185, 186; his role, 109–110;
his sin, 191–192; and Thanksgivings, 89.
See also Zadok: as *Moreh Ṣedeq*

Moses, 7–9, 28, 29, 31, 44–47, 82, 127, 129,
227–229, 240n, 245n, 248n

Muqammiz, David ben-Marwan al-, 127,
148, 149, 150, 152, 153

Nabonidus, Prayer of, 214

Nahawandi, Benjamin al-, 149, 269n

Nakedness, 41–42, 219

Nebuchadnezzar, 180

Nehemiah, 134, 207, 214, 215

New fruits. *See* First fruits

New heaven, 216, 221

New Jerusalem, 95–96, 224–225

New planting, 108, 114, 115, 119, 128, 181,
258n. *See also* Aaronide planting

New wine, 80, 97

Nicanor, 243n

Noah, 42, 53, 115, 153, 243n, 248n, 260n

Nudity. *See* Nakedness

Offerings. *See* Sacrifice

ᶜolam, 239n

Omer, waving of, 54, 55, 158, 165

Oniads, 181, 195

Onias, high priest, 201

Onias I, high priest, 171–173 *passim*

Onias II, high priest, 171–173 *passim,* 176,
220

Onias III, high priest, 171–173 *passim,* 182,
183, 194, 195, 197, 212, 272n

Orthography, 9, 207, 232n

Paschal lamb, 50–51, 61

Passover, 54, 156, 158

Peleg, 104

Pentateuch: as first Torah, 46, 47, 60, 96;
and Jubilees, 53, 60, 77, 245n; and
priestly education, 220; and Qumranic
Torah: differences, 2–3, 13, 14–15, 17, 20,
29–32, 53, 79, 85, 127, 157, 206, 222, 225,
227, 236n–237n, 263n, 281n; and Qumranic Torah: similarities, 14–15, 17, 82,
85, 126, 146, 207, 225, 227, 236n, 237n,
246n; as Torah, 17–18. *See also* Moses;
Torah

Pentecost. *See* Shavuot

Pentecontal seasons. *See* First fruits

Penuel, 40

Periodization, apocalyptic, 258n

Persian culture, 213–215

pešer, 89–90, 111, 189, 275n

Pesher Habakkuk, 89–91, 112, 185–193, 211,
218, 219, 264n, 277n

Pesher Nahum, 176, 199–200, 261n

Pesherite texts, 83, 89–94, 98, 146, 178, 197,
199, 211, 233n, 280n

Pharisees, 19, 30, 145, 146–147, 161, 163,
164–166, 174, 200–201, 209, 217, 233n,
265n, 271n

Philo, 157, 167, 268n

pišro, 110–111, 188, 200

Polygamy, 114, 119–120, 124–126, 126–127,
151, 152, 218, 261n. *See also* Bigamy;
Fornication

Polyhistor, Alexander. *See* Alexander Polyhistor

Poor, 132

Porphyry, 201

Prayer, 88–89

Priests and priesthood, 13, 14, 15, 85, 113,
115–116, 131, 139–140, 146, 194, 215, 216,
219, 220–221, 224, 263n. *See also* High
priests; Levites

Priestly Code, 2

Pronouns, use of, 3–9, 236n–237n

Property, 85, 103; renunciation of, 84, 94–95

Prophecy and political turmoil, 221–222
Psalms, 94, 233n
Psalms, Apocryphal, 269n
Pseudepigrapha and pseudonymity, 221, 233n, 234n
Pseudo-Eupolemus, 34
Ptolemies, 171, 172, 176, 184, 195, 201–202, 219; Ptolemy Euergetes, 172, 271n; Ptolemy IV Philopator, 173
Punishment, capital, 51
Purity, 16, 79, 83, 85, 95, 130–131, 133, 166, 228. *See also* Defilement
Qirqisani, 127, 148–155
Rabbanites, 148, 150, 154, 155, 156, 158, 160
Rechabites, 168–169, 225, 226
Redemption, 26–27, 221, 228
Remnant, 26
Repentance, 26, 262n
Resurrection, 144–146
Reward and punishment, 144–145, 235n
ris, 236n
Rockefeller Museum Mss., 205, 206, 207, 232n, 236n
Rome, 193, 196, 197
Rosh Hashanah, 54
Royal charter, 3, 14, 20–21, 25, 26, 31, 80, 146, 209, 222, 237n
Saadia Gaon, 156–157, 159, 269n
Sabbath, 39, 123–124, 134, 247n; offerings on, 48–50, 131, 152, 247n, 267n
Sabbatical year, 86
šabey, 262n
Sacred literature, 233n
Sacrifice and sacrifices, 18, 22, 48–53, 61, 73, 79–80, 86–87, 121, 132, 159, 162–163, 204, 208, 215, 222, 236n. *See also* Animals; Sabbath: offerings on
Sadducees, 136, 141, 144, 155, 156, 161–162, 165–166, 200–201, 226, 265n
Ṣadduqym, 136, 141, 153, 155, 160–162, 165–167, 269n, 270n. *See also* Zadokites
Sahl Abu al-Sari, 159
Salvation, 146
Scoffing priest, 109, 111, 114, 115, 118–119, 135, 137, 138, 181, 182, 183, 273n. *See also* Lying priest; Wicked priest
Sect. vs. commune, 256n

ṣedeq, 260n, 264n
Ṣedoqym. See Ṣadduqym
Seder Olam, 174, 177, 272n
Seleucids, 176, 193, 195, 196, 200, 201–202, 223, 274n
Septuagint, 18, 187, 234n, 249n, 250n
Serek literature, 111
Seven (the number), 38–39, 71, 237n, 242n, 249n
Shavuot, 53, 54, 55–56, 59, 60, 62, 153, 157, 158, 163–164, 268n
Simon, the Hasmonean, 177, 187
Simon, high priest, 41
Simon the Just I, 141, 143, 172, 173, 174, 175, 217, 273n
Simon the Just II, 173, 176, 182–183, 184, 194, 217, 218, 220, 273n
Sinai, Mount, 8–9, 13, 16, 28, 31, 33, 40, 44–45, 47, 91. *See also* Temple, eschatological: Sinai encampment
Solomon, 100
Song of Songs, 220, 275n
Sons of Zadok. See *Beney Ṣadoq*
Squareness, 39, 66, 71, 222, 225, 226
Sukkot, 54, 236n, 240n
Sun, 37–38, 39, 40, 57–58
Tabernacle of the wilderness, 23, 71, 76, 147, 210, 225, 235n, 244n
Tablets of the law, 44–46, 47, 60
Temple, eschatological, 21–30, 227, 244n; and Community Rule, 87–88; and Damascus Document, 135; description, 13–14, 65–77, 147; and Enoch, 36, 38–40; and First Temple, 8, 31, 78; and Florilegium, 93–94; as God's construction, 22–23, 27; and immortality, 146; and Jubilees, 45–47; and messianism, 216; and redemption, 226, 228; and Second Temple, 46; and Sinai encampment, 16, 80, 86, 223, 225–226; as spiritual temple, 233n, its squareness, 222; and wilderness tabernacle, 8, 31
Temple, First, 23, 31, 63–77, 97, 127–128, 130, 147, 216, 217–218, 236n, 258n, 272n
Temple, Second, 23, 30, 46, 75, 97, 128, 130, 174, 216–217, 272n
Testament of Levi, 61

Teaching in Judaism
220

Testaments of the Twelve Patriarchs, 110, 274n
Tetragrammaton, 9
Thanksgivings, 88–89, 98, 102, 105, 137, 146, 178, 225, 256n, 266n
Therapeutae, 157, 167, 226
Tithes, 52, 103, 131, 134, 135, 208, 247n
Tobiads, 42, 171–173, 181, 202, 220
Tobias, sheik of Ammon, 172
Tobit, Book of, 214, 280n
Torah, 17–18, 89, 221 (*See also* Tablets of the Law); and halakah, 233n–234n; "Last Torah", 46, 47, 56, 60, 61–62, 91, 96, 130; Qumranic Torah as equaling or surpassing Mosaic, 4–9, 15, 18–21, 97, 127, 135, 160, 203, 223; "Second Torah", 27, 30–32, 91, 92, 96, 239n (*See also* Mišneh Torah); Torah of the King, 20, 232n, 238n; Two Torahs, 24–27, 47, 60–61, 62, 77
Tosefta, 234n
Twelve (the number), 39, 242n
Twelve tribes, 14, 39, 66, 76, 81, 83, 225
Uncleanness. *See* Defilement
Urbanism, rejection of, 223–224, 225
Urim and Thummim, 113
War Rule, 33, 77–83, 97, 98, 146, 203, 204, 256n, 274n
Wealth. *See* Acquisitiveness
Wicked priest, 90, 91, 127, 138, 176–177, 181, 186, 187, 190–194, 196–198, 273n, 276n, 277n. *See also* Lying priest; Scoffing priest
Wilderness: forty years in, 82; idealization of, 224–225, 226
Wine and oil, 13, 30, 52, 53, 97, 134, 157, 158, 204. *See also* New wine
Wisdom, 219
Woman, captive, 15, 85
Wood-offering, 13, 30, 53, 134, 215, 242n

"Words of the Luminaries," 40
World to Come, 144, 145, 146, 147
Yaḥad, 33, 82, 83–98, 101, 102, 104, 110, 111, 134, 138, 178, 202, 203, 277n
Yodʿey ṣedeq, 129
Yoreh ṣedeq, 110, 129
Zadok (biblical priest), 112, 113–114, 116, 141
Zadok: and Antigonus of Soko, 141–148, 153, 175; in ARNA, 141–148; his contemporaries, 219; and Damascus Document, 181, 183; and Hasideans, 218; and high priesthood, 273n; and Karaites, 148–160; and mainstream Judaism, 222, 223; as messianic figure, 186, 226–227; as *Moreh Ṣedeq*, 99, 112, 116, 118–119, 129, 138–139, 140, 203, 228–229, 259n; and Moses, 227–229; his pedigree, 220; and Pesher Habakkuk, 277n; as prophet, 226; as founder of Qumranic sect, 118–119; as author of Qumranic Torah, 176, 203–204, 211, 226–227; as discoverer of Qumranic Torah, 119, 124, 176, 203, 262n; as sign of redemption, 128; and Sadducees, 265n; and Second Temple, 210; and Seleucids, 196; and Simon the Just, 273n; and the *Suda*, 167–168; his time of activity, 176, 211–212; his tomb, 100; as founder of Zadokites, 141–148
Zadokite fragments, 136, 181. *See also* Damascus Document
Zadokites, 143, 147, 148, 149, 152, 153, 156, 159, 161, 164–169, 175, 267n, 268n. See also *Beney Ṣadoq*
Zealots, 176, 220
Zedekiah, 26
Zeno papyri, 171, 172, 195
Zeus Olympus, 210, 216
Zion, Mount, 100
zugot, 175